Lecture Notes in Artificial Inte

T0250756

Edited by J. G. Carbonell and J. Siekmann

Subseries of Lecture Notes in Computer Science

Dietmar Seipel   Michael Hanus
Ulrich Geske   Oskar Bartenstein (Eds.)

Applications
of Declarative Programming
and Knowledge Management

15th International Conference
on Applications of Declarative Programming
and Knowledge Management, INAP 2004
and 18th Workshop on Logic Programming, WLP 2004
Potsdam, Germany, March 4-6, 2004
Revised Selected Papers

Series Editors

Jaime G. Carbonell, Carnegie Mellon University, Pittsburgh, PA, USA
Jörg Siekmann, University of Saarland, Saarbrücken, Germany

Volume Editors

Dietmar Seipel
Universität Würzburg, Institut für Informatik
Am Hubland, 97074 Würzburg, Germany
E-mail: seipel@informatik.uni-wuerzburg.de

Michael Hanus
Christian-Albrechts-Universität Kiel
Institut für Informatik und Praktische Mathematik
Olshausenstr. 40, 24098 Kiel, Germany
E-mail: mh@informatik.uni-kiel.de

Ulrich Geske
Fraunhofer FIRST
Kekulestr. 7, 12489 Berlin, Germany
E-mail: geske@first.fhg.de

Oskar Bartenstein
IF Computer Japan Limited
5-28-2 Sendagi, Bunkyo-ku, Tokyo, 113-0022, Japan
E-mail: oskar@ifcomputer.co.jp

Library of Congress Control Number: 2005923659

CR Subject Classification (1998): I.2.4, I.2, D.1.6

ISSN   0302-9743
ISBN-10   3-540-25560-5 Springer Berlin Heidelberg New York
ISBN-13   978-3-540-25560-4 Springer Berlin Heidelberg New York

Springer is a part of Springer Science+Business Media

springeronline.com

© Springer-Verlag Berlin Heidelberg 2005
Printed in Germany

Typesetting: Camera-ready by author, data conversion by Scientific Publishing Services, Chennai, India
Printed on acid-free paper   SPIN: 11415763   06/3142   5 4 3 2 1 0

Preface

This volume contains a selection of papers presented at the 15th International Conference on Applications of Declarative Programming and Knowledge Management, INAP 2004, and the 18th Workshop on Logic Programming, WLP 2004, which were held jointly in Potsdam, Germany, from March 4th to 6th, 2004.

Declarative programming is an advanced paradigm for the modeling and solving of complex problems. This specification method has become more and more attractive in recent years, for example, in the domains of databases, for the processing of natural language, for the modeling and processing of combinatorial problems, and for establishing knowledge-based systems for the Web.

The INAP conferences provide a forum for intensive discussions of applications of important technologies around logic programming, constraint problem solving, and closely related advanced software. They comprehensively cover the impact of programmable logic solvers in the Internet society, its underlying technologies, and leading-edge applications in industry, commerce, government, and social services.

The Workshops on Logic Programming are the annual meeting of the Society for Logic Programming (GLP e.V.). They bring together researchers interested in logic programming, constraint programming, and related areas like databases and artificial intelligence. Previous workshops have been held in Germany, Austria, and Switzerland.

The topics of the selected papers of this year's joint conference concentrate on three currently important fields: knowledge management and decision support, constraint programming and constraint solving, and declarative programming and Web-based systems.

During the last couple of years a lot of research has been conducted on the use of declarative programming for the management of knowledge-based systems and for decision support. Reasoning about knowledge wrapped in rules, databases, or the Web allows us to explore interesting hidden knowledge. Declarative techniques for the transformation, deduction, induction, visualization, or querying of knowledge, or data mining techniques for exploring knowledge have the advantage of high transparency and better maintainability compared to procedural approaches.

The problem when using knowledge to find solutions for large industrial tasks is that these problems have an exponential complexity, which normally prohibits the fast generation of exact solutions. One method that has made substantial progress over the last few years is the constraint programming paradigm. The declarative nature of this paradigm offers significant advantages for software engineering both in the implementation and in the maintenance phases. Different interesting aspects are in discussion: how can this paradigm be improved or combined with known, classical methods; how can practical problems be modelled as constraint problems; and what are the experiences of applications in really large industrial planning and simulation tasks?

An emerging topic in knowledge management is the use of the World Wide Web to distribute, store, and use knowledge. This spans vision, technology, and the application of non-monolithic cooperating Web-based systems. With respect to declarative programming, representation languages, transformation, and search procedures are of interest, and they are easily adaptable to the fast-changing content and structure of the Web, for example, in W3C Web services and queries. Other aspects are commercial Web-based consulting or the use of the Web as a platform for concurrent engineering or program development for effective distributed collaborative design.

The two conferences INAP 2004 and WLP 2004 were jointly organized at the University of Potsdam, Germany by the following institutions: the Society for Logic Programming (GLP e.V.), the Hasso Plattner Institute for Software Systems Engineering (HPI), and the Fraunhofer Institute for Computer Architecture and Software Technology (FhG FIRST). We would like to thank all authors who submitted papers and all conference participants for the fruitful discussions. We are grateful to the members of the Program Committee and the external referees for their timely expertise in carefully reviewing the papers, and we would like to express our thanks to the Hasso Plattner Institute for hosting the conference at the modern campus in the traditional atmosphere of Potsdam.

December 2004   Dietmar Seipel, Michael Hanus,
                                                 Ulrich Geske, Oskar Bartenstein

Organization

Program Chair

Dietmar Seipel   University of Würzburg, Germany

Organization

Ulrich Geske   Fraunhofer FIRST, Berlin, Germany
Thomas Linke   University of Potsdam, Germany
Wolfgang Severin   University of Potsdam, Germany
Armin Wolf   Fraunhofer FIRST, Berlin, Germany

Program Committee of INAP

Sergio A. Alvarez   Boston College, USA
Roman Barták   Charles University, Prague, Czech Republic
Oskar Bartenstein   IF Computer Japan, Japan
Joachim Baumeister   University of Würzburg, Germany
James P. Delgrande   Simon Fraser University, Canada
Robin Drogemuller   CSIRO, Australia
Shuichi Fukuda   Tokyo Metropolitan Institute of Technology, Japan
Rita Gavriloaie   Learning Lab Lower Saxony, Hannover, Germany
Nicola Henze   University of Hannover, Germany
Ulrich Geske   Fraunhofer FIRST, Germany
Geun-Sik Jo   Inha University, Korea
Thomas Linke   University of Potsdam, Germany
Steve Prestwich   4C/UCC, Ireland
Georg Ringwelski   4C/UCC, Ireland
Carolina Ruiz   Worcester Polytechnic Institute, USA
Torsten Schaub   University of Potsdam, Germany
Dietmar Seipel   University of Würzburg, Germany (Chair)
Paul Tarau   Binnet Corporation, USA
Armin Wolf   Fraunhofer FIRST, Germany
Akihiro Yamamoto   Kyoto University, Japan
Osamu Yoshie   Waseda University, Japan

Program Committee of WLP

Slim Abdennadher   German University Cairo, Egypt
Christoph Beierle   FernUniversität in Hagen, Germany

François Bry	University of München, Germany
Jürgen Dix	Technical University of Clausthal, Germany
Uwe Egly	Technical University of Vienna, Austria
Thomas Eiter	Technical University of Vienna, Austria
Burkhard Freitag	University of Passau, Germany
Thom Frühwirth	University of Ulm, Germany
Norbert E. Fuchs	University of Zürich, Switzerland
Ulrich Geske	Fraunhofer FIRST, Berlin, Germany
Michael Hanus	Christian Albrechts University Kiel, Germany (Chair)
Petra Hofstedt	Technical University of Berlin, Germany
Steffen Hölldobler	Technical University of Dresden, Germany
Ulrich Neumerkel	Technical University of Vienna, Austria
Dietmar Seipel	University of Würzburg, Germany
Armin Wolf	Fraunhofer FIRST, Berlin, Germany

External Referees for INAP and WLP

Christian Anger	Martin Atzmueller
Matthias Beck	Bernd Braßel
Ole Boysen	Tom Carchrae
Mona Gharib	Bernd Heumesser
Marbod Hopfner	Kathrin Konczak
Horst Reichel	Maged F. El Sayed
Armagan Tarim	Manfred Widera
Stefan Woltran	

Table of Contents

Knowledge Management and Decision Support

Constraint Programming and Constraint Solving

Declarative Programming and Web-Based Systems

Optimizing the Evaluation of XPath
Using Description Logics

Peter Baumgartner[1,2], Ulrich Furbach[1], Margret Gross-Hardt[1],
and Thomas Kleemann[1]

[1] Institut für Informatik, Universität Koblenz-Landau, D-56070 Koblenz, Germany
[2] Max-Planck-Institut für Informatik, D-66123 Saarbrücken
{peter, uli, margret, tomkl}@uni-koblenz.de

Abstract. The growing use of XML in commercial as well as non-commercial domains to transport information poses new challenges to concepts to access this information. Common ways to access parts of a document use XPath-expressions. We provide a transformation of DTDs into a knowledge base in Description Logic. We use reasoning capabilities grounded in description logics to decide if a given XPath can be satisfied by a document, and to guide the search of XML-Processors into possibly successful branches of the document, thus avoiding parts of the document that will not yield results. The extension towards object oriented subclassing schemes opens this approach towards OODB-queries. In contrast to other approaches we do not use any kind of graph representing the document structure, and no steps towards incorporation of the XML/OODB-processor itself will be taken.

Keywords: XML, XPath, Description Logics, automated reasoning, DTD, Schema.

1 Introduction

Within a short period of time XML has become a widely accepted standard for information interchange. Starting as a subset of SGML to transport structured text, the ease of understanding and using XML has promoted its use as an interchange format of rather large documents. This evolution has created the needs for a validation of documents against an according definition. Most common and basic validation is accomplished by XML-processors referring to a Document Type Definition (DTD). A DTD defines the structure of elements in the document, that references the DTD. We will detail the terms element and structure in the following chapters.

Beyond the need to validate data, several attempts have been made or are currently made to access parts of a document. One common idea in these attempts is the access of parts of a document following a path from its root to some subtrees. In general, these paths are not specified completely from the root to the subtree, but leave unspecified gaps to be filled by the XML query processor. Usually XML processors have to traverse the whole document tree to find instances of the specified parts of a path.

Based on DTD and XPath expressions we will provide a way to optimize this traversal. Actually, a XPath expression may be seen as a pattern that describes certain subtrees

D. Seipel et al. (Eds.): INAP/WLP 2004, LNAI 3392, pp. 1–15, 2005.

of the complete document. As already mentioned, current processors traverse the complete document in order to determine the appropriate subtrees. Instead, our goal is to follow only those parts that may result in desired data, but omit those paths that are guaranteed to fail. The idea is to exploit structural knowledge in order to determine the relevant parts of a document for a certain query. This allows to enhance other approaches based on indexing techniques in query processing. To this aim, we translate the DTD into a set of description logics (DL) formulae and the XPath query into a query in a logical representation. Questions about the satisfiability of a XPath in a document will be answered as well as queries of the starting element of subtrees, which may contain fillers for the path specification.

Recently, XML Schema [14] has evolved as a successor of DTDs. Basically, XML Schema addresses some shortcomings of DTDs; in particular XML Schema supports besides others user defined types and some aspects of object orientation. We will show the compatibility of our translation and reasoning with these sorts of object oriented extensions. This opens our approach towards the use of path completion techniques in object oriented databases as well as schema-based definitions of XML documents.

2   XML Documents

Starting as a specialisation of the Standard Generalized Markup Language (SGML) the eXtensible Markup Language (XML) was supposed to provide a better way of document markup than the widespread HyperText Markup Language (HTML). The *normative* definition of XML is available from the W3C [6]. In contrast to the fixed markup and its interpretation of HTML, the XML approach offers a standardized way to markup arbitrary documents. This may include redefined HTML documents but is not limited to this application.

A XML document consists of a prologue and an element, optionally followed by miscellaneous comments and processing instructions, that are not in the scope of this paper. An element is either an empty element or a sequence of a starting tag followed by content and an ending tag. Taken from [6]:

[1]	document	::=	prolog element Misc*
[39]	element	::=	EmptyElemTag | STag content Etag
[40]	STag	::=	'<' Name Attribute* '>'
[41]	Attribute	::=	Name '=' Attvalue
[42]	ETag	::=	'</' Name '>'
[43]	content	::=	CharData? ((element | Reference | CDSect | PI | Comment) CharData?)*
[44]	EmptyElemTag	::=	'<' Name Attribute* '/>'

Content by itself may again contain so called child-elements. Tags are identified by their names. We will use this name as the name of an element.

The W3C cares about character codings, white spaces and miscellaneous components. Because we are merely interested in the structure of the document we will omit these otherwise important details. The topmost element will be called root element. It spans almost all of the document, especially it contains all other elements. We expect all documents to be well-formed and valid, as explained in the following section.

Sample Document

According to the above mentioned productions and constraints a well-formed document may look like this:

```
<?xml version="1.0"?>
<!DOCTYPE university SYSTEM "university.dtd">
<university name="Universität Koblenz">
    <library>
        <book isbn="978123123">
            <author>  </author>
            <title>  </title>
        </book>
        <book isbn="978234234">
            <author>  </author>
            <title>  </title>
        </book>
    </library>
    <department name="cs"/>
    <department name="math"/>
    ...more descriptions...
</university>
```

The prologue specifies this document to be a XML document according to version 1.0. This is currently the only possible version. The second line specifies a document type definition. University is the root element of the document. This university element contains a library element, that contains several book elements, and several department elements. The department elements are empty elements. Empty elements are empty with respect to the content, but may contain attributes. The university, department and book elements contain attributes, i.e. name and isbn.

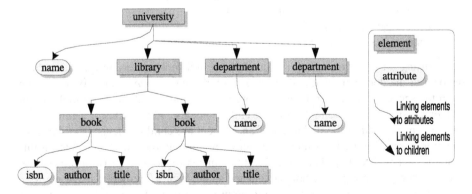

Fig. 1. Graphical Representation of Document

A XML document may be represented as a tree, see figure 1. The root element corresponds to the root of this tree. The elements are represented as nodes of the tree. An element is linked to its child elements and attributes. With respect to our query optimization task, we may omit the data of elements. Instead, we concentrate on the structure of documents. The following section introduces a common way to define possible structures.

3   Validation of Documents

Whenever XML is used to transport information between independent applications, which is most common in business-to-business communication, there is a need to validate the document structure. Validation of document structure means that the processor checks if the XML documents obey to the structure defined in the appropriate DTD. Validating XML processors offer standardized ways for this validation process. These processors use a Document Type Definition or a schema as a description of accepted elements, nesting of elements and type information. In the example document above (2nd line) we already introduced the reference to an external DTD. This Document Type Declaration names the root element, university in this case. DTDs may as well be inline. The advantage of external DTDs is that they are stored centrally and only once. Beyond these differences both kinds of DTDs provide the same set of definitions. DTDs are already known to SGML [12] and HTML documents. They do not provide significant type information or any aspect of object orientation. To overcome these insufficiencies XML schema has been introduced by the W3C. A schema introduces some basic type information and a limited support of object oriented concepts. We will start with DTDs and demonstrate afterwards the opportunities of extended type information.

A DTD for the sample document above may look like this

```
<!ELEMENT university (library, department*, #PCDATA)>
<!ATTLIST university name CDATA #REQUIRED)>
<!ELEMENT library (book)+>
<!ELEMENT department EMPTY>
<!ATTLIST department name CDATA #REQUIRED)>
<!ELEMENT book (author+, title, abstract?)>
<!ATTLIST book isbn CDATA #REQUIRED)>
<!ELEMENT author #PCDATA>
<!ELEMENT title #PCDATA>
```

Focusing on the structure of a document, we will not use any information about the data of the document that is described. So #PCDATA, CDATA and so on will not be in the scope of this paper. Crucial to our target of optimization and completion of path expressions are the definitions of the child elements and attributes of elements. All elements mentioned in the definition of an element are child elements. The sequence operator ',' may be used to establish a sibling relation among child elements. In this example author, title and abstract are child elements of book. isbn is an attribute of book. author is a sibling of author and title and so on. Figure 2 provides an overview.

For the purpose of this paper we limit our presentation to the abbreviated syntax for XPath. In this syntax, one does not have the possibility to express sibling relationships

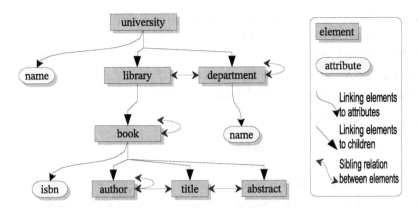

Fig. 2. Graphical Representation of DTD

directly. Therefore we omit these relations in the remaining of this paper although these relations between elements are covered by our approach.

Different from the tree like structure of the XML documents themselves, the description may contain cycles. A well known example of a cycle is the HTML table. The TD element is a child of an TR element, that is a child of the TABLE element. Because TABLE is part of arbitrary HTML content, TABLE is a possible child of TD. The reasoning capabilities used in our query optimization approach are robust against these cyclic definitions.

Even in our quite small example, DTD cycles can be found, e.g. the element author is a sibling of itself.

4   Picking the Parts

Common to almost all processing of documents is the addressing of parts of these. The basic idea of all addressing schemes is a path expression, that specifies the navigation through the document. These path expressions may be rooted or relative to an existing position in the document tree. Several notational variants have been developed. We will use the abbreviated XPath 2.0 notation, that is covered by a W3C-working-draft [15]. Path expressions following these recommendations are incorporated in XSLT, XQuery, CSS2 and other standards.

Path expressions are explained by the following rules taken from [15]:

path	::=	'//' relativePath | '/' relativePath | relativePath
relativePath	::=	stepExpr ('/' | '//') stepExpr
stepExpr	::=	'.' | '@' nameTest | '..' | nodeTest

The leading '/' and '//' construct a path starting at the document out of an relative path. '//' will expand to a path of zero or more steps. Step expressions access the current context node, its attributes by a preceding '@' the parent of an element, or perform node tests, ranging from simple element names to more complex expressions. Especially a wildcard '*' will match all child elements. A detailed description can be found in [15].

Because we restrict our path expressions to abbreviated syntax, the names of the axes are not mentioned, but inherently used. '.' uses the self axis. '..' uses the parent axis. The child axis will be used in nodeTest, as we will demonstrate with some examples:

/university/library will access the library element

//department will access the two department elements

several ways to access the book elements:

/university/*/* will access all grandchildren of the root

/university/*/book and /university/library/book will do the same

//book will also access the two book elements

//*[@isbn] this expression accesses all elements that have an isbn attribute

//*[author AND title] access all elements that have author and title child elements

The wildcard '*' and the universal path fragment '//' are a huge gain in comfort. A user may specify a correct path expression even if she does not know the structure in detail, as can be seen in the expression //book. Regardless of the structure, all book elements will be matched. This will happen regardless of how many totally different paths exist in the document. As a first approach, a XML processor may traverse the document and evaluate all constraints that a path expression contains. However, the larger the documents the worse this approach may become. We will provide decisions that guide the traversal towards those subtrees that may yield results with respect to the path expression. These decisions will be made based on the DTD of the document, using a description logics representation of the DTD.

The reasoning will also provide information about empty result sets. If you specify a path like //book[@isbn="987001001"] the XML processor will compare the isbn attribute of all book elements with the given string. In the above sample document no book element will fulfill this condition, and the result will be empty. But other documents according to the DTD may return results. This decision is made by the XML processor by comparing all book elements.

An additional empty path expression will be //book/library. Different from the first empty path expression this expression will never return any book elements, because the structure in question, library as a child of book, is a contradiction to the DTD. Again the reasoning capabilities in the logic representation state, that this expression will always be empty. Any traversal of the document may be omitted.

5   Description Logic for the Representation of DTDs

The target of our translation is a description logic (DL) that provides inverse and transitive roles and role hierarchies. Examples have been translated into input files for RACER [11] that offers services of a $\mathcal{SHIQ}$-reasoner. An alternative approach, described in Section 7.4, is based on a translation from DL to the input language of the KRHyper [16] Tableaux prover.

Number restrictions have not been used so far, although DTDs provide information about singular or multiple occurrences of child elements. These informations are dropped right now, because we didn't expect significant enhancements towards optimization of path expressions.

The building blocks of the DL used here are concepts and roles. Concepts, describing sets of the domain, may be seen as unary predicates, roles are binary predicates. In order to form new concepts, negation, conjunction and disjunction of existing concepts are allowed. The semantics of these constructors are defined as the complement with respect to the domain of the interpretation, intersection and union. The semantics of an existential restriction $\exists r.C$ is defined as $\{x \in \Delta^I | \exists y : (x,y) \in r^I \wedge y \in C^I\}$ where the domain Δ^I is a nonempty set of individuals in an interpretation I, with $C^I \subseteq \Delta^I$ and $r^I \subseteq \Delta^I \times \Delta^I$. Value restrictions $\forall r.C$ are defined as $\{x \in \Delta^I | \forall y : (x,y) \in r^I \rightarrow y \in C^I\}$.

An inverse role r^- is derived from r as $\{(x,y)|(y,x) \in r^I\}$. A role s is called a superrole of r if $r^I \subseteq s^I$. Transitivity of roles works as expected.

A *TBox* contains definitions of concepts as well as general inclusion axioms. A thorough introduction is given in [2, 1].

Besides terminological knowledge individual assignments are stated in an *ABox*. Individuals $a \in \Delta$ may be members of named concepts $a : C$, also written as $C(a)$, which results in $a^I \in C^I$, and role assertions $(a,b) : r$ or $r(a,b)$ are explained as $(a^I, b^I) \in r^I$.

Standard queries into a DL knowledge representation include subsumption of concepts, $C \sqsubseteq D$, and the satisfiability of concepts. The subsumption problem can be transformed to a satisfiability problem. Beyond these queries concerning the terminology most DL reasoners offer instance checking.

The TBox contains few concepts that correspond to the distinct parts of a DTD. The concepts of our translation will be the building blocks of the DTD like element, attribute and type. These concepts will be populated by the individual elements of the specific DTD during the translation process.

A type concept is almost absent for DTDs. The translation though allows for the integration of the enhanced typing capabilities of XML-schema. We give details later on, see section 7.3.

An important part of the TBox are the definitions of roles and their attributes. We introduce roles to be instantiated in the following translation step as well as roles that are superroles of these. Figure 3 depicts the role hierarchy.

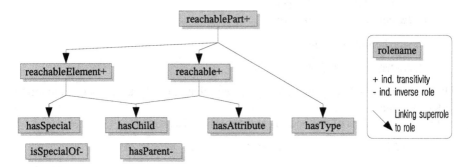

Fig. 3. The Role Hierarchy

Roles with an appended – are inverse roles, like hasParent is the inverse of hasChild. reachable is a superrole of hasChild and hasAttribute. The appended + indicates that this role is transitive.

6   The Optimization

Optimization in our approach is the detection of empty XPath expressions, which may be seen as a verification task, and the restriction of the document traversal to those parts, that may contain results conforming to the XPath expressions.

6.1   Translation of DTDs

The following translations demonstrate how we setup the ABox of our knowledge base from the DTD. The root element of the document and the corresponding DTD are mentioned in the prologue of the XML-file.

```
<!DOCTYPE rootelem Pointer_to_DTD>
```

This line leads to the ABox entry $(root, rootelem) : hasChild$. $root$ is an artificial individual that has the document's root element as a child. For further translation we analyze the appropriate DTD.

The description of the document structure contains information about the relationship of elements.

```
<!ELEMENT parent child1 child2 ...>
```

is translated to $(parent, child1) : hasChild$, $(parent, child2) : hasChild$ and so on. The according syntax would be (related parent child1 hasChild) for KRSS [13], that is used by RACER. In addition to these role assertions we have to declare parent, child1 and child2 as individuals of the element concept (e.g. $parent : element$.) A concept definition like (define-concept element (some hasChild top)) and (define-concept element (some hasParent element)) will do that automatically.

In terms of DL this will be performed by the general inclusion axioms:

$$\exists hasChild.\top \sqsubseteq element$$
$$\exists hasParent.element \sqsubseteq element$$

The special empty element

```
<!ELEMENT elem EMPTY>
```

will lead to the simple assertion $elem : element$, that reads (instance elem element) in the KRSS syntax.

Translation of lists of attributes is straight forward as well.

```
<!ATTLIST elem att1 type1 att2 type2 ...>
```

leads to the assertions $(elem, att1) : hasAttribute$, $(elem, att2) : hasAttribute$, $(att1, type1) : hasType$, and $(att2, type2) : hasType$. Again the definition (define-concept attribute (some hasType type)) will insure that att1 and att2 are elements of the concept attribute.

This is guaranteed by the inclusion axioms:

$$\exists hasAttribute.\top \sqsubseteq element$$
$$\exists hasAttribute^-.element \sqsubseteq attribute$$
$$\exists hasType.type \sqsubseteq attribute$$

Because of the limited number of types in DTDs, all types may be declared independent of the document: $PCDATA : type$, $CDATA : type...$

After these translation steps the ABox contains information about the structure of the DTD. Also, reachability of elements and attributes is encoded. While roles like hasChild correspond to the child-axis of XPath, the transitive superrole reflects the descendant axis.

6.2   Querying the Knowledge Base

The example above includes library as a role successor of university for the role hasChild. The element book is a role successor to library in hasChild. These relationships are valid for role reachable too because reachable is a superrole of hasChild. Due to the transitive attribute of reachable, book is a role successor of university.

The DL reasoner provides queries like (individuals-related? university book reachable) to ask, if the above mentioned relation is satisfied, i.e. book is a role successor of university for the role reachable. This query asks for $(university, book) : reachable$ in the usual notation of DL. Similarly, the query (individual-fillers book hasParent) reveals all possible parents of book. This query can be written as the concept description $\exists hasChild.\{book\}$ in the notation of DL. At first sight it looks like using nominals, which would be beyond the capabilities of DL reasoners like RACER. To solve this problem we introduce an additional concept named c_book. Furthermore we assert $book : c\_book$. With this individual concept RACER will carry out ABox reasoning without any difficulties.

Further reasoning support is provided to check the instances of concepts and the subsumption of concepts.

6.3   Empty Result Sets

With the Knowledge Base (KB) consisting of the TBox and the ABox our system is able to decide if a XPath expression will lead to an empty result set. There are two reasons why a XPath expression can be empty. First, the XPath expression may locate optional elements that are not in the specific document. Similarly, an expression will return an empty result, if the XPath expression incorporates comparisons to values of attributes that are not satisfied in the document. The second way to receive empty results are XPath expressions that try to locate elements in a structurally impossible way. With our reasoning capabilities we are able to find most of these necessarily empty expressions. The indication of an empty result due to the knowledge base therefore is a partial detection of empty results.

As an example, we consider the XPath expression /book and our example from above. In order to decide if the expression can return results one has to check if book is an individual of the concept element, i.e. book:element? If this is true we have to check if book is a role successor of hasChild to root. Obviously this is not the case, therefore the expression /book will be empty for all documents according to the DTD.

Changing the expression to //book will have an impact on the second condition. We will query if book is a role successor of reachable to root. This is true with respect to our DTD.

Determining if an expressions is empty is quite useful when expressions have to be evaluated, because these empty result sets are provided without any search in the document itself. Furthermore, the presence of permanently empty expressions in a software may be an indication that the expression is not useful or contains an error.

For more complex XPath expression, expressions can be combined to conjunctive conditions. //book/*@name is possibly not empty if the condition for //book is satisfied and book has a child that has an attribute 'name'.

We will show a way to combine these fragments in a single query (see Section 6.5.)

6.4   Optimizing Search in XML Documents

Beyond the ability to decide necessarily empty result sets we are able to predict in what parts of the document tree further search may be successful. Thus we avoid traversal of those parts of the documents that will not lead to results. In our simple expression //book the traversal of department elements cannot lead to any book elements. The DTD does not allow for it, and the knowledge base does not contain the pair $(department, book)$ in $reachableElement$. During traversal of the document tree the search can be limited to those elements (here library) that contain the requested structure made up of elements and attributes.

Our approach evaluates a concept expression to obtain all possible child elements of the current node of the traversal. If this concept expression returns an empty set, no further traversal of the subtree is required. Consequently, no traversable children of 'root' indicate an empty result of the XPath expression. This is equivalent to an unsatisfiable concept in terms of the used reasoners.

Additionally, the traversal of subtrees stops as soon as possible. If, for example, the structure is extended in a way that library may contain book elements as well as journal elements, the traversal will not deepen the search into the journal elements, even if there are no book elements present.

The extension of the concept expressions contains a maximal set of possible elements that have to be matched with the elements found in the document. Thus a query may be empty in a document even if the concept expression is not empty, because the structure allows for appropriate documents.

In our example (see Figure 1) the traversal of the document during the evaluation of the XPath expression //*[@isbn] is limited to the elements *university, library* and the two *book* elements. The other six elements are omitted.

6.5   How to Construct the Concept Expressions

In order to use the complete information provided by the XPath expression we choose a "bottom-up" approach to construct the DL concept expression. Some detailed patterns for this are shown in the following section. In a path like //library/*[@isbn] we will start at the end and construct a concept term for *[@isbn]. This term describes some elements, name unknown, that have an attribute named 'isbn'. The corresponding concept term is

$\exists hasAttribute.\{isbn\}$

Explicit values in a XPath expression like @isbn="987123123" are discarded because we focus on the structural decision. Stepping back to library we add

$\{library\} \sqcap \exists hasChild.\exists hasAttribute.\{isbn\}$

where the latter part contains the parents of the previous term that is intersected with the individual concept mentioned in the XPath expression. In case of an arbitrary element '*' no intersection or specialization will occur. To complete the task we add the '//' part, that is formed by the child elements of 'root' and the parents of the existing expression. These parents are either immediate or transitive parents.

$\exists hasParent.\{root\} \sqcap$
$\exists reachable.(\{library\} \sqcap \exists hasChild.\exists hasAttribute.\{isbn\})$

The resulting concept contains all child elements of the root that may lead to the elements in question. To guide the search of the XML processor one has to iterate the query after each step.

Regarding our sample DTD and the corresponding knowledge base, this expression would yield $\{university\}$. From this, we conclude that the expression in question is structurally possible. If the resulting concept is empty no search in the document will be needed.

Disjunctive or conjunctive connections of XPath expressions are easily transferred into union or intersection of the corresponding concept expressions. For instance, the XPath expression //*[@isbn OR @name] will be translated to

$\exists hasParent.\{root\} \sqcap$
$\exists reachable.(\exists hasAttribute.\{isbn\} \sqcup \exists hasAttribute.\{name\})$

by following the same ideas as in the above example. All of the above examples query the first element descending from the root. Upon the optimized traversal of the document tree the queries have to be iterated according to this traversal. This is mainly accomplished by the substitution of the starting element, here 'root', by the current document node and the adaption of the remaining XPath to the descent in the document as a non-optimized XPath processor has to do. The query then has to be modified with respect to the remaining XPath fragment.

7   Discussion

This sections discusses some restrictions of our approach as well as possible extensions especially with respect to XML schema.

7.1   Finite Model

While the number of possible paths is infinite in a cyclic structure, the set of possible child elements is finite. In fact every concept expression is a subset of the concept *element*.

7.2   Limitations

A strict limitation to all structural analysis are the "pointing" elements IDREF. These elements point to other elements based on an attribute identifier. Because no information is provided where they point to, the optimization is limited to the path from the root to the IDREF. At the referenced element an optimization or prediction may start with the remaining XPath expression.

The completion of the path through a XML document is performed on a step by step basis. The iteration of the completion is performed by the document processor. While this puts some tasks into the XML processor, the optimization is robust against cyclic structures.

Further improvements to decide if a query can lead to empty results might be derived from number restrictions. A structure with two Y-children in an X-element will not satisfy an expression X/Y[3], because there is no third Y-child in this structure. We have dropped these number restrictions because we did not find any XPath expression in our sample code base that accesses children this way, while the DTD description limits the number of child elements in an appropriate way.

7.3   Extensions

So far we have given patterns for the XPath expressions used in the abbreviated syntax. These expressions incorporate the child and parent axis. The transitive reachable role and its inverse cover the ancestor and descendant axis. To extend the knowledge base towards another axis we would simply have to introduce a role for the axis and integrate these roles into the translation of the DTD.

An important extension is the integration of a type system, which is introduced by XML schema. The type information is available on two levels. First, there are more types for attributes (44). This can easily be integrated by additional individuals in the type concept. Second, a type hierarchy is realized by certain concept subsumption. These types offer further refinement of the concept expressions. Similar to the expression $\exists\ hasAttribute.\{isbn\}$ we could easily use the hierarchy of types to query with concept expressions like $\exists hasAttribute.Number$. Using the subsumption of types, as in $NaturalNumber \sqsubseteq Number$, this query will provide all elements that have attributes of type *Number* or *NaturalNumber*. Unfortunately XPath does not provide any type conditions for attributes, although this information is available from schema.

On a second level XML schema introduces some very basic kind of extension and restriction mechanism of elements. We expect this feature to develop in an object oriented fashion, that might lead to a subsumption hierarchy of these typed elements. Currently we can deal with this typing mechanism through the roles hasSpecial and the inverse, or the above introduced subsumption.

An element s that extends an element g will be encoded as $(s, g) : isSpecialOf$. Elements s are reachable if an element g is reachable. The reachableElement role will cover both the child axis and a specialization relation between elements.

A fully object oriented typing might introduce the needs for nonmonotonic reasoning, beyond the capabilities of a standard DL system. Experiments with the first order prover KRHyper [3, 16, 10] indicate the ability to add the needed features.

7.4   Translation to Logic Programs

As mentioned above we have used the prover KRHyper [16] to answer the queries derived from translated XPath expressions and the structural description. Implementing the Hyper Tableau calculus [5], KRHyper tries to find a model of its input, which can be seen a disjunctive logic program. A possible source of disjunctions in the head of the program clauses are substitution groups, where every member of the group is a valid replacement for the head of the group in a path. A XPath expression may introduce disjunctions by the union of path elements.

In order to enable KRHyper with reasoning on description logics we employ a transformation into KRHyper's input language, domain restricted, stratified disjunctive logic programs. The transformation basically follows the standard relational transformation scheme, however making use of a nonmonotonic negation operator. See also [4], which describes a similar transformation.

In contrast to DL, the queries into the KB are performed now under the closed world assumption in these logic programs. Concerning the queries that are imposed by our approach, there will be no differences, because all concept expressions within the queries are bound by the concept "element".

We expect nonmonotonic negation to be an efficient way to translate the extension and restriction capabilities of XML schema. This is actually postponed to a future version of our translation. Although DL reasoners like RACER use highly optimized tableau algorithms, replacing the DL reasoner with the translation and using KRHyper improved the performance significantly.

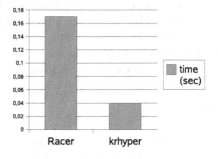

Fig. 4. Performance

The runtimes in figure 4 were measured on a comtemporary PC. The time includes the setup of the knowledge base and twenty queries according to an iterated evaluation of a XPath expression. The underlying DTD contained 25 element descriptions. The queries asked for subsets of element and the relation between individual elements, as indicated in section 6.2.

8   Conclusion

With the evolving use of DL reasoners in the field of the Semantic Web, the question arose if the optimization of the document processing has to use different reasoners or graph oriented tools. We have shown so far that a DL reasoner or a compatible reasoner is suitable for the task of predicting an empty result and the optimization of the document processing itself.

The structural decisions may be used in conjunction with indexing of the document. While indexing provides an efficient way to locate elements our approach will augment this by a preselection of possibly needed elements. Different from indexing our optimization may take place before any part of the document has been read.

With the ability to act as a reasoner about the semantic annotation of documents and the documents and their structure themselves a single reasoning component can be used to perform both tasks. This single tool concept may reduce overhead in system load and maintenance. The reduced learning effort, to understand the reasoning component, should help to promote the use of reasoning systems.

The use of a DL-representation for semistructured data is not new at all. In [9, 8] a thorough translation is presented that aims at a TBox representing the structure, and an ABox containing the content of such data. Our focus was the ability to guide an existing XPath processor through the document tree, not the processing of data. Furthermore the occurrence of cyclic structures introduces some challenges for this approach. In contrast to [7] we don't want to introduce an enhanced language for queries.

Our focus has led to the use of an ABox reflecting the structural properties of documents. Using the KRHyper prover we could get the results of 20 queries into a document structure within less than 0.04 seconds on an ordinary PC, including the setup of the knowledge base and the queries.

In contrast to a merely relational calculus, we did not want to sacrifice the ease of querying for a possible increase in speed, that is still in doubt.

Finally we have to admit that the reasoner has to catch up with the increasing complexity of the document's description and the reasoning task. The foreseeable task to integrate some kind of OO type system will lead to some needed improvements in the reasoner. The enhancements of the reasoning component may offer additional reasoning capabilities to all clients of the service. Focusing on a single system may speed up the process of improvement compared to the development of multiple services.

References

1. F. Baader, D. Calvanese, D. McGuinness, D. Nardi, and P. Patel-Schneider, editors. *Description Logic Handbook*. Cambridge University Press, 2002.
2. F. Baader and U. Sattler. An overview of tableau algorithms for description logics. *Studia Logica*, 69:5–40, 2001.
3. P. Baumgartner. Hyper Tableaux — The Next Generation. In H. de Swaart, editor, *Automated Reasoning with Analytic Tableaux and Related Methods*, volume 1397 of *LNAI*, pages 60–76. Springer, 1998.
4. P. Baumgartner, U. Furbach, M. Groß-Hardt, and T. Kleemann. Model Based Deduction for Database Schema Reasoning. In *KI 2004 - 27th German Conference on Artificial Intelligence*, LNCS. Springer Verlag, Berlin, Heidelberg, New-York, 2004. To appear.
5. P. Baumgartner, U. Furbach, and I. Niemelä. Hyper Tableaux. In *Proc. JELIA 96*, number 1126 in LNAI. European Workshop on Logic in AI, Springer, 1996.
6. T. Bray, J. Paoli, C. M. Sperberg-McQueen, and E. Maler. Extensible markup language (xml) 1.0 (second edition), w3c recommendation. http://www.w3.org/TR/REC-xml, 6 October 2000.
7. F. Bry and S. Schaffert. Towards a declarative query and transformation language for XML and semistructured data: Simulation unification. In *Proceedings of the Int. Conf. on Logic Programming (ICLP)*. Springer-Verlag LNCS, 2002.
8. D. Calvanese, G. D. Giacomo, and M. Lenzerini. Queries and constraints on semi-structured data. In *Proc. of CAiSE*, pages 434–438, 1999.

9. D. Calvanese, G. D. Giacomo, and M. Lenzerini. Representing and reasoning on XML Documents: a Description Logic Approach. *Journal of Logic and Computation*, pages 295–318, 1999.

10. J. Dix, U. Furbach, and I. Niemelä. Nonmonotonic Reasoning: Towards Efficient Calculi and Implementations. In A. Voronkov and A. Robinson, editors, *Handbook of Automated Reasoning*, pages 1121–1234. Elsevier-Science-Press, 2001.

11. V. Haarslev and R. Möller. RACER system description. *Lecture Notes in Computer Science*, 2083:701, 2001.

12. ISO8879:1986. Information processing – text and office systems – standard generalized markup language (sgml), 1986.

13. P. F. Patel-Schneider and B. Swartout. Description-logic knowledge representation system specification, Nov. 1993.

14. W3C. XML Schema - part 0 to part 2. http://www.w3.org/TR/xmlschema-0,-1,-2, 2001.

15. W3C. XML path language (XPath) 2.0. http://www.w3.org/TR/xpath20, 2002.

16. C. Wernhard. System Description: KRHyper. Fachberichte Informatik 14–2003, Universität Koblenz-Landau, Institut für Informatik, 2003.

Declaratively Querying and Visualizing Knowledge Bases in XML

Dietmar Seipel[1], Joachim Baumeister[1], and Marbod Hopfner[2]

[1] University of Würzburg, Institute for Computer Science,
Am Hubland, D – 97074 Würzburg, Germany
`{seipel, baumeister}@informatik.uni-wuerzburg.de`
[2] University of Tübingen, Wilhelm–Schickard Institute for Computer Science,
Sand 13, D – 72076 Tübingen, Germany
`hopfner@informatik.uni-tuebingen.de`

Abstract. The maintenance of large knowledge systems usually is a rather complex task. In this paper we will show that extensions or modifications of a knowledge base can be supported by appropriate visualizations techniques, e.g. by illustrating dependencies within the considered knowledge.

In particular, we introduce a declarative approach for querying and visualizing rule–based knowledge represented as XML documents; a knowledge engineer can extract and visually inspect parts of the knowledge base by ad–hoc declarations in a flexible manner.

Keywords: knowledge systems, rule bases, PROLOG, OWL, XML query / transformations, visualization.

1   Introduction

The extension and maintenance of large rule–based systems is a complex task. For instance, the deletion of redundant or incorrect rules is often very difficult to perform. Thus, transitive dependencies in which the rules are involved are not obvious at first sight, but they can effect the behaviour of the entire knowledge system.

In this paper we introduce a declarative approach for flexibly generating a suitable visualization of rule–based knowledge of various types, such as diagnosis rules, abstraction rules, and indication rules. For example, the dependency graph visualizes the rule base by depicting knowledge objects (e.g., findings or solutions) as nodes and rules as edges between them. The visualization of knowledge can be used, e.g., in the following scenarios:

- *Restructuring knowledge:* If the expert wants to remove or modify existing rules, then it is helpful to inspect all dependend knowledge objects (e.g., constrained findings and inferred solution objects) and rules, respectively. A visual representation of the dependencies can simplify the inspection of the knowledge base.
- *Validating knowledge:* The visual inspection of knowledge can be also helpful during the validation of the reasoning behavior of the knowledge system. In particular, the visualization of the derivation graph of a solution object defined by its deriving rules can assist the expert during a debugging session.

D. Seipel et al. (Eds.): INAP/WLP 2004, LNAI 3392, pp. 16–31, 2005.

– *Examining the knowledge design:* The design of the knowledge base can be simply analyzed by viewing the dependency graph. The interpretation of the results of this analysis is domain dependent. E.g., a subgraph connected to the remaining graph structure only by one node is an indicator for a vulnerable knowledge design, since a part of the implemented knowledge depends on a single object.

Besides the examples given above there exist many other applications for the visualization of rule bases. However, for the implementation of a visualization tool we face the problem that we cannot specify a predefined set of meaningful visualizations for rule bases, since the visualization depends on the requirements of the current task. Therefore, in a real–world environment a flexible and adaptive visualization tool is required for a reasonable application of visualization techniques.

In this paper we introduce a *declarative approach* for flexibly defining visualizations of rule bases. We assume the knowledge base to be available in an XML format. The declarative approach allows for a fast and compact ad–hoc definition of visualizations based on given requirements of the expert. We provide some exemplary queries and transformations for generating reports about the knowledge base in the form of HTML and graphs in GXL format, a standard format for graph–based structures [9]. In principle, our approach is not restricted to the visualization of rule bases; it can be generalized to arbitrary XML documents. E.g., in [8] we have described the tool VISUR/RAR for the visualization of procedural or declarative programs represented in XML structures, e.g., JAVA or PROLOG programs, and for reasoning about the structure of these programs.

The rest of the paper is organized as follows: In Section 2 we sketch a suitable XML representation of knowledge bases and motivate the processing of such XML structures. The visualization system VISUR is briefly introduced in Section 3. In Section 4 the declarative specification of visualizations is described by motivating examples. Our approach is not limited to a particular XML schema; in Section 5 we apply it to OWL based knowledge. In the conclusions we summarize the presented work and we outline some promising directions for future work.

2   Management of Knowledge Bases in XML

XML has been established as a frequently used standard for representing and interchanging data and knowledge. Consequently, various different markups have been proposed for formalizing explicit knowledge; OWL is a prominent example [15].

VISUR/RAR [7] is a system for managing and visualizing rule–based knowledge in XML notation. It is part of the DISLOG developers toolkit DDK, and it is based on the DDK–library FNQUERY [13] for querying, updating, and transforming XML data. The component RAR (*reasoning about rules*) is applied for query and modification tasks. The results of this task are handled by VISUR, which can *visualize* graphs given in the *Graph eXchange Language* GXL [9]; we have added some additional attributes to the GXL notation for configuring the graph display.

In this section we first introduce the XML schema that we are using for representing knowledge bases, and then we sketch the processing of knowledge bases using FN-QUERY.

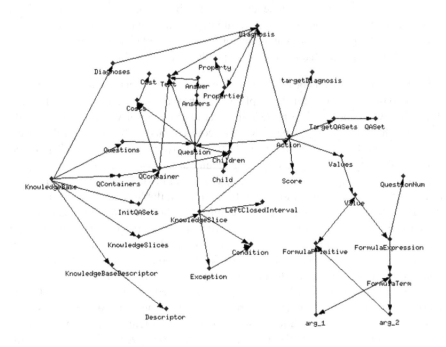

Fig. 1. Knowledge Schema Graph of D3

2.1   Knowledge Bases in XML

In our running example we work with a particular XML schema for knowledge bases, which is used by the D3 system. The expert system shell–kit D3 [11] has been applied successfully for building many diagnostic knowledge systems in the medical, the technical, and the biological domain.

The schema graph of D3 knowledge bases is depicted in Figure 1. The root tag is KnowledgeBase, and the important successor tags are KnowledgeBaseDescriptor (meta information about the given knowledge base), InitQASets (initial questions asked to the user of the system), Questions (questions to be asked to the user), Diagnoses (possible solutions derived by the system), and KnowledgeSlices (inferential knowledge connecting questions and diagnoses). All objects, e.g., diagnoses, questions, and rules, are identified by unique IDs in the XML representation of the knowledge base.

In Figure 2 a small excerpt of the SonoConsult knowledge base [10] is shown. SonoConsult is a fielded knowledge–based documentation and consultation system for medical sonography. Diagnoses and questions are described by a *text* containing the name of the knowledge object; for each question a list of the possible answers is given. The rules are *production rules*: if the given condition evaluates to true, then the production rule assigns a score category to the specified diagnosis.

▦ Diagnosis **P165**
    Text: *Chronische arterielle Verschlußkrankheit (I73.9)*

⚙ᵒᶜ Question **Msi250** (type OC)
    Text: *SI-Arterielle Verschlußkrankheit, Stadium nach Fontaine*
    Answers: (a1="*I*", a2="*II*", a3="*III*", a4="*IV*")

▲ Rule **Rfb3955** (ActionHeuristicPS)
    if (⚙ᵒᶜ Msi250=a2 *or* ⚙ᵒᶜ Msi250=a3 *or* ⚙ᵒᶜ Msi250=a4)
    then ▦ P165 *with* P6

Fig. 2. Excerpt of the Knowledge Base SonoConsult

The knowledge base SonoConsult contains about 8.000 rules. The rule with the ID *Rfb3955* from above is represented in XML as the following knowledge slice:

```
<KnowledgeSlice ID="Rfb3955" type="RuleComplex">
  <Action type="ActionHeuristicPS">
    <Score value="P6"/>
    <Diagnosis ID="P165"/>
  </Action>
  <Condition type="or">
    <Condition type="equal" ID="Msi250" value="Msi250a2"/>
    <Condition type="equal" ID="Msi250" value="Msi250a3"/>
    <Condition type="equal" ID="Msi250" value="Msi250a4"/>
  </Condition>
</KnowledgeSlice>
```

The condition of the rule *Rfb3955* evaluates to true if the question *Msi250* has one of the values *Msi250a2*, *Msi250a3*, or *Msi250a4*. In that case, the score *P6* is given to the diagnosis *P165*; due to this high score of *P6* the diagnosis will be considered as a possible solution. In general, the value range of the scores given to diagnoses is $SC = \{N7, \ldots, N1, P1, \ldots, P7\}$ with ascending categories $P1, \ldots, P7$ for confirming a diagnosis and categories $N1, \ldots, N7$ for disconfirming a diagnosis.

For many questions the value can be derived by another rule in the knowledge base, since the knowledge base can describe transitive paths for deriving a diagnosis. Then it is not necessary that the user enters this value. For a more detailed discussion of the applied knowledge representation we refer to [11].

2.2   Processing XML Knowledge Bases with FNQUERY

The library FNQUERY offers a variety of PROLOG predicates for *querying* and *transforming* XML documents and two different data structures, which we call field notation and database notation. In *field notation* a complex object can be represented as an *association list*

$$[a_1 : v_1, \ldots, a_n : v_n],$$

where a_i is an *attribute* and v_i is the associated *value*; this representation is well–known from the field of artificial intelligence. Using the field notation for semi–structured data with many attributes has got several advantages compared to ordinary PROLOG facts "$o(v_1, \ldots, v_n)$" : The sequence of attribute/value–pairs is arbitrary. Values can be accessed by attributes rather than by argument positions. Null values can be omitted, and new values can be added at runtime. In the PROLOG library FNQUERY this formalism has been extended to the *field notation* for XML documents: an XML element

$$\langle \text{Tag } a_1 = "v_1" \ldots a_n = "v_n" \rangle \text{ Contents } \langle /\text{Tag} \rangle$$

with the tag "Tag" can be represented as a PROLOG term Tag : As : C, where As is an association list for the attribute/value–pairs $a_i = "v_i"$, and C represents the contents, i.e., the subelements of the element. E.g., for the XML representation of the knowledge slice from Section 2.1 we obtain:

```
'KnowledgeSlice':['ID':'Rfb3955', type:'RuleComplex']:[
    'Action':[type:'ActionHeuristicPS']:[
        'Score':[value:'P6']:[],
        'Diagnosis':[ID:'P165']:[] ]
    'Condition':[type:or]:[
        'Condition':[
            type:equal, 'ID':'Msi250', value:'Msi250a2']:[],
        'Condition':[..., value:'Msi250a3']:[],
        'Condition':[..., value:'Msi250a4']:[] ] ]
```

Another way of representing XML in PROLOG is the *database notation*, which is based on the object–relational mapping: the attributes of a complex object o are represented by facts "$\text{attr}(o, a_i, v_i)$", and the subelements o' are stored in facts "$\text{ref}(o, t, n, o')$", where o' is the n–th subelement of o with the tag t. We are currently comparing the efficiency of query evaluation based on the two data structures.

The operations for *accessing* and *updating* an object O are the same for both representations. They use a binary infix predicate ": =", which evaluates its right argument and tries to unify the result with its left argument. Given an element tag E and an attribute A, we use the call X := O^E to select the E–subelement X of O, and we use Y := O@A to select the A–value Y of O; the application of selectors can be iterated, cf. path expressions in XML query languages [1]. On backtracking all solutions can be obtained.

```
?- KS =
    'KnowledgeSlice':[
        'ID':'Rfb3955', type:'RuleComplex']:[
        'Action':[type:'ActionHeuristicPS']:[
            'Score':[value:'P6']:[],
            'Diagnosis':[ID:'P165']:[] ]
        'Condition':[type:or]:[
            'Condition':[ ..., value:'Msi250a2']:[],
            'Condition':[ ..., value:'Msi250a3']:[],
            'Condition':[ ..., value:'Msi250a4']:[] ] ],
    Type := KS@type,
```

```
findall( Value,
    Value := KS^'Condition'^'Condition'@value,
    Values ).

Type = 'RuleComplex',
Values = ['Msi250a2', 'Msi250a3', 'Msi250a4']

Yes
```

To *update* the values of attributes or subelements, the call X := O*As is used, where As specifies the new elements or attribute/value–pairs in the updated object X. The following statements assign the value 'P3' to the score of an action:

```
?- A1 = 'Action':[type:'ActionHeuristicPS']:[
            'Score':[value:'P6']:[],
            'Diagnosis':[ID:'P165']:[] ],
   A2 := A1*[^'Score'@value:'P3'].

A2 = 'Action':[type:'ActionHeuristicPS']:[
        'Score':[value:'P3']:[],
        'Diagnosis':[ID:'P165']:[] ]

Yes
```

The library FNQUERY also contains additional, more *advanced methods*, such as the selection/deletion of all elements/attributes of a certain pattern, the transformation of subcomponents according to substitution rules in the style of XSLT, and the manipulation of path or tree expressions. Thus, FNQUERY can be used for transforming a given knowledge base into an arbitrary document, e.g., the GXL format for visualizing graphs.

3 Visualization of Knowledge Bases in VISUR

Queries and transformations on XML knowledge bases are applied using FNQUERY and RAR. The results of the transformation process are visualized by graphs and tables using the component VISUR. The system VISUR/RAR can significantly improve the development cycle of logic programming applications, and it facilitates the implementation of techniques for syntactically analyzing and visualizing a given knowledge base. For obtaining efficiency and for representing complex deduction tasks we have used techniques from deductive databases and non–monotonic reasoning.

The goal of the system VISUR/RAR is to support the application of *knowledge engineering* and *refactoring* techniques, and the further system development. VISUR/RAR facilitates program comprehension and review, design improvement by refactoring, the extraction of subsystems, and the computation of software metrics (such as, e.g., the degree of abstraction). When we apply it to rule–based knowledge systems, then it helps developers in becoming acquainted with the knowledge base by visualizing dependencies between different questions and diagnoses defined by the available rules. It is possible to analyse knowledge bases customized to the individual needs of a user, and to visualize the results graphically or in tables.

In previous papers [7, 8] we have shown how also JAVA source code represented in XML can be analysed using VISUR/RAR. In the future, we will gradually extend VI-SUR/RAR with additional features. We intend to implement sophisticated methods for *program analysis* from *software engineering* [4, 5, 6], and we want to integrate further *refactoring techniques* for XML knowledge bases, some of which have been described in [14] for PROLOG.

4   Declarative Specification of Visualizations

In this section we give motivating examples for visualizing XML knowledge bases using VISUR/RAR. As mentioned in the introduction, an appropriate visualization of the available knowledge depends on the current task. For large rule bases an exhaustive listing of all dependencies defined by the rules is not helpful, and also a focussing selection of the generated graph may be not meaningful. VISUR/RAR enables the developer of a rule base to flexibly generate visualizations in a declarative way; a visualization required for a specific task can be easily defined by a compact FNQUERY statement. In the following, we illustrate this by examples using the knowledge base of the SONO-CONSULT documentation and consultation system for medical sonography [10].

4.1   Neighbours of a Question

A frequent maintenance operation for knowledge systems considers the restructuring of an already available question. E.g., the value range of a choice question is extended or the question is refined by two more precise questions. Such a restructuring operation can be simplified by a preceding visual analysis of the considered question and its dependencies with other knowledge objects, respectively. The following declaration determines all neighbours of a specified question (here with ID *Msi250*) defined by incoming and outgoing derivation rules:

```
knowledge_base_to_neighbours_of_question(KB, Edges) :-
    findall( Edge,
        ( knowledge_base_to_neighbour_of_question(KB, Edge),
          edge_is_incident_with_node(Edge, 'Msi250') ),
        Edges ).

knowledge_base_to_neighbour_of_question(KB, Cid-Rid-Qid) :-
    Rule := KB^'KnowledgeSlices'^'KnowledgeSlice',
    Rid := Rule@'ID',
    'RuleComplex' := Rule@type,
    Cid := Rule^_^'Condition'@'ID',
    Qid := Rule^'Action'^'Question'@'ID'.
```

In Figure 3 the result of this declaration can be visualized using VISUR.
It is easy to see that the five questions *Mf249*, *Msi1851*, *Mf2206*, *Mf1849*, and *Mf1922*, derive a value for the question *Msi250* using the three rules *RADD430*, *RADD431*, and *RADD1834*. Furthermore, there exist four outgoing rules *Rfb3955*, *Rfb3949*, *Rfb3932*, and *Rfb2943*, that derive values for the diagnoses *P165*, *P1857*, *P2244*, and *P2221*, depending on the value of *Msi250*.

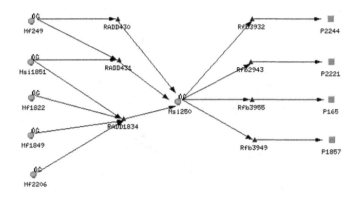

Fig. 3. Neighbours of Question Msi250

4.2   Derivation Tree of a Diagnosis

The visualization of a derivation tree for a specified diagnosis can be helpful during the validation task. Then, the debugging of an erroneous reasoning behavior (e.g.: a given diagnosis is not derived as a possible solution) is simplified by depicting its derivation graph. The following declaration generates the derivation tree for the diagnosis *P181*:

```
knowledge_base_to_rule_edges(KB, Edges) :-
    findall( Edge,
        knowledge_base_to_rule_edge(KB, Edge),
        Edges_2 ),
    reaching_edges('P181', Edges_2, Edges).

knowledge_base_to_rule_edge(KB, Cid-Rid-Qid) :-
    Rule := KB^'KnowledgeSlices'^'KnowledgeSlice',
    Rid := Rule@'ID',
    'RuleComplex' := Rule@type,
    Cid := Rule^_^'Condition'@'ID',
    Qid := Rule^'Action'^_@'ID'.
```

The resulting VISUR presentation is depicted in Figure 4.

For example, the derivation tree shows that the diagnosis *P181* is directly derived by the two rules *Rfb1831* and *Rfb1822*.

4.3   Compact Views of Knowledge Bases

Another possible application of the presented work is the transformation of an existing knowledge base into a more compact XML representation: existing XML structures and tags are combined or deleted in order to remove redundant or uninteresting information. The result of such a transformation can for instance be used for reporting issues.

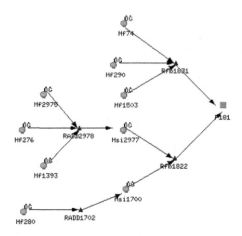

Fig. 4. Derivation Tree of Diagnosis P181

The following declarations shrink the verbose representation of *or* and *equal* conditions by condensing disjunctions $Q = a_1 \vee \ldots \vee Q = a_n$ of equalities to more readable set conditions $Q \in \{\, a_1, \ldots, a_n \,\}$.

```
knowledge_base_view(KB_1, KB_2) :-
    Substitution = [
        (X:As:Es)-('Condition':[type:X|As]:Es),
        Y-X-shorten_value_by_id(X, Y),
        In-Or-or_condition_to_in_condition(Or, In) ],
    fn_transform_elements_fixpoint(Substitution, KB_1, KB_2).

or_condition_to_in_condition(Or, In) :-
    fn_item_parse(Or, or:[]:Equals),
    first(Equals, equal:['ID':Id, value:_]:[]),
    maplist( d3_equal_to_in(Id),
        Equals, Vs ),
    In = in:['ID':Id]:Vs.

equal_to_in(Id, Equal, In) :-
    fn_item_parse(Equal, equal:['ID':Id, value:V]:[]),
    In = element:[value:V]:[].
```

The predicate `fn_transform_elements_fixpoint/3` of the library FNQUERY offers a powerful substitution mechanism: E.g., the substitution

```
(X:As:Es)-('Condition': [type:X|As]:Es)
```

transforms a `'Condition'`–element of `type` X with the further attributes As and the subelements Es into a new element with the tag X, the attributes As and the subelements Es; the substitution

```
In-Or-or_condition_to_in_condition(Or, In)
```

transforms an XML element `Or = or:[]:Equals`, such that all conditions in the list `Equals` have the same `'ID'`, into a new element `In = in:['ID':Id]:Vs`, where `Vs` contains elements `element:[value:V]:[]` with their different values.

When applied to the rule *Rfb3955* given in Section 2.1 the resulting knowledge slice is the following, which is more compact and readable than the original representation:

```
<KnowledgeSlice ID="Rfb3955" type="RuleComplex">
  <Action type="ActionHeuristicPS">
    <Score value="P6"/>
    <Diagnosis ID="P165"/>
  </Action>
  <in ID="Msi250">
    <element value="a2"/>
    <element value="a3"/>
    <element value="a4"/>
  </in>
</KnowledgeSlice>
```

Our declarative query processing techniques can also be applied for producing an overview of the knowledge base in a reader–friendly format. Figure 5 displays an excerpt of the SonoConsult rule base in HTML format, which was also generated using the FNQUERY library (see Figure 2 for another excerpt).

Rule **Rfb3956** (ActionHeuristicPS)
  if ($\mathscr{C}^c$ Msi158 = a8 *and* $\mathscr{C}^c$ M768 = a1 *and* $\mathscr{C}^c$ Msi1510 = a1)
  then ▪ P320 *with* P6

Rule **Rfb3955** (ActionHeuristicPS)
  if ($\mathscr{C}^c$ Msi250 ∈ { a2, a3, a4 })
  then ▪ P165 *with* P6

Rule **Rfb3918** (ActionHeuristicPS)
  if ($\mathscr{C}^c$ Mf333 ∈ { a1, a2 })
  then ▪ P529 *with* P6

Rule **Rfb3917** (ActionHeuristicPS)
  if ($\mathscr{C}^c$ Mf333 ∈ { a3, a4 })
  then ▪ P530 *with* P6

Rule **Rfb4036** (ActionHeuristicPS)
  if ($\mathscr{C}^c$ Mf4027 = a2 *and* $\mathscr{C}^c$ Mf1915 = a1)
  then ▪ P4025 *with* P3

Fig. 5. Rules of SonoConsult in Compact Form

4.4   Static Analysis of the Knowledge Base

For examining the *knowledge design* it is interesting to have statistics about the complexities of the diagnostic rules of the knowledge base. The following PROLOG rule determines the number of findings for each rule condition of SonoConsult:

```
knowledge_base_to_condition_statistics(KB, Numbers) :-
    findall( N,
        ( Slice := KB^_^'KnowledgeSlice',
          knowledge_slice_to_conditions(Slice, Conditions),
          length(Conditions, N) ),
        Numbers ).

knowledge_slice_to_conditions(Slice, Conditions) :-
    findall( Condition,
        ( ( Condition := Slice^'Condition'
        ; Condition := Slice^_^'Condition' ),
          _ := Condition@'ID',
          _ := Condition@value ),
        Conditions ),
    !.
```

The computation took about 1 minute. Due to the wildcard in the path expression KB^_^'KnowledgeSlice' the system tests for each element in the Sono-Consult knowledge base whether it has the tag 'KnowledgeSlice'. Interestingly,

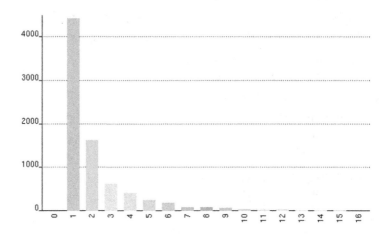

Fig. 6. Findings in Rule Conditions

Table 1. Size of Rule Conditions

Size	0	1	2	3	4	5–9	10–19	20–50
Number	0	4.437	1.629	636	417	692	198	14

in our current implemantation only half of the computation time was spend on the calls `knowledge_slice_to_conditions(Slice, Conditions)`, whereas the other half was needed to find out that there exist no further `'KnowledgeSlice'` elements in the knowledge base. We could save this time by automatically completing the path expression to `KB^'KnowledgeSlices'^'KnowledgeSlice'` based on the available schema knowledge. Note that the other wildcard in the path expression `Slice^_^'Condition'` is necessary to find deeply nested subconditions.

The chart in Figure 6 was created using XPCE–PROLOG. It shows the numbers of rules (y–axis) having a certain number of findings (x–axis) in their condition.

The following (partially aggregated) Table 1 shows that most of the rules, namely 7.119, have between 0 and 4 findings in their conditions, and that only 906 rules have at least 5 findings in their conditions. Interestingsly, there was even one rule condition with 192 findings and one with 204 findings, respectively.

5   Knowledge Bases in OWL

In the previous sections we have discussed a proprietary XML schema for representing real–world knowledge bases. However, with the advent of the *semantic web* the demand for a standard representation of knowledge has been increasingly identified, which has resulted in the introduction of RDF(S)[1] and OWL [2] [15]; for a recent introduction to the concepts and techniques of the semantic web we refer to [2]. It has been repeatedly shown that the application of such standards significantly simplifies the interchange and reuse of knowledge – not only in the context of the web.

Compared to the schema presented in Section 2, XML–based notions like OWL additionally allow for the standardized representation of *semantic meta–knowledge*, e.g., hierarchical relationships and semantic constraints like disjointness properties. In this section, we will show an OWL–based representation of the previously described Sono-Consult knowledge base. In general, OWL documents are relatively verbose. Thus, we will apply FNQUERY to such documents for creating abbreviated reports in PROLOG syntax.

An OWL document is typically defined by the following template:

```
<?xml version="1.0" encoding="UTF-8" ?>
<rdf:RDF
  xmlns="http://d3web.de/ontology#"
  xmlns:rdf="http://www.w3.org/1999/02/22-rdf-syntax-ns#"
  xmlns:rdfs="http://www.w3.org/2000/01/rdf-schema#"
  xmlns:owl="http://www.w3.org/2002/07/owl#">

  << OWL Classes >>
  << OWL Object Properties >>
  << Knowledge Instances >>

</rdf:RDF>
```

---

[1] resource description framework (schema).
[2] ontology web language.

In the following we represent some interesting aspects from the SonoConsult domain in OWL.

OWL Classes

Basic entities of the knowledge representation are defined as OWL classes (some semantic annotation is omitted):

```
<owl:Class rdf:ID="question"/>
<owl:Class rdf:ID="answer"/>
<owl:Class rdf:ID="diagnosis"/>
<owl:Class rdf:ID="rule"/>
<owl:Class rdf:ID="diagnosticRule">
  <rdfs:subClassOf rdf:resource="#rule"/>
</owl:Class>
<owl:Class rdf:ID="ruleCondition"/>
<owl:Class rdf:ID="condOr">
  <rdfs:subClassOf rdf:resource="#ruleCondition"/>
</owl:Class>
<owl:Class rdf:ID="condChoiceEqual">
  <rdfs:subClassOf rdf:resource="#ruleCondition"/>
</owl:Class>
<owl:Class rdf:ID="questionChoice">
  <rdfs:subClassOf rdf:resource="#question"/>
</owl:Class>
<owl:Class rdf:ID="answerChoice">
  <rdfs:subClassOf rdf:resource="#answer"/>
</owl:Class>
```

An OWL element

```
<owl:Class rdf:ID="C">
   <rdfs:subClassOf rdf:resource="#S"/>
</owl:Class>
```

which indicates that C is a class and that C is a subclass of S, is represented in PRO-LOG as a term C --> S; if there is no rdfs:subClassOf element, then it is simply represented as C.

```
owl_classes([
  question, answer, diagnosis,
  rule, diagnosticRule --> rule,
  ruleCondition,
  condOr --> ruleCondition,
  condChoiceEqual --> ruleCondition,
  questionChoice --> question,
  answerChoice --> answer ]).
```

Based on the ontological knowledge we can make query evaluation in FNQUERY more flexible. E.g., it is now possible to evaluate a path expression

```
KB^_^rule^ruleCondition
```

to obtain both condOr and condChoiceEqual elements, since both classes are subclasses of ruleCondition.

OWL Properties

In the following we show only a small part of the existing OWL properties for the defined classes. We distinguish *data type* properties using standard primitive representation based on XMLSchema, and *object properties* that are based on other OWL classes:

```
<owl:DatatypeProperty rdf:ID="questionText">
  <rdfs:domain rdf:resource="#question"/>
  <rdfs:range rdf:resource="XMLSchema#string"/>
  <rdf:type rdf:resource="&owl;FunctionalProperty"/>
</owl:ObjectProperty>

<owl:ObjectProperty rdf:ID="questionCond">
  <rdfs:domain rdf:resource="#condChoiceEqual"/>
  <rdfs:range rdf:resource="#questionChoice"/>
  <rdf:type rdf:resource="&owl;FunctionalProperty"/>
</owl:ObjectProperty>

<owl:ObjectProperty rdf:ID="answerCond">
  <rdfs:domain rdf:resource="#condChoiceEqual"/>
  <rdfs:range rdf:resource="#answerChoice"/>
  <rdf:type rdf:resource="&owl;FunctionalProperty"/>
</owl:ObjectProperty>
```

The following PROLOG representation of the properties is much more readable than the OWL representation, and much more compact (by a factor of 4–5); notice, that we have shown only a small portion of the corresponding OWL data:

```
owl_data_type_properties(functional, [
  questionText: question --> 'XMLSchema#string',
  answerText: answer --> 'XMLSchema#string' ]).

owl_object_properties(functional, [
  questionCond: condChoiceEqual --> questionChoice,
  answerCond: condChoiceEqual --> answerChoice,
  diagnosisRuleAction: diagnosticRule --> ruleAction,
  diagnosisAction: diagnosticRuleAction --> diagnosis,
  ruleScore: diagnosticRuleAction --> score ]).
```

Obviously, the OWL representation can be restored from the PROLOG representation using simple PROLOG rules.

SonoConsult Knowledge

The following OWL instance of a diagnostic rule represents an excerpt from the Sono-Consult knowledge base:

```
<diagnosticRule rdf:ID="Rfb3955">
  <ruleCondition>
    <condOr rdf:ID="c1">
```

```
        <subConditions>
          <condChoiceEqual rdf:ID="sc1">
            <questionCond rdf:resource="#Msi250"/>
            <answerCond rdf:resource="#Msi250a2"/>
          </condChoiceEqual>
        </subConditions>
        ...
      </condOr>
    </ruleCondition>
    <diagnosticRuleAction>
      <diagnosisAction rdf:resource="#P165"/>
      <ruleScore rdf:resoucre="#P6"/>
    </diagnosticRuleAction>
  </diagnosticRule>
```

It is easy to see that FNQUERY can also be applied for stating declarative queries based on OWL documents. In contrast to the proprietary XML format used in the previous sections, we additionally can utilize *semantic information*, e.g. the subclass information.

6   Conclusions

In this paper we have presented a declarative approach for querying and visualizing rule–based knowledge. We have introduced a possible XML representation for rule bases and we have briefly described the system VISUR/RAR: The component RAR allows for compact queries and transformations on XML documents based on FNQUERY. This is used here, e.g., for transforming a specified part of an XML knowledge base into GXL or HTML format. The component VISUR in turn uses GXL documents for graph–based visualizations. The applicability of VISUR/RAR was demonstrated by motivating examples taken from a real–world application. Additionally, we have shown that FN-QUERY can also be applied to OWL documents which allow for a deeper declaration of the semantics contained in the represented knowledge.

In the future we are planning to generalize the presented work to further types of knowledge, e.g., case–based knowledge and model–based knowledge. Furthermore, the usability of the system can be increased by improving the interactivity between the user and the system. E.g., extended browsing techniques for the generated visualizations are necessary.

References

1. *S. Abiteboul, P. Bunemann, D. Suciu:* Data on the Web – From Relations to Semi–Structured Data and XML, Morgan Kaufmann, 2000.
2. *G. Antoniou, F. van Harmelen:* A Semantic Web Primer, MIT Press, 2004.
3. *S. Ceri, G. Gottlob, L. Tanca:* Logic Programming and Databases, Springer, 1990.
4. *S. Diehl (Ed.):* Software Visualization: International Seminar, Dagstuhl Castle, Germany, Springer LNCS 2269, 2002.

5. *H. Erdogmus, O. Tanir (Eds.):* Advances in Software Engineering – Comprehension, Evaluation, and Evolution, Springer, 2002.
6. *M. Fowler:* Refactoring – Improving the Design of Existing Code, Addison–Wesley, 1999.
7. *M. Hopfner, D. Seipel:* Reasoning about Rules in Deductive Databases, Proc. 17th Workshop on Logic Programming WLP 2002.
8. *M. Hopfner, D. Seipel, J. Wolff von Gudenberg:* Comprehending and Visualising Software based on XML Representations and Call Graphs, Proc. 11th IEEE International Workshop on Program Comprehension IWPC 2003.
9. *R. Holt, A. Winter, A. Schürr:* GXL: Towards a Standard Exchange Format, Proc. Working Conference on Reverse Engineering WCRE 2000, http://www.gupro.de/GXL/
10. *M. Hüttig, G. Buscher, T. Menzel, W. Scheppach, F. Puppe, H.-P. Buscher:* A Diagnostic Expert System for Structured Reports, Quality Assessment, and Training of Residents in Sonography, Medizinische Klinik, 2004.
11. *F. Puppe:* Knowledge Reuse among Diagnostic Problem–Solving Methods in the Shell–Kit D3, International Journal of Human–Computer Studies (49), 1998.
12. *A. Serebrenik, B. Demoen:* Refactoring Logic Programs, Proc. Intl. Conference on Logic Programming ICLP 2003 (Poster Session).
13. *D. Seipel:* Processing XML Documents in PROLOG, Proc. 17th Workshop on Logic Programming WLP 2002.
14. *R. Seyerlein:* Refactoring in Deductive Databases Applied to the Information System Qualimed, Diploma Thesis (in German), University of Würzburg, 2001.
15. *M. Smith, C. Welty, D. McGuinness:* OWL Web Ontology Language Guide, February 2004, http://www.w3.org/TR/2004/REC-owl-guide-20040210/
16. *J. Wielemaker, A. Anjewierden:* Programming in XPCE/PROLOG http://www.swi-prolog.org/

SQL Based Frequent Pattern Mining with FP-Growth

Xuequn Shang, Kai-Uwe Sattler, and Ingolf Geist

Department of Computer Science,
University of Magdeburg,
P.O.BOX 4120, 39106 Magdeburg, Germany
{shang, kus, geist}@.iti.cs.uni-magdeburg.de

Abstract. Scalable data mining in large databases is one of today's
real challenges to database research area. The integration of data mining with database systems is an essential component for any successful
large-scale data mining application. A fundamental component in data
mining tasks is finding frequent patterns in a given dataset. Most of the
previous studies adopt an *Apriori*-like candidate set generation-and-test
approach. However, candidate set generation is still costly, especially
when there exist prolific patterns and/or long patterns. In this study
we present an evaluation of SQL based frequent pattern mining with a
novel frequent pattern growth (*FP-growth*) method, which is efficient
and scalable for mining both long and short patterns without candidate
generation. We examine some techniques to improve performance. In addition, we have made performance evaluation on DBMS with IBM DB2
UDB EEE V8.

1   Introduction

Mining frequent patterns in transaction databases has been studied popularly
in data mining research. Most of the previous studies adopt an *Apriori*-like
candidate set generation-and-test approach [3, 7, 8], which is based on an anti-
monotone *Apriori* heuristic: if any length k pattern is not frequent in the
database, its length (k+1) super-pattern can never be frequent. The above
Apriori heuristic achieves good performance gain by reducing significantly the
size of candidate sets. However, in situations with prolific frequent patterns, long
patterns, or quite low minimum support thresholds, this kind of algorithm may
still suffer from the following two nontrivial costs:

1. It is costly to handle a huge number of candidate sets.
2. It is tedious to repeatedly scan the database and check a large set of candidates by pattern matching, which is especially true for mining long patterns.

Recently, an *FP-tree* based frequent pattern mining method [4], called *FP-
growth*, developed by Han et al achieves high efficiency, compared with *Apriori*-
like approach. The *FP-growth* method adopts the divide-and-conquer strategy,

D. Seipel et al. (Eds.): INAP/WLP 2004, LNAI 3392, pp. 32–46, 2005.

uses only two full I/O scans of the database, and avoids iterative candidate generation.

The integration of data mining with database systems is an emergent trend in database research and development area. This is particularly driven by the following reasons.

- Explosion of the data amount stored in databases such as Data Warehouses.
- Database systems provide powerful mechanisms for accessing, filtering, indexing data. Rather than devising specialized parallelization, one can potentially exploit the underlying SQL parallelization. The DBMS support for check-pointing and space management can be especially valuable for long-running mining algorithms on huge volumes of data.
- SQL-aware data mining systems have ability to support ad-hoc mining, ie., allowing to mine arbitrary query results from multiple abstract layers of database systems or Data Warehouses.
- These techniques need to be re-implemented in part if the data set in main-memory approaches does not fit into the available memory.

Data mining on large relational databases has gained popularity and its significance is well recognize. However the performance of SQL based data mining is known to fall behind specialized implementation since the prohibitive nature of the cost associated with extracting knowledge, as well as the lack of suitable declarative query language support. Main-memory algorithms employ sophisticated in-memory data structures and try to reduce the scan of data as few times as possible while SQL based algorithms either require several scans over the data or require many and complex joins between the input tables. There are some SQL based approaches proposed to mine frequent patterns [9, 12], but they are on the base of *Apriori*-like approach which suffer from the inferior performance since the candidate-generation-and-test operation. This fact motivated us to examine if we can get efficient performance by the utilization of SQL based frequent pattern mining using *FP-growth*-like approach. We propose mining algorithms based on *FP-growth* to work on DBMS and compare the performance of these approaches using synthetic datasets.

The remainder of this paper is organized as follows: In section 2, we introduce the method of *FP-tree* construction and *FP-growth* algorithm. In section 3, we discuss different SQL based frequent pattern mining implementations using *FP-growth*-like approach. Experimental results of the performance test are given in section 4. We present related work in section 5 and finally conclude our study and point out some future research issues in section 6.

2   Frequent Pattern Tree and Frequent Pattern Growth Algorithm

The frequent Pattern mining problem can be formally defined as follows. Let $I = \{i_1, i_2, ..., i_m\}$ be a set of items, and DB be a transaction database, where each transaction T is a set of items and $T \subseteq I$. An unique identifer, called its TID, is assigned with each transaction. A transaction T contains a pattern P, a set of items in I, if $P \subseteq T$. The support of a pattern P is the number of transactions containing P in DB. We say that P is a frequent pattern if $P's$ support is no less than a predefined minimum support threshold ξ.

In [4], frequent pattern mining consists of two steps:

1. Construct a compact data structure, frequent pattern tree (FP-tree), which can store more information in less space.
2. Develop an *FP-tree* based pattern growth (FP-growth) method to uncover all frequent patterns recursively.

2.1   Construction of *FP-Tree*

The construction of *FP-tree* requires two scans on transaction database. The first scan accumulates the support of each item and then selects items that satisfy minimum support. In fact, this procedure generates frequent 1-items and then stores them in frequency descending order. The second scan constructs *FP-tree*.

An *FP-tree* is a prefix-tree structure storing frequent patterns for the transaction database, where the support of each tree node is no less than a predefined minimum support threshold ξ. It consists of one root labelled as "*null*", a set of *item-prefix subtrees* as the children of the root, and a *frequent-item-header*

Table 1. A transaction database DB and $\xi = 3$

TID	Items	Frequent Items
1	a, c, d, f, g, i, m, o	c, f, a, m, o
2	a, b, c, f, l, m, n	c, f, a, b, m
3	b, f, h, j, n	f, b
4	$b, c, k, o,$	c, b, o
5	a, c, e, f, l, m, o	c, f, a, m, o

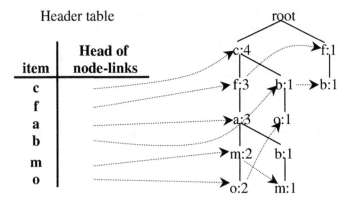

Fig. 1. An *FP-tree* for Table 1

table. Each node in the *item-prefix subtree* consists of three fields: *item-name*, *count*, and *node-link*. Where *node-link* links to the next node in the *FP-tree* carrying the same item-name, or null if there is none. For any frequent item a_i, all the possible frequent patterns that contain a_i can be obtained by following a_i's node-links, starting from a_i's head in the *FP-tree* header. The frequent items in each path are stored in their frequency descending order.

   FP-tree is a highly compact and a much smaller than its original database, and thus saves the costly database scans in the subsequent mining processes. Let us give an example with five transactions. Let the transaction database DB, be the first two columns of Table 1 and the minimum support threshold be 3. The last column of Table 1 collects all frequent 1-items ordered in frequency descending order. One may construct an *FP-tree* as in Figure 1.

2.2   FP-Growth

Based on *FP-tree* structure, an efficient frequent pattern mining algorithm, *FP-growth* method is proposed, which is a divide-and-conquer methodology: decompose mining task into smaller ones, and only need sub-database test.

   FP-growth performed as follows:

– For each node in the *FP-tree* construct its conditional pattern base, which is a "subdatabase" constructed with the prefix subpath set co-occurring with the suffix pattern in the *FP-tree*. *FP-growth* traverses nodes in the *FP-tree* from the least frequent item in L;
– Construct conditional *FP-tree* from each conditional pattern base;
– Execute the frequent pattern mining recursively upon the conditional *FP-tree*. If the conditional *FP-tree* contains a single path, simply enumerate all the patterns.

With the *FP-tree* in Figure 1, the mining process and result is listed in Table 2.

Table 2. Mining of all-patterns based on *FP-tree*

Item	Conditional Pattern Base	Conditional FP-tree	Frequent Pattern
o	$\{(m:2, a:2, f:2, c:2),$ $(b:1, c:1)\}$	$\langle c:3 \rangle$	$c\ o:3$
m	$\{(a:2, f:2, c:2),$ $\{(b:1, a:1, f:1, c:1)$	$\langle c:3, f:3, a:3 \rangle$	$c\ m:3,\ f\ m:3$ $a\ m:3$
b	$\{(a:1, f:1, c:1), (f:1)\}$	ϕ	ϕ
a	$\{(f:3, c:3)\}$	$\langle c:3, f:3 \rangle$	$c\ a:3,\ f\ a:3$
f	$\{(c:3)\}$	$\langle c:3 \rangle$	$c\ f:3$
c	ϕ	ϕ	ϕ

3   Frequent Pattern Mining Based on SQL

Although an *FP-tree* is rather compact, it is unrealistic to construct a main memory-based *FP-tree* when the database is large. However using RDBMSs provides us the benefits of using their buffer management systems specifically developed for freeing the user applications from the size considerations of the data. And moreover, there are several potential advantages of building mining algorithms to work on RDBMSs as described in Introduction. An interesting alternative is to store an *FP-tree* in a relational table and to propose algorithms for frequent patterns mining based on such a table. We studied two approaches in this category - *FP*, *EFP* (Extended Frequent Pattern). They are different in the process of constructing frequent pattern tree table, named *FP*. *FP* approach checks each frequent item of each transaction table one by one to decide whether it should be inserted into the table *FP* or not to construct *FP*. *EFP* approach introduces an extended frequent pattern table, named *EFP*, which collects the set of frequent items and their prefix items of each transaction, thus table *FP* can generate from *EFP* by combining the items which share a common prefix.

Transaction data, as the input, is transformed into a table *T* with two column attributes: transaction identifier (*tid*) and item identifier (*item*). For a given *tid*, typically there are multiple rows in the transaction table corresponding to different items in the transaction. The number of items per transaction is variable and unknown during table creation time.

3.1   Construction of the *FP* Table

FP-tree is a good compact tree structure. In addition, it has two properties: node-link property (all the possible frequent patterns can be obtained by following each frequent's node-links) and prefix path property (to calculate the frequent patterns for a node a_i in a path, only the prefix sub-path of a_i in P need to be accumulated). For storing the tree in a RDBMS a flat table structure is necessary. According to the properties of *FP-tree*, we represent an *FP-tree* by a table *FP* with three column attributes: item identifier (*item*), the number of transactions that contain this item in a subtree (*count*), and item prefix subtree (*path*). The field *path* is beneficial not only to construct the table *FP* but also to find all frequent patterns from *FP*. In the construction of table *FP*, the field *path* is an important condition to judge if an item in frequent item table *F* should be inserted into the table *FP* or not. If an item does not exist in the table *FP* or there exist the same items as this item in the table *FP* but their corresponding *path* are different, insert the item into table *FP*. Otherwise, update the table *FP* by incrementing the item's count by 1. In the process of mining frequent patterns using *FP*, we need to recursively construct conditional frequent pattern table, named *ConFP*, for each frequent item. Due to the *path* column of *FP* storing the set of prefix items of each frequent item, it's easy to find the items which co-occur with this item by deriving all its *path* in the table *FP*.

The process of the table FP construction is as following:

1. Transfer the transaction table T into table T', in which infrequent items are excluded. The size of the transaction table is a major factor in the cost of joins involving T. It can be reduced by pruning the non-frequent items from the transactions after the first pass. We insert the pruned transactions into table T' which has the same schema as that of T. In the subsequent passes, join with T can be replaces by join with T'. This could result in improved performance especially for datasets which contains lot of non-frequent items. SQL query using to generate T' from T in figure 2.

```
insert into T'
select t.id, t.item from T t,
    ((select item, count(*) from T
     group by item
     having count(*) ≥ minsupp
     order by count(*) desc ) as F (item, count))
where t.item = F.item
```

Fig. 2. SQL query to generate T'

```
Algorithm 1 (table FP construction)
  Input: a transferred transaction table T'
  Output: a table FP
  Procedure:
    curcnt := 1;
    curpath := null;
    find distinct tid from the table T'
    for each item i_k of the first tid
        insert i_k with curcnt and curpath into the table FP;
        curpath += i_k;
    insertFP (items);

  insertFP (items)
    if FP has an item f == i_1 (the first item in the items) and f. path == null
        for each item i_k in the items
            insert i_k with curcnt and curpath into the table FP;
            curpath += i_k;
    else
        for each item i_k in the items
            if FP has an item f == i_k and f. path == i_k. path
                curcnt = i_k. count + 1;
                update the table FP;
            else
                insert i_k into the table FP;
            curpath += i_k;
```

Fig. 3. Algorithm for constructing table FP

2. Construct the table FP. Frequent items in T' are sorted in descending order by frequency. (If the frequent ones are sorted in their frequency descending order, there are better chances that more prefix items can be shared.) Each frequent item is tested as follows.
   - If the item does not have the same *item* and *path* as those in the FP, insert it into the FP as a new item with the *count* being 1.
   - Otherwise, update the FP by increasing the *count* by 1.

The algorithm for constructing the table FP is show in Figure 3.

3.2   Finding Frequent Pattern from *FP*

After the construction of a table FP, we can use this table to efficiently mine the complete set of frequent patterns. For each frequent item i we construct its conditional pattern base table PB_i, which has three column attributes $(tid, item, count)$. The table PB_i includes items that co-occur with i in the table FP. As we said above, the path attribute in the table FP represent the information of prefix subpath set of each frequent itemset in a transaction. So this process is implemented by a select query to get all corresponding counts and paths, then split these paths into multiple items with the same count. This can be achieved as follows.

```
select count, path from FP where item = i;
for each count cnr, path p
    id := 1;
    item[ ] = split(p);
    for each item j in item[ ]
        insert into PBᵢ values (id, cnr, j);
    id += 1;
```

Then we construct the table $ConFP_i$ from each conditional pattern base table PB_i using the same algorithm as the table FP construction, and mine recursively in the table $ConFP_i$. We start from the frequent item with the minimum frequency. The similar procedure goes on until the last one.

Further optimization can be exploring if the FP table has a single path. In this case, all the frequent patterns associated with it can be mined by enumeration of all the combinations of the items in FP. Let us examine an example in Table 3. Thus, the following set of frequent patterns is generated, $\{(a:3), (f:3), (c:3), (a\ f:3), (a\ c:3), (f\ c:3), (a\ f\ c:3)\}$.

The algorithm of finding frequent patterns from table FP is showed in Figure 4.

3.3   *EFP* Approach

In the whole procedure, the construction of table FP (table $ConFP$) is a time-consuming procedure. The important reason is that each frequent item must be tested one by one to construct the table FP (table $ConFP$). In that case, the test process is inefficient.

Table 3. An FP table has a single path

$Item$	$Count$	$Path$
a	3	$null$
f	3	$null : a$
c	3	$null : a : f$

Algorithm 2 (FindFP)
  Input: table FP constructed based on Algorithm 1 and table F collects all
        frequent itemsets.
  Output: table $Pattern$, which collects the complete set of frequent patterns.
  Procedure:
  If items in the table FP in a single path
    combine all the items with prefix, insert into $Pattern$;
  else
    for each item i in the table F
      construct table $ConFP_i$;
      if $ConFP_i \neq \phi$
        call FindFP($ConFP_i$);

Fig. 4. Algorithm for finding frequent patterns from table FP

From the above discussions, we expect significant performance improvement
by introducing an extended FP table, called EFP, which has the same format
as table FP ($item, count, path$). We can obtain EFP by directly transforming
frequent items in the transaction table T'. We initialize the path of the first
frequent item i_1 in each transaction and set it as $null$. The path of the second frequent item i_2 is $null : i_1$, and the path of the third frequent item i_3
is $null : i_1 : i_2$, and so on. Table EFP represents all information of frequent
itemsets and their prefix path of each transaction. We combine the items with
identical path to get the table FP. However, compare to the construction of
table FP, we do not need to test each frequent item to construct the table
EFP and can make use of the database powerful query processing capability.
The construction of table EFP can be implemented using a recursive query as
follows.

```
for each tid id
    select item from T'
    where id = id
        create table temp (id int, iid int, item varchar(20) )
    iid := 1;
    for each item i
        insert into temp values( iid, i )
        iid += 1;
```

with fp (item, path, nsegs) as
((select item, cast ('null' as varchar (200)), 1 from temp
    where iid = 1)
union all
(select t.item, cast (f.path ∥' :' ∥ f.item as varchar (200)), f.nesgs+1
    from fp f, temp t
    where t.iid = f.nsegs+1 and
    f.nesgs ¡ iid))
insert into EFP select item, path from FP

For example, with the transactions in Table 1, we get a table FP and a table EFP in Figure 5.

Item	Count	Path
c	4	null
f	3	null : c
a	3	null : c : f
m	2	null : c : f : a
o	2	null : c : f : a : m
b	1	null : c : f : a
m	1	null : c : f : a : b
f	1	null
b	1	null : f
b	1	null : c
o	1	null : c : b

(a) An FP table for Table 1

Item	Path
c	null
f	null : c
a	null : c : f
m	null : c : f : a
o	null : c : f : a : m
c	null
f	null : c
a	null : c : f
b	null : c : f : a
m	null : c : f : a : b
f	null
b	null : f
c	null
b	null : c
o	null : c : b
c	null
f	null : c
a	null : c : f
m	null : c : f : a
o	null : c : f : a : m

(b) An EFP table
for Table 1

Fig. 5. Table FP and table EFP for Table 1

Basically, EFP table is larger than FP table especially there are lots of items share the prefix strings. However, from the performance aspect, the construction of EFP is more efficient than that of FP since the former avoid checking each item of each transaction one by one. The SQL statement of construct FP from EFP is illustrated as follows.

insert into FP
select item, count(*) as count, path from EFP
group by item, path

3.4   Using SQL with Object-Relational Extension

In the following section, we study approaches that use object-relational extension in SQL to improve performance. We consider an approach that use a table function path. As a matter of fact, all approaches above have to materialize its temporary table namely T' and PB'. Those temporary tables are only required in the construction of table FP and table $ConFP$. They are not needed for generating the frequent patterns. So we further use subquery instead of temporary tables. The data table T is scanned in the (id, item) order and combined with frequent itemsets table F to remove all infrequent items and sort in support descending order as F, and then passed to the user defined function Path, which collects all the prefixes of items in a transaction. SQL query to generate FP using the user defined function Path as follows:

insert into FP select $tt_2.item$, tt_2.count (*), $tt_2.path$
from (select $T.id$, $T.item$ from T, F
where $T.item = F.item$
order by $T.id$, $F.count$ desc) as tt_1,
table (Path ($tt_1.id$, $tt_1.item$)) as tt_2
group by $tt_2.item$, $tt_2.path$
order by $tt_2.path$

4   Performance Evaluation

4.1   Dataset

We use synthetic transaction data generation with program describe in *Apriori* algorithm paper [3] for experiment. The nomenclature of these data sets is of the form TxxIyyDzzzK, where xx denotes the average number of items present per transaction, yy denotes the average support of each item in the data set and zzzK denotes the total number of transactions in K (1000's). We report experimental results on four data sets, they are respectively T5I5D1K, T5I5D10K, T25I10D10K, T25I20D100K.

The first dataset consists of 1 thousand transactions, each containing an average of 5 items and the average size of potentially frequent itemsets is 5.

The following two datasets consist of 10 thousand transactions. Each containing an average of 5 items and 25 items. The average size of the maximal potentially frequent itemsets is 5 and 10 respectively .

The last one consists of 100 thousand transactions with an average 25 number of items per transaction and the average length of potentially frequent patterns is 20. There exist exponentially numerous frequent itemsets in this data set when the support threshold goes down. There are pretty long frequent itemsets as well as a large number of short frequent itemsets in it. It is a relatively dense dataset and contains mixtures of short and long frequent itemsets.

4.2   Performance Comparison

Our experiments were performed on DBMS with IBM DB2 UDB EEE V8. For comparison, we also implemented two approaches as follows.

1. A loose-coupling approach, in which access to data stored in RDBMS was provided through a JDBC interface. The procedure of an *FP-tree* build and pattern growth is implemented in memory.
2. A *k-way join* approach based on *Aprioti* algorithm, as proposed in [12]. In *K-way join*, the candidate generation phase computes a set of potential frequent k-itemsets C_k from F_{k-1}. The statement of candidate generation is illustrated in Figure 6.

insert into C_k select $I_1.item_1, \ldots, I_1.item_{k-1}, I_2.item_{k-1}$
from $F_{k-1}I_1, F_{k-1}I_2$
where $I_1.item_1 = I_2.item_1$ and
             $\vdots$
             $I_1.item_{k-2} = I_2.item_{k-2}$ and
             $I_1.item_{k-1} < I_2.item_{k-1}$

Fig. 6. Candidate generation phase in SQL-92

The support counting phase uses k instances of the transaction table and joins it k times with itself and with a single instance of C_k to filter out those itemsets from C_k that appear more frequently in the given set of transactions than the minimum support and store them in F_k. The statement of *K-Way join* is illustrated in Figure 7.

insert into F_k select $item_1, \ldots, item_k$, count(*)
from C_k, T $t_1, \ldots$ T t_k
where t_1.item = $C_k.item_1$ and
             $\vdots$
             t_k.item = $C_k.item_k$ and
             t_1.tid = t_2.tid and
             $\vdots$
             $t_k - 1$.tid = t_k.tid
group by $item_1, item_2 \ldots item_k$
having   count(*) $\geq minsupp$

Fig. 7. Support counting by *K-Way join*

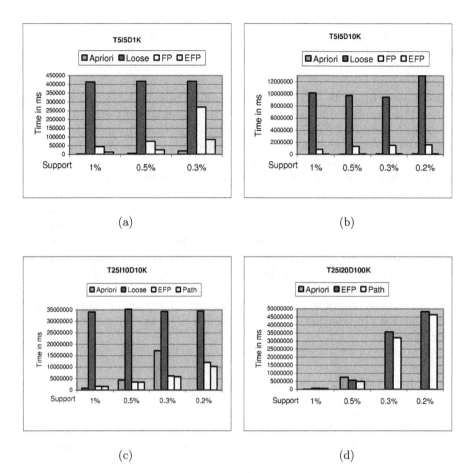

(a)   (b)

(c)   (d)

Fig. 8. Comparison of four approaches. In (c), for *k-way join* approach with the support value of 0.2% , and in (d), for *Loose* and *k-way join* approach with the support value of 0.3% and 0.2%, the running times were so large that we had to abort the runs in many cases

We built (id, item), (item id) index on the data table T and (item) index on the frequent itemsets table F, table FP , and table EFP. The goal was to let the optimizer choose the best plan possible.

In figure 8 (a)(b) we show the total time taken by the four approaches on data set T5I5D1K and T5I5D10K: *K-way join* approach, *loose-coupling* approach, SQL-based FP, and improved SQL-based EFP (without object-relational extension in SQL). From the graph we can make the following observation: *K-way join*, FP, EFP has the better performance than loose-coupling approach. EFP approach can get competitive performance out of FP implementation. An important reason for superior performance of EFP over FP is the avoid testing each frequent item one by one in the construction of table FP. For instance, for dataset T5I5D10K with the support value of 0.5%, in the FP approach, almost

50% of execution time belongs to the construction of table FP. However, in the EFP approach, almost less 24% of execution time belongs to the construction of table FP. Since the recursive construction of table $ConFP$ use the same method as the construction of table FP. In that case, the overall execution time is highly reduced.

In data set T5I5D10K, as the support threshold is high, the frequent items are short and the number of item is not large. The advantages of EFP over $Apriori$ are not so impressive. EFP is even slightly worse than $Apriori$. However, as the support threshold goes down, the gap is becoming wider. When the support threshold is low, the number of frequent patterns as well as that of candidates are non-trivial. In contrast, EFP avoid candidates generation and test. That is why EFP can get significant performance improvement.

We compare the four approaches on data sets T25I10D10K and T25I20D100K: K-way join approach, loose-couple approach, EFP approach, and $Path$ approach using a user defined table functions (Path). Figure 8 (c)(d) shows the results of experiments. From the graph we can make the following observation: EFP and $Path$ approach can get better performance than K-way join on large data sets or long patterns. The main reason is that generating candidate-k table C_k is time-consuming procedure when T is large or minimum support threshold is quite low. In addition, with the extended SQL we can get the improved performance.

5   Related Work

The work on frequent pattern mining started with the development of the AIS algorithm, and was further modified and extended in [3]. Since then, there have been several attempts in improving the performance of these algorithms. [7] presents a hash based algorithm, which is especially effective for the generation of candidate set for large 2-itemsets. [8] presents a partition algorithm, which improve the overall performance by reducing the number of passes needed over the complete database to at most two. [1] presents a $TreeProjection$ method, which represents frequent patterns as nodes of a lexicographic tree and uses the hierarchical structure of the lexicographic tree to successively project transactions and uses matrix counting on the reduced set of transactions for finding frequent patterns. [4] builds a special tree structure in main memory to avoid multiple scans of database. However, most of these algorithms are applicable to data stored in flat files. The basic characteristics of these algorithms are that they are main memory algorithms, where the data is either read directly from flat files or is first extracted from the DBMS and then processed in main memory.

Recently researchers have started to focus on issues related to integrating mining with databases. There have been language proposals to extend SQL to support mining operators. The data mining Query Language DMQL [5] proposed a collection of such operators for classification rules, characteristics rule, association rules, etc. The Mine Rule operator [6] was proposed for a generalized version of the association rule discover problem. [2] presents a methodology for tightly-coupled integration of data mining applications with a relational database system. [9] has tried to highlight the implications of various architecture alternatives for coupling data mining with relational database systems. They have also compared the performance of the SQL-92 architecture with SQL-OR based architecture, and they are on the base of *Apriori*-like approach.

6   Summary and Conclusion

We have implemented SQL based frequent pattern mining using *FP-growth*-like approach. We represent *FP-tree* using a relational table *FP* and proposed a method to construct this table. To improve its performance, a table called *EFP* is introduced, which is in fact stores all information of frequent item sets and their prefix path of each transaction. And then, table *FP* can derived from table *EFP*. Compare to the construction of *FP*, the process of the construction of *EFP* avoid testing each frequent item one by one. We next experimented with an approach that made use of the object-relational extensions like table function. The experimental results show that SQL based frequent pattern mining approach using *FP-growth* can get better performance than *Apriori* on large data sets or long patterns.

There remain lots of further investigations. We plan to implement our SQL based frequent pattern mining approach on parallel RDBMS, and to check how efficiently our approach can be parallelized and speeded up using parallel database system. Additionally, we will investigate an SQL based algorithm which combine *Apriori* and *FP-growth* to scale both small and large data sets.

References

1. R. Agarwal, C. Aggarwal, and V. Prasad. A tree projection algorithm for generation of frequent itemsets. Journal of Parallel and Distributed Computing(Special Issue on High Performance Data Mining), 2000.
2. R. Agrawal and K. Shim. Developing tightly-coupled data mining application on a relational database system. In Proc.of the 2nd Int. Conf. on Knowledge Discovery in Database and Data Mining, Portland,Oregon, 1996.
3. R. Agrawal, R. Srikant. Fast algorithms for mining association rules. In Proc. of the 20st VLDB Conference, Santiago, Chile, pp.487-499, 1994.
4. J. Han, J. pei, and Y. Yin. Mining frequent patterns without candidate generation. In Proc. of the ACM SIGMOD Conference on Management of data, 2000.
5. J. Han, Y. Fu, W. Wang, K. Koperski, and O. Zaiane. DMQL: A data mining query language for relational database. In Proc. Of the 1996 SIGMOD workshop on research issues on data mining and knowledge discovery, Montreal, Canada, 1996.
6. M. Houtsma and A. Swami. Set-oriented data mining in relational databases. DKE, 17(3): 245-262, December 1995.
7. R. Meo, G. Psaila, and S. Ceri. A new SQL like operator for mining association rules. In Proc. Of the 22nd Int. Conf. on Very Large Databases, Bombay, India, 1996.

8. J. S. Park, M. Chen, and P. S. Yu. An effective hash based algorithm for mining association rules. In Proc. of the ACM SIGMOD Conference on Management of data, pp.175-186, 1995.

9. I. Pramudiono, T. Shintani, T. Tamura and M. Kitsuregawa. Parallel SQL based associaton rule mining on large scale PC cluster: performance comparision with directly coded C implementation. In Proc. Of Third Pacific-Asia Conf. on Knowledge Discovery and Data Mining, 1999.

10. R. Rantzau. Processing frequent itemset discovery queries by division and set containment join operators. DMKD03: 8th ACM SIGMOD Workshop on Research Issues in Data Mining and Knowledge Discovery, 2003.

11. A. Savsere, E. Omiecinski, and S. Navathe. An efficient algorithm for mining association rules in large databases. In Proc. of the 21st VLDB Conference, 1995.

12. S. Sarawagi, S. Thomas, and R. Agrawal. Integrating mining with relational database systems: alternatives and implications. In Proc. of the ACM SIGMOD Conference on Management of data, Seattle,Washinton,USA, 1998.

13. K. Sattel and O. Dunemann. SQL database primitives for decision tree classifiers. In Proc. Of the 10nd ACM CIKN Int. Conf. on Information and Knowledge Management, Atlanta,Georgia, 2001.

14. S. Thomas and S. Chakravarthy. Performance evaluation and optimization of join queries for association rule mining. In Proc. DaWaK, Florence, Italy, 1999.

15. H. Wang and C. Zaniolo. Using SQL to build new aggregates and extenders for Object-Relational systems. In Proc. Of the 26th Int. Conf. on Very Large Databases, Cairo,Egypt, 2000.

16. T. Yoshizawa, I. Pramudiono, and M. Kitsuregawa. SQL based association rule mining using commercial RDBMS (IBM DB2 UDB EEE). In Proc. DaWaK, London, UK, 2000.

Incremental Learning of Transfer Rules
for Customized Machine Translation

Werner Winiwarter

Faculty of Computer Science,
University of Vienna, Liebiggasse 4, A-1010 Vienna, Austria
`werner.winiwarter@univie.ac.at`
`http://www.ifs.univie.ac.at/~ww/`

Abstract. In this paper we present a machine translation system, which translates Japanese into German. We have developed a transfer-based architecture in which the transfer rules are learnt incrementally from translation examples provided by a user. This means that there are no handcrafted rules, but, on the contrary, the user can customize the system according to his own preferences. The translation system has been implemented by using Amzi! Prolog. This programming environment had the big advantage of offering sufficient scalability even for large lexicons and rule bases, powerful unification operations for the application of transfer rules, and full Unicode support for Japanese characters. Finally, the application programming interface to Visual Basic made it possible to design an embedded translation environment so that the user can use Microsoft Word to work with the Japanese text and invoke the translation features directly from within the text editor. We have integrated the machine translation system into a language learning environment for German-speaking language students to create a Personal Embedded Translation and Reading Assistant (PETRA).

1 Introduction

For language students and other people interested in Japanese documents, the Web makes available a wealth of information. In general, after reaching a certain level of linguistic competence in a foreign language, the reading of written material represents an excellent way to improve the fluency by learning new terminology or grammatical structures in their natural context with comparatively little effort.

However, this approach to language acquisition, which works so well with many languages, is seriously hampered by the complexity of the Japanese writing system. Japanese texts are a mixture of the two syllabaries *hiragana* and *katakana* as well as the Japanese versions of Chinese characters called *kanji*. The two syllabaries are relatively easy to learn with only 46 different characters each, but there are several thousand, mostly quite complex kanji of which the pronunciations or *readings* often depend on the textual context. Another severe

D. Seipel et al. (Eds.): INAP/WLP 2004, LNAI 3392, pp. 47–64, 2005.
© Springer-Verlag Berlin Heidelberg 2005

Japanese sentence:

これは、片面だけに字を書いて、同じ大きさに切りそろえたものを、
何枚も革のひもでとじた。

Roman transcription:

Kore wa, katamen dake ni ji o kaite, onaji ookisa ni kirisoraeta mono o,
nan mai mo kawa no himo de tojita.

Human translation into German:

Man hat es nur einseitig beschrieben und mehrere auf gleiche Größe
zurechtgeschnittene Blätter mit Lederriemen zusammengebunden.

Human translation into English:

It was written on only one side, and several sheets, trimmed to the same size,
were bound together with leather laces.

Machine translation by WorldLingo
(www.worldlingo.com/products_services/worldlingo_translator.html):

Dieses, den Brief auf gerade die eine Seite, die schreibend, die sie in die
gleiche Größe trimmt, geschlossen vielen mit der Zeichenkette des Leders.

This, writing the letter on just the one side, those which it trims in the same size,
closed many with the string of the leather.

Machine translation by Excite
(www.excite.co.jp/world/url/):

This is leather many sheets about what wrote the character only to one side
and was cut to an even length in the same size. With a string It closed.

Machine translation by @nifty
(www.nifty.com/globalgate/):

This wrote the character only to one side and also closed many things cut to
an even length in the same size with the string of leather.

Machine translation by TransLand
(www.brother.co.jp/jp/honyaku/demo/index.html):

A letter was written only to the settlement side, and this じ how many sheets
of things which cut it into the same size and which was completed with the
leather string, too.

Machine translation by iTranslator
(itranslator.mendez.com/BGSX/BGSXeng_us-EntryPage.htm):

For this, as writing a character, I cut and leveled it for a similar size for one
side only, and any sheets are ひもでとじた of a leather.

Machine translation by 訳せ!!ゴマ
(ai2you.com/goma/):

This bound the one, that writes only to one side and evenly cut a/the
character to the same size with the strings of many sheets of leather.

Fig. 1. Example output of machine translation systems

problem in Japanese is that the individual words are not separated by spaces so
that the reader has to guess the word boundaries.

All these difficulties make reading and translating Japanese sentences a cum-
bersome and tedious process. If the reader reaches an inscrutable text passage,

he must first guess where an unknown word starts and then consult a dictionary. To look up the word in a bilingual dictionary is quite straightforward as long as the reader is sure about the correct pronunciation, otherwise he has to consult a kanji dictionary, which lists kanji and their readings categorized by 214 basic elements or *radicals*. The retrieval of this kanji information is again a time-consuming task, especially because the radicals appear in different shapes depending on the position within the kanji.

Online documents have the great advantage that they enable the use of convenient tools, which assist the reader in comprehending the meaning of the Japanese text. Today, there exist several Web sites that offer information about kanji as well as English or German translations of Japanese words as pop-up hints just by pointing with the mouse at a certain text position, e.g. POPjisho[1] or Rikai[2]. Even if these tools are very useful, there are still often problems with the correct segmentation and the retrieval of conjugated words.

In a previous project we developed a reading tool for the use within Microsoft Word. We implemented this environment by using Amzi! Prolog, which provides full Unicode support so that Japanese characters can be used freely in the Prolog source code. Its application programming interface to Visual Basic enabled us to embed the Prolog program into the text editor. The implemented functionality of our reading tool included correct segmentation, the lookup of conjugated words, and the addition of new word definitions. This application represented also an evaluation of the scalability of Amzi! Prolog. We could achieve excellent performance although we searched 6,355 entries extracted from the kanji dictionary KANJIDIC[3], 100,014 entries from the Japanese-English dictionary EDICT[4], and 190,251 entries from the Japanese-German dictionary WaDokuJT[5].

Another, less satisfying observation with using our reading environment was that even with all this information available, it was still often not possible to correctly reproduce the intended meaning of a Japanese text. The main reason for this lies in the complexity of the translation task for the language pair Japanese–German caused by the very different grammars of the two languages. Whereas German grammar has a very specific system of declensions and conjugations to express number, gender, case, tense, mood, voice, etc., Japanese is highly ambiguous regarding most of these features, e.g. there exist no articles to indicate gender or definiteness, no declension to indicate number or case, and only two tenses. The ambiguity is further increased dramatically by the extensive use of ellipsis in Japanese. Therefore, a machine translation system requires sophisticated disambiguation techniques [1, 17, 19, 20] and anaphoric resolution strategies [12, 16, 18, 27].

---

[1] http://www.popjisyo.com

[2] http://www.rikai.com/perl/Home.pl

[3] http://www.csse.monash.edu.au/~jwb/kanjidic.html

[4] http://www.csse.monash.edu.au/~jwb/edict.html

[5] http://www.wadoku.de

Instead of a lengthy discussion of the state of the art of systems available for Japanese translation, we show the results of an entertaining experiment in Fig. 1. The figure lists the attempts of several machine translation programs to translate a sentence about producing a parchment codex. We could only find one program that also translates into German, all others translate only into English. All the examples are taken from free online translation Web sites, except the last entry, which was produced by a commercial product.

As can be seen, the results are far from satisfactory. All the systems are certainly not suitable for fully automatic high quality machine translation. It is sometimes even hard or impossible to grasp the exact meaning of a Japanese sentence from the mutilated translations.

This unsatisfactory situation was the motivation for us to meet the challenge of developing a high quality machine translation system from Japanese into German. In our approach the system learns the transfer rules incrementally from translation examples by using structural matching between the syntax trees. This way the user can customize the system according to his personal preferences. If the user is not satisfied with a translation result, he can simply correct the translation and activate the adaptive learning module, which results in an update of the translation rule base.

We have integrated our machine translation system with the previously developed reading tool to create the *Personal Embedded Translation and Reading Assistant (PETRA)*. PETRA's main aim is to assist German-speaking language students in reading and translating Japanese documents. PETRA offers the students valuable information, which the students apply to solve the translation task at hand. This encourages a bidirectional knowledge transfer so that the students play an active role during their whole interaction with PETRA. Therefore, studying Japanese becomes more interesting and entertaining.

The rest of the paper is organized as follows. In Sect. 2 we first provide a brief discussion of related work. Then we give an overview of the system architecture in Sect. 3 before we describe the technical details of the individual components of our translation environment in Sect. 4, i.e. tokenization, parsing, learning, transfer, and generation. Finally, we close the paper with concluding remarks and an outlook on future work.

2   Related Work

Research on machine translation has a long tradition (for good overviews see [7, 8, 9, 11, 22]). The state of the art in machine translation is that there are quite good solutions for narrow application domains with a limited vocabulary and concept space. For more general use only systems for very similar language pairs promise to produce output that is acceptable or at least comprehensible. It is the general opinion that fully automatic high quality translation without any limitations on the subject and without any human intervention is far beyond the scope of today's machine translation technology, and there is serious doubt that it will be ever possible in the future [10].

This is true for *transfer-based* machine translation systems, which try to find mappings between specific language pairs, and even more so for *interlingua-based* machine translation systems aiming to find a language-independent representation that mediates among arbitrary languages. The latter are also often referred to as *knowledge-based* machine translation systems [15, 23, 24] because in most cases a semantic representation of the sentence meaning is used as interlingua. The most ambitious initiative in this direction is probably UNL[6]; one recent system limited to the translation of Japanese, Spanish, and Arabic texts into English is GAZELLE [6].

It is very disappointing to have to notice that the translation quality has not much improved in the last 10 years [28]. One main obstacle on the way to achieving better quality is seen in the fact that most of the current machine translation systems are not able to learn from their mistakes. Most of the translation systems consist of large static rule bases with limited coverage, which have been compiled manually with huge intellectual effort. All the valuable effort spent by users on post-editing translation results is usually lost for future translations.

As a solution to this knowledge acquisition bottleneck, *corpus-based* machine translation tries to learn the transfer knowledge automatically on the basis of large bilingual corpora for the language pair (for a good survey and discussion see [14]). *Statistical* machine translation [3, 4] basically translates word-for-word and rearranges the words afterwards in the right order. Such systems have only been of some success for very similar language pairs. For applying statistical machine translation to Japanese several hybrid approaches have been proposed that also make use of syntactic knowledge [29, 30].

The most prominent approach for the translation of Japanese has been *example-based* machine translation [21, 26]. The basic idea is to collect translation examples for phrases and to use a best match algorithm to find the closest example for a given source phrase. The translation of a complete sentence is then built by combining the retrieved target phrases. The different approaches vary in the representation of the translation examples. Whereas some approaches store structured representations for all concrete examples [2], others explicitly use variables to produce generalized templates [5, 13]. However, the main drawback remains that most of the representations of translation examples used in example-based systems of reasonable size have to be manually crafted or at least reviewed for correctness [25].

To summarize, we are faced with the dilemma that by relying on the available approaches one can either spend several years of effort in creating hand-coded transfer rules or a knowledge-based interlingua – ending up with a large knowledge base that is difficult to maintain – or put one's trust in statistical machine translation based on huge bilingual corpora resulting in mediocre translations caused by the use of inaccurate approximations. Example-based machine translation somehow offers a compromise: one can choose how much effort one wants

---

[6] `www.undl.org`.

to invest in adding or correcting translation examples in order to improve the translation quality.

3   System Architecture

In our approach we use translation examples provided by the user to learn the transfer rules incrementally by using structural matching between the corresponding syntax trees. There were several considerations that guided us towards this design choice:

- as our aim was to develop a domain-independent machine translation system, an interlingua-based approach was out of the question,
- we did not have the resources to manually build a large transfer rule base, also a handcrafted rule base is in conflict with our need for flexible adaptation,
- we had no huge bilingual corpus available for Japanese–German, also the insufficient data quality of today's large corpora would interfere with our demand for high quality translations,
- even if we had an adequate corpus, the poor results achieved by statistical techniques and the manual effort to compile translation templates of sufficient quality for the use in example-based machine translation prohibit the use of existing approaches,
- in our opinion there exists no "perfect" translation but only a preferred one for a certain user, therefore we aim at full customization of our machine translation system,

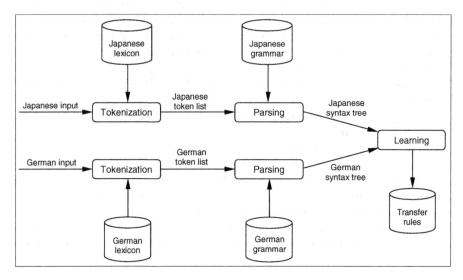

Fig. 2. Learning mode

- the interactive improvement of translation results has also an important pedagogical benefit for the language students because it turns a boring translation task into an entertaining hands-on experience,
- the structured representation in the syntax trees proved to be an efficient input to the learning algorithm, and we can display the trees to language students as additional valuable information.

The operation of our machine translation system can be divided into a learning mode and a translation mode. In the *learning mode* (see Fig. 2) we derive new transfer rules by using a Japanese–German sentence pair as input. Both sentences are first analyzed by the *tokenization* modules, which produce the correct segmentations into word tokens associated with their part-of-speech (POS) tags. Both token lists are then transformed into syntax trees by the *parsing* modules. The syntax trees represent the input to the *learning* module, which uses a structural matching algorithm to discover new transfer rules.

In the *translation mode* (see Fig. 3) we translate a Japanese sentence into the corresponding German sentence by invoking the *transfer* module. It applies the transfer rules stored in the rule base to transform the Japanese syntax tree into the corresponding German syntax tree. Finally, the task of the *generation* module is to produce the surface form of the German sentence as a character string. Of course, the user can correct the translation result and activate the learning mode to incrementally improve the quality of the transfer rule base.

In Sect. 4 we give a more detailed technical description of the individual modules. We illustrate their mode of operation by using the sentence in Fig. 1 as a running example throughout the rest of this paper.

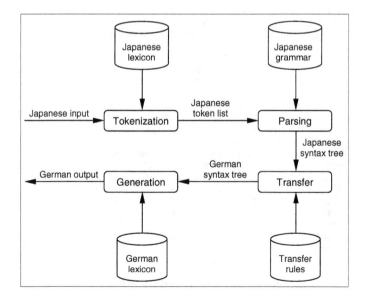

Fig. 3. Translation mode

4   System Description

4.1   Tokenization

The task of the tokenization module is to analyze the surface string of a sentence, to divide the string into words, to lemmatize the words (i.e. to reduce inflectional and variant forms of a word to their base form), and to annotate the base forms with POS tags. Figure 4 shows the token list for our example sentence. The demonstrative pronoun "kore" is an anaphoric reference to "the parchment", which was introduced before in the Japanese text. The *ta*-form of a verb indicates English past tense (expressed as perfect tense in German), whereas the *te*-form is the connective form. The expression "nan mai mo" (literally "what thin objects also") means "several sheets" in this context.

Japanese sentence:
これは、片面だけに字を書いて、同じ大きさに切りそろえた
ものを、何枚も革のひもでとじた。
Segmentation:
これ|は|、|片面|だけ|に|字|を|書いて|、|同じ|大きさ|に|切りそろえた|
もの|を|、|何|枚|も|革|の|ひも|で|とじた|。
Roman transcription:
Kore wa, katamen dake ni ji o kaite, onaji ookisa ni kirisoraeta
mono o, nan mai mo kawa no himo de tojita.

これ/dpr	demonstrative pronoun – kore – it
は/par	particle – wa – (topic indicator)
、/cma	comma
片面/nou	noun – katamen – one side
だけ/suf	suffix – dake – only
に/par	particle – ni – on
字/nou	noun – ji – character
を/par	particle – o – (direct object indicator)
書く/vte	verb te-form – kaku – to write
、/cma	comma
同じ/ano	adjectival noun – onaji – same
大きさ/nou	noun – ookisa – size
に/par	particle – ni – to
切りそろえる/vta	verb ta-form – kirisoraeru – to trim
もの/nou	noun – mono – thing
を/par	particle – o – (direct object indicator)
、/cma	comma
何/ipr	interrogative pronoun – nan – what
枚/cou	counter – mai – thin object
も/par	particle – mo – also
革/nou	noun – kawa – leather
の/par	particle – no – (attribution indicator)
ひも/nou	noun – himo – lace
で/par	particle – de – with
とじる/vta	verb ta-form – tojiru – to bind together
。/per	period

Fig. 4. Example of Japanese token list

Since Japanese writing does not use word delimiters (such as space characters), we have to represent a Japanese sentence as one single atom during segmentation. We have to find and remove the correct word token that is the left subatom of the sentence:

```
segment(Sentence, [BaseForm/POS|TokenList]) :-
    find_token(Sentence, BaseForm, WordLength, POS),
    remove_token(Sentence, WordLength, TokenList).
```

To remove the word token from the sentence we use the information about the word length to calculate the subatom that has to be extracted. Then we continue recursively with the retrieval of the next word token. The recursion ends when the word length equals the length of the remaining partial sentence:

```
remove_token(Sentence, WordLength, []) :-
    atom_length(Sentence, WordLength).
remove_token(Sentence, WordLength, TokenList) :-
    atom_length(Sentence, SentenceLength),
    StartPos is 1 + WordLength,
    RestLength is SentenceLength - WordLength,
    sub_atom(String, StartPos, RestLength, RestSentence),
    segment(RestSentence, TokenList).
```

For the identification of the correct word token we retrieve all words from the Japanese lexicon that are left subatoms of the sentence. From the list of word candidates we choose the correct word by applying some disambiguation rules. The default choice is the longest matching sequence:

```
find_token(Sentence, BaseForm, WordLength, POS) :-
    findall(W:B:P, find_word(Sentence, W, B, P), Candidates),
    select_word(Candidates, BaseForm, WordLength, POS).
```

The retrieval of a word from the Japanese lexicon is performed by matching it with the beginning of the sentence:

```
find_word(Sentence, Word, Word, POS) :-
    jap_lex_entry(Word, POS),
    atom_length(Word, WordLength),
    sub_atom(Sentence, 1, WordLength, Word).
```

Since Japanese has quite a complex system of conjugations for verbs and adjectives, we also have to search for all concatenations of word stems and endings for these two word classes. The base form of conjugated words is computed by concatenating the stem and the correct base form ending depending on the conjugation class:

```
find_word(Sentence, Word, BaseForm, POS) :-
    jap_lex_verbadj(Stem, ConjClass),
    atom_length(Stem, StemLength),
    sub_atom(Sentence, 1, StemLength, Stem),
    jap_ending(ConjClass, Ending, POS),
    atom_length(Ending, EndLength),
    StartPos is StemLength + 1,
    sub_atom(Sentence, StartPos, EndLength, Ending),
    atom_concat(Stem, Ending, Word),
    jap_baseform_ending(ConjClass, BaseFormEnding),
    atom_concat(Stem, BaseFormEnding, BaseForm).
```

The tokenization of Japanese sentences requires a lot of processing power, but is solved by Amzi! Prolog even for large lexicons without any problems.

Compared to this, tokenization of German sentences is quite a trivial task. It can be solved by simply using the predicate string_tokens to transform the sentence into a list of tokens, which can then be lemmatized separately. Figure 5 shows the German token list for our translation example. Some ambiguities regarding syntactic features are resolved later during parsing. For example, for the noun "Lederriemen" plural and singular forms are identical so that the decision about the correct number is left to the parsing module. Within the PETRA environment, the language students can consult the token lists to offer them valuable information at the word level.

German sentence:
Man hat es nur einseitig beschrieben und mehrere auf gleiche Größe zurechtgeschnittene Blätter mit Lederriemen zusammengebunden.

man/npr	indefinite pronoun – one
haben/apr	auxiliary verb present tense – to have
es/pep	personal pronoun – it
nur/adv	adverb – only
einseitig/apo	adjective positive comparison – on one side
beschreiben/vpp	verb past participle – to write
und/con	conjunction – and
mehrere/npr	indefinite pronoun – several
auf/prp	preposition – to
gleich/apo	adjective positive comparison – same
Größe/nsg	noun singular – size
zurechtschneiden/vap	verb attributive past participle – to trim
Blatt/npl	noun plural – sheet
mit/prp	preposition – with
Lederriemen/nsp	noun singular or plural – leather lace
zusammenbinden/vpp	verb past participle – to bind together
. /per	period

Fig. 5. Example of German token list

4.2   Parsing

The parsing modules compute the syntactic structure of sentences from their
token lists. One interesting property of Japanese grammar is that it uses post-
positions instead of prepositions and that the predicate is at the end of the
sentence. Therefore, it is easier to parse a Japanese sentence from right to left.
Figure 6 shows the syntax tree for our example sentence. As can be seen, the
POS tag for conjugated word forms is indicated as feature `hwf` (head word form).

hew	ver	とじる		head word – verb – tojiru – to bind together
hwf	vta			head word form – verb ta-form
pob	hew	nou	ひも	postpositional object – head word – noun – himo – lace
	php	par	で	phrase particle – particle – de – with
	anp	hew	nou 革	attributive noun phrase – head word – noun – kawa – leather
dob	hew	nou	もの	direct object – head word – noun – mono – thing
	amo	hew	cou 枚	amount – head word – counter – mai – thin object
	php	par	も	phrase particle – particle – mo – also
	qua	ipr	何	quantity – interrogative pronoun – nan – what
	avp	hew	ver 切りそろえる	attributive verb phrase – head word – verb – kirisoraeru – to trim
	hwf	vta		head word form – verb ta-form
	pob	hew	nou 大きさ	postpositional object – head word – noun – ookisa – size
	php	par	に	phrase particle – particle – ni – to
	aap	hew	ano 同じ	attributive adjective phrase – head word – adjectival noun – onaji – same
pcl	hew	ver	書く	preceding clause – head word – verb – kaku – to write
	hwf	vte		head word form – verb te-form
	dob	hew	nou 字	direct object – head word – noun – ji – character
	adp	hew	nou 片面	adverbial phrase – head word – noun – katamen – one side
	php	par	に	phrase particle – particle – ni – on
	asf	suf	だけ	attributive suffix – suffix – dake – only
	sub	dpr	これ	subject – demonstrative pronoun – kore – it

Fig. 6. Example of Japanese syntax tree

We use the Definite Clause Grammar (DCG) preprocessor of Amzi! Prolog
to write the grammar rules. Instead of using a fixed structure to represent the
syntax tree, we opted for a more flexible and robust representation by using *sets*
modeled as Prolog lists. A sentence is a set of constituents, and each constituent
is a compound term of arity 1 with the constituent name as principal functor
and the argument being either

– a *simple constituent* (`feature_value` or `word/word_class`) or
– a *complex constituent* (set of subconstituents).

This flexible representation has the advantage that it is compact, because
empty optional constituents are not stored explicitly, and is not affected by the
ordering of the different subconstituents. The latter is important for a robust
and effective realization of the transfer module so that the transfer rules can
change the syntax tree without having to consider any sequencing information.

During parsing we collect arguments for all possible subconstituents and then
eliminate empty subconstituents by using the predicate `compress` to remove all
list entries with argument `nil`.

In the following we show some (strongly simplified) grammar rules for a noun phrase with an optional attributive suffix and an optional attributive noun phrase (we use the Roman transcription of the particle "no" just in this example):

```
noun_phrase(NP) --> attr_suffix(Asf), [N/nou], attr_np(Anp),
    {compress([hew(N), asf(Asf), anp(Anp)], Np)}.
attr_suffix(Asf) --> [Asf/suf].
attr_suffix(nil) --> [].
attr_np(Anp) --> [no/par], noun_phrase(Anp).
attr_np(nil) --> [].
```

To facilitate the matching between Japanese and German syntax trees (see Sect. 4.3) we tried to align the German grammar as best as possible with the Japanese one. Therefore, we also parse German sentences from right to left. For that purpose we have to perform a preprocessing step on the token list in which we shift all prepositions to the end of prepositional phrases so that they are parsed first. Figure 7 shows the German syntax tree for our translation example. As mentioned in Sect. 4.1 we resolve ambiguous feature values during parsing, e.g. now we can assign the correct number plural to "Lederriemen".

hew	ver	zusammenbinden			head word – verb – to bind together
ten	per				tense – perfect
pob	hew	nou	Lederriemen		prepositional object – head word – noun – leather lace
	php	prp	mit		phrase particle – preposition – with
	det	nod			determiner type – no determiner
	num	plu			number – plural
dob	hew	nou	Blatt		direct object – head word – noun – sheet
	det	nod			determiner type – no determiner
	num	plu			number – plural
	aip	npr	mehrere		attributive indefinite pronoun – indefinite pronoun – several
	avp	hew	ver	zurechtschneiden	attributive verb phrase – head word – verb – to trim
		ten	per		tense – perfect
		pob	hew	nou	Größe	prepositional object – head word – noun – size
			php	prp	auf	phrase particle – preposition – to
			det	nod		determiner type – no determiner
			num	sng		number – singular
			aap	hew	adj	gleich	attributive adjective phrase – head word – adjective – same
				com	pos	comparison – positive
sub	npr	man			subject – indefinite pronoun – one
pcl	hew	ver	beschreiben		preceding clause – head word – verb – to write
	ten	per			tense – perfect
	php	con	und		phrase particle – conjunction – and
	pap	hew	adj	einseitig	predicative adjective phrase – head word – adjective – on one side
		com	pos		comparison – positive
		aav	adv	nur	attributive adverb – adverb – only
	dob	pep	es		direct object – personal pronoun – it

Fig. 7. Example of German syntax tree

For displaying the parsing trees to the user we have implemented one generic display module for both Japanese and German syntax trees, which is also able to deal with mixed representations caused by missing coverage of the transfer rule base. This way we can show the limitations of the translation system to the language student who can easily fix them with an update of the rule base.

4.3   Learning

The learning module traverses the Japanese and German syntax trees and derives new transfer rules, which are added to the rule base. For that purpose we have implemented generic predicates for the simultaneous navigation in two complex constituents. We start to search for new rules at the sentence level before we look for corresponding constituents to continue the search for finer-grained transfer rules recursively. We always perform a complete traversal, i.e. new rules are learnt even if they are not required for the translation of the Japanese sentence in order to extract as much information as possible from the example.

We distinguish between four different types of transfer rules for simple constituents (SC) and complex constituents (CC). The transfer rules are stored as facts in Prolog:

- `tr_sc(C1,C2,A1,A2)`: changes the SC C1(A1) to C2(A2),
- `tr_asc(A1,A2)`: changes the argument of an SC from A1 to A2,
- `tr_cc(C1,C2,Hew,Req1,Req2)`: changes the CC C1(A1), A1=Req1∪Opt, to C2(A2), A2=Req2∪Opt, if hew(Hew)∈A1,
- `tr_acc(Hew,Req1,Req2)`: changes the argument of a CC from A1=Req1∪Add to A2=Req2∪Add if hew(Hew)∈A1.

`Hew` serves as index for the fast retrieval of matching rules and the reduction of the number of rules that have to be analyzed. For transfer rules of type `tr_acc` any additional subconstituents are allowed in `Add`, whereas `Opt` in rules of type `tr_cc` can only contain certain optional subconstituents. Transfer rules for complex constituents can use shared variables for unification in `Req1` and `Req2`. In addition to those four generic rule types, we also use several more specific types, e.g. for the correct translation of conjunctions and syntactic features.

Figure 8 shows the transfer rules that we can learn from our translation example. We omit the default rules for deriving the perfect tense from the head word form `vta`, for deriving the conjunction "und" from the head word form `vte`, and for inserting the indefinite pronoun "man" for the missing subject. The suffix "dake" is an optional subconstituent, which can extend the set of required subconstituents in Rule 8. Rule 1 and Rule 4 are two examples of transfer rules that use shared variables for unification.

The principal steps for performing the structural matching between two complex constituents are:

- we either derive transfer rules of type `tr_asc` for the head word or transfer rules of type `tr_acc` for head/modifier combinations,
- we derive transfer rules of type `tr_sc` or `tr_cc` to translate a Japanese subconstituent into a different German subconstituent,
- we search for corresponding subconstituents and apply the matching recursively to those subconstituents,
- we derive transfer rules for conjunctions and syntactic features.

Each rule is validated against the existing rules to resolve all conflicts arising from adding the new rule to the rule base. The resolution is achieved by making the conflicting rules more specific.

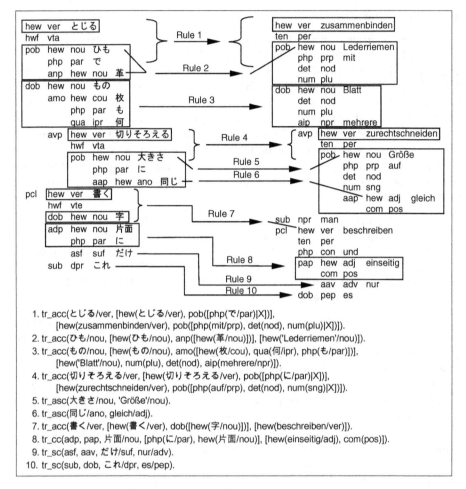

Fig. 8. Example of learning transfer rules

4.4   Transfer

The transfer module traverses the Japanese syntax tree and searches for transfer rules that can be applied. The flexible definition of the rules enables a robust processing of the syntax tree. One rule only changes certain parts of a constituent into the German equivalent, other parts are left unchanged to be transformed later on. Thus, our transfer algorithm deals efficiently with a mixture of Japanese–German, which gradually turns into a correct German syntax tree.

To translate the argument A1 of a constituent C(A1) into A2 we have defined the predicate tf_arg(C, A1, A2). For simple constituents we just apply transfer rules of type tr_asc, for complex constituents we first apply transfer rules of type tr_acc (predicate tf_acc(A1, A2)) as well as rules for conjunctions and syntactic features before we recursively call the predicate tf_sub(Csub, A1, A2) for the translation of each subconstituent Csub(Asub):

```
tf_sub(Csub, A1, A2) :-
    find_subconstituent(Csub, A1, Asub),
    tf_sub_arg(Csub, Asub, A1, A2).
tf_sub(_, A, A).
```

The predicate find_subconstituent retrieves the argument Asub for the subconstituent Csub(Asub). It fails if no subconstituent with constituent name Csub is included in A1. The predicate tf_sub_arg first tries to apply rules of type tr_sc and tr_cc to replace the Japanese subconstituent with a different German subconstituent before it recursively calls the predicate tf_arg to translate the argument Asub:

```
tf_sub_arg(Csub, Asub, A1, A2) :-
    tr_sc(Csub, Csub2, Asub, Asub2),
    replace_subconstituent(Csub, Csub2, A1, Asub2, A2).
tf_sub_arg(Csub, Asub, A1, A2) :-
    tf_cc(Csub, Csub2, Asub, Asub2),
    replace_subconstituent(Csub, Csub2, A1, Asub2, A2).
tf_sub_arg(Csub, Asub, A1, A2) :-
    tf_arg(Csub, Asub, Asub2),
    Asub \== Asub2,
    replace_arg_subconstituent(Csub, A1, Asub2, A2).
tf_sub_arg(_, _, A, A).
```

To apply transfer rules of type tr_acc we retrieve the head word from A1 as index for the access to matching transfer rules and then call split to unify the subconstituents in Req1 with the corresponding subconstituents in A1:

```
tf_acc(A1, A2) :-
    find_subconstituent(hew, A1, Hew),
    tr_acc(Hew, Req1, Req2),
    split(A1, Req1, Add),
    append(Req2, Add, A2).
tf_acc(A, A).
```

The predicate split takes every subconstituent in Req1, retrieves the corresponding subconstituent in A1 and unifies the two structures. This way we can guarantee that the unification is not affected by the order of the subconstituents in Req1 and A1. As a byproduct of this sorting procedure, split returns the set of additional subconstituents Add=A1\Req1, i.e. all subconstituents in A1 that were not retrieved. Figure 9 shows an example of the application of a transfer rule of type tr_acc with a shared variable for unification (Rule 4 in Fig. 8). The predicate tf_cc for the application of transfer rules of type tr_cc is defined in a similar way.

```
tr_acc(切りそろえる/ver,
        [hew(切りそろえる/ver), pob([php(に/par)|X])],
        [hew(zurechtschneiden/ver), pob([php(auf/prp), det(nod), num(sng)|X])]).
Req1 =  [hew(切りそろえる/ver), pob([php(に/par)|X])]
Req2 =  [hew(zurechtschneiden/ver), pob([php(auf/prp), det(nod), num(sng)|X])]
A1 =    [pob([php(に/par), hew(大きさ/nou), aap([hew(同じ/ano)])]),
        hwf(vta), hew(切りそろえる/ver)]
Req1' = [hew(切りそろえる/ver), pob([php(に/par),
                hew(大きさ/nou), aap([hew(同じ/ano)])])]
Add =   [hwf(vta)]
Req2' = [hew(zurechtschneiden/ver), pob([php(auf/prp), det(nod), num(sng),
                hew(大きさ/nou), aap([hew(同じ/ano)])])]
A2 =    [hew(zurechtschneiden/ver), pob([php(auf/prp), det(nod), num(sng),
                hew(大きさ/nou), aap([hew(同じ/ano)])]), hwf(vta)]
```

Fig. 9. Example of the application of a transfer rule

4.5   Generation

To generate the surface form of a German sentence, we traverse the syntax tree in
a top-down fashion. For each complex constituent we transform its argument into
a list of surface strings, which is computed recursively from its subconstituents
as nested list and flattened afterwards. The syntactic features to compute the
correct determiners and the declensions and conjugations of German words are
partly included in the German syntax tree, e.g. number or tense, and partly
retrieved from the German lexicon, e.g. gender. In the following we show the
(strongly simplified) predicate to generate the list of surface strings for a noun
phrase (the predicate find_optional_subconstituent returns nil if it cannot
find the subconstituent):

```
generate_np(nil, _, []).
generate_np(NP, Case, StringList) :-
    find_subconstituent(hew, NP, Hew/nou),
    find_subconstituent(det, NP, Det),
    find_subconstituent(num, NP, Num),
    ger_lex_noun(Hew, Gender, DeclClass),
    generate_det(Det, Num, Case, Gender, Determiner),
    find_optional_subconstituent(aap, NP, Aap),
    generate_aap(Aap, Det, Num, Case, Gender, Adjective),
    generate_hew(Hew, Num, Case, DeclClass, Noun),
    flatten([Determiner, Adjective, Noun], StringList).
generate_np(_, _, []).
```

After the complete traversal of the syntax tree, the resulting flat list of surface
strings is transformed into a single character string by inserting spaces where
appropriate.

Finally, we provide some means for the resolution of simple intersentential
anaphora by storing candidates for antecedents in previous sentences, e.g. to
compute the correct surface form of a personal pronoun.

5 Conclusion

In this paper we have presented a customizable machine translation system, which incrementally learns transfer rules from translation examples provided by a user. We have completed the implementation of the translation system and the integration into the language learning environment PETRA. We are now in the process of filling the transfer rule base with the help of several language students from the University of Vienna. So far, the feedback from the students has been very positive. For some, PETRA has already become an invaluable companion throughout their language studies.

Whereas at the moment language students are our main target audience, we hope to reach a level of linguistic competence in the near future that will make it also possible for non-specialist users to benefit from our translation environment. In addition to constantly extending the coverage of our machine translation system, future work will also concentrate on a thorough evaluation of the system according to the FEMTI[7] framework.

References

1. Bond, F., Ogura, K., Kawaoka, T.: Noun phrase reference in Japanese-to-English machine translation. Proceedings of the 7th International Conference on Theoretical and Methodological Issues in Machine Translation, Leuven, Belgium (1995)
2. Brockett, C. et al.: English-Japanese example-based machine translation using abstract linguistic representations. Proceedings of the COLING-2002 Workshop on Machine Translation in Asia, Taipei, Taiwan (2002)
3. Brown, P.: A statistical approach to machine translation. Computational Linguistics **16(2)** (1990) 79–85
4. Brown, P. et al.: The mathematics of statistical machine translation: Parameter estimation. Computational Linguistics **19(2)** (1993) 263–311
5. Furuse, O., Iida, H.: Cooperation between transfer and analysis in example-based framework. Proceedings of the 14th International Conference on Computational Linguistics, Nantes, France (1992) 645–651
6. Germann, U.: Making semantic interpretation parser-independent. Proceedings of the 3rd AMTA Conference, Longhorne, USA (1998) 286–299
7. Hutchins, J.: Machine Translation: Past, Present, Future. Ellis Horwood (1986)
8. Hutchins, J.: Machine translation over 50 years. Histoire epistémologie langage **23(1)** (2001) 7–31
9. Hutchins, J.: Has machine translation improved? Some historical comparisons. Proceedings of the 9th MT Summit, New Orleans, USA (2003) 181–188
10. Hutchins, J.: Machine translation and computer-based translation tools: What's available and how it's used. In: Bravo, J. M., ed.: A New Spectrum of Translation Studies. University of Valladolid (2003)
11. Hutchins, J., Somers, H.: An Introduction to Machine Translation. Academic Press (1992)
12. Isozaki, H., Hirao, T.: Japanese zero pronoun resolution based on ranking rules and machine learning. Proceedings of the Conference on Empirical Methods in Natural Language Processing, Sapporo, Japan (2003) 184–191

---

[7] www.isi.edu/natural-language/mteval/.

13. Kaji, H., Kida, Y., Morimoto, Y.: Learning translation examples from bilingual text. Proceedings of the 14th International Conference on Computational Linguistics, Nantes, France (1992) 672–678
14. Knight, K.: Automatic knowledge acquisition for machine translation. AI Magazine **18(4)** (1997) 81–96
15. Leavitt, J. R. R., Lonsdale, D. W., Franz, A. M.: A reasoned interlingua for knowledge-based machine translation. Proceedings of the 10th Canadian Conference on Artificial Intelligence, Banff, Canada (1994)
16. Murata, M., Isahara, H., Nagao, M.: Pronoun resolution in Japanese sentences using surface expressions and examples. Proceedings of the ACL-99 Workshop on Coreference and its Applications, Maryland, USA (1999)
17. Murata, M., Nagao, M.: Determination of refential property and number of nouns in Japanese sentences for machine translation into English. Proceedings of the 5th International Conference on Theoretical and Methodological Issues in Machine Translation, Kyoto, Japan (1993) 218–225
18. Murata, M., Nagao, M.: Resolution of verb ellipsis in Japanese sentence using surface expressions and examples. Proceedings of the Natural Language Processing Pacific Rim Symposium, Phuket, Thailand (1997) 75–80
19. Murata, M. et al.: An example-based approach to Japanese-to-English translation of tense, aspect, and modality. Proceedings of the 8th International Conference on Theoretical and Methodological Issues in Machine Translation, Chester, United Kingdom (1999) 66–76
20. Murata, M. et al.: A machine-learning approach to estimating the referential properties of Japanese noun phrases. Proceedings of the CICLing-2001 Conference on Intelligent Text Processing and Computational Linguistics, Mexico City, Mexico (2001)
21. Nagao, M.: A framework of a mechanical translation between Japanese and English by analogy principle. In: Elithorn, A., Banerji, R., eds.: Artificial and Human Intelligence. NATO Publications (1984)
22. Newton, J., ed.: Computers in Translation: A Practical Appraisal. Routledge (1992)
23. Nirenberg, S. et al.: Machine Translation: A Knowledge-Based Approach. Morgan Kaufmann Publishers (1992)
24. Onyshkevych, B., Nirenburg, S.: A lexicon for knowledge-based MT. Machine Translation **10(1-2)** (1995) 5–57
25. Richardson, S. et al.: Overcoming the customization bottleneck using example-based MT. Proceedings of the ACL Workshop on Data-driven Machine Translation, Toulouse, France (2001) 9–16
26. Sato, S.: Example-Based Machine Translation. PhD thesis, Kyoto University (1991)
27. Seki, K., Atsushi, F., Ishikawa, T.: A probabilistic method for analyzing Japanese anaphora integrating zero pronoun detection and resolution. Proceedings of the 19th International Conference on Computational Linguistics, Taipei, Taiwan (2002) 911–917
28. Somers, H., ed.: Computers and Translation: A Translator's Guide. John Benjamins (2003)
29. Watanabe, T., Imamura, K., Sumita, E.: Statistical machine translation based on hierarchical phrase alignment. Proceedings of the 9th International Conference on Theoretical and Methodological Issues in Machine Translation, Keihanna, Japan (2002) 188–198
30. Yamada, K.: A Syntax-Based Statistical Translation Model. PhD thesis, University of Southern California (2002)

Quality Measures and Semi-automatic Mining of Diagnostic Rule Bases

Martin Atzmueller, Joachim Baumeister, and Frank Puppe

Department of Computer Science,
University of Würzburg, 97074 Würzburg, Germany
Phone: +49 931 888-6739, Fax: +49 931 888-6732
{atzmueller, baumeister, puppe}@informatik.uni-wuerzburg.de

Abstract. Semi-automatic data mining approaches often yield better results than plain automatic methods, due to the early integration of the user's goals. For example in the medical domain, experts are likely to favor simpler models instead of more complex models. Then, the accuracy of discovered patterns is often not the only criterion to consider. Instead, the simplicity of the discovered knowledge is of prime importance, since this directly relates to the understandability and the interpretability of the learned knowledge.

In this paper, we present quality measures considering the understandability and the accuracy of (learned) rule bases. We describe a unifying quality measure, which can trade-off small losses concerning accuracy vs. an increased simplicity. Furthermore, we introduce a semi-automatic data mining method for learning understandable and accurate rule bases. The presented work is evaluated using cases from a real world application in the medical domain.

1   Introduction

Automatic methods for learning rules commonly perform well concerning the classification accuracy of the learned models. However, often the understandability of the learned patterns is poor, which is problematic if the learned knowledge should be manually processed in further steps. Semi-automatic approaches often yield better results than plain automatic methods, due to the early integration of the user's goals. In such semi-automatic scenarios the learned knowledge is not used as a black-box reasoning engine, but can be refined incrementally by other techniques, e.g., human interpretation.

Furthermore, semi-automatic learning methods can incorporate additional background knowledge for further quality improvements. When guiding the knowledge discovery process, it often turns out that user interests concerning the accuracy of the learned knowledge are not related to other aspects, e.g., simplicity of the patterns [1, 2]. So, the knowledge discovery method should take both accuracy and simplicity of the learned knowledge into account.

In this paper, we present quality measures for rating the simplicity and the accuracy of a learned rule base, and we briefly introduce a semi-automatic learning method for simple scoring rules. Besides the discussed quality measures we propose a unifying quality measure balancing the accuracy and the understandability of a given rule base.

D. Seipel et al. (Eds.): INAP/WLP 2004, LNAI 3392, pp. 65–78, 2005.

It is worth noticing, that the presented measures are not only applicable to scoring rules but can be easily generalized to other rule-based approaches, e.g., association rules. However, in this paper we focus on the application of scoring rules.

Our implementation and evaluation is based on the knowledge-based documentation and consultation system for sonography SONOCONSULT [3]. The cases are detailed descriptions of findings of the examination(s), together with the inferred diagnoses (concepts). The cases acquired using SONOCONSULT have a high quality regarding the derived diagnoses as evaluated by medical experts (cf. [3]).

The rest of the paper is organized as follows: In Section 2 we define the basic notions used in this paper, and we introduce diagnostic scores implemented by scoring rules as an intuitive concept for representing diagnostic knowledge. In Section 3 we present simplicity measures for diagnostic scores and scoring rules. These measures are used to determine the understandability of the learned knowledge. We present a unifying quality measure taking both the simplicity and the accuracy of the rule base into account. In Section 4 we outline a method for learning diagnostic scores, and discuss additional background knowledge that is applicable to the learning task. An evaluation using a real-world case base is given in Section 5. We conclude the paper in Section 6 discussing the presented work, and we show promising directions for future work.

2   Diagnostic Scores Using Scoring Rules – An Overview

We first give an introduction to the applied knowledge representation before discussing appropriate quality measures and semi-automatic learning methods. Let Ω_Q be the universe set of all questions available in the problem domain. In the context of machine learning methods, questions are commonly called *attributes*. A value $v \in dom(q)$ assigned to a question $q \in \Omega_Q$ is called a *finding*, and we call $\Omega_{\mathcal{F}}$ the set of all possible findings in the given problem domain. A finding $f \in \Omega_{\mathcal{F}}$ is denoted by $q{:}v$ for $q \in \Omega_Q$ and $v \in dom(q)$. The set $F_q \subseteq \Omega_{\mathcal{F}}$ of possible findings for a given question q is defined as $F_q = \{f \in \Omega_{\mathcal{F}} \mid f = q{:}v \wedge v \in dom(q)\}$. Each finding $f \in \Omega_{\mathcal{F}}$ is defined as a possible input of a diagnostic knowledge system.

Let d be a *diagnosis* representing a possible output of a diagnostic knowledge system. We define $\Omega_{\mathcal{D}}$ to be the universe of all possible diagnoses for a given problem domain. With respect to a given problem a symbolic state

$$dom(d) = \{not\ probable,\ undefined,\ probable\}$$

is assigned to a diagnosis $d \in \Omega_{\mathcal{D}}$.

A *case* c is defined as a tuple $c = (\mathcal{F}_c, \mathcal{D}_c, \mathcal{I}_c)$, where $\mathcal{F}_c \subset \Omega_{\mathcal{F}}$ is the set of observed findings for the given case. The set $\mathcal{D}_c \subseteq \Omega_{\mathcal{D}}$ contains the diagnoses describing the solution of the case c, and $\mathcal{I}_c$ contains additional (meta-) information describing the case c in more detail. The set of all possible cases for a given problem domain is denoted by Ω_C. For the learning task we consider a case base $CB \subseteq \Omega_C$ containing all available cases that have been solved previously.

Diagnostic scores, e.g., [4, 5] are a rather wide spread formalism for medical decision making. For inferring a diagnosis a limited number of findings is used in a regular and simple to interpret manner. In its simplest form, each observed finding individually contributes one point to an account. If the total score of the account exceeds a given threshold, then the diagnosis is established. Diagnostic scores are commonly implemented using scoring rules, which are used to derive a specific diagnosis. A *simple scoring rule r* is denoted by $r = f \xrightarrow{s} d$, where $f \in \Omega_{\mathcal{F}}$ is a finding, and $d \in \Omega_{\mathcal{D}}$ is the target diagnosis. For each rule a symbolic confirmation category $s \in \Omega_{scr}$ is attached with $\Omega_{scr} \in \{ S_3, S_2, S_1, 0, S_{-1}, S_{-2}, S_{-3} \}$. Formally, a diagnostic score $DS(d)$ for a diagnosis $d \in \Omega_{\mathcal{D}}$ is defined as the set of scoring rules $r \in \mathcal{R}$ that contain d in their rule action, i.e., $DS(d) = \{r \in \mathcal{R} \mid r = f \xrightarrow{s} d \wedge f \in \Omega_{\mathcal{F}}\}$. Let Ω_R be the universe of all possible rules for the sets $\Omega_{\mathcal{F}}$, $\Omega_{\mathcal{D}}$ and Ω_{scr}. Then, we call $\mathcal{R} \subseteq \Omega_R$ the *rule base* containing the inferential knowledge of the problem domain.

Confirmation categories of scoring rules are used to represent a qualitative degree of uncertainty. In contrast to quantitative approaches, e.g., Bayesian methods, symbolic categories state the degree of confirmation or disconfirmation for a diagnosis. In this way, a symbolic category s expresses the uncertainty for which the observation of finding f will confirm/disconfirm the diagnosis d. Whereas $s \in \{S_1, S_2, S_3\}$ stand for confirming symbolic categories in ascending order, the categories $s \in \{S_{-1}, S_{-2}, S_{-3}\}$ are ascending categories for disconfirming a diagnosis. A rule with category 0 has no effect on the diagnosis' state, and therefore is usually omitted from the rule base. It is worth noticing, that the value range Ω_{scr} of the possible symbolic categories is not fixed. For a more detailed (or coarse) representation of confirmation the value range may be extended (or reduced).

For a given case $c \in \Omega_C$ the final state of each diagnosis $d \in \Omega_{\mathcal{D}}$ is determined by evaluating the available scoring rules $r \in \mathcal{R}$ targeting d. Thus, rules $r = f \xrightarrow{s} d$ contained in $\mathcal{R}$ are activated, iff f is observed in case c, i.e., $f \in \mathcal{F}_c$. The symbolic categories of the activated rules are aggregated by adding the categories in a way, so that four equal categories result in the next higher category (e.g., $S_1 + S_1 + S_1 + S_1 = S_2$), and so that two equal categories with opposite sign nullify (e.g., $S_1 + S_{-1} = 0$). For a more detailed or coarse definition of Ω_{scr} the aggregation procedure may be adapted. A diagnosis is assumed to be *probable* (i.e., part of the final solution of the case), if the aggregated score is greater or equal than the symbolic category S_3. Analogously, a diagnosis is assumed to be *not probable*, if the aggregated score is less or equal than the symbolic category S_{-3}.

Scoring rules have proved to be useful in large medical knowledge bases, e.g., in the INTERNIST/QMR project [6]. In our own work with the shell-kit D3, scores have been applied successfully in many (large) knowledge system projects, e.g., in a biological application [7] or in medical domains [3] and technical domains [4] using generalized scores.

3 Quality Measures for Diagnostic Rule Bases

When we consider the quality of the learned knowledge in the semi-automatic setting, then we are not only interested in classification accuracy, but also in understandability of the learned patterns. Understandability, unexpectedness, actionability, surprisingness, validity and simplicity measured on rules, or patterns in general, are several interestingness measures used in data mining research [8, 9].

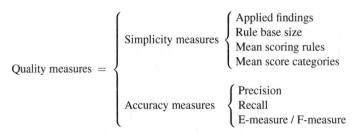

Fig. 1. Quality measures for (scoring) rule bases

Validity is most often measured, and together with the simplicity it can be regarded as an objective measure. We will focus on these measures, for which we assess the accuracy, corresponding to validity. The understandability of the learned scores is typically defined by its simplicity, which can be measured with respect to the learned scoring rules in the rule base $\mathcal{R} \subseteq \Omega_R$. If the learned rules have a low complexity, then it is easier for the expert/user to understand the corresponding scores.

In general, a score is considered to be the more complex, the more findings it contains. This directly corresponds to the number of learned rules per diagnosis. An overall impression of the simplicity of the learned scores is given by the total number of learned rules. Furthermore, as a global simplicity measure we count the total number of findings used in scoring rules of the rule base. Usually a moderate number of findings is considered more comprehensible than a large number of findings. Similarly, the comprehensibility of a score also depends on the number of the applied distinct score categories: a smaller (mean) number of different confirmation categories is usually easier to survey and to interpret by the expert, than a larger number of distinct confirmation categories. Figure 1 depicts an overview of the presented measures considering the simplicity and accuracy of (scoring) rule bases.

In the following, we discuss simplicity measures and accuracy measures for diagnostic scores in more detail. Based on these measures we develop a unifying quality measure combining the aspects of both, the simplicity and the accuracy of (scoring) rule bases.

3.1   Simplicity Measures

It is difficult to determine the simplicity of a rule base by only one measure. For defining *global* simplicity measures, we consider the rule base as a whole. *Local* variants, considering a specific knowledge item, i.e., a diagnostic score, can be defined accordingly. In contrast to the local simplicity measures the use of global measures is appropriate for comparing the understandability of different (learned) rule bases. We consider the following issues and define corresponding functions applied on scoring rule bases.

- APPLIED FINDINGS: Number of findings used in the rule base; the rule base is much simpler to survey, if fewer findings are used to describe the scores.
- RULE BASE SIZE: Overall number of learned scoring rules; obviously the number of scoring rules is a direct measure for the complexity of the learned knowledge. However, for a more detailed analysis of the rule base complexity the applied

classes of confirmation categories should be considered. Thus, the interpretation of scoring rules categorically establishing or excluding a diagnosis, i.e., S_3, S_{-3}, is very simple, when compared to scoring rules with less certain confirmation categories, e.g., S_1, S_{-1}.

Therefore, it is suggestive to define a weighting function $w : \Omega_{scr} \rightarrow I\!N$ for the confirmation categories. In the context of our work we defined $w(s) = 1$ for $s \in \{S_3, S_{-3}\}$, and $w(s) = 2$ otherwise, i.e., we define a category $s \in \Omega_{scr} \setminus \{S_3, S_{-3}\}$ to be twice as complex as the categories S_3, S_{-3}, which are categorically (de)establishing a diagnosis.

In summary, the measure RULE BASE SIZE is simply defined by the count of the rules contained in the rule base. A more refined measure RULE BASE SIZE for a rule base $\mathcal{R} \subseteq \Omega_R$ is defined as follows

$$\text{RULE BASE SIZE}(\mathcal{R}) = \sum_{r \in \mathcal{R}} w\big(category(r)\big) . \tag{1}$$

- MEAN SCORING RULES: This measure gives the mean number of rules for scoring a single diagnosis, and can be derived from RULE BASE SIZE. Fewer scoring rules for a diagnosis are much simpler to understand than more rules. Similar to the measure RULE BASE SIZE, it can be computed using the weighted categories or by directly counting the number of rules.
- MEAN SCORE CATEGORIES: Mean number of different confirmation categories applied for scoring a single diagnosis. A smaller number of distinct categories allow for a much simpler interpretation of the diagnosis score, since confirmation strengths of the findings contributing to a score are less distributed. This measure is indirectly dependent on the global number of different confirmation categories defined, i.e., $|\Omega_{scr}|$. A small universe of possible confirmation categories allows for a simpler distinction between the single categories.

In addition to the simplicity measures, the second part of the quality measures for the semi-automatic learning task are measures concerning the accuracy.

3.2 Accuracy Measures

There exists a variety of methods for assessing the accuracy of individual rules, or the entire rule base. Several factors need to be considered. For a two-class prediction problem, e.g., predicting a single diagnosis, we have to consider four possible outcomes, shown in the following table.

	Predicted Class = YES	Predicted Class = NO
Actual Class = YES	*True Positive*	*False Negative*
Actual Class = NO	*False Positive*	*True Negative*

The true positives and true negatives are correct classifications. If the class is incorrectly predicted as 'YES' while it is in fact 'NO', then we have a false positive. Likewise, if the class is incorrectly predicted as negative while it is in fact positive, then we have a false negative. In the following, TP, FP, TN, and FN denote the number of true positives, false positives, true negatives, and false negatives, respectively.

For measuring the different trade-offs between correct and false classifications, there exist several measures like *sensitivity* ($TP/(TP+FN)$), *specificity* ($TN/(TN+FP)$) from diagnosis, or likewise *precision* ($TP/(TP + FP)$) and *recall* (same as sensitivity) from information theory. For the different measures the trade-off between these classification alternatives has to be taken into account. The *success rate*, or *efficiency*, is a widely used measure: $(TP + TN)/(TP + TN + FP + FN)$. However, a single diagnosis, which is not predicted very frequently, and which also does not occur very frequently as the correct diagnosis of a case, might get a better rating, than a diagnosis which occurs more frequently. This is especially relevant, if we apply a case base with multiple disorders, as experienced in our evaluation setting. Therefore we used an adaptation of the *E-measure* (cf. [10]), for all applied diagnoses $d \in \Omega_{\mathcal{D}}$.

In our context of multiple disorders as case solutions, precision and recall are defined as follows

$$prec(\mathcal{D}_c, \mathcal{D}_p) = \frac{|\mathcal{D}_c \cap \mathcal{D}_p|}{|\mathcal{D}_p|}, \qquad recall(\mathcal{D}_c, \mathcal{D}_p) = \frac{|\mathcal{D}_c \cap \mathcal{D}_p|}{|\mathcal{D}_c|}, \qquad (2)$$

where $\mathcal{D}_c \subseteq \Omega_{\mathcal{D}}$ is the correct solution and $\mathcal{D}_p \subseteq \Omega_{\mathcal{D}}$ specifies the proposed, derived solution. The *E-measure* itself is defined as follows

$$E(\mathcal{D}_c, \mathcal{D}_p) = 1 - \frac{(\beta^2 + 1) \cdot prec(\mathcal{D}_c, \mathcal{D}_p) \cdot recall(\mathcal{D}_c, \mathcal{D}_p)}{\beta^2 \cdot prec(\mathcal{D}_c, \mathcal{D}_p) + recall(\mathcal{D}_c, \mathcal{D}_p)}. \qquad (3)$$

Then, the *F-measure* (cf. [11–Ch. 5]), the harmonic mean between recall and precision, is defined as follows

$$F(\mathcal{D}_c, \mathcal{D}_p) = 1 - E_{\beta=1}(\mathcal{D}_c, \mathcal{D}_p), \qquad (4)$$

where $\beta \in [0; \infty[$ denotes the relative weight of precision vs. recall. The *F-measure* uses a value of $\beta = 1$ to give an equal weight to recall and precision.

In contrast to the *E-measure*, higher values of the *F-measure* correspond to higher classification accuracy, which is more suitable for combining the accuracy measure and the simplicity measure into the unified quality measure defined below.

3.3   A Unifying Quality Measure for Semi-automatic Learning Methods

In a semi-automatic scenario the user wants to obtain an overview of the quality of the learned knowledge. Concerning accuracy and simplicity of the learned knowledge often there is a trade-off between these two measures. Then, accurate learned models are quite complex, while simpler ones lack performance. Therefore, it is suggestive to balance the two measures. Also user quality standards need to be taken into account regarding the simplicity, since the simplicity is subjective to the user's goals and is also dependent on the applied domain. We combine a normalized simplicity measure and the accuracy measure into a single quality measure.

For the simplicity measure we first define a local simplicity measure SCORING RULES, which gives the absolute number of scoring rules for scoring a single specific diagnosis. Then, the function SCORING RULES($DS(d)$) returns the number of scoring rules learned for the specified diagnostic score $DS(d)$. For the definition of the unifying quality measure QM we first introduce a normalized simplicity measure $NSM(DS(d))$ concerning a single diagnostic score $DS(d)$, which is defined as follows

$$NSM(DS(d)) = 1 - \frac{\text{SCORING RULES}(DS(d)) - 1}{\text{SCORING RULES}(DS(d)) + \gamma}, \quad (5)$$

where γ is a generalization parameter, with default value $\gamma = 1$. If γ is set to larger values, then larger scores will get an increased simplicity value. Since $NSM(DS(d)) \in [0; 1]$, the maximum value $NSM(DS(d)) = 1$ is obtained, if a diagnosis d is predicted with a single rule, i.e., if the score has the size one.

We propose to combine this measure with the accuracy in a term similar to the F-measure balancing both measures. Then, the unifying quality measure $QM : 2^{\Omega_R} \rightarrow [0; 1]$ for a rule base $\mathcal{R}$ is defined as follows,

$$QM(\mathcal{R}) = \frac{1}{|\Omega_{\mathcal{D}}|} \sum_{d \in \Omega_{\mathcal{D}}} \frac{(\alpha^2 + 1) \cdot NSM(DS(d)) \cdot ACC(DS(d))}{\alpha^2 \cdot NSM(DS(d)) + ACC(DS(d))}, \quad (6)$$

where the function $ACC(DS(d))$ calculates the accuracy of the specified diagnostic score $DS(d)$ using the F-measure. The factor α is a weight balancing simplicity vs. accuracy. We used $\alpha = 1$ for our experiments to assign an equal weight to the simplicity and the accuracy.

Related Work. Favoring simple rules is in line with a classic principle of inductive learning methods called Ockham's Razor [12]. Existing interestingness measures applying this principle generate compact rules [13], for example, where the number of rules, the number of conditions in a rule, and the classification accuracy of a rule are taken into account. A general measure discussed by Freitas [9] takes the size of the disjuncts of a rule into account. Due to the fact that we only consider simple scoring rules not containing disjuncts, this measure is not applicable to diagnostic scores. We purely concentrate on the syntactic elements contained in the rule base $\mathcal{R}$. For a localized evaluation, we propose a unifying quality measure, which combines both aspects, i.e., the simplicity and the accuracy. This measure with fixed upper and lower bounds provides a first intuitive evaluation for the user.

4   Learning Diagnostic Scores

In the following we first describe diagnostic profiles utilized in the learning method. Then, we briefly discuss necessary data preprocessing steps for the learning task. After that we outline the method for inductive learning of diagnostic scores.

4.1   Constructing Diagnostic Profiles

Diagnostic profiles describe a compact representation for each diagnosis. A diagnostic profile P_d for a diagnosis $d \in \Omega_{\mathcal{D}}$ contained in a case base CB is defined as the set of tuples

$$P_d = \{(f, freq_{f,d}) \mid f \in \Omega_{\mathcal{F}} \land freq_{f,d} \in [0,1]\},$$

where $f \in \Omega_{\mathcal{F}}$ is a finding and $freq_{f,d} \in [0,1]$ represents the frequency with which the finding f occurs in conjunction with d in the case base CB. Only findings f are stored that occur frequently with the diagnosis d.

We construct diagnostic profiles by first learning coarse frequency profiles such that the finding frequencies are determined according to the given case base. Thus, learning diagnostic profiles entails, that each profile will initially contain all findings which occur together with the profile's diagnoses. Therefore, also seldom findings occur in the plain profile. However, we want to construct a profile only containing the typical findings for a given diagnosis. Thus, we apply a statistical pruning method, removing unfrequent findings. After that, a diagnostic profile contains at least all relevant findings for the specified diagnosis. For a more detailed discussion we refer to [14].

4.2   Basic Algorithm for Learning Diagnostic Scores

The basic algorithm for learning diagnostic scores can only handle discrete valued attributes. If no partitions of continuous attributes were defined by the expert, then we applied a *k-means* clustering method (e.g., described in [15]) with a default k of 5, for the discretization of continuous attributes.

In the following, we outline the method for learning diagnostic scores: we first have to identify dependencies between findings and diagnoses. In general, all possible combinations between diagnoses and findings have to be taken into account. However, in order to reduce the search space we only consider the findings occurring most frequently with the diagnosis. Thus we constrain the set of *important* findings using diagnostic profiles. In summary, we basically apply three steps for learning a diagnostic scoring rule:

1. Identify a dependency between a finding $f \in \Omega_{\mathcal{F}}$ and a diagnosis $d \in \Omega_{\mathcal{D}}$
2. Rate this dependency and map it to a symbolic category $s \in \Omega_{scr}$
3. Finally, construct a diagnostic rule: $r = f \xrightarrow{s} d$

This basic procedure is applied in Algorithm 1, and explained below in more detail.

Identify Dependencies. For each diagnosis $d \in \Omega_{\mathcal{D}}$, we create a diagnostic profile containing the most frequent findings occurring with the diagnosis. We consider all attributes (questions) in the profile selecting the findings which are observed in the case base. For each finding $f = q{:}v$ we apply the χ^2-*test for independence* for binary variables, i.e., variable D for diagnosis d and variable F for finding f, respectively. D and F measure if d and f occur in a case. If they occur the respective variable is true and false otherwise. The χ^2-test for independence, is applied using a certain threshold χ^2_α corresponding to confidence level α. We construct the following four-fold contingency table for the binary variables:

	$D = true$	$D = false$
$F = true$	a	b
$F = false$	c	d

The frequency counts denoted in the table are defined as follows:

$$a = N(D = true \wedge F = true), \; b = N(D = false \wedge F = true),$$
$$c = N(D = true \wedge F = false), \; d = N(D = false \wedge F = false),$$

Algorithm 1. Learning Simple Diagnostic Scores

Require: Case base $CB \subseteq \Omega_C$
1: **for all** diagnoses $d \in \Omega_D$ **do**
2:     Learn a diagnostic profile P_d
3:     **for all** attributes $q \in \{q \mid q \in \Omega_Q, \exists f \in F_q, f \in P_d)\}$ **do**
4:         **for all** findings $f \in F_q$ **do**
5:             Construct binary variables D, F for d and f, which measure if d and f occur in cases
                of the case base CB.
6:             Compute $\chi^2_{fd} = \chi^2(F, D)$
7:             **if** $\chi^2_{fd} \geq \chi^2_\alpha$ **then**
8:                 Compute the correlation/ϕ_{fd} coefficient $\phi_{fd} = \phi(F, D)$
9:                 **if** $|\phi_{fd}| \geq threshold_c$ **then**
10:                    Compute the quasi-probabilistic score qps,
                       $qps = sgn(\phi_{fd}) * prec(r)(1 - FAR(r))$ using the pseudo-rule: $f \rightarrow d$
11:                    Map the qps-score to a symbolic category s using a conversion table
12:                    Apply background knowledge to validate the diagnostic scoring rule, if available
13:                    Create a diagnostic scoring rule (if valid): $f \xrightarrow{s} d$

---

where $N(cond)$ is the number of times the condition $cond$ is true for cases $c \in C$. For binary variables the formula for the χ^2-test simplifies to

$$\chi^2(F, D) = \frac{(a + b + c + d)(ad - bc)^2}{(a + b)(c + d)(a + c)(b + d)} . \tag{7}$$

We require a certain minimal support threshold for a finding f co-occurring with diagnosis d. The default threshold is set to 5, i.e., the finding has to occur together with the diagnosis at least five times. Generally, for small sample sizes, we apply the Yates' correction for a more accurate result.

For all dependent tuples (F, D) we derive the quality of the dependency, i.e., the strength of the association using the ϕ-coefficient,

$$\phi(F, D) = \frac{ad - bc}{\sqrt{(a + b)(c + d)(a + c)(b + d)}}, \quad \phi(F, D) \in [-1; 1], \tag{8}$$

which is a correlation measure between two binary variables. We use it to discover positive or negative dependencies. A positive value of $\phi(F, D)$ signifies a positive association, whereas a negative value signifies a negative one. If the absolute value of $\phi(F, D)$ is less than a certain threshold $threshold_c$, i.e., $|\phi(F, D)| < threshold_c$, then we do not consider this weak dependency for rule generation. For the remaining dependencies we generate rules described as follows: If $\phi(F, D) < 0$, then we obtain a negative association between the two variables, and we generate a rule $f \xrightarrow{s} d$ with a negative category s. If $\phi(F, D) > 0$, then we construct a rule $f \xrightarrow{s} d$ with a positive category s.

Mapping Dependencies. For determining the exact symbolic confirmation category of the remaining rules r, we utilize two measures used in diagnosis: The *precision* and the *false alarm rate (FAR)*; the precision of a rule r is defined as

$$prec(r) = TP/(TP + FP), \tag{9}$$

whereas the false alarm rate *FAR* for a rule r is given by

$$FAR(r) = FP/(FP + TN), \tag{10}$$

where the symbols TP, TN, FP denote the number of *true positives*, *true negatives*, and *false positives*, respectively. These can easily be extracted from the contingency table. For a positive dependency between the finding f and the diagnosis d, we see that $TP = a$, $TN = d$ and $FP = b$. For a negative dependency we try to predict the absence of the diagnosis d, so in this setting we obtain $TP = b$, $TN = c$ and $FP = a$.

To score the dependency, we first compute a *quasi probabilistic score (qps)* which we then map to a symbolic category. The numeric *qps* score for a rule r is computed as follows

$$qps(r) = sgn\big(\phi(D, F)\big) * prec(r)\big(1 - FAR(r)\big). \tag{11}$$

We achieve a tradeoff between the accuracy of the diagnostic scoring rule to predict a disease measured against all predictions and the proportion of false predictions.

It is worth noting, that often the *true positive rate (TPR)* – which is also known as *recall/sensitivity* – is used in combination with the FAR as a measure of accuracy. However, this is mostly applicable to standard rules, which usually contain more complex rule conditions than scoring rules applied in diagnostic scores. Since a diagnostic score is a combination of several diagnostic scoring rules, which support each other in establishing a diagnosis, their accuracy needs to be assessed on localized regions of the diagnosis space. Therefore, precision is more suggestive, since it does not take the entire diagnosis space into account, but it only measures the accuracy of the localized prediction.

To ease interpretability of the discovered knowledge, we restrict the mapping process to only six different symbolic confirmation categories, three positive and three negative. The *qps*-scores are then mapped to the symbolic categories according to the following conversion table ($\varepsilon \approx 0$):

$qps(r)$	$category(r)$	$qps(r)$	$category(r)$
$[-1.0, -0.9)$	$\rightarrow S_{-3}$	$(\varepsilon, 0.5)$	$\rightarrow S_1$
$[-0.9, -0.5)$	$\rightarrow S_{-2}$	$[0.5, 0.9)$	$\rightarrow S_2$
$[-0.5, -\varepsilon)$	$\rightarrow S_{-1}$	$[0.9, 1.0]$	$\rightarrow S_3$

We accept the loss of information to increase the understandability and to facilitate a user-friendly adaptation of the learned diagnostic scores.

Including Background Knowledge. The presented algorithm can be augmented with additional background knowledge in order to achieve better learning results. We introduce abnormality information and partition class knowledge as appropriate background knowledge.

If *abnormality* information about attribute values is available, then each value v of a question q is attached with an abnormality label. It explains, whether $v \in dom(q)$ is describing a normal or an abnormal state of the question. For example, consider the attribute *temperature* with the value range: $dom(temperature) = \{normal, marginal,$

high}. The values *normal* and *marginal* denote normal values of the question, whereas the value *high* describes an abnormal value. We will use these abnormalities, for further reducing the size of the generated rule base.

We apply two heuristics for pruning, which are motivated by the diagnostic situation that a normal value of an attribute usually is not responsible for causing a diagnosis, while an abnormal value may. Let $r = q{:}v \xrightarrow{s} d$ be a scoring rule. If $s \in \Omega_{scr}$ denotes a positive category and v is a normal value of attribute q, then we omit rule r, since findings describing normal behavior usually should not increase the confirmation of a diagnosis. Furthermore, if s denotes a negative category and v is an abnormal value of attribute q, then we likewise omit rule r because an abnormal finding usually should not decrease the confirmation of a diagnosis, but possibly increases the confirmation of other diagnoses. Thus, we apply the heuristics above in order to reduce the size of the learned rule base, and to increase its quality with respect to its interpretability.

As a second type of background knowledge the expert can provide *partition class* knowledge describing how to divide the set of diagnoses and attributes into partially disjunctive subsets, i.e., partitions. These subsets correspond to certain problem areas of the application domain. For example, in the medical domain of sonography, we have subsets corresponding to problem areas like *liver*, *pancreas*, *kidney*, *stomach*, and *intestine*. This knowledge is especially useful when diagnosing multiple faults. Since a case may contain multiple diagnoses, attributes occurring with several diagnoses will be contained in several diagnostic profiles. We reduce noise and irrelevant dependencies by pruning such discovered dependencies $f \rightarrow d$, for which f and d are not in the same partition class.

5   Evaluation

We evaluated the presented method with cases taken from a fielded medical application. The applied SONOCONSULT case base contains 1340 cases, with a mean of diagnoses $M_d = 4.32 \pm 2.79$ and a mean of relevant findings $M_f = 76.89 \pm 20.59$ per case. SONOCONSULT [3] is a knowledge-based documentation and consultation system for sonography. It is developed and maintained by the domain experts using the shell-kit D3 [16]. The quality of the derived diagnoses is very good as checked by medical experts in a medical evaluation (cf. [3]).

For the evaluation of our experiments we adopted the F-measure introduced in Section 3, adapted to the multiple disorder problem occurring in the applied case base. Furthermore, a stratified 10-fold cross-validation method was applied. We performed two experiments to determine the impact of including background knowledge into the learning process. For experiment *E0* we applied no background knowledge at all. To demonstrate how the utilization of knowledge improves the results we used both partition class knowledge and abnormality knowledge for experiment *E1*. We created several sets of scores depending on the parameter $threshold_c$, which describes the correlation threshold used in the learning algorithm. Two criteria – accuracy and simplicity – as outlined in Section 3, were used to define the quality of the scores.

The results are presented in the following tables. Column $threshold_c$ specifies the correlation threshold, QM_1 shows the combined quality measure with the default parameter $\gamma = 1$, whereas QM_5 and QM_{10} show the measure with a parameter $\gamma = 5$ and $\gamma = 10$, respectively. *MR* corresponds to the measure MEAN SCORING RULES, attached with standard deviation. *RBS* describes the measure RULE BASE SIZE with total number of rules in addition to the number of weighted rules in parentheses (as described in Section 3.1). The column *SC* corresponds to the measure MEAN SCORE CATEGORIES. Column *AF* shows the number of applied findings, i.e., the values of the measure APPLIED FINDINGS. Finally, we depict the accuracy of the rule base using the F-measure in column *ACC*.

Experiment E0: no knowledge used

$threshold_c$	QM_1	QM_5	QM_{10}	ACC	RBS *(w)*	MR	AF	SC
0.2	0.15	0.33	0.46	0.94	2201 (3798)	30.58 ± 16.83	395	3.49
0.3	0.21	0.41	0.54	0.92	1510 (2466)	20.97 ± 10.59	348	3.20
0.4	0.27	0.49	0.61	0.90	1069 (1647)	14.85 ± 7.02	297	2.98
0.5	0.34	0.56	0.68	0.89	770 (1101)	10.70 ± 4.90	247	2.67
0.6	0.40	0.61	0.72	0.83	594 (789)	8.24 ± 3.51	207	2.32
0.7	0.51	0.70	0.77	0.81	369 (413)	5.13 ± 2.13	158	1.44

Experiment E1: using partition class and abnormality knowledge

$threshold_c$	QM_1	QM_5	QM_{10}	ACC	RBS *(w)*	MR	AF	SC
0.2	0.39	0.59	0.68	0.88	594 (990)	8.25 ± 5.00	180	2.60
0.3	0.45	0.64	0.72	0.86	437 (693)	6.07 ± 3.30	153	2.38
0.4	0.51	0.68	0.75	0.85	328 (495)	4.56 ± 2.15	131	2.12
0.5	0.58	0.72	0.77	0.84	240 (335)	3.34 ± 1.36	113	1.78
0.6	0.62	0.73	0.77	0.78	188 (245)	2.61 ± 1.04	101	1.49
0.7	0.68	0.75	0.77	0.76	131 (149)	1.81 ± 0.70	81	1.10

The evaluation shows that applying background knowledge helps to improve the simplicity of the learned rule base significantly, i.e., by suppressing or pruning rules. However, the accuracies of the learned rule bases in experiment *E1* compared to experiment *E0* are slightly lower, but this is countered by the significant increase in rule base simplicity evidenced by the individual values for the combined quality measure *QM*.

Looking at both experiments *E0* and *E1*, the high values of the accuracy for low values of $threshold_c$ and the large number of rules per diagnosis indicate overfitting of the learned knowledge. This is domain dependent and therefore the expert needs to tune the threshold carefully. With greater values for $threshold_c$ less rules are generated, since only strong dependencies are taken into account. If $threshold_c$ is too high, i.e., if too many rules are pruned, this obviously degrades the accuracy of the learned scores. In our experiments this occurs for $threshold_c = 0.6$, for which the accuracy decreases significantly in comparison to $threshold_c = 0.5$. Furthermore, the number of rules per diagnosis (MR) is reduced considerably without decreasing the accuracy (ACC) significantly from $threshold_c = 0.2$ to $threshold_c = 0.5$. Analogously, the number of applied findings (AF) is reduced with an increasing value of $threshold_c$ but a decreasing accuracy. Column SC indicates that the number of applied confirmation categories is reduced by an increased $threshold_c$, i.e., simpler scoring rules are learned.

These findings are also reflected in the unifying quality measure. It is easy to see that the balance between the scores' accuracy and simplicity depends on the generalization parameter γ. QM_1 has a stronger increase from $threshold_c = 0.6$ to $threshold_c = 0.7$ than QM_5 since the size of the score, i.e., the number of rules has a higher impact. This depends on the priorities of the user: If $\gamma = 1$, then we have a strong bias favoring minimal scores, one rule per diagnosis in the best case. If γ is set to higher values, then we generalize this, such that the accuracy is more important. This can be seen in experiment $E1$ for $\gamma = 10$ considering thresholds $0.5, 0.6$, and 0.7, where the increased score simplicity is balanced by the decrease in score accuracy. In the case of such a plateau, the user has to consult the detailed quality measures to trade-off accuracy vs. simplicity. Additionally the user also can tune the quality measure with respect to the parameter α, i.e., the weighting factor which trades-off simplicity vs. accuracy. Then, either a clear cut-off point is found, where the quality measure has a maximum value, or the appropriate cut-off point has to be selected from a limited number of options, in the case of a plateau, i.e., a set of equal values.

6   Conclusion

Standard learning methods usually concentrate on the accuracy of the learned patterns. In this paper, we described quality measures focussing on the understandability, i.e., simplicity of the learned knowledge. Additionally, a unifying quality measure also takes the accuracy of the learned knowledge into account. This measure allows for a first quick evaluation of the learned patterns. The measure can be fine-tuned guided by the user's expectations and goals. This is especially important in the context of semi-automatic learning methods, which can be refined incrementally taking different amounts of background knowledge into account.

As an example of such a semi-automatic approach, we outlined a method for learning simple diagnostic scores, and presented an evaluation of the proposed method using a case base from a real-world application in the medical domain. This demonstrated the applicability of the presented simplicity measures and the unifying quality measure balancing simplicity and accuracy aspects.

In the future, we are planning to apply the measures to other rule-based representations of knowledge, such as subgroup patterns. Additionally, interpretation and evaluation of the learned knowledge together with the proposed quality measures by medical experts should further demonstrate the usefulness of these measures.

References

1. Ho, T., Saito, A., Kawasaki, S., Nguyen, D., Nguyen, T.: Failure and Success Experience in Mining Stomach Cancer Data. In: International Workshop Data Mining Lessons Learned, International Conf. Machine Learning. (2002) 40–47 1
2. Gamberger, D., Lavrac, N.: Expert-Guided Subgroup Discovery: Methodology and Application. Journal of Artificial Intelligence Research **17** (2002) 501–527 1
3. Huettig, M., Buscher, G., Menzel, T., Scheppach, W., Puppe, F., Buscher, H.P.: A Diagnostic Expert System for Structured Reports, Quality Assessment, and Training of Residents in Sonography. Medizinische Klinik **99** (2004) 117–122 1, 1, 2, 5, 5

 4. Puppe, F., Ziegler, S., Martin, U., Hupp, J.: Wissensbasierte Diagnosesysteme im Service-Support (Diagnostic Knowledge Systems for the Service-Support). Springer Verlag (2001) 2, 2
 5. Ohmann, C., et al.: Clinical Benefit of a Diagnostic Score for Appendicitis: Results of a Prospective Interventional Study. Archives of Surgery **134** (1999) 993–996 2
 6. R., M., Pople, H.E., Myers, J.: Internist-1, an Experimental Computer-Based Diagnostic Consultant for General Internal Medicine. NEJM **307** (1982) 468–476 2
 7. Neumann, M., Baumeister, J., Liess, M., Schulz, R.: An Expert System to Estimate the Pesticide Contamination of Small Streams using Benthic Macroinvertebrates as Bioindicators, Part 2. Ecological Indicators **2** (2003) 391–401 2
 8. Tuzhilin, A.: Usefulness, Novelty, and Integration of Interestingness Measures. Chapter 19.2.2. In: Klösgen, Zytkow: Handbook of Data Mining and Knowledge Discovery. Oxford University Press, New York (2002) 3
 9. Freitas, A.A.: On Rule Interestingness Measures. Knowledge-Based Systems **12** (1999) 309–325 3, 3.3
10. Lewis, D.D., Gale, W.A.: A Sequential Algorithm for Training Text Classifiers. In: Proc. of the 17th ACM International Conference on Research and Development in Information Retrieval (SIGIR 94), London, Springer (1994) 3–12 3.2
11. Witten, I.H., Frank, E. In: Data Mining: Practical Machine Learning Tools and Techniques with Java Implementations . Morgan Kaufmann (1999) 3.2
12. Mitchell, T.: Machine Learning. McGraw-Hill Comp. (1997) 3.3
13. Yen, S.J., Chen, A.L.P.: An Efficient Algorithm for Deriving Compact Rules from Databases. In: Ling, Masunaga: Proceedings of the 4th International Conference on Database Systems for Advanced Applications-95, World Scientific (1995) 364–371 3.3
14. Baumeister, J., Atzmueller, M., Puppe, F.: Inductive Learning for Case-Based Diagnosis with Multiple Faults. In: Advances in Case-Based Reasoning. Volume 2416 of LNAI. Springer-Verlag, Berlin (2002) 28–42 Proceedings of the 6th European Conference on Case-Based Reasoning (ECCBR-2002). 4.1
15. Han, J., Kamber, M.: Data Mining: Concepts and Techniques. Morgan Kaufmann Publishers, San Mateo, California (2000) 4.2
16. Puppe, F.: Knowledge Reuse Among Diagnostic Problem-Solving Methods in the Shell-Kit D3. Int. J. Human-Computer Studies **49** (1998) 627–649 5

An Evaluation of a Rule-Based Language for Classification Queries

Dennis P. Groth

Indiana University School of Informatics,
Bloomington, IN 47408, USA
dgroth@indiana.edu

Abstract. This paper provides results from a usability experiment comparing two different database query languages. The research focuses on a specific type of query task, namely classification queries. Classification is the process of assigning input data to discrete classes according to application specific criteria. While SQL can be used to perform classification tasks, we seek to discover whether a different type of query language offers any advantages over SQL. We present a rule-based language, which organizes the queries in a logical way. The rule based language is specifically designed to support classification tasks. The usability experiment measures the effectiveness, efficiency and satisfaction of novice and expert users performing a variety of classification tasks. The results show that while both approaches are usable for classification tasks, the rule-based approach was preferred by expert users.

1   Introduction

Classification is the process of assigning input data to discrete classes according to application specific criteria. Simple examples abound for this type of task. For example, employees in an employee database may be classifed according to their salary into "High", "Medium" and "Low" classes.

In this research we consider classifications that are definable by the user in two ways. First, a classification is *definable* if the class values are explicitly assigned. The definition can be stated in the form of a series of *If .. Then* statements. For example, consider the following sentences that define the employee salary classification:

1. If an employee's salary is less than $30,000 then assign the employee to the "low" salary class.
2. If an employee's salary is between $30,000 and $60,000 then assign the employee to the "medium" salary class.
3. If an employee's salary is more than $60,000 then assign the employee to the "high" salary class.

A classification is *derivable* if the class values are assigned according to a calculation. For example, we can assign employees to classes using the state-

D. Seipel et al. (Eds.): INAP/WLP 2004, LNAI 3392, pp. 79–97, 2005.

ment $SalaryClass = floor(Salary/1000)$, which effectively "bins" employees into salary ranges.

This research considers schemes that may be either definable or derivable to the extent that a user can describe the classification in some declarative form. We do not consider algorithmic techniques encountered in data mining, such as automatic cluster detection or discretization, which are described in [5, 4].

In this research we present a declarative language that supports both definable and derivable classifications. We call the language a Mapping Query Language (MQL), since the user declares the mappings between the input data and the classifications. The language has a syntax that succinctly describes the classifications according to a set of rules. A BNF grammar is provided as an appendix to this paper. We compare our approach with an Structured Query Language (SQL) approach in a controlled usability experiment.

The usability experiment seeks to determine whether one approach is superior to another in a controlled fashion. Previous experiments have compared equivalent systems. That is, each system was fully equivalent in expressive power, differing in syntactic form, or in interaction style. This research differs from previous approaches in that the language we describe is strictly weaker than SQL. Nevertheless, by focusing on a specific work task (classification) the systems are comparable.

This paper is structured as follows. Section 1.1 provides pointers to the relevant literature most closely related to this work. Section 2 provides a brief description of the rule-based language. In Section 3 we describe the setup for our experiment. Section 4 provides the results from the usability experiments. Lastly, in Section 5 we provide directions for future research activities and summarize our findings.

1.1   Related Work

In this section we describe the relevant work that is related to this research. First, from a query language perspective, our approach is based on Datalog. Descriptions of the theoretical aspects of Datalog can be found in database texts, such as [1]. A comprehensive description of logic-based query languages is described by Vianu in [10]. There are numerous references for SQL, including general texts [1, 7] as well as language standards [3]. From a data mining perspective, SQL has been used in support of various techniques. With regards to classification tasks, very little work has focused on relational query languages, with the exception being [6].

There have been numerous examples in the literature related to usability of query languages. The approaches tend to follow a fairly standard experimental design, in which two query languages are compared. Early work by Reisner et. al. [9] forms the basis for many other experiments. Surveys that provide a compilation of multiple experiments were provided by Reisner [8] and Welty [11]. A study by Yen and Scamell [13] comparing SQL to Query By Example (QBE) serves as the basis of our experiment design. More recently, comparisons of diagramatic languages to SQL have been presented, including work by Catarci [2].

2   The Rule-Based Language

Conceptually, we view the process of classifying data as shown in Figure 1. The class values that are assigned can be expressed with database queries. We will continue with the employee salary example for the purposes of describing our approach.

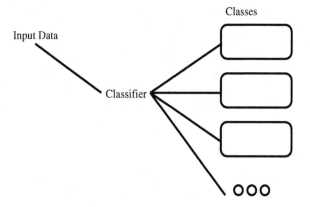

Fig. 1. The classification process

We assume a basic familiarity with relational database processing. Data is stored in tables that are described by their schema, which is a finite set of attribute names. Given a table **r** over attributes $R = \{A, B, C, \ldots\}$, let $t \in \mathbf{r}$ be a tuple. A query q is a mapping from input schema to an output schema.

Our rule-based language specifies queries in the form of a finite list of rules. Each rule is of the form $Head \leftarrow Body$, with the following semantics. The body of a rule is a boolean expression involving attribute names and constants, as well as a small number of supported functions. For example, basic mathematical functions such as addition and subtraction are supported. The head of a rule is an expression like the body, except that it is not restricted to a $\{0, 1\}$ result. Each rule head in a query must of the same data type. We refer to the set of attributes used in the rules as the schema of the query.

Let $P = \{p_1, \ldots, p_k\}$ be a rule query and **r** be a table. For each $t \in \mathbf{r}$, let $Head(t)$ be the value of the expression $Head$ when given t as input. $Body(t)$ is defined in the same manner. The output schema of P is $R \cup Class$, where R is the schema of the input table and $Class$ is the class value assigned to each tuple.[1] The following rule query defines the employee salary classification.

---

[1] The implementation provides the user with a mechanism for defining a unique name for *Class*.

$'Low' \leftarrow Salary < 30000$
$'Medium' \leftarrow Salary >= 30000$ and $Salary <= 60000$
$'High' \leftarrow Salary > 60000$

Rules are evaluated in the order that they are defined. In addition, we support two different interpretation strategies. Queries may be interpreted *functionally* or *relationally*. Under a functional interpretation, rules are evaluated until a success is encountered. In contrast, a relational interpretation will evaluate every rule, which provides for a single input tuple to be mapped to multiple classes.

We support two special types of rules to provide greater control over the process. A rule of the form *Except* ← *Body* excludes input tuples from further processing. A rule of the form *Head* ← *Else* allows for a tuple to be mapped if all of the preceding rules failed. A BNF syntax description of the language is provided as an appendix to this paper.

By design, the rule-based query language is restricted in terms of the types of queries that can be expressed. While it is similar to Datalog in terms of its syntax, we do not support recursive queries or negation in the head of the rule. With these restrictions, the queries can be executed in linear time by processing one tuple at a time.

2.1   Equivalence to SQL

Each rule query is equivalent to an SQL query involving set operations. The proof of this equivalence is based on a transformation from the rule-based language to SQL. Rather than providing the proof we provide a sketch of the transformation process here. First, note that the body of a rule is essentially the same as the SQL where clause. The head of a rule is the same as the SQL select clause. The following SQL query is equivalent to the rule query that classifies employee salaries.

```
Select "Low", * from employee where salary < 30000
   Union
Select "Medium", * from employee where salary >= 30000 and salary <=60000
   Union
Select "High", * from employee where salary > 60000
```

Special care must be taken to support the *Except* and *Else* rules by creating more complicated where clauses in the SQL queries. From a processing perspective, it is likely that SQL queries used for classification tasks will be less efficient than the rule-based process. Note that the SQL queries may require multiple passes through the input data. In addition, using SQL in support of classification tasks may require complex queries to be written, which may be beyond the end-user's ability.

2.2   Classification as Visualization Mapping

The rule language is envisioned as a component within the visualization pipeline [12] that supports the mapping of data into a visual representation. Our process implements maps as relations that are used to transform input data into a form that is more useful for visualization purposes. The input data to be mapped is represented by relation and is physically stored as a table in the database. The contents of the map depend on the application, as specified by the user. Note that the map controls how data appears in the visualization, but remains separate from the data itself.

A map is used to add order and scale to the data that is desired to be visualized. The mapping process is conceptualized in Figure 2. For example, the input data is "mapped" to a point in the display based on the contents of the map. In this case, we use a two-dimensional scatterplot only as a means to illustrate the mapping process. The approach we present here is independent of any particular choice of graphical display technique.

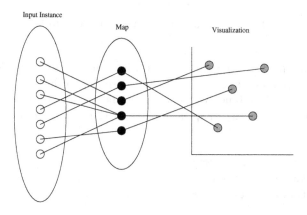

Fig. 2. The mapping process

Formally, a map is a relation instance **s** over schema S. **s** is applied to data through the use of a relational join operator. Our approach places no restriction on the type of join being performed, allowing for the specific requirements of the visualization problem to be satisfied by a user specified join.

To describe the concepts behind the mapping process we will use an example based on the instance of the *Customer* relation shown in Figure 3. Note that the schema of *Customer* contains a mixture of categorical and numeric attributes.

CustomerId	State	AnnualSales	Employees
1	IN	1000	2500
7	IL	2000	1150
5	CA	500	6000
75	FL	6500	579
:	:	:	:

Fig. 3. An example *Customer* relation

The visualization we are interested in viewing is a two-dimensional scatterplot of annual sales compared to geographic region. The sales amount is a numeric value that maps naturally to our display. However, the geographic region must be derived from the state attribute. To accomplish this, consider the map shown in Figure 4, which we will refer to as **StateMap**.

State	StateOrder
AK	1
HI	1
CA	2
OR	2
WA	2
⋮	⋮

Fig. 4. A map that orders states from West to East

In this example, the map associates with each state a natural number, which adds both order and scale to the categorical value of the state. The application process combines the map with the *Customer* relation by using a natural join. In SQL this map is applied to the original data with the following query:

```
Select   Customer.*, StateMap.StateOrder
From     Customer, StateMap
Where    Customer.State = StateMap.State
```

In order to generate the desired visualization we execute the following aggregate query, which extracts the "mapped" state value and the annual sales for each customer. The resulting visualization is shown in Figure 5. The color for each point is derived from the *Frequency* attribute of the aggregate query.

```
Select   vis.StateOrder, vis.AnnualSales, count(*) as Frequency
From     (Select   Customer.*, StateMap.StateOrder
          From     Customer, StateMap
          Where    Customer.State = StateMap.State) vis
Group By vis.StateOrder, vis.AnnualSales
```

This approach to mapping provides flexibility in a number of ways. First, changes to the visualization can be effected by simply changing the map, and not the base data. Second, multiple maps can be defined for the same data, allowing for reuse of data in multiple contexts.

There are many ways that a map may be constructed. For example, simple SQL insert statements are sufficient to populate the map used previously. The following, partial sequence of SQL insert statements creates **StateMap**.

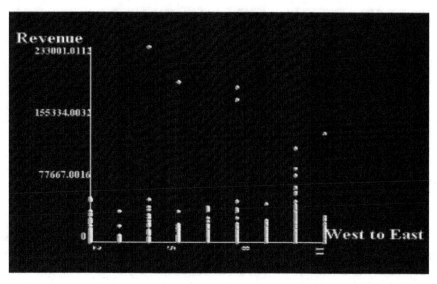

Fig. 5. An example visualization using the mapped value

```
Insert Into StateMap Values ('AK', 1)
Insert Into StateMap Values ('HI', 1)
Insert Into StateMap Values ('CA', 2)
      . . .
```

While construction of the map can be accomplished with SQL statements, it is important to note that a user's proficiency with the formulation of queries serves as an effective upper-bound on the complexity of problems that can be addressed using this technique. To address this issue, we propose a declarative approach for specifying maps that shields the user from the SQL syntax. The remainder of this section provides an example of how the user applies maps.

2.3   Mapping Example

In this subsection we provide a description of the prototype system's implementation of the mapping process. Using the application manager interface, a user adds various objects to the desktop. In order to give a flavor for the process that a user employs, we provide a series of screen captures for a simple application. In the left pane of Figure 6, the user right-clicks with the mouse on the desktop and a popup menu is displayed. The menu provides access to the various objects that can be placed on the desktop. The right pane shows a list of available input data sources, in the form of user-defined queries.

The example data we are using is unemployment data, downloaded from the U.S. Department of Commerce. The data is comprised of $(Year, Month, Rate)$ triples for years 1948-2001. The data is already numeric, but we will still apply a map to the month field in order to demonstrate the process. In particular, we will map the months of the year to quarters, using the following rules:

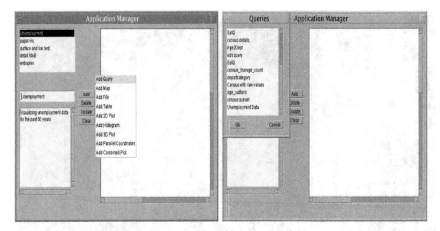

Fig. 6. The user right-clicks with their mouse to see a menu of available application objects. Selecting "Add Query", the user is presented a list of available queries that can be visualized

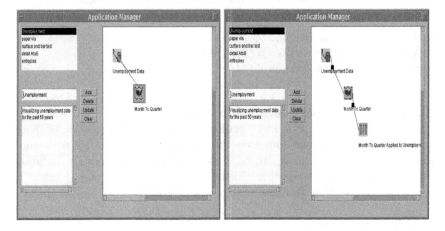

Fig. 7. The user uses the mouse to connect an input data source to a map. After the map has been applied to the input data, a new object is automatically added to the desktop

```
1 <- month <= 3
2 <- month <= 6
3 <- month <= 9
4 <- Else
```

Using the same process as before, the user adds the map to the desktop. Then, as shown in Figure 7, the user right clicks on the query object and selects the "Connect" option. Then, the user moves the mouse over the map object and clicks the mouse button. Feedback is provided to the user during this process

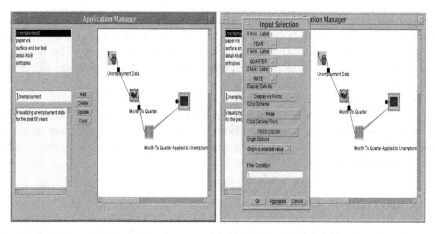

Fig. 8. The user adds a plotting object to the desktop and connects the mapped data to the plotting object. The user is then presented with options based on the input data and the type of plot

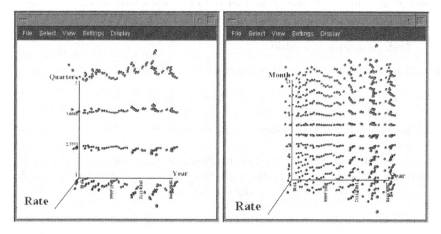

Fig. 9. The left pane shows the mapped unemployment data within a 3D scatterplot. The right pane shows the original data in its unmapped form

by coloring the connecting line from the query to the map. If two application objects are connectable, the color of the line is green, otherwise it is red and the user cannot connect the objects. When the objects are connected the server component applies the map the input data. The right pane of the figure shows the result of the operation, in which a new object is added to the desktop that represents the input data transformed according to the map.

With the map applied to the data we can plot the data using similar steps. In Figure 8 the user adds a plotting object to the application, in this case a 3D plot. After connecting an input data source to the 3D plot object, the user is presented with display options based on the input data and the plot object.

The user can select any of the input attributes as the data being visualized. In addition, the user can select how the data is to be displayed. For example, the user can choose to display the data as spheres in the 3D space. The user has control over the color of objects, which can be based on an attribute of the input data, or a derived value such as frequency.

With the data connected to the plot object and the appropriate options selected, the user can view the resulting visualization by right-clicking on the plot object and selecting "View". Figure 9 shows the unemployment data in using a 3D scatterplot display. The original, unmapped data is shown in the right pane of the figure.

3   Experiment Design

In order to understand the usefulness of our approach we have performed a controlled usability experiment. This experiment seeks to quantify a user's ability to solve classification tasks with either SQL or the rule-based language. The focus is targeted only at classification tasks, and is not a broad comparison of fully equivalent systems. SQL was chosen as the most appropriate comparative tool due to its predominant use by both expert and novice users.

3.1   Independent Variables

The independent variables used to control the experiment were:

1. User skill level (Low, Medium-Low, Medium-High, High)
2. Query language (SQL, Rule-Based Language)
3. Query complexity (Less complex, More complex)

Subjects for the experiment were recruited from a one-semester course in database systems as well as professional programmers. Table 1 describes how user skill levels were assigned as well as the number of subjects in each skill level.

Half of the subjects performed classification tasks using either SQL or the rule language. The use of SQL and the rule language was balanced within the groups. The same problems were attempted by each user. Query complexity was based on the type of classification being performed. The complexity of the task was calculated based on a model answer for the problem as formulated in the rule-based language. A complexity score for a rule is defined according to the

Table 1. The base of experimental subjects

User Description	Skill Level	Number
Undergraduate Student	Low	27
Graduate Student	Medium-Low	28
Professional experience < 3 years	Medium-High	6
Professional experience >= 3 years	High	4

combined complexity of the head and the body, each of which is given a score of 1 (simple) or 2 (complex). An expression is simple if it involves only constants or simple boolean comparisons, otherwise it is complex. The total complexity score for a task is given by summing the score for each rule. The score for our running example would be 6 - each rule involves only simple expressions and there are 3 rules.

Tasks below the mean score for all tasks are considered less complex, while tasks that score above the mean are considered more complex. It is important to note that the queries required to solve most of the tasks in this experiment would be classified as complex in the previously reported experiments due to their use of set operations.

3.2 Environment and Evaluation

While we have a fully functioning implementation of the rule-based language, we decided to administer the experiment by using a paper and pencil exam. This technique has been frequently employed in previous experiments, and benefits from being efficiently administered to multiple subjects simultaneously. Prior to participating in the exam, each subject filled out a short demographic question-aire, which identified their skill level.

The exam was comprised of twelve classification problems against three different datasets. The datasets were described in terms of the input schema of the table. The problems were worded in the form of english sentences describing the desired classification.

Each subject was provided a training manual for the tool they were to use to solve the classification tasks. Each user had some experience with writing SQL queries, so the SQL training material focused on the writing of queries invloving set operations. The rule-based language training materials were slightly longer due to syntax differences. Both training manuals contained an identical set of example classification tasks as well as solutions. After reviewing the training materials the users were asked to solve the twelve classification problems.

The professional developers (expert users) were asked to complete both versions of the test. The order of exposure was controlled, ensuring that half of the expert subjects first used SQL and then used the rule-based language. The other half reversed this order of exposure. After completing both tests, the expert users completed a satisfaction survey comparing the two approaches.

3.3 Subject Group Comparison

Because of the design of the experiment, there are several groups whose characteristics need to be considered. Table 2 provides a summary of the information provided by the subjects that reported GPA's. A test for homogeneity of variances showed that the subject groups were comparable ($p < .10$).

The professional programmers were not asked to provide GPA's. Instead, they were asked to report their work experience (in years) with databases. As a group, the professional programmers averaged 4.2 years of experience.

Table 2. The average GPA and number of database courses for the student subjects

Subject Description	Average GPA (SD)	Average Experience (SD)
Undergraduate Student	3.35 (0.47)	1.18 (0.62)
Graduate Student	3.64 (0.31)	1.00 (0.85)

Table 3. Possible scores assigned to each problem solution

Score	Description
3	Correct solution
2	Essentially correct solution (typographical errors)
1	Partially correct solution (missing conditions)
0	Incorrect solution, or unsolved

3.4   Dependent Variables

The dependent variables we measured with this experiment were: 1. User Accuracy, and 2. User Satisfaction.

Accuracy is a quantitave measurement of the user's ability to solve classification problems with a specific tool. Satisfaction is a qualitative measurement of the user's feelings towards using a specific tool to solve classification problems. We did not measure the time required to solve each problem for two reasons. First, measuring time would have required the use of either an SQL interface as well as the implemented rule-based system. The queries are more efficiently processed using the rule-based system, which we believe would unduly influence the satisfaction measurement. Second, interacting with either system introduces possible side-effects to the accuracy measurements. For example, subjects may fail to get the syntax of the query exactly correct and become frustrated with either system leading to fewer problems attempted.

We determined the accuracy of a user's solution using a technique similar to [13]. Each problem was assigned the lowest of the possible scores shown in Table 3.

The scoring method is intentionally coarse. Each subject's total score was computed by totaling their score for each problem and dividing by the maximum number of possible points.

User satisfaction was determined by using a qualitative assessment survey. Two surveys were completed by each student. The first survey was completed after reviewing the training material. The second survey was completed after completing the exam problems.

3.5   Hypotheses

Figure 10 provides the hypotheses we seek to test with this experiment. By convention, each hypothesis is stated in its negative form.

The expert users were the only subjects that evaluated both approaches. As a result, the between-groups comparisons are limited to the first approach

H1: There will be no difference in accuracy based on tool selection.

H2: There will be no difference in accuracy based on user skill level.

H3: There will be no difference in accuracy based on task complexity level.

H4: There will be no interaction between user skill level and task complexity on accuracy.

H5: There will be no interaction between user skill level and tool selection on accuracy.

H6: There will be no interaction between task complexity level and tool selection on accuracy.

H7: There will be no difference in satisfaction based on tool selection.

H8: There will be no difference in satisfaction based on user skill level.

H9: There will be no difference in satisfaction based on task complexity level.

H10: There will be no interaction between user skill level and tool selection on satisfaction.

H11: There will be no difference on user satisfaction for expert users based on the order of exposure.

Fig. 10. Experimental hypotheses

evaluated by the expert users. Within-groups comparisons are based on the order of exposure for expert users.

4   Results

In this section we report the results of the experiment. In the following subsections we report: 1. Efficiency, 2. Accuracy, 3. Satisfaction, 4. Professional programmers.

The statistical test employed for this analysis was the standard T-Test. The significance level employed for all tests was 0.10. Note that the risk associated with making a type I error with either approach is small.

4.1   Efficiency

Often, usability experiments of this type will measure the efficiency with which users can solve problems. Efficiency may be measured in terms of time; however, for this experiment time was a constraint placed upon the user. Consequently, the time involved in solving problems would have a more significant effect on effectiveness measures, since the lack of time to solve all of the problems would preclude users from fully completing the problems. This was certainly the case with the student subjects, with only two subjects providing solutions for every problem.

A different measure of effectiveness which can be reported for this experiment is the number of steps involved in solving problems with each system. For example, a smaller number of steps with one system may indicate an improvement efficiency . The problems given to the users in this experiment involved similar steps with either system:

1. Identify the classes to be generated.
2. Define a condition for each class.
3. Define the output value to be generated for each condition.
4. Construct a simple query in SQL or the Rule language.
5. Put the queries or rules in the correct order.

Syntactically, the solutions had the same number of rules or queries. For this experiment, then, the systems are not separable. In the future, more elaborate experiments could be constructed to more closely measure the cognitive impact of these languages.

It is clear that the rule language is less verbose than SQL, which allows for a comparison on this basis. For example, the following rule program classifies patients according to their age:

$'Newborns' \leftarrow Age < 3$
$'Children' \leftarrow Age \geq 3 \text{ AND } Age \leq 12$
$'Adolescents' \leftarrow Age \geq 13 \text{ AND } Age \leq 18$
$'Adults' \leftarrow Age \geq 19 \text{ AND } Age \leq 65$
$'Elderly' \leftarrow Age > 65$

The equivalent SQL query is much more verbose:

```
Select "Newborns", * from Patient where Age < 3
  Union
Select "Children", * from Patient where Age >= 3 and Age <= 12
  Union
Select "Adolescents", * from Patient where Age >= 13 and Age <= 18
  Union
Select "Adults", * from Patient where Age >= 19 and Age <= 65
  Union
Select "Elderly", * from Patient where Age > 65
```

A word count (each term) of the rule language yields 37 words, while the SQL query has 61 words. Using this measure, the SQL queries were all longer than the rule programs. The average word count for the rule programs was 29.2 words, while the average for the SQL queries was 44.8 words.

Even though the rule language has the propensity to be more efficient using this measure, it is difficult to draw any direct conclusions. It is more likely that the experiment has revealed this in an indirect way. For instance, it is plausible that the lower satisfaction scores for SQL are related to the length of the solutions.

4.2   Accuracy

Table 4 shows the accuracy scores for each subject group.

The low scores for the students is related to the limited time that was provided for the exam. The difference in performance between the undergraduate and

Table 4. Mean accuracy scores for each group, as a percent of total (standard deviation)

Subject	SQL	Mapping Language
Undergraduate Student	27 (17)	37 (10)
Graduate Student	26 (19)	24 (21)
Professional	97 (0.1)	96 (0.2)

Table 5. Statistical tests of the accuracy results (Hypothesis 1 - 3)

Hypothesis	t (critical value)	Result (p)
H1	-0.56 (±1.665)	Not Rejected ($p > .10$)
H2: Undergrad	-1.86 (±1.708)	Rejected ($p < .10$)
H2: Grad	0.29 (±1.706)	Not Rejected ($p > .10$)
H2: Prof - 1	0.44 (±1.86)	Not Rejected ($p > .10$)
H2: Prof - 2	0.26 (±1.86)	Not Rejected ($p > .10$)
H3: SQL	2.4 (±1.665)	Rejected ($p < .10$)
H3: MQL	1.82 (±1.665)	Rejected ($p < .10$)

graduate student subjects is interesting. Note that the performance of graduate and undergraduate students is indistinguishable when using SQL. However, when using the mapping language, the undergraduate students performed better.

The lack of a similar relationship between accuracy scores for graduate students is a result of 4 students that did not get any problem correct. When omitting these students the average accuracy score for graduate students increases to 34% (SD 17), which tracks more accurately with the undergraduate result. The best explanation we have is based on the mix of students in the graduate class, which has a higher number of international students. It is possible that a language barrier was the primary influencer of the lower scores for these students. Since we did not control for this variable, we retained these students scores, rather than removing them from our result.

Table 5 reports the statistical tests for Hypothesis 1 - 3. Each result was tested at a 0.10 significance level. When the hypothesis is rejected, we report the lowest significance level, even though our a priori test was at 0.10. For the professional programmers we report both parts of the experiment: Prof-1 refers to the first exam, Prof-2 refers to the second exam. For Hypothesis 3, we tested both SQL and the mapping language.

The undergraduate students accuracy scores were higher for the mapping language. However, the trend on accuracy as experience increases indicates that either tool can be used to solve such classification problems. This is a positive result for the mapping language, since the subjects had no prior knowledge of the language. Future work certainly needs to consider the effect of experience with the mapping language.

The results for Hypothesis 3 show that complexity of the solution does impact the accuracy. However, the actual result is counterintuitive - subjects were more

Table 6. Mean satisfaction scores (1=Best, ..., 5=Worst) for the SQL group. (standard deviation)

Subject	Pre-Exam	Post-Exam
Undergraduate Student	1.82 (0.65)	2.45 (0.67)
Graduate Student	1.92 (0.80)	2.48 (0.81)
Professional	1.90 (0.78)	2.62 (0.56)

Table 7. Mean satisfaction scores (1=Best, ..., 5=Worst) for the Mapping Language group. (standard deviation)

Subject	Pre-Exam	Post-Exam
Undergraduate Student	2.09 (0.78)	2.01 (0.92)
Graduate Student	1.83 (0.57)	2.42 (0.58)
Professional	2.10 (0.60)	2.03 (0.68)

Table 8. Statistical tests of the satisfaction results (Hypothesis 4 and 5)

Hypothesis	t (critical value)	Result (p)
H4	1.69 ($\pm$1.665)	Rejected ($p < .10$)
H5: Undergrad	-1.45 ($\pm$1.708)	Not Rejected ($p > .10$)
H5: Grad	0.22 ($\pm$1.706)	Not Rejected ($p > .10$)
H5: Prof - 1	1.53 ($\pm$1.86)	Not Rejected ($p > .10$)
H5: Prof - 2	-0.86 ($\pm$1.86)	Not Rejected ($p > .10$)

accurate with complex solutions. This was especially true with SQL. In retrospect, controlling for complexity in the way we did is probably faulty. Note that the more complex solutions were shorter, which most likely skewed the results.

4.3   Satisfaction

Table 6 shows the results of the satisfaction surveys for the SQL group. Table 7 shows the results of the satisfaction surveys for the Mapping Language group.

What is interesting about the satisfaction scores is the relationship between the pre-exam and post-exam scores. For the SQL group, the post-exam score is higher. Again, the undergraduate students are interesting, in that their post-exam score is actually lower than the pre-exam score. Omitting the same 4 students as we previously omitted still resulted in a higher post-exam satisfaction score for the graduate students, although not as high as the SQL, graduate student group.

We compared the satisfaction scores to a target satisfaction score of 2.0, which would indicate that the user subjectively believes that the tool is a "good" tool to use. The statistical test employed was a standard T-Test with degrees of freedom set to the size of the sample minus 1. As a group, the SQL group's post-exam satisfaction scores indicated that SQL was not as good as they initially believed. For the Mapping Language group, only the Graduate students exhibited the same behavior.

Table 9. Statistical tests of the satisfaction results (Hypothesis 6, 7 and 8)

Hypothesis	t (critical value)	Result (p)
H6	-0.01 (±1.86)	Not Rejected ($p > .10$)
H7	-1.68 (±1.86)	Not Rejected ($p > .10$)
H8	6.11 (±1.833)	Rejected ($p < .10$)

Table 8 reports the statistical results for Hypothesis 4 and 5. Again, we distinguish between the professional programmer's first and second exams.

Hypothesis 4 was rejected. Note that this result compares the mean satisfaction score to 2.0 for the post-exam satisfaction survey. This result is influenced by the decreased satisfaction in SQL. For Hypothesis 5 the results do not consider the tool. Rather, they simply indicate that either tool is subjectively considered to be a good tool to solve classification problems.

4.4   Details of the Professional Programmer Experiment

In this subsection we report the results of statistical testing of Hypothesis 6 - 8. These hypotheses consider whether there is any difference in accuracy and satisfaction for the professional programmers when given both tools to solve problems. Table 9 reports the statistical results for these hypotheses.

Professional programmers had no problem with solving the problems with either tool, so there is no surprise about the accuracy hypothesis (H6). The satisfaction hypothesis (H7) is close to rejection. Again, the trend indicates that the subjects were less satisfied with SQL.

The significant result from Hypothesis 8 is based on a preference survey administered after using both tools. The raw data was scored on a 1 to 5 scale:

1: Strong preference for SQL.
2: Preference for SQL.
3: No preference.
4: Preference for MQL.
5: Strong preference for MQL.

The professional programmers preferred the mapping language, with a mean preference score of 3.7 (sd 0.35). The mean score indicates a somewhat weak preference for the mapping language. However, for the type of problem (classifications) no subject had a preference for SQL. This is especially positive for MQL, since the subjects had no prior knowledge of the language.

5   Conclusion and Future Work

The usability experiment showed that the mapping language could be used by both experienced and lesser experienced users with about as much accuracy as SQL. This in itself is encouraging, since the mapping language was a new concept for the subjects. The subjects were satisfied with both SQL and the mapping language. In general, the subjects were more satisfied with the mapping language.

We took advantage of the time the professional programmers made available for the study. Ideally, we would have liked many more professionals to participate in the study. The professionals had a strong preference for the mapping language for all types of classification tasks. At the same time, they tended to like SQL, since they had much more experience with it. The professionals were able to envision the benefits of the mapping language, which translated into the higher preference scores.

For future work, we are investigating a web service implementation of the process. This approach would allow for users to submit rule programs and data files for mapping. A web service approach may allow for optimizations to occur that are not feasible in the current implementation. In addition, we are looking at a continuous processing implementation for data streams, in which the process must necessarily look at a tuple only once.

References

1. ABITEBOUL, S., HULL, R., AND VIANU, V. *Foundations of Databases*. Addison-Wesley, 1995.
2. CATARCI, T. What happened when database researchers met usability. *Information Systems 25*, 3 (2000), 177–212.
3. DATE, C. J., AND DARWEN, H. *A Guide to the SQL Standard*. Addison-Wesley, Reading, Mass., 1993.
4. HAN, J., AND KAMBER, M. *Data Mining: Concepts and Techniques*. Morgan Kaufmann, 2001.
5. HAND, D., MANNILA, H., AND SMYTH, P. *Principles of Data Mining*. The MIT Press, 2001.
6. MEIER, A., SAVARY, C., SCHINDLER, G., AND VERYHA, Y. Database schema with fuzzy classification and classification query language. In *Computational Intelligence: Methods and Applications* (2001).
7. RAMAKRISHNAN, R. *Database Management Systems*. McGraw-Hill, 1998.
8. REISNER, P. Human factors studies of database query languages: A survey and assessment. *ACM Computing Surveys 13*, 1 (1981), 13–31.
9. REISNER, P., BOYCE, R., AND CHAMBERLIN, D. Human factors evaluation of two database query languages - square and sequel. In *Proceedings of the National Computer Conference* (1975), pp. 447–452.
10. VIANU, V. Rule-based languages. *Annals of Mathematics and Artificial Intelligence 19* (1997), 215–259.
11. WELTY, C., AND STEMPLE, D. Human factors comparison of a procedural and a nonprocedural query language. *ACM Transactions on Database Systems 6*, 4 (1981), 626–649.
12. WRIGHT, H., BRODLIE, K., AND BROWN, M. The dataflow visualization pipeline as a problem solving environment. In *Virtual Environments and Scientific Visualization '96*, M. Göbel, J. David, P. Slavik, and J. J. van Wijk, Eds. Springer-Verlag Wien, 1996, pp. 267–276.
13. YEN, M., AND SCAMELL, R. A human factors experimental comparison of SQL and QBE. *IEEE Transactions on Software Engineering 19*, 4 (1993), 390–402.

Appendix

<MAP_PROGRAM>	::=	<RULE> [<Line Feed> <RULE>]*
<RULE>	::=	<HEAD> "<-" <BODY>
<HEAD>	::=	<EXPRESSION>
	|	"Except"
<BODY>	::=	<BOOLEAN_EXPR> | "Else" | Null
<BOOLEAN_EXPR>	::=	<CONDITIONAL_EXPR> [<BOOLEAN_OPERATOR> <CONDITIONAL_EXPR>]*
	|	["NOT"] "(" <BOOLEAN_EXPR> [<BOOLEAN_OPERATOR> <BOOLEAN_EXPR>]* ")"
<BOOLEAN_OPERATOR>	::=	"AND" | "OR"
<CONDITIONAL_EXPR>	::=	<STATEMENT> [<RELATION> <STATEMENT>]
<STATEMENT>	::=	["NOT"] <EXPRESSION>
<RELATION>	::=	"<" | "<=" | ">" | ">=" | "=" | "!="
<EXPRESSION>	::=	<EXPRESSION> [<OPERATOR> <EXPRESSION>]*
	|	"(" <EXPRESSION> ")"
	|	<FUNCTION> | <ELEMENT>
<OPERATOR>	::=	"+" | "-" | "*" | "/" | "?" | "&" | "#" | "|"
<FUNCTION>	::=	"ABS(" <EXPRESSION> ")"
	|	"FLOOR(" <EXPRESSION> ")"
	|	"CEIL(" <EXPRESSION> ")"
	|	"SQRT(" <EXPRESSION> ")"
	|	"GRAYCODE(" <EXPRESSION> ["," <EXPRESSION>]* ")"
	|	"LENGTH(" <EXPRESSION> ")"
	|	"SUBSTRING(" <EXPRESSION> "," <EXPRESSION> "," <EXPRESSION> ")"
<ELEMENT>	::=	<VARIABLE> | <CONSTANT> | "(" <EXPRESSION> ")"
<VARIABLE>	::=	$A_i \in R$
<CONSTANT>	::=	number | "string"

Deductive and Inductive Reasoning on Spatio-Temporal Data

Mirco Nanni[1], Alessandra Raffaetà[2], Chiara Renso[1],
and Franco Turini[3]

[1] ISTI CNR - Pisa
{nanni, renso}@isti.cnr.it
[2] Dipartimento di Informatica - Università Ca' Foscari Venezia
raffaeta@dsi.unive.it
[3] Dipartimento di Informatica - Università di Pisa
turini@di.unipi.it

Abstract. We present a framework for a declarative approach to spatio-temporal reasoning on geographical data, based on the constraint logical language STACLP, which offers deductive and inductive capabilities. It can be exploited for a deductive rule-based approach to represent domain knowledge on data. Furthermore, it is well suited to model trajectories of moving objects, which can be analysed by using inductive techniques, like clustering, in order to find common movement patterns. A sketch of a case study on behavioural ecology is presented.

1 Introduction

New technologies in the field of mobile computing and communication can provide a wealth of spatio-temporal information. Collected data are useful as far as they can be used to analyse phenomena and to take informed decisions. Inductive methods can be exploited for data analysis since they are capable to extract implicit knowledge from raw observations. However, extracted patterns are very seldom geographic knowledge prêt-à-porter: it is necessary to reason on patterns and on pertinent background knowledge, evaluate pattern interestingness, refer them to geographic information.

The first step for allowing one to make a profitable use of data and extracted patterns is to provide a query language for them. The query language has to be flexible enough both to represent the kind of knowledge we wish to extract from the spatio-temporal data and to express how such a knowledge can be induced. From this viewpoint, a logic based query language is a good candidate in terms of flexibility and expressive power. Furthermore, we believe that the query language, even more in the case of spatio-temporal data, must be able to handle not only data but also rules, and exhibit both deductive and inductive capabilities. Rules can be used to represent general knowledge about the collected data, and deductive capabilities can provide answers to queries that require some inference besides the crude manipulation of the data. Induction can help in

D. Seipel et al. (Eds.): INAP/WLP 2004, LNAI 3392, pp. 98–115, 2005.
© Springer-Verlag Berlin Heidelberg 2005

extracting implicit knowledge from data and, according to its impressive success for knowledge discovery in database field, it can provide a powerful support to decision making. The approach we propose here is a first step towards a framework where a representational and a query language for spatio-temporal data mining are integrated on a logic programming basis. Such a framework must allow to represent raw data, to encode methods for pattern extraction and to support reasoning over background knowledge to permit the integration of other related georeferenced data and of extracted patterns.

To support both deductive and inductive reasoning on spatio-temporal data, the framework exploits STACLP (Spatio-Temporal Annotated Constraint Logic Programming) [34], a language based on constraint logic programming, extended with annotations. Constraint logic programming provides the deductive capabilities, and annotations allow a neat representation of temporal, spatial and spatio-temporal knowledge. On this ground, knowledge extraction methods can be implemented thus providing the required inductive capabilities.

Our proposal fits in a new and promising research field, that is the integration of declarative paradigms and systems for dealing with spatial and/or temporal information, such as spatial databases and Geographical Information Systems (GISs). In the literature we can find other attempts to exploit the deductive capabilities of logics to *reason* on geographic data [47, 41, 1, 16, 27].

Information induction over spatio-temporal data is far from being a mature field, yet. In recent years, many algorithms and applications have been investigated, which deal with spatial data (e.g., [10, 19, 31, 25]) *or* temporal data (e.g., [42, 15, 22]), either extending ideas coming from relational data mining or introducing new concepts of patterns and new computational approaches. On the contrary, only a limited number of proposals are actually available on mining methods which exploit both the spatial and the temporal components of data. In Section 2 a brief review is provided.

Section 3 introduces the language STACLP and Section 4 focuses on the representation of trajectories as a paradigmatic example of spatio-temporal objects. In Section 5 we sketch how STACLP allows us to solve a case study concerning behavioural ecology by using the deductive capabilities of the language, and the inductive capabilities implementing a clustering method. Finally, Section 6 draws some conclusions and outlines future research directions.

2   Related Work

While a lot of effort has been spent in developing extensions of logic programming languages capable to manage time [32], the logic based languages for the handling of spatial information only deal with the qualitative representation and reasoning about space (see e.g. [37]). And also the few attempts to manipulate time and space have led to languages for qualitative spatio-temporal representation and reasoning [46]. On the other hand, temporal [44, 11] and spatial [18, 33] database technologies are relatively mature, although, also in the database area, their combination is far from straightforward [5].

Our spatio-temporal language is based on the design principles of MuTA-CLP [27, 35]. In MuTACLP temporal information is represented by annotations whereas spatial information is encoded into the formulae, by using constraints. This leads to a mismatch of conceptual levels and a loss of simplicity. In STA-CLP we overcome this mismatch, by defining a uniform setting where spatial information is represented by means of annotations, so that the advantages of using annotations apply to the spatial dimension as well. Moreover, STACLP is close to the approaches based on constraint databases [4, 7, 16]. From a database point of view, logic programs can represent deductive databases, i.e. relational databases enriched with intensional rules, constraint logic programs can represent constraint databases [21], and thus STACLP can represent spatio-temporal constraint databases. The spatio-temporal proposals in [4, 16] are extensions of languages originally developed to express only spatial data. Thus the high-level mechanisms they offer are more oriented to query spatial data than temporal information. In fact, they can model only definite temporal information and there is no support for periodic, indefinite temporal data. On the contrary, STACLP provides several facilities to reason on temporal data and to establish spatio-temporal correlations. For instance, it allows one to describe *continuous* change in time as well as [7] does, whereas both [4] and [16] can represent only *discrete* changes. Also indefinite spatial and temporal information can be expressed in STACLP, a feature supported only by the approach in [26].

Spatio-temporal data mining is a subfield of data mining and knowledge discovery, aimed at the extraction of spatial and temporal patterns and relationships not explicitly contained in the database. Introducing a spatial and/or temporal component to data has two main effects: on one hand, the complexity of the data mining task is highly increased, requiring to adopt suitable measures to contain the computation time; on the other hand, space and time are not simple attributes, since they have a specific semantics, and thus new, ad hoc analysis tools should be developed to take full advantage of such information.

In the last ten years, several mining algorithms for temporal data have been presented in literature. Among the mainstream research subfields, we mention the mining of frequent patterns in transactional, timestamped databases such as sequential patterns [3] and episodes [28], and the large area of time series mining: time series classification [15, 8], sequential association rules [9, 20], clustering [17, 22] and anomaly detection [48].

Several approaches have also been proposed for mining spatial data (see [29], [40] for reviews of recent results): spatial trend detection [10], clustering [19], outlier detection [31, 39], association/co-location rules [25, 38] and classification [24, 10].

In the context of spatio-temporal data mining, where the spatial and temporal component are expected to be used together, [2] suggests two main kinds of information to induce: *meta-rules*, i.e., regularities shown along time by the rules obtained in each snapshot, and *evolution rules*, i.e., rules computed over pre-computed spatio-temporal features of entities. So far, only a limited number of concrete proposals are available for the mining of spatio-temporal data, such as sequential patterns [45], movement prediction [43] and clustering [30, 23, 14, 12]. In this work, in particular, a clustering algorithm for trajectories is designed within the STACLP system, following the solution described in [30]. However a few alternative approaches can be found in literature: [23] considers generic sequences together with a conceptual hierarchy over the sequence elements, used to compute both the cluster representatives and the distance between two sequences. In [14], a model-based clustering method for continuous trajectories is proposed, which puts together objects which can be obtained from a common core trajectory by adding noise with normal distribution. Finally, [12] proposes a general mapping from any data space to an Euclidean space, where any standard clustering algorithm can be applied.

3   STACLP: A Spatio-Temporal Language

In this section we present the language STACLP [34], which extends Temporal Annotated Constraint Logic Programming [13], a constraint logic programming language with temporal annotations, by adding spatial annotations. The pieces of spatio-temporal information are given by pairs of annotations which specify the spatial extent of an object at a certain time period. The use of annotations makes time and space explicit, but avoids the proliferation of spatial and temporal variables and quantifiers. Moreover, it supports both definite and indefinite spatial and temporal information, and it allows one to establish a dependency between space and time, thus permitting to model continuously moving points and regions.

Let us start by describing the temporal and spatial domain underlying STACLP. Time can be discrete or dense. Time points are totally ordered by the relation $\leq$. We denote by $\mathcal{T}$ the set of time points and we suppose to have a set of operations (e.g., the binary operations $+$, $-$) to manage such points. The time-line is left-bounded by 0 and open to the future, with the symbol ∞ used to denote a time point that is later than any other. A *time period* is an interval $[r, s]$ with $r, s \in \mathcal{T}$ and $0 \leq r \leq s \leq \infty$, which represents the convex, non-empty set of time points $\{t \mid r \leq t \leq s\}$. Thus the interval $[0, \infty]$ denotes the whole time line.

Analogously space can be discrete or dense and we consider as spatial regions *rectangles* represented as $[(x_1, x_2), (y_1, y_2)]$, where (x_1, y_1) and (x_2, y_2) denote the lower-left and upper-right vertex of the rectangle. Precisely, $[(x_1, x_2), (y_1, y_2)]$ models the region $\{(x, y) \mid x_1 \leq x \leq x_2, y_1 \leq y \leq y_2\}$. Rectangles are the two-dimensional counterpart of convex sets of time points.

Annotated formulae are of the form $A\,\alpha$ where A is an atomic formula and α an annotation. We define three kinds of temporal and spatial annotations inspired by similar principles:

at T and **atp** (X, Y) are used to express that a formula holds in a time or spatial point, respectively.

th I, **thr** R are used to express that a formula holds *throughout*, i.e., at *every* point, in the temporal interval or the spatial region, respectively.

in I, inr R are used to express that a formula holds at *some* point(s) - but we may not know exactly which - in the interval or the region, respectively. They account for indefinite information.

The set of annotations is endowed with a partial order relation $\sqsubseteq$. Given two annotations α and β, the intuition is that $\alpha \sqsubseteq \beta$ if α is "less informative" than β in the sense that for all formulae A, $A\beta \Rightarrow A\alpha$. This partial order is used in the definition of new inference rules. In addition to Modus Ponens, STACLP has the two inference rules below:

$$\frac{A\,\alpha \quad \gamma \sqsubseteq \alpha}{A\,\gamma} \quad rule\ (\sqsubseteq) \qquad\qquad \frac{A\,\alpha \quad A\,\beta \quad \gamma = \alpha \sqcup \beta}{A\,\gamma} \quad rule\ (\sqcup)$$

The rule $(\sqsubseteq)$ states that if a formula holds with some annotation, then it also holds with all annotations that are smaller according to the partial ordering. The rule $(\sqcup)$ says that if a formula holds with some annotation α and the same formula holds with another annotation β then it holds with the least upper bound $\alpha \sqcup \beta$ of the two annotations.

Next, we introduce the *constraint theory for temporal and spatial annotations*. A constraint theory is a non-empty, consistent first order theory that axiomatises the meaning of the constraints. Besides an axiomatisation of the total order relation $\leq$ on the set of points, the constraint theory includes the axioms defining the partial order on temporal and spatial annotations.

(at th)	at $t = $ th $[t, t]$
(at in)	at $t = $ in $[t, t]$
(th $\sqsubseteq$)	th $[s_1, s_2] \sqsubseteq$ th $[r_1, r_2] \Leftrightarrow r_1 \leq s_1,\ s_2 \leq r_2$
(in $\sqsubseteq$)	in $[r_1, r_2] \sqsubseteq$ in $[s_1, s_2] \Leftrightarrow r_1 \leq s_1,\ s_2 \leq r_2$
(atp thr)	atp $(x, y) = $ thr $[(x, x), (y, y)]$
(atp inr)	atp $(x, y) = $ inr $[(x, x), (y, y)]$
(thr $\sqsubseteq$)	thr $[(x_1, x_2), (y_1, y_2)] \sqsubseteq$ thr $[(x'_1, x'_2), (y'_1, y'_2)] \Leftrightarrow$
	$\qquad\qquad x'_1 \leq x_1,\ x_2 \leq x'_2, y'_1 \leq y_1,\ y_2 \leq y'_2$
(inr $\sqsubseteq$)	inr $[(x'_1, x'_2), (y'_1, y'_2)] \sqsubseteq$ inr $[(x_1, x_2), (y_1, y_2)] \Leftrightarrow$
	$\qquad\qquad x'_1 \leq x_1,\ x_2 \leq x'_2, y'_1 \leq y_1,\ y_2 \leq y'_2$

The first two axioms state that th I and in I are equivalent to at t when the time period I consists of a single time point t. Next, if a formula holds at every point of a time period, then it holds at every point in all sub-periods of that period ((th $\sqsubseteq$) axiom). On the other hand, if a formula holds at some points of a time period then it holds at some points in all periods that include this period ((in $\sqsubseteq$) axiom). The axioms for spatial annotations are analogously defined.

Spatio-temporal annotations are obtained by combining spatial and temporal annotations. More precisely, if *Spat* denotes the set of spatial annotations built from atp, thr and inr and *Temp* denotes the set of temporal annotations built from at, th and in, then spatio-temporal annotations are of the kind $\alpha\beta$ and $\beta\alpha$ where $\alpha \in Spat$ and $\beta \in Temp$, with the obvious componentwise order, i.e., whenever $\alpha_1 \sqsubseteq_{Spat} \alpha_2$ and $\beta_1 \sqsubseteq_{Temp} \beta_2$ then $\alpha_1\beta_1 \sqsubseteq \alpha_2\beta_2$ and $\beta_1\alpha_1 \sqsubseteq \beta_2\alpha_2$.

The constraint theory presented above is enriched to include the axiomatisation of the least upper bound on spatio-temporal annotations. The reader is referred to [34] for a more detailed presentation.

Now we can introduce the clausal fragment of STACLP, which can be used as an efficient spatio-temporal programming language. It consists of clauses of the following form:

$$A\,\alpha\beta \leftarrow C_1, \ldots, C_n, B_1\,\alpha_1\beta_1, \ldots, B_m\,\alpha_m\beta_m \quad (n, m \geq 0)$$

where A is an atom, α, α_i, β, β_i are (optional) temporal and spatial annotations, the C_j's are constraints, and the B_i's are atomic formulae. Constraints C_j cannot be annotated. A *STACLP program* is a finite set of STACLP clauses.

Example 1. Assume that a person is described by his/her name, the activity and the spatial position(s) in a *certain time interval.* For instance, from 1am to 10am John sleeps, then he goes skiing up to 4pm, while Monica skies from noon to 4pm. This can be expressed by means of the following clauses.

```
does(john,sleep) atp (200,700) th [1am,10am].
does(john,ski) inr [(500,2000),(1000,2000)] th [10am,4pm].
does(monica,ski) inr [(500,800),(800,2000)] th [12am,4pm].
place(ski_shop) thr [(700,900),(1200,1400)].
```

Notice that the spatial location is expressed by using an `atp` annotation when the exact position is known, and by an `inr` annotation if we can only delimit the area where the person can be found. Furthermore, a place can be described by its name and its area represented by a `thr` annotation.

An example of query is: *Where is John while Monica is at the ski shop?*, encoded in the following way:

```
does(john,_) inr R th I, does(monica,_) inr R1 th I, place(ski_shop) thr R1.
```

This query is a composition of a spatial join and a temporal join.

4 Representing Trajectories

One of the basic forms of spatio-temporal information is given by spatio-temporal objects, namely objects which move along time within a spatial environment.

From an abstract point of view, the movement of a spatio-temporal object o – i.e., its *trajectory* – can be represented by a continuous function of time which, given a time instant t, returns the position at time t of the object in a d-dimensional space (typically $d \in \{2, 3\}$). Formally $o : \mathbb{R}^+ \to \mathbb{R}^d$.

In a real-world application, however, object movements are given by means of a finite set of *observations* – or *control points* –, i.e. a finite subset of points taken from the actual continuous trajectory. Moreover, it is reasonable to expect that observations are taken at irregular rates within each object, and that there is not any temporal alignment between the observations of different objects. As a result, it is possible to have couples of objects for which at all time points the observation of at least one of the objects is missing. A very basic operation such as the comparison between objects, then, cannot be performed by simply comparing their raw observations. To allow the comparison between objects, an (approximate) reconstruction of their full trajectory is needed. Among the several possible solutions, we will focus on *Local interpolation*. According to this method, although there is not a global function describing the whole trajectory, objects are assumed to move between the observed points following some rule. For instance, a linear interpolation function models a straight movement with constant speed, while other polynomial interpolations can represent smooth changes of direction. The above mentioned linear (local) interpolation, in particular, seems to be a quite standard approach to the problem (see, e.g., Chomicki and Revesz's parametric 2-spaghetti model [7]).

Now, let us show how trajectories can be modelled in STACLP. Given an object o, the *observations* that describe its trajectory is a finite set of triplets (x, y, t), where x and y are the coordinates of the object tracked at time t. The trajectory reconstruction through linear interpolation can be easily represented by equations of the following form, which define the (x, y) coordinates of an object at time $t \in [t_1, t_2]$:

$$(x - x_1)(t_2 - t_1) - (x_2 - x_1)(t - t_1) = 0, \; and$$
$$(y - y_1)(t_2 - t_1) - (y_2 - y_1)(t - t_1) = 0$$

where (x_1, y_1, t_1) and (x_2, y_2, t_2) are two consecutive location points (i.e., there are not other locations in the time interval $[t_1, t_2]$).

Specifically, the N locations of each object o, (x_i, y_i, t_i) for $i = 1, \ldots, N$, can be represented by the following N STACLP facts:

```
fix(o) atp (x1, y1) at t1.
    ⋮
fix(o) atp (xN, yN) at tN.
```

Such locations will define the *core* of the trajectory of object o, which is then *completed* by defining all the intermediate points through linear interpolation using the following STACLP rules:

```
traj(O) atp (X, Y) at T :- fix(O) atp (X, Y) at T.
traj(O) atp (X, Y) at T :- fix(O) atp (X1, Y1) at T1,
                           fix(O) atp (X2, Y2) at T2,
                           succ(T1,T2), T1 < T < T2,
                           X=(X1(T2-T)+X2(T-T1))/(T2-T1),
                           Y=(Y1(T2-T)+Y2(T-T1))/(T2-T1).
```

In the body of the second rule, approximate points (x, y) are computed by using the equation for the line passing through two given points, shown above. The presence of the (standard) *successor* predicate succ, defined as true for all and only the couples of (strictly) consecutive location points, ensures that no other observation exists between times t_1 and t_2, i.e., the interpolation is performed only between consecutive location points.

5   Spatio-Temporal Analysis in STACLP

In this section we sketch a case study about behavioural ecology, the science which studies animal behaviour with special interest in the relation to the environment where animal lives. This is definitely an appealing application domain for our framework since the problems coped with require the analysis of large spatio-temporal datasets.

Typically, biologists collect information tracking the movement of animals by means of special radio-collars thus building large datasets containing spatio-temporal locations, called *fixes*. Each fix includes the identifier of the animal, the position expressed by the spatial coordinates X, Y and the time T of the location. The set of fixes allows us to view animals as spatio-temporal objects.

To experiment the usefulness of our framework for spatio-temporal analysis, we coped with some relevant problems in behavioural ecology of the crested porcupines. In particular, we focused on determining the estimated position of the den whenever its real location is unknown, detecting how the life area of the animal, called *home range*, changes along the time, discovering the relationships existing among individuals, or assessing whether and to what extent an event (e.g. a change in a crop cover, meteorological or geo-morphological occurrence) defined in time and space, has caused variations in the movement of the monitored animals. Such questions emerged from a research leaded by biologists from the University of Siena about the behavioural ecology of crested porcupines in the Maremma Regional Park (Tuscany, Italy) [6]. It is worth recalling that the crested porcupine is mainly nocturnal, lives in natural or artificial burrows and there is very few information available on the behaviour of such species. For this reason there is currently much interest, in the animal ecology field, in studying its habits.

Here we will describe only how changes in the home range of the animals can be discovered and how relationships among individuals can be established. The last problem includes a wide range of cases such as finding pairs of individuals of different sex that move together and possibly share the same den (couples), or groups of individuals that move together (herds), or couple/groups of individuals that avoid each other (territoriality). In facing such issues, we can highlight the benefits of STACLP. First of all, the language allows for a high level representation and manipulation of time as well as space thus providing primitive support for reasoning on spatio-temporal data. Secondly, it allows us to mix inductive and deductive steps in order to perform complex kinds of analysis on the behaviour of crested porcupines.

Section 5.1 below focuses on deduction, showing how the deductive capability of our language allows us to select the animals which are likely to be a couple and to detect changes in the home range. Section 5.2, instead, is devoted to introduce mechanisms to support inductive analysis, describing how these tools can be successfully used in our case study.

5.1   Deductive Analysis in STACLP

To model the spatio-temporal locations of each crested porcupine we define a collection of facts of the kind:

```
fix(id) atp (x,y) at t.
```

specifying the position x,y, and the time t (expressed in seconds) of a location for the animal identified by id.

Below we will show the STACLP code that implements the expert criteria by which we successfully solve the questions of interest. To focus on the knowledge representation ability of the language, the rules are slightly simplified by removing some implementation details, but the code can be made executable by a simple precompilation step. The rules extensively use the Prolog meta-predicate findall(X,G,L) which computes the list L of elements X that satisfy the goal G.

For understanding the habits and the social behaviour of animals, it is extremely relevant to discover the relationships existing among individuals. To assess the degree of association among individuals the inter-individual distance between animals localised at the same time is computed. Two fixes are called *contemporary* if they refer to locations of animals in the same place and at the same time, i.e., a kind of spatio-temporal closeness among individuals is considered. Since the tracking technique usually presents several sources of error, in the analysis two fixes are assumed to be *contemporary* if they fall within a given time interval and the corresponding locations are within a certain distance. The effective values for the temporal and spatial thresholds are established by biologists (and they can be varied if the results are not satisfactory).

Analysing this kind of inter-individual distance between animals, it is possible to make hypotheses about which animals can be considered a couple, form a herd, or avoid other individuals. For instance, two animals of different sex are likely to be a couple in a given day if a high quantity of contemporary fixes for the two animals is found in such a day. The following code implements the described criteria to determine a couple.

```
fixes_in_day(Id1,Id2,R,S,N) at T :-
    findall(c(Id1,Id2), (fix(Id1) atp(X1,Y1) at T1,
                         fix(Id2) atp(X2,Y2) at T2,
                         sex(Id1, S1), sex(Id2, S2), S1 != S2,
                         contem(X1,Y1,X2,Y2,R,S,T1,T2) at T),
           L),
    length(L,N).

contem(X1,Y1,X2,Y2,Rad,Sec,T1,T2) at T:-
                   in_day(T1) at T, in_day(T2) at T,
                   dist(X1,Y1,X2,Y2,D), D<Rad, abs(T2-T1)<Sec.
```

```
couple(Id1,Id2,R,S,Ratio) at T :-
                porcupine(Id1), porcupine(Id2),
                fixes_in_day(Id1,Id2,R,S,N) at T,
                fixes_in_day(Id1,Id2,1000000,S,M) at T,
                Ratio is (N/M).
```

The predicate `fixes_in_day` returns the number N of contemporary fixes in a day T for the pair of crested porcupines `Id1,Id2`. Two fixes are considered contemporary if they are in the same day (predicate `in_day`) and their spatial and temporal distance is bounded by R and S respectively, as encoded by the predicate `contem`. Finally, the predicate `couple` returns the ratio between the number of contemporary fixes of the crested porcupines `Id1,Id2` and the number of observations of `Id1,Id2` within S seconds at arbitrary distance (concretely this is obtained by setting a very large bound for the distance parameter) in the day T.

Another basic objective in the analysis of animal behaviour is a better understanding of how the animals change their *home ranges* along time. This goal requires, among other tasks, the detection of seasonal variations of the home ranges, both in location and size, and also, to infer the factors determining the dimensions of home ranges for these species. A simple approach to face this problem consists of partitioning the time period covered by the analysis, $[t_{start}, t_{end}]$, into consecutive time sub-intervals of appropriate duration ΔT, thus evaluating the home ranges within each sub-interval, and analysing the sequence of results obtained. However, in general, determining a suitable value for ΔT results to be not easy. On one hand, it has to be large enough to allow the computation of a significant home range, but, on the other one, it has to be small enough to catch swift changes. A solution to this problem is to calculate home ranges in a "continuous" way within a given time interval (e.g., a season). The "continuity" can be obtained by replacing the time partitioning approach, described above, with a temporal *sliding window*: now, two parameters δ_t and W_t are defined, and home ranges are computed on overlapping time intervals, each of duration W_t and each shifted of δ_t w.r.t. the previous one, starting from interval $[t_{start}, t_{start} + W_t]$. We assume that `Wt <= t_end - t_start`, i.e., at least one of such intervals can fit in `[t_start,t_end]`.

```
homerange(Fix_list, Home) :- <ad hoc query/external call>

home(Id, Home) at t_start:- findall((X,Y),
    fix(Id) atp (X,Y) in [t_start, t_start+Wt], Fix_list),
    homerange(Fix_list, Home).
home(Id, Home) at T:- home(Id, _) at T_prev,
        T=T_prev+δt, T + Wt <= t_end,
        findall((X,Y),
                fix(Id) atp (X,Y) in [T, T+Wt],
                Fix_list),
        homerange(Fix_list, Home).
```

Given a list of fixes, the predicate `homerange` returns the corresponding home range Home by simply calling a routine provided by an external application. More details on the use of built-in predicates to directly invoke external functions can be found in [27, 35].

The predicate `home` returns the home range `Home` for an animal `Id` at regular time points, i.e. at `t_start` and at time points shifted from `t_start` of a multiple of δt. The first rule states that the home range for animal `Id` at the time instant `t_start` is obtained by finding all the fixes included in the interval `[t_start, t_start+Wt]` and then applying the home range routine to these fixes. The second rule manages the remaining time points and is defined in a similar way: it computes the home range using the fixes within the interval `[T, T+Wt]`, provided that `T` is shifted from `t_start` by a multiple of δt and `T+Wt <= t_end`.

It is worth noting that computing home ranges over a sliding window produces a *smoothly-evolving* home range, which is perfectly analogous to the smooth curve obtained by applying any (of the several well known) sliding window-based smoothing operator on a time series. Such operators have a wide application in several fields, such as noise-reduction filters in signal processing tools. In this sense, the sequence of home ranges obtained for an object o can be viewed as an alternative, improved representation of its trajectory. Therefore, depending on how home ranges are computed and the complexity of their representation, they can be used in some analysis tasks in place of the original trajectory, in order to improve the quality of the results (e.g., in any analysis where the global *trend* of o's movement is relevant, while its single movements are uninteresting and potentially misleading). This represents an interesting direction for future work.

5.2   Inductive Analysis in STACLP

As shown in the previous subsection, deductive reasoning can be useful to solve analysis problems which essentially require to find entities and values having some, possibly complex, properties.

However, when dealing with sophisticated analysis tasks, it is quite common to meet concepts and abstract entities whose definition through deductive rules can be extremely difficult. In many cases, a suitable solution to the problem at hand requires the *extrapolation* of new pieces of information from those already available. In other words, knowledge induction capabilities can be needed to properly tackle some difficult problems.

For this reason, we will show how the STACLP language can be fruitfully used to support induction capabilities, such as data mining algorithms. In this section we show (i) how a basic data mining tool, the k-means clustering algorithm, specifically tailored around trajectories, can be defined as STACLP rules, and (ii) how it can be used to provide an alternative solution to the problem of discovering couples and herds.

Clustering. The clustering task is aimed at identifying clusters embedded in the data, i.e. to partition (although not necessarily in a crisp way) the dataset into collections of data objects, such that within each partition the objects are "similar" to one another, while they are "different" from the objects contained in other partitions.

Among the classical clustering algorithms, K-means is one of the best known and widely used, for its simplicity and its low computational complexity. It is a centre-based algorithm, meaning that clusters are represented by means of artificial objects (the *centres* or *representatives*) which summarise the properties of all the objects in their cluster. The k-means algorithm is essentially an iterative convergence process which tries to find "stable" centres: it starts with k random centres, and then, at each iteration (i) each object is associated with the closest centre, and (ii) new centres are computed. The algorithm ends when the centres are stable, i.e. they do not change any more from an iteration to the next one.

The general k-means clustering schema can be instantiated to a specific k-means algorithm by specifying the two key operations used in the schema: (i) computing the distance between two objects, and (ii) computing the representative of a set of objects (i.e., the centre of a cluster). Different definitions for these two steps can yield completely different notions of clustering.

The STACLP language allows to implement a k-means algorithm in a very compact, well structured and readable form. In what follows, we show the most high level rules of such implementation. For ease of presentation, we assume that k is the (fixed) number of clusters to find, and all objects to be clustered have an Id of the form "objs(name_of_object)".

```
objs_to_cluster(O_list) :-
          findall(X, (fix(X) atp (_,_) at _, X=objs(_)), O_list).

assign(It, [], []).
assign(0,[A1|A],[Obj1|Objs]) :- K=random(k),
        A1=cluster(Obj1,K), assign(0, A, Objs).
assign(It,[A1|A],[Obj1|Objs]) :- It>0, closest(It-1, Obj1, Clust),
        A1=cluster(Obj1,Clust), assign(It, A, Objs).
```

The objs_to_cluster predicate defines the set of objects to be clustered. In the example instantiation given above, all objs(_) objects having some fixes defined were selected. For any iteration It, the assign predicate associates every object with its closest cluster centre, based on the results recursively obtained at the previous iteration, representing this information as terms of the form cluster(object_ID, cluster_number). At iteration zero, the assignment object-cluster is random.

```
closest(Iter, Obj, Clust) :- best_dist(Iter, Obj, k, Clust, D).

best_dist(Iter, Obj, 1, 1, D) :- distance(centre(Iter, 1), Obj, D).
best_dist(Iter, Obj, K, Clust, D) :- K>1,
            distance(centre(Iter, K), Obj, D1),
            best_dist(Iter, Obj, K-1, Clust2, D2),
            if D1 < D2 then Clust=K, D=D1
                       else Clust=Clust2, D=D2.
```

Here the selection of the closest cluster centre is implemented, simply scanning all the k centres obtained for the previous iteration, searching for the minimum value of the distance w.r.t. the object to assign. Here it appears the `distance` predicate, defined later in this section. In the following last set of rules, the centre of each cluster for any iteration is defined by setting its coordinates to the average values taken by all objects in the cluster (notice that a predicate `sum_pairs` is used to sum the single components of couples: since it is quite trivial to implement, its definition is omitted).

```
fix(centre(Iter,K)) atp (X,Y) at T :-
    objs_to_cluster(O_list), assign(Iter, A, O_list),
    member(cluster(Obj,K), A), fix(Obj) atp (_, _) at T,
    compute_avg_position(A, K, T, X, Y).

compute_avg_position(A, K, T, X, Y) :-
    findall((X1, Y1),
        (member(cluster(O,K),A), traj(O) atp (X1, Y1) at T), L),
    sum_pairs(L, (Xsum, Ysum)), length(L,N), N>0,
    X=Xsum/N, Y=Ysum/N.

fix(centre(K)) atp (X,Y) at T :-
            fix(centre(max_n_iters, K)) atp (X,Y) at T.

assignments(A) :- objs_to_cluster(O_list),
                assign(max_n_iters, A, O_list).
```

Notice that in the definition of `compute_avg_position`, the `traj` predicate is used to interpolate the position of objects, since the fixes of an object could be not aligned to the fixes of the others. The final result of the clustering process is represented by the cluster assignments (see the `assignments` predicate) and the means of the centres obtained when the maximum number of iterations has been reached – in particular, such centres will coincide with a local minimum of the clustering process if the algorithm converges in less than `max_n_iters` iterations.

The distance between objects can be defined in several ways, depending, e.g., on the meaning given to clusters or the coarseness allowed in the computation. One example of coarse but simple distance has been implicitly given in the previous section, where the similarity between two animals were defined as the percentage of mutually contemporary fixes (see the `couple` predicate in Section 5.1). In that case, only the explicit information on fixes has been exploited, not considering the whole trajectory followed by objects. A different and more precise solution, then, should take into account the position of objects for each time instant. Following this idea, a simple general approach to compute the distance $D(o_1, o_2)$ between two objects o_1 and o_2, whose positions along time $o_1(t)$ and $o_2(t)$ are defined over a time interval T, can be described by the following expression:

$$D(o_1, o_2) = \Phi(d_{o_1, o_2})\big|_T$$

where the first parameter of the schema, $d_{o_1,o_2}(t)$, is a distance measure between $o_1(t)$ and $o_2(t)$, and the second one, $\Phi(f)|_T$, is a functional computed over function f and domain T and returns a real value. In the STACLP rules given below, $d()$ is instantiated as the Euclidean distance on $\mathbf{R}^2$, and $\Phi()$ is the *average* functional, thus modelling $D(o_1, o_2)$ as the average Euclidean distance between o_1 and o_2. However, such parameters are modular components of the clustering algorithm, and therefore can be easily instantiated with other functions, as those described in [30], thus defining new distance notions for $D(o_1, o_2)$.

Computing the average Euclidean distance between moving objects requires to calculate an integral of the Euclidean distance formula over a given time interval $[t_s, t_e]$. Thanks to the linear interpolation model adopted, such computation can be realised in linear time w.r.t. the number of fixes of each object [30]. This is due to the fact that the integration interval can be broken down to subintervals, and in each of them the integral can be symbolically solved and thus computed in constant time. The following rules essentially find such subintervals, use a predicate compute_sub (not described here, as well as sort_without_duplicates, for sake of brevity) to compute local integrals, and aggregate them.

```
distance(O1,O2,D) :- collect_fixes(O1,O2,Fixes),
                integral(O1,O2,Fixes,Int), D=I/(t_e-t_s).

collect_fixes(O1,O2,Fixes) :-
                findall(T, fix(O1) atp (_,_) at T, L1),
                findall(T, fix(O2) atp (_,_) at T, L2),
                append(L1,L2,L).
                sort_without_duplicates(L, Fixes).

integral(O1,O2,[_],0).
integral(O1,O2,[T1|[T2|T]], Int) :-
   traj(O1) atp (X11,Y11) at T1, traj(O1) atp (X12,Y12) at T2,
   traj(O2) atp (X21,Y21) at T1, traj(O2) atp (X22,Y22) at T2,
   compute(X11, Y11, X12, Y12, X21, Y21, X22, Y22, T1, T2, Int1),
   integral(O1,O2,[T2|T], Int2), Int = Int1 + Int2.
```

Knowledge Discovery on Trajectories. In this section we provide a very compact STACLP program which shows how using the clustering tool can yield an alternative, more sophisticated, solution to the problem of discovering animal couples or herds.

In Section 5.1, a fully deductive approach has already been presented, where a simple criterion was adopted, based on contemporary fixes, to discover animal couples. A more precise and general solution to the problem can be achieved by noticing that animal couples and animal herds are groups of animal which, in general, move together. This can be straightforwardly rephrased saying that animal herds are clusters of animal individuals whose mutual distance is, on average, small. This leads to the following STACLP formalisation, where trajectories of animals are clustered using the k-means algorithm, and focusing on a time interval $[t_s, t_e]$:

```
objs_to_cluster(O_list) :-
        findall(X, (fix(X) atp (_,_) at _, X=cut_obj(_)), O_list).
```

```
fix(cut_obj(O)) atp (X,Y) at t_s :- traj(obj(O)) atp (X,Y) at t_s.
fix(cut_obj(O)) atp (X,Y) at t_e :- traj(obj(O)) atp (X,Y) at t_e.
fix(cut_obj(O)) atp (X,Y) at T :- T > t_s, T<t_e,
                                    fix(obj(O)) atp (X,Y) at T.
```

```
cluster_member(K,O_list) :- findall( Obj,
            (assignments(A), member(cluster(Obj,K), A)),
            O_list).
```

```
couples([Obj1, Obj2]) :- cluster_member(_, [Obj1, Obj2]),
                    sex(Obj1, S1), sex(Obj2, S2), S1 != S2.
```

```
herds(O_list) :- cluster_member(_, O_list),
                length(O_list, N), N>=min_herd_size.
```

The first rule redefines the `objs_to_cluster` predicate in order to cluster the new `cut_obj(O)` objects, obtained by clipping the trajectories of the original `obj(O)` objects on the $[t_s, t_e]$ time interval. Such task is accomplished, for each object, by (i) selecting those of its fixes which fall within the time interval, and (ii) interpolating the position of the object on the extremes of the time interval. Notice that, to such purpose, in the first case the rules which define `fix(cut_obj(O))` make use of the `fix` predicate (third clause), while in the second case the `traj` predicate is invoked. The `cluster_member` predicate provides the list of objects belonging to a cluster and it is exploited to find out couples and herds by checking the size of clusters. In the rules defining couples and herds, we assumed (i) to be interested in clusters of two individuals of different sex, and that (ii) a necessary (and sufficient) condition for a group of animals to be a herd is that its size is not smaller that a given threshold. Of course, it is easy to insert more complex conditions on the properties of the group and of the animals it contains (e.g., checking the respect of given proportions in the number of male and female individuals).

6 Conclusions

The main aim of the framework we presented is to provide the user with high level mechanisms to represent and reason on spatio-temporal data. The peculiarity of this approach is that it exhibits both deductive and inductive capabilities, thus offering the possibility to make analysis both exploiting domain expert rules and general background knowledge (deduction), and driven by observations (induction). Furthermore we sketched how this approach can be successfully applied to a concrete case study concerning behavioural ecology that well represents these two kinds of reasoning.

We are currently improving the implementation of STACLP, which is at a prototype stage and lacks of optimisation techniques. As a future research direction we are moving towards the introduction of other knowledge discovery techniques, such as classification and frequent patterns, in this framework. This leads to challenging and interesting research problems as well as a wide range of possible applications related to mobile devices. As an example, classification applied to trajectories can be exploited to predict the future direction of a moving object. Detecting frequent patterns of a number of trajectories representing car movements can allow to identify routes with high traffic density depending on the time of the day.

Another promising direction we intend to address concerns qualitative spatio-temporal reasoning. Starting from some preliminary results presented in [36], we aim at defining forms of qualitative reasoning on trajectories thus providing support for *qualitative spatio-temporal reasoning*, possibly enriched with uncertainty information. As an example, a typical qualitative spatio-temporal query can be to find out whether, when and with which degree of certainty a given trajectory crosses a specific area.

Acknowledgements. We thank T. Ceccarelli and A. Massolo for providing us the case study and F. Fornasari and B. Furletti who collaborated in the implementation of the system.

References

1. A.I. Abdelmoty, N.W. Paton, M.H. Williams, A.A.A. Fernandes, M.L. Barja, and A. Dinn. Geographic Data Handling in a Deductive Object-Oriented Database. In *DEXA Conf.*, volume 856 of *LNCS*, pages 445–454. Springer, 1994.
2. T. Abraham. *Knowledge Discovery in Spatio-Temporal Databases.* PhD thesis, School of Computer and Information Science, Faculty of Information Technology, University of South Australia, 1999.
3. R. Agrawal and R. Srikant. Mining sequential patterns. In Philip S. Yu and Arbee S. P. Chen, editors, *Eleventh International Conference on Data Engineering*, pages 3–14, Taipei, Taiwan, 1995. IEEE Computer Society Press.
4. A. Belussi, E. Bertino, and B. Catania. An extended algebra for constraint databases. *IEEE TKDE*, 10(5):686–705, 1998.
5. M.H. Böhlen, C.S. Jensen, and M.O. Scholl, editors. *Spatio-Temporal Database Management*, volume 1678 of *Lecture Notes in Computer Science*. Springer, 1999.
6. T. Ceccarelli, D. Centeno, F. Giannotti, A. Massolo, C. Parent, A. Raffaetà, C. Renso, S. Spaccapietra, and F. Turini. The behaviour of the Crested Porcupine: the complete case study. Technical report, DeduGIS - EU WG, 2001.
7. J. Chomicki and P.Z. Revesz. Constraint-Based Interoperability of Spatiotemporal Databases. *GeoInformatica*, 3(3):211–243, 1999.
8. P. Cotofrei. Statistical temporal rules. In *Proc. of the 15th Conf. on Computational Statistics*, 2002.
9. G. Das, K.-I. Lin, H. Mannila, G. Renganathan, and P. Smyth. Rule discovery from time series. In *Proc. of the Fourth International Conference on Knowledge Discovery and Data Mining - KDD98*, pages 16–22, 1998.

10. M. Ester, H.-P. Kriegel, and J. Sanders. Algorithms and applications for spatial data mining. In *[29]*, pages 160–187.

11. O. Etzion, S. Jajodia, and S. Sripada, editors. *Temporal Databases: Research and Practice*, volume 1399 of *Lecture Notes in Computer Science*. Springer, 1998.

12. C. Faloutsos and K.-I. Lin. Fastmap: a fast algorithm for indexing of traditional and multimedia databases. In *SIGMOD Conf.*, pages 163–174. ACM, 1995.

13. T. Frühwirth. Temporal Annotated Constraint Logic Programming. *Journal of Symbolic Computation*, 22:555–583, 1996.

14. S. Gaffney and P. Smyth. Trajectory clustering with mixture of regression models. In *KDD Conf.*, pages 63–72. ACM, 1999.

15. P. Geurts. Pattern extraction for time series classification. *Lecture Notes in Computer Science*, 2168:115–127, 2001.

16. S. Grumbach, P. Rigaux, and L. Segoufin. Spatio-Temporal Data Handling with Constraints. *GeoInformatica*, 5(1):95–115, 2001.

17. S. Guha, N. Mishra, R. Motwani, and L. O'Callaghan. Clustering data streams. In *IEEE Symposium on Foundations of Computer Science*, pages 359–366, 2000.

18. R.H. Güting. An Introduction to Spatial Database Systems. *VLDB Journal*, 3(4):357–400, 1994.

19. J. Han, M. Kamber, and A. K. H. Tung. Spatial clustering methods in data mining: a survey. In *[29]*, pages 188–217.

20. S. K. Harms, J. Deogun, and T. Tadesse. Discovering sequential association rules with constraints and time lags in multiple sequences. In *Proc. of the 13th Int. Symposium on Methodologies for Intelligent Systems*, pages 432–441, 2002.

21. P.C. Kanellakis, G.M. Kuper, and P.Z. Revesz. Constraint query languages. *Journal of Computer and System Sciences*, 51(1):26–52, 1995.

22. E. Keogh, J. Lin, and W. Truppel. Clustering of Time Series Subsequences is Meaningless: Implications for Previous and Future Research. In *Proceedings of the 3rd IEEE International Conference on Data Mining*, pages 115–122, 2003.

23. A. Ketterlin. Clustering sequences of complex objects. In *KDD Conf.*, pages 215–218. ACM, 1997.

24. K. Koperski. *A Progressive Refinement Approach to Spatial Data Mining*. PhD thesis, Simon Frasery University, 1999.

25. K. Koperski and J. Han. Discovery of spatial association rules in geographic information databases. In *Advances in Spatial Databases, Proc. of 4th Symp. SSD'95*, volume 951 of *LNCS*, pages 47–66, Berlin, 1995. Springer-Verlag.

26. M. Koubarakis and S. Skiadopoulos. Tractable Query Answering in Indefinite Constraint Databases: Basic Results and Applications to Querying Spatiotemporal Information. In *[5]*, pages 204–223, 1999.

27. P. Mancarella, A. Raffaetà, C. Renso, and F. Turini. Integrating Knowledge Representation and Reasoning in Geographical Information Systems. *International Journal of GIS*, 18(4):417–446, June 2004.

28. H. Mannila, H. Toivonen, and A. I. Verkamo. Discovery of frequent episodes in event sequences. *Data Mining and Knowledge Discovery*, 1(3):259–289, 1997.

29. H. J. Miller and J. Han, editors. *Geographic Data Mining and knowledge Discovery*. Taylor & Francis, 2001.

30. M. Nanni. *Clustering Methods for Spatio-Temporal Data*. PhD thesis, Dipartimento di Informatica, Università di Pisa, 2002.

31. R. T. Ng. Detecting outliers from large datasets. In *[29]*, pages 218–235.

32. M. A. Orgun and W. Ma. An Overview of Temporal and Modal Logic Programming. In *ICTL'94*, volume 827 of *LNAI*, pages 445–479. Springer, 1994.

33. J. Paredaens. Spatial databases, the final frontier. In *ICDT'95*, volume 893 of *LNCS*, pages 14–32. Springer, 1995.
34. A. Raffaetà and T. Frühwirth. Spatio-Temporal Annotated Constraint Logic Programming. In *PADL'01*, volume 1990 of *LNCS*, pages 259–273. Springer, 2001.
35. A. Raffaetà, C. Renso, and F. Turini. Enhancing GISs for Spatio-Temporal Reasoning. In *ACM GIS'02*, pages 35–41. ACM Press, 2002.
36. A. Raffaetà, C. Renso, and F. Turini. Qualitative Spatial Reasoning in a Logical Framework. In *AI*IA Conf.*, volume 2829 of *LNAI*, pages 78–90, 2003.
37. D. Randell, Z. Cui, and A. Cohn. A Spatial Logic based on Regions and Connection. In *KR1992*, pages 165–176. Morgan Kaufmann, 1992.
38. S. Shekhar and Y. Huang. Discovering spatial co-location patterns: A summary of results. In *Advances in Spatial and Temporal Databases, 7th International Symposium, SSTD 2001*, volume 2121 of *LNCS*, pages 236–256, 2001.
39. S. Shekhar, C.-T. Lu, and P. Zhang. Detecting graph-based spatial outliers: algorithms and applications (a summary of results). In *Proc. of the 7th ACM SIGKDD international conference on Knowledge discovery and data mining*, pages 371–376. ACM Press, 2001.
40. S. Shekhar, P. Zhang, R. R. Vatsavai, and Y. Huang. Research accomplishments and issues on spatial data mining. In *White paper of the Geospatial Visualization and Knowledge Discovery Workshop*, Lansdowne, Virginia, 2003. http://www.ucgis.org/Visualization/.
41. S. Spaccapietra, editor. *Spatio-Temporal Data Models & Languages (DEXA Workshop)*. IEEE Computer Society Press, 1999.
42. R. Srikant and R. Agrawal. Mining sequential patterns: generalisations and performance improvements. In *Proc. of the 5th Int. Conf. on Extending Database Technology (EDBT'96)*, volume 1057 of *LNCS*, pages 3–17, 1996.
43. N. Sumpter and A. Bulpitt. Learning spatio-temporal patterns for predicting object behaviour. *Image and Vision Computing*, 18(9):697–704, 2000.
44. A. Tansel, J. Clifford, S. Gadia, S. Jajodia, A. Segev, and R. Snodgrass editors. *Temporal Databases: Theory, Design, and Implementation*. Benjamin/Cummings, 1993.
45. I. Tsoukatos and D. Gunopulos. Efficient mining of spatiotemporal patterns. In *Advances in Spatial and Temporal Databases, 7th International Symposium, SSTD 2001*, volume 2121 of *LNCS*, pages 425–442, 2001.
46. F. Wolter and M. Zakharyaschev. Spatio-temporal representation and reasoning based on RCC-8. In *KR2000*, pages 3–14. Morgan Kaufmann, 2000.
47. M. F. Worboys. *GIS - A Computing Perspective*. Taylor & Francis, 1995.
48. T. Yairi, Y. Kato, and K. Hori. Fault detection by mining association rules from house-keeping data. In *Proc. of International Symposium on Artificial Intelligence, Robotics and Automation in Space*, 2001.

Mining Semantic Structures in Movies

Kimiaki Shirahama, Yuya Matsuo, and Kuniaki Uehara

Graduate School of Science and Technology, Kobe University,
Nada, Kobe, 657-8501, Japan
{kimi, yuya, uehara}@ai.cs.scitec.kobe-u.ac.jp

Abstract. 'Video data mining' is a technique to discover useful patterns from videos. It plays an important role in efficient video management. Particularly, we concentrate on extracting useful editing patterns from movies. These editing patterns are useful for an amateur editor to produce a new, more attractive video. But, it is essential to extract editing patterns associated with their semantic contents, called 'semantic structures'. Otherwise the amateur editor can't determine how to use the extracted editing patterns during the process of editing a new video.

In this paper, we propose two approaches to extract semantic structures from a movie, based on two different time series models of the movie. In one approach, the movie is represented as a multi-stream of metadata derived from visual and audio features in each shot. In another approach, the movie is represented as one-dimensional time series consisting of durations of target character's appearance and disappearance. To both time series models, we apply data mining techniques. As a result, we extract the semantic structures about shot transitions and about how the target character appears on the screen and disappears from the screen.

1   Introduction

Advances in multimedia technologies have yielded a vast amount of video data. For efficient video management, 'video data mining' has attracted much research interest in recent years. Video data mining is a technique to discover useful patterns from videos. For example, [16] extracted patterns of news and commercial video clips for content-based video retrieval and browsing. [13] extracted patterns of object motions for monitoring a surveillance video. Also, for extracting interesting patterns from movies, [12] proposed the mining framework by using already existing audio and video analysis techniques. But, they didn't report the use of the extracted interesting patterns. In our case, considering that a lot of video materials are left behind for the lack of video editing knowledge, we have been trying to discover useful editing patterns from movies [1].

Video editing is a process of selecting and joining various shots to create a final video sequence. Here, a shot is a sequence of video frames which are contiguously recorded by a single camera. Although there is no absolute rule to present a certain semantic content (e.g. happiness, sadness, violence etc),

D. Seipel et al. (Eds.): INAP/WLP 2004, LNAI 3392, pp. 116–133, 2005.

some editing patterns make it easy to convey a specific semantic content to the viewers. Particularly, in the field of movie production, there are a lot of editing patterns which have been employed for a long time and known to successfully convey editor's intention to the viewers [10]. Therefore, useful editing patterns extracted from movies can be used by an amateur video editor to produce a new, more attractive video.

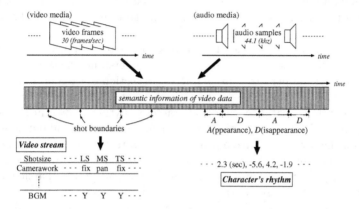

Fig. 1. Our two time series models of video data for semantic structure extraction

It is essential to extract editing patterns associated with their semantic contents, which we didn't discuss the problem in [1]. In [1], we extracted the editing patterns from a movie, called 'cinematic rules', such as "a long distance shot with a duration of about 6 seconds followed by a middle distance shot about 4 seconds". But, as described in [1], although the extracted cinematic rules are essential to make the movie meaningful, they don't especially characterize any kind of semantic contents. As a result, an amateur editor can't determine how to use the extracted cinematic rules during the process of editing a new video. Considering this problem, in this paper, we concentrate on extracting useful editing patterns associated with their semantic contents, called 'semantic structures'.

Video data like a movie is 'unstructured'. It does not have a clear structure to describe its rich and complicated semantic information [11]. This unstructured nature of video data is caused by the characteristics of video and audio media, both of them being known as 'continuous media'. As shown in Fig. 1, video or audio media consists of a sequence of media quanta (i.e. video frames or audio samples), and it conveys its meaning only when media quanta are continuously presented in time. So, the semantic information of video data conveyed through video and audio media is time-dependent. Furthermore, temporal relationships among semantic (information) contents are ambiguous and ill-defined.

Considering the above unstructured nature of video data, we firstly organize a movie into a time series model which is relevant for the extraction of semantic structures. This is one of the most important task since it constructs the building blocks of the movie, and converts the movie from a raw material to data with reasonable semantic information [13].

In this paper, we propose two approaches to extract semantic structures from a movie, based on two different time series models of the movie. In section 3, considering the editing process where the movie editor connects various shots with certain meanings, we represent the movie as a multi-stream, called 'video stream' shown in Fig. 1. Here, one stream is a sequence of metadata derived from visual and audio media in each shot. Then we extract semantic structures about shot transitions. We call these semantic structures 'syntactical association rules'.

Rather than the above shot transitions, character's appearance and disappearance are more essential for the viewer to understand the semantic information about what happens to that character. In section 4, we represent the movie as one-dimensional time series consisting of durations of target character's appearance and disappearance, called 'character's rhythm' shown in Fig. 1. Based on character's rhythm, we extract the semantic structures about how he/she appears on the screen and disappears from the screen. One interval where character's rhythm roughly stays constant defines a semantically meaningful episode where the character performs a particular action and plays a particular role in the movie. We call this semantic structure 'topic continuity'.

In the next section, we clarify the semantic structures we aim to extract. We also describe some extensions of our video data mining approach from the previous work [1]. In section 3 and 4, we present a method for extracting syntactical association rules from a video stream and a method for extracting topic continuities based on character's rhythm, respectively. Examples of extracted semantic structures are shown in section 5. Finally, we conclude this paper in section 6, by giving some current research issues and future works.

2   Semantic Structures

We plan to mine the following two types of semantic structures from movies.

Syntactical Association Rules: A syntactical association rule defines syntactical shot transitions for presenting a certain semantic content. An example of a syntactical association rule is "two types of shots are connected one after the other in a battle scene, where one shot presents the leading character close to the camera with a long duration and the other presents the secondary character distant from the camera with a short duration". In order to extract such syntactical association rules, a shot is indexed by the 'raw-level' metadata (*Shotsize*, *Camerawork*, and *Duration*) and the 'semantic-level' metadata (*Character*, *BGM (BackGround Music)* and *SE (Sound Effect)*).

In [1], we extracted frequent editing patterns from a movie, called 'cinematic rules'. Specifically, a cinematic rule is defined as a pattern in the video stream, where the corresponding shot sequence of metadata frequently appears in the same form. But, this definition is too rigid to extract syntactical association rules. First, two shot transitions which are used to present a certain semantic content may be slightly different (i.e. the corresponding two shot sequences have slightly different metadata in the video stream), because one of them are varied according to some semantically minor factors. For example, in the above battle scene, depending on the leading (or secondary) character's action, a few shots may take shorter (or longer) durations. Secondly, editing patterns which are certainly used to present some specific semantic contents are ignored by measuring the importance of a editing pattern by its frequency. Considering the above drawbacks, we define a syntactical association rule as a pattern in the video stream, where the corresponding shot sequence contains shots with a strong correlation among themselves, which is supported by the appearance of several shot sequences similar to that syntactical association rule. Based on this definition, we can extract syntactical association rules in more flexible and effective way.

Topic Continuities: A 'topic' is an interval, where one semantically meaningful episode of a target character is presented. For example, the target character talks to someone or makes love with a partner in the topic. In such a topic, character's rhythm which consists of durations of target character's appearance and disappearance, is assumed to roughly stay constant. So, we index semantic-level metadata for each shot, representing intervals where the target character appears on the screen and intervals where he/she disappears from the screen. We will show that a topic is semantically meaningful in terms of the continuity of target character's action and his/her role in the movie. Thus, we can know the outline about how target character appears on the screen and disappears from the screen, in order to present his/her semantically meaningful episode.

[7] proposed an efficient method to extract topics of a target subject from an e-mail stream, based on rates of message arrivals relevant to the target subject. In [1], by using rates of target character's appearances instead of those of relevant message arrivals, we extracted topics from a movie. But, this approach deals too coarsely with the semantic information about the target character in the movie. Here, the semantic information of the movie is provided as a continuous function of time, because the video and audio media are continuous media (see Fig. 1). On the other hand, the semantic information of an e-mail stream is provided as a discrete function of time, because each message emerges at a single time point and makes sense by itself. So, in the e-mail stream, no semantic information about a target subject is provided between consecutive time points of relevant message arrivals. But, in the movie, the interval between the time points of two consecutive appearances of the target character includes two semantically different intervals, his/her appearance interval and disappearance interval. In order to more precisely capture the semantic information about the target character, we propose character's rhythm and extract topics based on it.

The above raw-level and semantic-level metadata can be automatically identified by existing techniques. For example, [16] automatically extracts one type of semantic object of interest in a video (e.g. human being, cars, and airplanes), and tracks it across video frames. So. [16] can be used to detect intervals where a target character appears on the screen and intervals where he/she disappears from the screen. However, our goal is to discover useful editing patterns from movies. We thus manually index the above metadata to extract reliable editing patterns (see [12] where several audio and video analysis techniques useful for indexing the above row-level and semantic level metadata are introduced).

3   Mining Syntactical Association Rules in Video Streams

Since a shot doesn't make sense by itself, a movie editor connects various shots during an editing process in order to convey the editor's intention to the viewer. So, several shot transitions are associated with the semantic contents that the movie editor wants to present, that is, syntactical association rules are used. For example, suppose a scene where the leading character and the secondary one are standing face to face and fighting. Here, the editor uses the tight shots (TS) with long durations, where the leading character appears close to the camera. In contrast, the editor uses the loose shots (LS) with short durations, where the secondary character appears distant from the camera. This is one of the syntactical association rules to present a battle scene, where the leading character is more emphasized than the second one.

In order to extract syntactical association rules described above, each shot is indexed by the following row-level and semantic-level metadata;

Shotsize: *Shotsize* is selected according to the distance from the camera to the objects. *Shotsize* is classified into loose shot (LS), medium shot (MS) and tight shot (TS). TS and LS are the shots taken by approaching to and leaving from the object, respectively.

Camerawork: *Camerawork* means camera movement including its direction. We consider the following seven types of *Cameraworks*; Fix, RightPan, LeftPan, UpPan, DownPan, ZoomIn, and ZoomOut.

Duration (*sec*): *Duration* ($= (EndFrameNo - StartFrameNo) / 30$) means the duration of the shot. The value of *Duration* is classified according to the distribution of each shot's length. The shot duration plays an important role to convey the meaning of the shot.

Character: *Character* represents the name of a character who appears on the screen.

BGM: *BGM* represents whether the background music is present or not in the shot. The editors use *BGM* with a certain intention. For example, even in scenes of the same type, rhythms of *Duration*s in these scenes may be different from each other, depending on the presence of *BGM*.

SE (Sound Effect): *SE* represents whether the sound which adds some effects to the scene (e.g. a gunshot, an explosion, a strike and so on) is present or not in the shot. The *SE* also influences the rhythm of *Duration*s in a scene. For example, a scene with many sounds is assumed to be a battle scene, and therefore they should be edited in a fast rhythm.

Shot No.	1	2	3	4	5	6	7	8	9	10	11	12	13	14		
Shotsize	LS	MS	TS	MS	LS	MS	TS	TS	LS	MS	MS	LS	MS	TS		
Camerawork	fix	fix	fix	pan	fix	pan	fix	fix	fix	fix	pan	fix	fix	fix	·	·
Duration[sec]	1.5	2	3	4	2	3	2	3	6	3	10	2	4	5	·	·
Character	A	B	A	-	A	B	A	B	A	-	A	A	B	A	·	·
BGM	Y	Y	Y	Y	Y	Y	Y	Y	Y	-	-	-	-	-	·	·
SE	Y	-	-	-	Y	Y	-	-	Y	Y	Y	Y	Y	-	·	·

→ *time*

Fig. 2. Video stream indexed by the raw-level and semantic-level metadata

As illustrated in Fig. 2, we formulate the video stream that is a multi-stream data indexed by the above raw-level and semantic-level metadata. Shot *No.1* represents the content that *"Shotsize* is *LS, Camerawork* is *fix, Duration* of Shot *No.1* is 1.5 *seconds*, the *Character A* is displayed on the screen, and *BGM* and *SE* are present in this shot". Since the pattern extraction algorithm from the multi-stream data needs to consider vast amounts of candidate patterns, the work of extracting significant patterns from the multi-stream data takes huge amount of time. Therefore, it is essential to develop an effective algorithm which reduces the amount of redundant calculation [9]. Especially, in order to count the frequency of a candidate pattern, the method introduced in [1] unwisely searches all positions in the multi-stream, where data in many positions don't obviously match that candidate pattern.

From now, we present a new mining method to effectively extract the significant patterns from a multi-stream data, such as the video stream in Fig. 2. Our method searches the significant patterns in the multi-stream with the following procedure.

1. **Generate the candidate pattern whose length is 1.** After scanning the symbols in the multi-stream data, our method generates the group of the possible candidate patterns whose length is 1. That is, these candidate patterns are the unique sets of symbols which occur at the same time in the multi-stream. For example, in the video stream in Fig. 2, a unique set of metadata indexed for each shot, such as (*Shotsize* = LS, *Camerawork* = fix, *Duration* = 1.5, *Character* = A, *BGM* = Y, *SE* = Y), (MS, fix, 2, B, Y, -), is a candidate pattern of length 1.

2. **For each candidate pattern, determine the search positions where the candidate pattern may occur in the multi-stream.** In order to improve the efficiency of this procedure, our method employs Boyer-Moore approach [3] which is known as one of the fastest string matching algorithms. For the candidate pattern P ($= p_1p_2 \cdots p_m$) and a focused stream S ($= s_1s_2 \cdots s_n$) of length m and n respectively, it can complete the string matching in average time order complexity $O(\frac{n}{m} \log_k m)$, where k is the number of symbols.

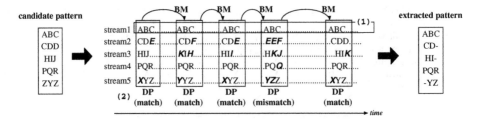

Fig. 3. The mining method using Boyer-Moore approach by focusing on stream (1) and Dynamic Programming (2)

Suppose the current candidate pattern is $\{(A, C, H, P, Z) \Rightarrow (B, D, I, Q, Y) \Rightarrow (C, D, J, R, Z)\}$ in Fig. 3. As shown in (1) in Fig. 3, by applying Boyer-Moore approach to the stream 1 being focused, our method effectively searches the symbol "ABC" that is the candidate pattern of stream 1, and detects the five search positions where "ABC" occurs in stream 1. In the next procedure, at these search positions, our method performs matching between the candidate pattern and the original data in stream 2, 3, 4 and 5.

3. **At all the positions determined in procedure 2, perform matching between each candidate pattern and the original data, using dynamic programming algorithm.**
   As can be seen from Fig. 3, at the detected search positions, the original data differs from the candidate pattern in stream 2, 3, 4 and 5. In Fig. 3, the symbols in the original data which don't match the candidate pattern are emphasized by bold and italic fonts. Like this, the candidate pattern is rarely completely matched by the original data. In a movie, various factors such as a change of character's action and an occasional SE affect the editing patterns. Nevertheless, the fundamental editing patterns are assumed to be preserved. So, we adopt approximate string matching between the candidate pattern and the original data by dynamic programming algorithm.
   The dynamic programming algorithm (DP) for approximate string matching [5] computes the edit distance between two strings A and B of length m_1 and m_2, respectively. For these strings, DP computes a matrix $C_{0...m_1, 0...m_2}$ that consists of $m_1 + 1$ columns and $m_2 + 1$ rows. The value $C_{i,j}$ holds the edit distance between $A_{1...i}$ and $B_{1...j}$. A_i is the symbol of A at i-th position. $A_{i...j}$ represents a substring of A enclosed between i-th and j-th symbols.

$$C_{i,0} \leftarrow i, \quad C_{0,j} \leftarrow j \tag{1}$$
$$\begin{aligned} C_{i,j} \leftarrow if \quad & A_i = B_j \quad then \quad C_{i-1,j-1}, \\ & else \quad 1 + \min(C_{i-1,j-1}, C_{i-1,j}, C_{i,j-1}) \end{aligned} \tag{2}$$

The edit distance $ed(A, B)$ is the final value of C_{m_1, m_2}. The rationale of the formula is that if $A_i = B_j$ then the cost to convert $A_{1...i}$ into $B_{1...j}$ is the cost of converting $A_{1...i-1}$ into $B_{1...j-1}$. Otherwise, we have to select one among three choices: (a) convert $A_{1...i-1}$ into $B_{1...j-1}$ and replace A_i by B_j. (b) convert $A_{1...i-1}$ into $B_{1...j}$ and delete A_i, or (c) convert $A_{1...i}$ into $B_{1...j-1}$ and insert B_j. At all the positions determined in procedure 2, we perform the same matching process.

(2) in Fig. 3 represents that our method performs matching from stream 2 to 5 between the candidate pattern and the original data at the five search positions. During this matching, our method counts the number of search positions, whose edit distances between the candidate pattern and original data are less or equal than the pre-specified maximal cost. In Fig. 3, where the maximal cost is set to 4, the original data is matched by the candidate pattern at the four out of the five search positions. The number of these matching positions is used to measure the significance of the candidate pattern in the next procedure.

4. **Remove the non-significant patterns from the group of candidate patterns by using $J-measure$.** *J-measure* represents the average amount of information content contained in a candidate pattern with the following equation [6];

$$J(B;A) = P(A)*\left\{ P(B|A)\log_2\frac{P(B|A)}{P(B)} + (1-P(B|A))\log_2\frac{1-P(B|A)}{1-P(B)} \right\}.$$
(3)

Here, B is the last column of the candidate pattern and A is the remaining columns. For the candidate pattern in Fig. 3, $A = \{(A,C,H,P,Z) \Rightarrow (B,D,I,Q,Y)\}$ and $B = (C,D,J,R,Z)$. $P(A)$ and $P(B)$ represent the probabilities of A's and B's appearances, respectively. $P(B|A)$ represents the conditional probability of B's appearance, given that A appears. The first term $(P(A))$ measures the frequency of the candidate pattern in the multi-stream. The second term (surrounded by the braces) expresses the degree of dissimilarity between a prior probability $(P(B))$ and a posterior probability conditioned on A $(P(B|A))$ (this is known as the cross-entropy). *J-measure* is larger if a candidate pattern is more frequent and has a stronger connection between the conditional part (A) and the consequential part (B). Therefore, we use *J-measure* to measure how significant a candidate pattern is. Candidate patterns that don't satisfy the threshold value are regarded as non-significant and can be removed from the group of candidate patterns.

By using *J-measure*, we can extract not only "general" patterns which frequently appear in the overall range of the multi-stream, but also "specialized" patterns which don't appear frequently but are confirmed by the occurrences of conditional parts in this multi-stream. For example, in our case of extracting syntactical association rules from a video stream, the pattern $((Shotsize = TS, Camerawork = fix) \Rightarrow (TS, fix) \Rightarrow (TS, fix))$ is a general pattern which is frequently used in most of conversation scenes. On the other hand, the pattern $((Shotsize = TS, Duration = long, Character = A) \Rightarrow (LS, short, B) \Rightarrow (TS, long, A))$ is a specialized pattern which is used in some battle scenes.

5. **Generate candidate patterns whose length is incremented by 1, and repeat procedure 2 while candidate patterns still exist.** Generate the new candidate patterns whose lengths are incremented by 1, using the remaining candidate patterns. Go back to procedure 2.

We can obtain a set of candidate patterns whose $J - measures$ are larger than the threshold value. Suppose that the candidate pattern $\{(A, C, H, P, Z) \Rightarrow (B, D, I, Q, Y) \Rightarrow (C, D, J, R, Z)\}$ is extracted in Fig. 3. This means that the patterns similar to this candidate pattern are significant in Fig. 3. Furthermore, by checking the symbols which frequently matched the original data in procedure 3, we can know which part is significant in an extracted candidate pattern, such as $\{(A, C, H, P, -) \Rightarrow (B, D, I, Q, Y) \Rightarrow (C, -, -, R, Z)\}$ in Fig. 3. In this way, we extract the syntactical association rules from a video stream. In addition, the above mining method can reduce about 40% of calculation time compared with the method described in [1].

4   Extracting Topics Based on Character's Rhythm

In this section, we describe a technique for extracting topic continuities which defines semantically meaningful episodes from the perspective of a target character in the movie. First of all, we explain how character's appearance and disappearance patterns serve for conveying to the viewer what happens to the target character, by using Fig. 4. Fig. 4 represents the several shots from Alfred Hitchcock's movie "PSYCHO", where there are two characters, *Marion* and *Norman*. In the bottom row of the table in Fig. 4, A and D indicate *Marion*'s appearance and disappearance in a shot, respectively.

In a movie, each character definitely has his/her own 'action flow'. Character's action flow presents 'actions' and 'surrounding events' to the viewer. An action means an action that the target character performs during his/her appearance. A surrounding event means other characters' actions or changes of surrounding settings during target character's disappearance. Consider *Marion*'s action flow in Fig. 4. In *Marion*'s appearance in *shot 207*, her action is driving her car. In *Marion*'s disappearance in *shot 208*, the surrounding event is that, looming light is to be seen outside her car. Also, at the end of *shot 254*, the surrounding event is, *Norman* talks to *Marion* who disappears from the screen.

Each action or surrounding event in character's action flow, must be consistent with the previous one. For example, *Marion*'s action in *shot 209* (she glances outside while driving her car) is relevant to the reaction to the surrounding event in *shot 208*. *Marion*'s action in *shot 251* (she listens to *Norman*) is relevant to

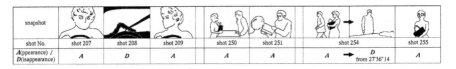

Fig. 4. Several shots from Alfred Hitchcock's movie PSYCHO

the reaction to her previous action in *shot 250* (she talks to *Norman*). These consistent connections in *Marion*'s action flow allow the viewer to understand why she glances outside her car or why she listens to *Norman*. So, the connections of target character's actions and surrounding events over a certain period, construct his/her semantically meaningful episode, that is a 'topic'.

Meanwhile, the movie editor determines the duration of a target character's action (i.e. his/her appearance) is determined based on his/her action and situation. Similarly, the duration of a surrounding event (i.e. target character's disappearance) reflects other characters' actions and situations, while the target character disappears from the screen. Consequently, we can assume that, as long as the target character performs similar actions in a particular situation, where other characters perform similar actions as surrounding events (i.e. in a topic), character's rhythm which consists of durations of target character's appearance and disappearance, roughly stays constant.

From the above discussion, a topic is characterized by a certain 'interaction' between the target character and other characters. A change of such an interaction is naturally reflected in character's rhythm. As a simple example, suppose a conversation scene where the target character talks with other characters. This example consists of the following three topics; firstly the target character mainly talks to one of the other characters, secondly all characters talk to each other, and thirdly the target character just looks at other characters' talking. It is easily conceivable that durations of target character's disappearance in the second (or third) topic are distinctly longer than those of the first (or second) topic, because the number of other characters' talking actions in his/her disappearance significantly increases. Thus, extracting topics where character's rhythm is relatively constant reveals his/her semantically meaningful episodes.

To implement the above concept, we index metadata for each shot, representing intervals where a target character appears and intervals where he/she disappears. Some metadata indexed for *Marion*, are shown in Fig. 4, where except *shot 254*, she appears or disappears throughout the entire period of a shot (indexed by A or D). *Marion*'s rhythm from *shot 194* to *267* can be drawn as shown in Fig. 5, by scanning durations of her appearance and disappearance one by one. Starting from the leftmost in Fig. 5, the small circles correspond to *Marion*'s appearance or disappearance in *shot 207, 208, 209, 250, 251, start of 254, end of 254,* and *255*, respectively (Fig. 4). A positive value indicates the duration of *Marion*'s appearance, and a negative value indicates the duration of her disappearance.

The best example reflecting our assumption of character's rhythm is the interval from *Marion*'s *198th* to *226th* disappearance (*topic 2*). In *topic 2*, the durations of *Marion*'s appearance and disappearance are shown as alternating positive and negative values with very similar amplitudes. Corresponding to this *Marion*'s constant rhythm, she drives her car in a rainy night in *topic 2*. But, character's rhythm may be rugged in a topic, because the topic may include some different character's actions and surrounding events. For example, in *topic 3* (*Marion* calls *Norman* after reaching his motel), *Marion* walks around looking

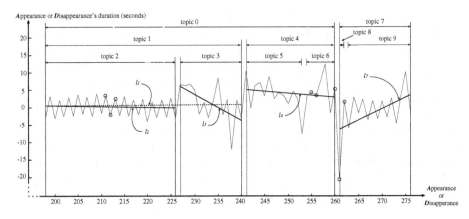

Fig. 5. Our rhythmic model of character's actions and surrounding events

for *Norman* and she waits impatiently beeping the horn. So, we need to extract topics where character's rhythm is relatively constant with some degree of error.

We extract topics by employing time series segmentation method [4]. Our method recursively divides a segment of character's rhythm into two sub-segments in a top-down approach, beginning from the whole range of his/her rhythm. In each recurrence, our method examines whether character's rhythm in a segment is constant or not, by using the following "correlation measure".

Suppose we approximate the values of character's rhythm in a segment (y_i) by the least-square regression line ($\hat{y_i} = bx_i + a$, such as the straight lines in Fig. 5). The correlation of character's rhythm in the segment is estimated by the 'Sum of Residual Squares ($SRS_{segment} = \sum (y_i - \hat{y_i})^2$)', where a smaller $SRS_{segment}$ means a stronger correlation. In each recurrence, by applying the correlation measure to a segment and sub-segments, our method evaluates the constancy of character's rhythm with the following procedure:

1. **Find the optimal pair of sub-segments within a segment, which satisfies the following condition:**

$$\min(SRS_{sub-segment1} + SRS_{sub-segment2}) \qquad (4)$$

For every possible pair of sub-segments within the segment, $SRS_{sub-segment1}$ and $SRS_{sub-segment2}$ are computed by detecting the respective least-square regression lines. Our method finds the optimal pair of sub-segments which minimizes the sum of $SRS_{sub-segment1}$ and $SRS_{sub-segment2}$. According to the property of the correlation measure described above, character's rhythm is well correlated with different least-square regression lines. That is, the segment is supposed to have different types of rhythms in the optimal pair of sub-segments.

Here, we assume that if the segment has a constant rhythm, the values of appearance and disappearances' durations are relatively uniformly distributed around the least-square regression line, such as *topic 2* in Fig. 5. In such a case, any pair of sub-segments will have similar types of rhythms associated with

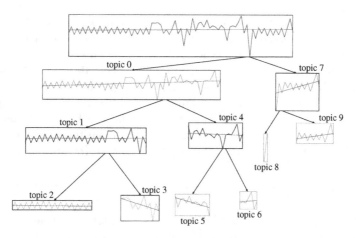

Fig. 6. The resulting tree of topics to be extracted from *Marion*'s rhythm in Fig. 5

least-square regression lines similar to that of the original segment. So, the difference between the rhythms in the optimal pair of sub-segments can be used for the evaluation of the constancy of character's rhythm in a segment.

2. **Decide whether the segment should be divided into the optimal pair of sub-segments in the following way:**

$$R\_SRS_{segment} = SRS_{segment} - \min(SRS_{sub-segment1} + SRS_{sub-segment2}).$$

$$\implies \begin{cases} \textbf{If } R\_SRS_{segment} > threshold, \textbf{ then } divide\ the\ segment. \\ \textbf{Else } don't\ divide\ the\ segment\ any\ more. \end{cases} \quad (5)$$

A more precise approximation of character's rhythm, by dividing the segment into the optimal pair of sub-segments, generates a "Reduction of $SRS_{segment}$ ($R\_SRS_{segment}$)". $R\_SRS_{segment}$ is larger than the *threshold* if the segment has considerably different types of rhythms in the optimal pair of sub-segments. In Fig. 5, *Marion*'s rhythm in *topic 2* and *topic 3* (which are selected as the optimal pair) are completely different, so R_SRS_{topic1} is larger than the *threshold*. In such a segment, character's rhythm is not regarded as constant, and our method divides the segment into the optimal pair of sub-segments.

On the other hand, $R\_SRS_{segment}$ is smaller than the *threshold* if there is no considerable difference between rhythms in the optimal pair for the segment, such as *topic 2* in Fig. 5. In such a segment, character's rhythm is regarded as constant, and our method no longer divides the segment.

Finally, we can obtain a binary tree of topics where character's rhythm is constant at multiple abstraction levels. Fig. 6 shows that *Marion*'s rhythm in Fig. 5 is divided into more precisely constant rhythms. Correspondingly, a part of PSYCHO is divided into more localized topics from *Marion*'s perspective. In Fig. 5, *Marion*'s rhythm is relatively constant in *topic 2* (*Marion* drives car in a rainy night) and *topic 7* (*Marion* talks to *Norman* in her room). But, although *topic 4* (*Marion* checks in *Norman*'s motel) and *topic 7* can be thought as *Marion*'s semantically meaningful episodes, they are over-divided due to extremely long durations of her disappearance compared to other durations. In these long durations of *Marion*'s disappearance, *Norman* suspects *Marion* in *topic 4* and he moves around her room before talking to her in *topic 7*, respectively. While this kind of temporal change of character's rhythm can be thought as an editing technique, we need to develop a method which can robustly extract topics including such temporal changes of character's rhythm (i.e. outliers).

5   Experiments

We implemented the methods stated in section 3 and 4, and mainly analyzed two movies, "PSYCHO" and "Star Wars Episode I" directed by Alfred Hitchcock and George Lucas, respectively. Also, we analyzed some additional movies. Since our experimental movies are very famous and popular, we considered that there are many useful editing patterns to persuasively convey editor's intentions to the viewer, that is, semantic structures.

5.1   Syntactical Association Rules

We implemented the method stated in section 3 to extract the syntactical association rules. The following presents some examples of syntactical association rules that our mining method extracted from the movie PSYCHO.

1. **Fast rhythm with BGM and rapid transition of Shotsizes:** The rhythm of *Durations* is associated with the presence of *BGM* and the way of a transition of *Shotsizes*. The rapid transition of *Shotsizes* ($LS \Rightarrow TS, TS \Rightarrow LS$) in a *BGM* scene induces a fast rhythm of *Durations*. In this movie, this pattern characterized by the visual leap (rapid transition of *Shotsizes*), speedy deployment (fast rhythm of *Durations*) and *BGM*, is often used in tense scenes.
2. **Constant rhythm with BGM and constant transition of Shotsizes:** In contrast with case 1, the constant transition of *Shotsizes* ($LS \Rightarrow LS$, $MS \Rightarrow MS$, $TS \Rightarrow TS$) in a *BGM* scene induces a constant rhythm of *Durations*, in most cases, a slow rhythm. This pattern characterized by using constant *Shotsizes* and *Durations* in a *BGM* scene, is often used to smoothly present a conversation of two *Characters*.
3. **Long Durations of Pan shots in a BGM scene:** *Durations* of *Pan* shots in a *BGM* scene are longer than those of a non-*BGM* scene. Especially, a *Pan* shot with a long *Duration* is used to thoroughly present the action of one *Character* who appears on the screen. Furthermore, this pattern is got more effective by involving *BGM*.

The following shows the examples of syntactical association rules in the movie Star Wars Episode I.

1. **Fast rhythm with BGM and SE in a scene:** The editing patterns are influenced by whether *BGM* or *SE* (Sound Effect) is present or not in a scene. Even in similar scenes, a *BGM* scene is edited in a fast rhythm of *Durations* compared with a non-*BGM* scene. Non-*BGM* scenes generally contain long conversation scenes, and these scenes are edited in slow rhythms. On the other hand, a scene with *BGM* or *SE* generally contains a lot of quick *Cameraworks*, and the scene is obviously edited in a fast rhythm of *Durations*.

2. **Character's appearance:** The editing patterns are influenced by which *Character* appears in a scene. In a scene where rapid transitions of *Shotsizes* are used frequently, the leading *Character* appears in close shots (*TS*) with long *Durations*. On the other hand, the secondary *Character* appears in distant shots (*LS*) with short *Durations*. This pattern characterized by changing *Shotsizes* and *Durations* depending on each character, is often used in battle scenes.

3. **Intelligible Camerawork in a fast rhythm scene:** Especially in a scene edited in a fast rhythm of *Durations*, the editor connects shots whose *Cameraworks* have the same direction. That is, it is inappropriate to follow a shot with *RightPan* by a shot with *LeftPan* in a scene edited in a fast rhythm of *Durations*, because this inconsistent connection in the fast rhythm confuses the viewers.

Finally, we present some examples of syntactical association rules in the movie "Seven Samurai" directed by Akira Kurosawa. Although George Lucas is said to be influenced by Akira Kurosawa, their editing patterns are quite different.

1. **Shot connection without TS:** In most of scenes, the editor does not use *TS*, but uses distant shots such as *MS* and *LS*.

2. **Slow rhythm with BGM at the beginning or the end of a scene:** The beginning or end of a scene is presented in a slow rhythm of *Durations* by using *BGM*. This editing pattern is often used at the beginning or the end of a silent scene.

3. **Using TS with BGM in a conversation scene:** In a conversation scene with *BGM*, *TS* is often used with a long *Duration*.

5.2 Topic Continuities

By the method described in section 4, we extracted topic continuities of leading characters, *Marion* in PSYCHO, *Qui-Gon* in Star Wars Episode I, and *Roger* in another Alfred Hitchcock's movie "North By Northwest". For giving a clear summary of our experiments, we use a 'specific topic' which is considered as a semantically relevant atomic episode of a target character. And we use a 'long-running topic' which is a large topic generalized by some specific topics. Our experiments shows that, by using the temporal information about target character's appearance and disappearance, we could extract almost all specific topics, but we could not successfully extract long-running topics. We summarize our experimental results of topic extraction by using Fig. 7. Here, the topics which

a) a part of Qui-Gon's rhythm

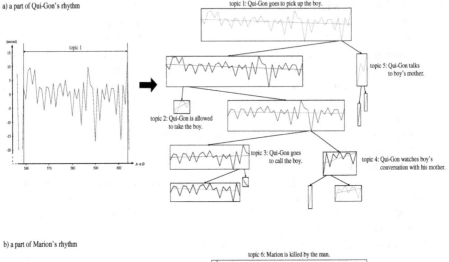

b) a part of Marion's rhythm

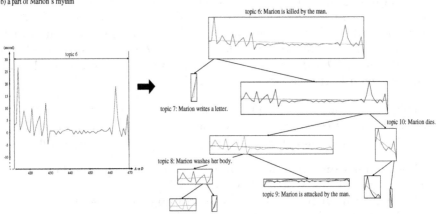

Fig. 7. The parts of the resulting trees extracted for *Qui-Gon*'s (a) and *Marion*'s (b) rhythms

can be considered as semantically meaningful episodes of *Qui-Gon* and *Marion*, are manually annotated by human interpretation.

In Fig. 7 (a), *topic 1* is a long-running topic including four specific topics *topic 2 ~ 5*. These specific topics reveal the interactions between *Qui-Gon* and other characters. For example, *Qui-Gon*'s rhythm has different patterns in *topic 3* and *topic 4*, because the duration of *Qui-Gon*'s disappearance suddenly becomes very long at the beginning of *topic 4*. And this change in *Qui-Gon*'s rhythm corresponds to a great change in his actions. That is, although *Qui-Gon* was a principal actor in *topic 3*, after this point of change, he plays a secondary role in *topic 4*. Since the editor can use only a single video stream to present the story of a movie, it can be thought that a duration of target character's disappearance reflects his/her importance. Thus, a specific topic is considered as semantically meaningful, because it is sensitive to changes of target character's role in the movie.

On the other hand, a duration of target character's appearance reflects his/her action. As can be seen from Fig. 7 (b), at the beginnings of *topic 9* and *topic 10*, the durations of *Marion*'s appearance dramatically change. And, these changes of *Marion*'s rhythm are confirmed by changes of her actions too. Like this, a specific topic is not only sensitive to changes of target character's role, but also sensitive to changes of his/her action. In this way, one roughly constant rhythm of a target character defines a specific topic in terms of the continuity of his/her action and role in the movie. Although the degree of constancy of the rhythm in each specific topic is different, almost all specific topics can be preserved in the resulting tree where character's rhythm is constant at multiple abstraction levels. Furthermore, by investigating specific topics, we can know the outline about how the target character appears on the screen and disappears from the screen in order to present his/her semantically meaningful episodes.

However, our method is not efficient for extracting long-running topics such as *topic 1* and *topic 6* in Fig. 7. The reason is that, the resulting tree cannot preserve semantic relationships between consecutive topics. For example, taking a close look at Fig. 7 (a), the positions of *topic 4* and *topic 5* are distant, although they are very close in the following semantic content, "both topics happen in boy's house". Consequently, two consecutive specific topics whose semantic contents are different from each other, have the same parent topic in the resulting tree.

6   Conclusion and Future Work

In this paper, we extracted two types of semantic structures, syntactical association rules and topic continuities, by applying data mining techniques to movies organized into time series models of raw-level and semantic-level metadata. By using the extracted semantic structures in our video editing support system [2], the system becomes able to help an amateur produce a new, more attractive video. But, there are some issues and future works to be further explored, which are summarized as follows:

In section 3, we proposed a method for effectively extracting syntactical association rules from a video stream, by adopting Boyer-Moore approach, dynamic programming and *J-measure*. Our method can perform fast matching between a candidate pattern and the original data and eliminate non-significant patterns from the group of candidate patterns. But, our method seems to be still too rigid to extract useful editing patterns of shots associated with their semantic contents. The weakest point is that our method invariably searches a sequence of shots where the last shot can be predicted by the preceding sub-sequence. That is, we assume that a certain semantic content is always presented in the same temporal order of shots, but it is obviously impractical. Therefore, we may need to deal with a video stream from a different perspective. For example, it may be better to firstly segment a video stream into sub-sequences of shots (e.g. [8] introduces an unsupervised segmentation algorithm in categorical time series). And then, we classify these sub-sequences into groups which have similar distributions of shots indexed by raw-level and semantic level metadata.

In section 4, we proposed a method for extracting topic continuities based on character's rhythm. For a target character, our method extracts the binary tree of topics where his/her rhythm is constant at multiple abstraction levels. From this resulting tree, we could extract almost all specific topics as semantically meaningful episodes of the target character. But, at present, we extract specific topics by investigating the resulting tree with our own sights. To solve this issue, we aim to calculate the importance score for each topic, by modifying the importance measure introduced in [15]. By using the importance measure, we can assign large importance scores to topics with our desired properties. Our experiments show that a specific topic is a topic which is as long as possible and in which character's rhythm is as constant as possible. Thus, by using importance measure, we may extract only topics with large importance scores as specific topics. Furthermore, by classifying segments of character's rhythm in extracted specific topics, we may extract patterns of character's rhythm which characterize certain types of episodes.

References

1. Y. Matsuo, K. Shirahama and K. Uehara: Video Data Mining: Extracting Cinematic Rules from Movie. In Proc. of 4th International Workshop on Multimedia Data Mining MDM/KDD. (2003) 18-27
2. M. Kumano, Y. Ariki, M. Amano, K. Uehara, K. Shunto and K. Tsukada: Video Editing Support System Based on Video Grammar and Content Analysis. In Proc. of 16th International Conference on Pattern Recognition. (2002) 346-354
3. R. Boyer and S. Moore: A Fast String Searching Algorithm. Communications of the ACM. Vol. 20 (1977) 762-772
4. V. Guralnik and J. Srivastava: Event Detection from Time Series Data. In Proc. of the 5th ACM SIGKDD International Conference on Knowledge Discovery and Data Mining. (1999) 33-42
5. G. Navarro and R. Baeza-Yates: Fast Multi-Dimensional Approximate Pattern Matching. In Proc. of the 10th Annual Symposium on Combinatorial Pattern Matching, Lecture Notes in Computer Science, Vol. 1645. Springer. (1999) 243-257
6. P. Smyth and R. M. Goodman: An Information Theoretic Approach to Rule Induction from Databases. IEEE Transactions on Knowledge and Data Engineering, Vol. 4, Issue 4. (1992) 301-316
7. J. Kleinberg: Bursty and Hierarchical Structure in Streams. In Proc. of the 8th ACM SIGKDD International Conference on Knowledge Discovery and Data Mining. (2002) 91-101
8. P. Cohen, B. Heeringa and N. Adams: An Unsupervised Algorithm for Segmenting Categorical Timeseries in Episodes. In Proc. of ESF Exploratory Workshop on Pattern Detection and Discovery in Data Mining, Lecture Notes in Artificial Intelligence. Vol. 2447. Springer. (2002) 49-62

9. F. Hoppner: Discovery of Core Episodes from Sequences Using Generalization for Defragmentation of Rule Sets. In Proc. of ESF Exploratory Workshop on Pattern Detection and Discovery in Data Mining, Lecture Notes in Artificial Intelligence. Vol. 2447. Springer. (2002) 199-213

10. D. Arijon: Grammar of File Language. Focal Press Limited Publishers. (1976)

11. A. Hampapur: Designing Video Data Management Systems. Ph.D dissertation, University of Michigan. (1995)

12. D. Wijesekera and D. Barbara: Mining Cinematic Knowledge: Work in Progress. In Proc. of the International Workshop on Multimedia Data Mining. (2000) 98-103

13. J. Oh and B. Bandi: Multimedia Data Mining Framework for Raw Video Sequences. In Proc. of 3th International Workshop on Multimedia Data Mining MDM/KDD. (2002) 1-10

14. J. Pan and C. Faloutsos: VideoCube: a novel tool for video mining and classification. In Proc. of 5th ICADL conference. (2002) 194-205

15. S. Uchihashi, J. Foote, A. Girgensohn and J. Boreczky: Video Manga: Generating Semantically Meaningful Video Summaries. In Proc. of 7th ACM Multimedia 1999. (1999) 383-392

16. J. Fan and Y. Ji: Automatic Moving Object Extraction toward Content-Based Video Representation and Indexing. Jour. of Visual Communications and Image Representation, Vol. 12, No. 3. (2001) 217-239

Solving Alternating Boolean Equation Systems in Answer Set Programming

Misa Keinänen and Ilkka Niemelä

Dept. of Computer Science and Engineering,
Lab. for Theoretical Comp. Science,
Helsinki University of Technology,
P.O. Box 5400, FI-02015 HUT, Finland
{Misa.Keinanen, Ilkka.Niemela}@hut.fi

Abstract. In this paper we apply answer set programming to solve alternating Boolean equation systems. We develop a novel characterization of solutions for variables in disjunctive and conjunctive Boolean equation systems. Based on this we devise a mapping from Boolean equation systems with alternating fixed points to normal logic programs such that the solution of a given variable of an equation system can be determined by the existence of a stable model of the corresponding logic program. The technique can be used to model check alternating formulas of modal μ-calculus.

1 Introduction

Model checking is a verification technique aimed at determining whether a system model satisfies desired properties expressed as temporal logic formulas. In recent years, research on model checking has addressed large scale verification problems, which are often solved by special purpose verification tools.

Yet it has been demonstrated that also logic programming systems can successively be applied to the construction of practical model checkers, like e.g. in [10, 5, 13]. In the present paper, we continue this line of research and restrict the attention to the model checking problem of modal μ-calculus [12], and in particular to its formulation as *Boolean equation systems* [1, 18, 23]. The research topic belongs to the area of formal verification, but more specifically it addresses effective ways of solving systems of fixed point equations.

The modal *μ-calculus* is an expressive logic for systems verification, and has been widely studied in the recent model checking literature (e.g. [3] gives a general exposition). Boolean equation systems provide here a useful framework, because μ-calculus expressions can easily be translated into this more flexible formalism (see [1, 3, 18] for the standard translations). The complexity of μ-calculus model checking is an important open problem; no polynomial time algorithm has been discovered. On the other hand, it is shown in [6, 7] that the problem is in the complexity class NP ∩ co-NP (and is known to be even in UP ∩ co-UP [11], where UP is the class of problems decided by unambiguous polynomial time nondeterministic Turing machines, see [21]).

D. Seipel et al. (Eds.): INAP/WLP 2004, LNAI 3392, pp. 134–148, 2005.
© Springer-Verlag Berlin Heidelberg 2005

In this paper we propose an answer set programming (ASP) based approach for solving alternating Boolean equation systems. In ASP a problem is solved by devising a mapping from a problem instance to a logic program such that models of the program provide the answers to the problem instance [14, 19, 20]. We develop such a mapping from alternating Boolean equation systems to logic programs providing a basis for a model checking technique for μ-calculus logic.

Previously, answer set programming has been applied to solve Boolean equation systems in [13] where it is argued that alternating Boolean equation systems can be solved by translating them to propositional normal logic programs, and computing stable models which satisfy certain criteria of preference. Moreover, it is shown in [13] how alternation-free Boolean equation systems can be mapped to stratified logic programs, which can be directly solved in linear time, preserving the complexity [2] of model checking alternation-free fragment of μ-calculus. However, the approach proposed in [13] does not preserve the polynomial time complexity [9] of solving disjunctive and conjunctive Boolean equation systems.

We reduce the problem of solving alternating Boolean equation systems to computing stable models of normal logic programs. This is achieved by devising an alternative mapping from Boolean equation systems to normal logic programs so the solution for a given variable in an equation system can be determined by the existence of a stable model of the corresponding logic program. Our translation is such that it ensures polynomial time complexity of solving both disjunctive and conjunctive alternating systems, and hence preserves the complexity of model checking many important fragments of μ-calculus, like $L1$ and $L2$ investigated in [4, 6, 7].

The paper is organized as follows. In the following section we introduce basic notions of Boolean equation systems. In Section 3 we state some properties of Boolean equation systems which are important in solving them. In Section 4 we review stable model semantics of normal logic programs. In Section 5 we show how alternating Boolean equation systems can be solved using answer set programming techniques. In Section 6 we discuss some initial experimental results. Finally, Section 7 contains conclusive remarks.

2   Boolean Equation Systems

We will give in this section a short presentation of Boolean equation systems. Essentially, a Boolean equation system is an ordered sequence of fixed point equations over Boolean variables, with associated signs, μ and ν, specifying the polarity of the fixed points. The equations are of the form $\sigma x = \alpha$, where α is a positive Boolean expression. The sign, σ, is μ if the equation is a least fixed point equation and ν if it is a greatest fixed point equation.

Let $\mathcal{X} = \{x_1, x_2, ..., x_n\}$ be a set of Boolean variables. The set of *positive Boolean expressions* over $\mathcal{X}$ is denoted by $B(\mathcal{X})$, and given by the grammar:

$$\alpha ::= 0 \mid 1 \mid x \in \mathcal{X} \mid \alpha_1 \wedge \alpha_2 \mid \alpha_1 \vee \alpha_2$$

where 0 stands for *false* and 1 for *true*. We define the syntax of Boolean equation systems as follows.

Definition 1 (The syntax of a Boolean equation system). *A Boolean equation is of the form $\sigma_i x_i = \alpha_i$, where $\sigma_i \in \{\mu, \nu\}$, $x_i \in \mathcal{X}$, and $\alpha_i \in B(\mathcal{X})$. A Boolean equation system is an ordered sequence of Boolean equations*

$$((\sigma_1 x_1 = \alpha_1)(\sigma_2 x_2 = \alpha_2), ..., (\sigma_n x_n = \alpha_n))$$

where the left-hand sides of the equations are all different. We assume that the order on variables and equations are in synchrony, and that all right-hand side variables are from $\mathcal{X}$.

The priority ordering on variables and equations of a Boolean equation system is important for it ensures the existence of a unique solution. The semantical interpretation of Boolean equation systems is such that each system $\mathcal{E}$ has a uniquely determined solution, which is a valuation assigning a constant value in $\{0,1\}$ to variables occurring in $\mathcal{E}$. More precisely, the solution is a truth assignment to the variables $\{x_1, x_2, ..., x_n\}$ satisfying the fixed-point equations such that the right-most equations have higher priority over left-most equations (see e.g. [1,18]). In particular, we are interested in the value of the left-most variable x_1 in the solution of a Boolean equation system. Such a local solution can be characterized in the following way.

Let α be a closed positive Boolean expression (i.e. without occurrences of variables in $\mathcal{X}$). Then α has a uniquely determined value in the set $\{0,1\}$ which we denote by $\|\alpha\|$. We define a substitution for positive Boolean expressions. Given Boolean expressions $\alpha, \beta \in B(\mathcal{X})$, let $\alpha[x/\beta]$ denote the expression α where all occurrences of variable x are substituted by β simultaneously.

Similarly, we extend the definition of substitutions to Boolean equation systems in the following way. Let $\mathcal{E}$ be a Boolean equation system over $\mathcal{X}$, and let $x \in \mathcal{X}$ and $\alpha \in B(\mathcal{X})$. A substitution $\mathcal{E}[x/\alpha]$ means the operation where $[x/\alpha]$ is applied simultaneously to all right-hand sides of equations in $\mathcal{E}$. We suppose that substitution $\alpha[x/\alpha]$ has priority over $\mathcal{E}[x/\alpha]$.

Definition 2 (The local solution to a Boolean equation system). *The solution to a Boolean equation system $\mathcal{E}$, denoted by $[\![\mathcal{E}]\!]$, is a Boolean value inductively defined by*

$$[\![\mathcal{E}]\!] = \begin{cases} \|\alpha[x/b_\sigma]\| & \text{if } \mathcal{E} \text{ is of the form } ((\sigma x = \alpha)) \\ [\![(\mathcal{E}')[x/\alpha[x/b_\sigma]]]\!] & \text{if } \mathcal{E} \text{ is of the form } (\mathcal{E}'(\sigma x = \alpha)) \end{cases}$$

where b_σ is 0 when $\sigma = \mu$, and b_σ is 1 when $\sigma = \nu$.

The following example illustrates the definition of the solution.

Example 1. Let $\mathcal{X}$ be the set $\{x_1, x_2, x_3\}$ and assume we are given a Boolean equation system

$$\mathcal{E}_1 \equiv ((\nu x_1 = x_2 \wedge x_1)(\mu x_2 = x_1 \vee x_3)(\nu x_3 = x_3)).$$

The local solution, $[\![\mathcal{E}_1]\!]$, of variable x_1 in $\mathcal{E}_1$ is given by

$$
\begin{aligned}
&[\![((\nu x_1 = x_2 \wedge x_1)(\mu x_2 = x_1 \vee x_3)(\nu x_3 = x_3))]\!] = \\
&[\![((\nu x_1 = x_2 \wedge x_1)(\mu x_2 = x_1 \vee x_3)[x_3/1]]\!] = \\
&[\![((\nu x_1 = x_2 \wedge x_1)(\mu x_2 = x_1 \vee 1))]\!] = \\
&[\![((\nu x_1 = x_2 \wedge x_1)[x_2/x_1 \vee 1]]\!] = \\
&[\![(\nu x_1 = (x_1 \vee 1) \wedge x_1)]\!] = \|((1 \vee 1) \wedge 1)\| = 1
\end{aligned}
$$

3   Properties of Boolean Equation Systems

In this section, we discuss important concepts concerning Boolean equation systems. We also state some facts about Boolean equation systems which turn out to be useful in the computation of their solutions.

The *size* of a Boolean equation system is inductively defined as $|(\sigma x = \alpha)\mathcal{E}| = 1 + |\alpha| + |\mathcal{E}|$, where $|\alpha|$ is the number of variables and constants in α, and the size of an empty equation system is 0.

A Boolean equation system $\mathcal{E}$ is in a *standard form* if each right-hand side expression α_i consists of a disjunction $x_i \vee x_j$, a conjunction $x_i \wedge x_j$, or a single variable x_i. As pointed out in [18], for each system $\mathcal{E}$ there is another system $\mathcal{E}'$ in the *standard form* such that $\mathcal{E}'$ preserves the solution of $\mathcal{E}$ and has size linear in the size of $\mathcal{E}$. In the sequel we restrict to standard form Boolean equation systems.

Given a Boolean equation system, we define a variable *dependency graph* similar to a *Boolean graph* in [1], which provides a representation of the dependencies between the variables.

Definition 3 (A dependency graph). *Let $\mathcal{E}$ be a standard form Boolean equation system:*

$$((\sigma_1 x_1 = \alpha_1)(\sigma_2 x_2 = \alpha_2)\ldots(\sigma_n x_n = \alpha_n)).$$

The dependency graph of $\mathcal{E}$ is a directed graph $G_{\mathcal{E}} = (V, E)$ where

- *$V = \{i \mid 1 \leq i \leq n\}$ is the set of nodes*
- *$E \subseteq V \times V$ is the set of edges such that for all equations $\sigma_i x_i = \alpha_i$:*
  $(i, j) \in E$ iff a variable x_j appears in α_i.

We say that a variable x_i *depends on* variable x_j in a Boolean equation system $\mathcal{E}$, if the dependency graph $G_{\mathcal{E}}$ of $\mathcal{E}$ contains a directed path from node i to node j. It is said that two variables x_i and x_j are *mutually dependent*, if x_i depends on x_j and vice versa. A Boolean equation system is *alternation free*, if x_i and x_j are mutually dependent implies that $\sigma_i = \sigma_j$ holds. Otherwise, the Boolean equation system is said to be *alternating*. An important notion of Boolean equation systems is *alternation depth*, and we take the standard definition of alternation depth which can be found in Definition 3.34 of [18].

We say that a variable x_i is *self-dependent*, if x_i depends on itself such that no variable x_j with $j < i$ occurs in this chain of dependencies. More precisely, the notion of self-dependency can be defined in the following way.

$$\nu x_1 = x_2 \wedge x_1$$
$$\mu x_2 = x_1 \vee x_3$$
$$\nu x_3 = x_3$$

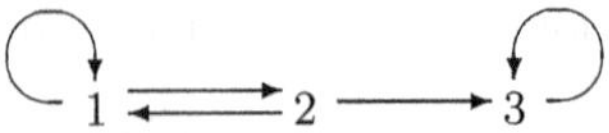

Fig. 1. The dependency graph of Boolean equation system $\mathcal{E}_1$ in Example 1

Definition 4. *Given a Boolean equation system $\mathcal{E}$, let $G = (V, E)$ be its dependency graph and $k \in V$. We define the graph $G{\restriction}k = (V{\restriction}k, E{\restriction}k)$ by taking*

- $V{\restriction}k = \{i \in E \mid i \geq k\}$
- $E{\restriction}k = \{\langle i, j\rangle \in E \mid i \geq k \text{ and } j \geq k\}$.

The variable x_k is self-dependent in the system $\mathcal{E}$, if node k is reachable from itself in the graph $G{\restriction}k$.

Example 2. Consider the Boolean equation system $\mathcal{E}_1$ of Example 1. The dependency graph of $\mathcal{E}_1$ is depicted in Figure 1. The system $\mathcal{E}_1$ is in standard form and is alternating, because it contains alternating fixed points with mutually dependent variables having different signs, like x_1 and x_2 with $\sigma_1 \neq \sigma_2$. Notice that two variables are mutually dependent when they appear on the same cycle in the dependency graph. The variables x_1 and x_3 of $\mathcal{E}_1$ are self-dependent, but x_2 is not as $G{\restriction}2 = (\{2, 3\}, \{(2, 3), (3, 3)\})$ contains no loop from node 2 to itself.

The variables of a standard form Boolean equation system can be partitioned in *blocks* such that any two distinct variables belong to the same block iff they are mutually dependent. Consequently, each block consists of such variables whose nodes reside on the same strongly connected component of the corresponding dependency graph. The dependency relation among variables extends to blocks such that block B_i depends on another block B_j if some variable occurring in block B_i depends on another variable in block B_j. The resulting dependency relation among blocks is an ordering. For example, the system $\mathcal{E}_1$ of Example 1 can be divided in two blocks, $B_1 = \{x_1, x_2\}$ and $B_2 = \{x_3\}$ such that the block B_1 depends on the block B_2. In Mader [18], there are two useful lemmas (Lemma 6.2 and Lemma 6.3) which allow us to solve all blocks of standard form Boolean equation systems one at a time. The basic idea is that we start by solving blocks that do not depend on any other block. For each solved block we can substitute its solution to blocks depending on it and thus iteratively solve them. Alternation-free blocks of standard form Boolean equation systems can be trivially solved in linear time in the size of the blocks [2]. Thus, we focus here on devising a technique to solve an alternating block of standard form Boolean equations, for which no polynomial time solution technique is known.

We call an equation $\sigma_i x_i = \alpha_i$ *disjunctive* if its right-hand side α_i is a disjunction. A standard form Boolean equation system is said to be *disjunctive* if all its equations $\sigma_i x_i = \alpha_i$ are either *disjunctive* or $\alpha_i \in \mathcal{X}$. Similarly, a Boolean equation $\sigma_i x_i = \alpha_i$ is *conjunctive* if its right-hand side α_i is a conjunction. A standard form Boolean equation system is *conjunctive* if all its equations $\sigma_i x_i = \alpha_i$ are conjunctive or $\alpha_i \in \mathcal{X}$.

The following lemmas form the basis for our answer set programming based technique to solve standard form Boolean equation systems with alternating fixed points. For a disjunctive (conjunctive respectively) form Boolean equation systems we have:

Lemma 1 (Lemma 4.2 of [9]). *Let $\mathcal{E}$ be a disjunctive (conjunctive) Boolean equation system in the standard form. Then the following are equivalent:*

1. $[\![\mathcal{E}]\!] = 1$ *(or $[\![\mathcal{E}]\!] = 0$ respectively)*
2. *There is a variable x_j in $\mathcal{E}$ such that $\sigma_j = \nu$ ($\sigma_j = \mu$) and:*
   (a) x_1 depends on x_j, and (b) x_j is self-dependent.

From each Boolean equation system $\mathcal{E}$ containing both disjunctive and conjunctive equations we may construct a new Boolean equation system $\mathcal{E}'$, which is either in a disjunctive or in a conjunctive form. To obtain from $\mathcal{E}$ a disjunctive form system $\mathcal{E}'$, we remove in every conjunctive equation of $\mathcal{E}$ exactly one conjunct; otherwise the system $\mathcal{E}$ is unchanged. The dual case is similar. For any standard form Boolean equation system having both disjunctive and conjunctive equations we have:

Lemma 2. *Let $\mathcal{E}$ be a standard form Boolean equation system. Then the following are equivalent:*

1. $[\![\mathcal{E}]\!] = 0$ *(or $[\![\mathcal{E}]\!] = 1$ respectively)*
2. *There is a disjunctive (conjunctive) system $\mathcal{E}'$ with the solution $[\![\mathcal{E}']\!] = 0$ ($[\![\mathcal{E}']\!] = 1$ respectively) which can be constructed from $\mathcal{E}$.*

Proof. We only show that (2) implies (1) for the conjunctive case. The other direction can be proved by a similar argument and also follows directly from Proposition 3.36 in [18].

Define a *parity game* in the following way. Given a standard form Boolean equation system $\mathcal{E} = ((\sigma_1 x_1 = \alpha_1), (\sigma_2 x_2 = \alpha_2), ..., (\sigma_n x_n = \alpha_n))$, we define a game $\Gamma_{\mathcal{E}} = (V, E, P, \sigma)$ where V and E are exactly like in the dependency graph of $\mathcal{E}$ and

- $P : V \rightarrow \{I, II\}$ is a player function assigning a player to each node; for $1 \leq i \leq n$, P is defined by $P(i) = I$ if α_i is conjunctive and $P(i) = II$ otherwise.
- $\sigma : V \rightarrow \{\mu, \nu\}$ is a parity function assigning a sign to each node; for $1 \leq i \leq n$, σ is defined by $\sigma(i) = \mu$ if $\sigma_i = \mu$ and $\sigma(i) = \nu$ otherwise.

A *play* on the game graph is an infinite sequence of nodes chosen by players I and II. The play starts at node 1. Whenever a node n is labelled with $P(n) = I$, it is player I's turn to choose a successor of n. Similarly, if a node n is labelled with $P(n) = II$, it is player II's turn to choose a successor of n. A *strategy* for a player i is a function which tells i how to move at all decision nodes, i.e. a strategy is a function that assigns a successor node to each decision node belonging to player i. Player I *wins* a play of the game if the smallest node that is visited infinitely often in the play is labelled with μ, otherwise player II wins.

We say that a player has a *winning strategy* in a game whenever she wins all the plays of the game by using this strategy, no matter how the opponent moves. According to Theorem 8.7 in [18], player II has a winning strategy for game on $\Gamma_{\mathcal{E}}$ with initial vertex 1 iff the solution of $\mathcal{E}$ is $[\![\mathcal{E}]\!] = 1$.

So suppose there is a conjunctive equation system $\mathcal{E}'$ obtained from $\mathcal{E}$ by removing exactly one disjunct from all equations of the form $\sigma_i x_i = x_j \vee x_k$ such that $[\![\mathcal{E}']\!] = 1$. We can construct from $\mathcal{E}'$ a winning strategy for player II in the parity game $\Gamma_{\mathcal{E}}$. For all nodes i of $\Gamma_{\mathcal{E}}$ where it is player II's turn to move, define a strategy for II to be $str_{II}(i) = j$ iff $\sigma_i x_i = x_j$ is an equation of $\mathcal{E}'$. That is, the strategy str_{II} for II is to choose in every II labelled node of $\Gamma_{\mathcal{E}}$ the successor which appears also in the right-hand side expression of the i-th equation in $\mathcal{E}'$.

It is then straightforward to verify that for the game on $\Gamma_{\mathcal{E}}$ with initial node 1 player II wins every play by playing according to str_{II}. By Lemma 1, the system $\mathcal{E}'$ does not contain any μ labelled variables that depend on x_1 and are self-dependent. The crucial observation is that the dependency graph of $\mathcal{E}'$ contains all and only those paths which correspond to the plays of the game $\Gamma_{\mathcal{E}}$ where the strategy str_{II} is followed. Consequently, there cannot be a play of the game $\Gamma_{\mathcal{E}}$ starting from node 1 that is won by player I and where player II plays according to str_{II}. It follows from Theorem 8.7 in [18] that the solution of $\mathcal{E}$ is $[\![\mathcal{E}]\!] = 1$. $\qquad\square$

Example 3. Recall the Boolean equation system $\mathcal{E}_1$ of Example 1. There is only one conjunctive equation $\nu x_1 = x_2 \wedge x_1$, yielding two possible disjunctive Boolean equation systems which can be constructed from $\mathcal{E}_1$:

- if we throw away the conjunct x_2, then we obtain:

$$\mathcal{E}_1' \equiv ((\nu x_1 = x_1)(\mu x_2 = x_1 \vee x_3)(\nu x_3 = x_3))$$

- if we throw away the conjunct x_1, then we obtain:

$$\mathcal{E}_1'' \equiv ((\nu x_1 = x_2)(\mu x_2 = x_1 \vee x_3)(\nu x_3 = x_3)).$$

Using Lemma 1, we can see that these disjunctive systems have the solutions $[\![\mathcal{E}_1']\!] = [\![\mathcal{E}_1'']\!] = 1$. By Lemma 2, a solution to $\mathcal{E}_1$ is $[\![\mathcal{E}_1]\!] = 1$ as expected.

In Section 5 we will see the application of the above lemmas to give a compact encoding of the problem of solving alternating Boolean equation systems as the problem of finding stable models of normal logic programs.

4   Stable Models of Normal Logic Programs

For encoding Boolean equation systems we use normal logic programs with the stable model semantics [8]. A normal rule is of the form

$$a \leftarrow b_1, \ldots, b_m, \text{not } c_1, \ldots, \text{not } c_n. \tag{1}$$

where each a, b_i, c_j is a ground atom. Models of a program are sets of ground atoms. A set of atoms Δ is said to satisfy an atom a if $a \in \Delta$ and a negative literal not a if $a \notin \Delta$. A rule r of the form (1) is satisfied by Δ if the head a is satisfied whenever every body literal $b_1, \ldots, b_m,$ not $c_1, \ldots,$ not c_n is satisfied by Δ and a program Π is satisfied by Δ if each rule in Π is satisfied by Δ.

Stable models of a program are sets of ground atoms which satisfy all the rules of the program and are justified by the rules. This is captured using the concept of a *reduct*. For a program Π and a set of atoms Δ, the reduct Π^Δ is defined by

$$\Pi^\Delta = \{a \leftarrow b_1, \ldots, b_m. \mid a \leftarrow b_1, \ldots, b_m, \text{not } c_1, \ldots, \text{not } c_n. \in \Pi, \\ \{c_1, \ldots, c_n\} \cap \Delta = \emptyset\}$$

i.e., a reduct Π^Δ does not contain any negative literals and, hence, has a unique subset minimal set of atoms satisfying it.

Definition 5. *A set of atoms Δ is a stable model of a program Π iff Δ is the unique minimal set of atoms satisfying Π^Δ.*

We employ two extensions which can be seen as compact shorthands for normal rules. We use *integrity constraints*, i.e., rules

$$\leftarrow b_1, \ldots, b_m, \text{not } c_1, \ldots, \text{not } c_n. \tag{2}$$

with an empty head. Such a constraint can be taken as a shorthand for a rule

$$f \leftarrow \text{not } f, b_1, \ldots, b_m, \text{not } c_1, \ldots, \text{not } c_n.$$

where f is a new atom. Notice that a stable model Δ satisfies an integrity constraint (2) only if at least one of its body literals is not satisfied by Δ.

For expressing the choice of selecting exactly one atom from two possibilities we use *choose-1-of-2 rules* on the left which correspond to the normal rules on the right:

$$1 \{a_1, a_2\} 1. \qquad\qquad a_1 \leftarrow \text{not } a_2. \quad a_2 \leftarrow \text{not } a_1. \quad \leftarrow a_1, a_2.$$

Choose-1-of-2 rules are a simple subclass of cardinality constraint rules [22]. The Smodels system (http://www.tcs.hut.fi/Software/smodels/) provides an implementation for cardinality constraint rules and includes primitives supporting directly such constraints without translating them first to corresponding normal rules.

5   Solving Boolean Equation Systems in ASP

The overall idea of our approach is as follows. Given a standard form Boolean equation system $\mathcal{E}$, we partition its variables into blocks so that variables are in the same block iff they are mutually dependent. The partition can be constructed in linear time on the basis of the dependencies between the variables. Like argued in Section 3, the variables can be solved iteratively one block at a time.

If all variables in a single block have the same sign, i.e. the block is alternation free, the variables in this block can be trivially solved in linear time (see e.g. [2, 17]). So we only need to concentrate on solving alternating blocks containing mutually dependent variables with different signs. Consequently, we present here a technique to solve an alternating Boolean equation system which applies Lemmas 1-2 from Section 3.

In order to reduce the resolution of alternating Boolean equation systems to the problem of computing stable models of logic programs we define a translation from equation systems to normal logic programs. Consider a standard form, alternating Boolean equation system $\mathcal{E}$. We construct a logic program $\Pi(\mathcal{E})$ which captures the solution $[\![\mathcal{E}]\!]$ of $\mathcal{E}$. Suppose that the number of conjunctive equations of $\mathcal{E}$ is less than (or equal to) the number of disjunctive equations, or that no conjunction symbols occur in the right-hand sides of $\mathcal{E}$. The dual case goes along exactly the same lines and is omitted.[1] The idea is that $\Pi(\mathcal{E})$ is a ground program which is polynomial in the size of $\mathcal{E}$. We give a compact description of $\Pi(\mathcal{E})$ as a program with variables. This program consists of the rules

$$solve(1). \tag{3}$$
$$depends(Y) \leftarrow dep(X, Y), solve(X). \tag{4}$$
$$depends(Y) \leftarrow depends(X), dep(X, Y). \tag{5}$$
$$reached(X, Y) \leftarrow nu(X), dep(X, Y), Y \geq X. \tag{6}$$
$$reached(X, Y) \leftarrow reached(X, Z), dep(Z, Y), Y \geq X. \tag{7}$$
$$\leftarrow depends(Y), reached(Y, Y), nu(Y). \tag{8}$$

extended for each equation $\sigma_i x_i = \alpha_i$ of $\mathcal{E}$ by

$$dep(i, j). \qquad\qquad \text{if } \alpha_i = x_j \tag{9}$$
$$dep(i, j).\ dep(i, k). \qquad\qquad \text{if } \alpha_i = (x_j \vee x_k) \tag{10}$$
$$1\ \{dep(i, j), dep(i, k)\}\ 1. \qquad\qquad \text{if } \alpha_i = (x_j \wedge x_k) \tag{11}$$

and by $nu(i).$ for each variable x_i such that $\sigma_i = \nu$.

Example 4. Recall the Boolean equation system $\mathcal{E}_1$ of Example 1. The program $\Pi(\mathcal{E}_1)$ consists of the rules 3-8 extended with rules:

$$1\ \{dep(1, 2), dep(1, 1)\}\ 1.$$
$$dep(2, 1).\ dep(2, 3).$$
$$dep(3, 3).$$
$$nu(1).\ nu(3).$$

---

[1] This is the case where the number of disjunctive equations of $\mathcal{E}$ is less than the number of conjunctive equations, or where no disjunction symbols occur in the right-hand sides of $\mathcal{E}$.

The idea is that for the solution $[\![\mathcal{E}]\!]$ of $\mathcal{E}$, $[\![\mathcal{E}]\!] = 0$ iff $\Pi(\mathcal{E})$ has a stable model. This is captured in the following way. The system $\mathcal{E}$ is turned effectively into a disjunctive system by making a choice between $dep(i,j)$ and $dep(i,k)$ for each conjunctive equation $x_i = (x_j \wedge x_k)$. Hence, each stable model corresponds to a disjunctive system constructed from $\mathcal{E}$ and vice versa. Then by Lemmas 1 and 2 the main result can be established.

Theorem 1. *Let $\mathcal{E}$ be a standard form, alternating Boolean equation system. Then $[\![\mathcal{E}]\!] = 0$ iff $\Pi(\mathcal{E})$ has a stable model.*

Proof. Consider a system $\mathcal{E}$ and its translation $\Pi(\mathcal{E})$. The rules (9–11) effectively capture the dependency graphs of the disjunctive systems that can be constructed from $\mathcal{E}$. More precisely, there is a one to one correspondence between the stable models of the rules (9–11) and disjunctive systems that can be constructed from $\mathcal{E}$ such that for each stable model Δ, there is exactly one disjunctive system $\mathcal{E}'$ with the dependency graph $G_{\mathcal{E}'} = (V, E)$ where $V = \{i \mid dep(i,j) \in \Delta \text{ or } dep(j,i) \in \Delta\}$ and $E = \{(i,j) \mid dep(i,j) \in \Delta\}$.

Now it is straightforward to establish by the splitting set theorem [15] that each stable model Δ of $\Pi(\mathcal{E})$ is an extension of a stable model Δ' of the rules (9–11), i.e., of the form $\Delta = \Delta' \cup \Delta''$ such that in the corresponding dependency graph there is no variable x_j such that $\sigma_j = \nu$ and x_1 depends on x_j and x_j is self-dependent. By Lemma 2 $[\![\mathcal{E}]\!] = 0$ iff there is a disjunctive system $\mathcal{E}'$ that can be constructed from $\mathcal{E}$ for which $[\![\mathcal{E}']\!] = 0$. By Lemma 1 for a disjunctive system $\mathcal{E}'$, $[\![\mathcal{E}']\!] = 1$ iff there is a variable x_j such $\sigma_j = \nu$ and x_1 depends on x_j and x_j is self-dependent. Hence, $\Pi(\mathcal{E})$ has a stable model iff there is a disjunctive system $\mathcal{E}'$ that can be constructed from $\mathcal{E}$ whose dependency graph has no variable x_j such that $\sigma_j = \nu$ and x_1 depends on x_j and x_j is self-dependent iff there is a disjunctive system $\mathcal{E}'$ with $[\![\mathcal{E}']\!] \neq 1$, i.e., $[\![\mathcal{E}']\!] = 0$ iff $[\![\mathcal{E}]\!] = 0$. □

Similar property holds also for the dual program, which allows us to solve all alternating blocks of standard form Boolean equation systems.

Although $\Pi(\mathcal{E})$ is given using variables, for the theorem above a finite ground instantiation of it is sufficient. For explaining the ground instantiation we introduce a relation $depDom$ such that $depDom(i,j)$ holds iff there is an equation $\sigma_i x_i = \alpha_i$ of $\mathcal{E}$ with x_j occurring in α_i. Now the sufficient ground instantiation is obtained by substituting variables X, Y in the rules (4–6) with all pairs i, j such that $depDom(i,j)$ holds, substituting variables X, Y, Z in rule (7) with all triples l, i, j such that $nu(l)$ and $depDom(i,j)$ hold and variable Y in rule (8) with every i such that $nu(i)$ holds. This means also that such conditions can be added as domain predicates to the rules without compromising the correctness of the translation. For example, rule (7) could be replaced by $reached(X, Y) \leftarrow nu(X), depDom(Z, Y), reached(X, Z), dep(Z, Y), Y \geq X$. Notice that such conditions make the rules domain restricted as required, e.g., by the Smodels system.

6   Experiments

In this section, we describe some experimental results on solving alternating Boolean equation systems with the approach presented in the previous section. We demonstrate the technique on two series of examples which are solved using the Smodels system as the ASP solver. Unfortunately, we were not able to compare this method to other approaches as we did not find any implementation capable of handling Boolean equation systems with high alternation depths.

We also experimented with another ASP system, DLV (release 2004–05–23 available on http://www.dbai.tuwien.ac.at/proj/dlv/), as the underlying ASP solver but ran into performance problems as explained below.

The times reported are the average of 3 runs of the time for Smodels 2.26 to find the solutions as reported by the /usr/bin/time command on a 2.0Ghz AMD Athlon running Linux. The time needed for parsing and grounding the input with lparse 1.0.13 is included.

The encoding used for the benchmarks is that represented in Section 5 with a couple of optimizations. Firstly, when encoding of dependencies as given in rules (9–11) we differentiate those dependencies where there is a choice from those where there is not, i.e., for each equation $\sigma_i x_i = \alpha_i$ of $\mathcal{E}$ we add

$ddep(i, j).$ if $\alpha_i = x_j$
$ddep(i, j).ddep(i, k).$ if $\alpha_i = (x_j \vee x_k)$
$1 \{cdep(i, j), cdep(i, k)\} 1. \ depDom(i, j). \ depDom(i, k).$ if $\alpha_i = (x_j \wedge x_k)$

instead of rules (9–11). Secondly, in order to make use of this distinction and to allow for intelligent grounding, rules (4–7) are rewritten using the above predicates as domain predicates in the following way.

$depends(Y) \leftarrow ddep(X, Y), solve(X).$
$depends(Y) \leftarrow depDom(X, Y), cdep(X, Y), solve(X).$
$depends(Y) \leftarrow depends(X), ddep(X, Y).$
$depends(Y) \leftarrow depends(X), depDom(X, Y), cdep(X, Y).$
$reached(X, Y) \leftarrow nu(X), ddep(X, Y), Y \geq X.$
$reached(X, Y) \leftarrow nu(X), depDom(X, Y), cdep(X, Y), Y \geq X.$
$reached(X, Y) \leftarrow nu(X), reached(X, Z), ddep(Z, Y), Y \geq X.$
$reached(X, Y) \leftarrow nu(X), depDom(Z, Y), reached(X, Z), cdep(Z, Y), Y \geq X.$

All benchmark encodings are available at http://www.tcs.hut.fi/Software/ smodels/tests/inap2004.tar.gz.

The first series deals with solving alternating Boolean equation systems of increasing size and alternation depth. The problem is taken from [18–p.91] and consists of finding the solution of the left-most variable x_1 in Fig. 2. The example is such that a Boolean equation system with n equations has the alternation depth n. The solution of the system is such that $[\![\mathcal{E}]\!] = 1$ which can be obtained by determining the existence of a stable model of the corresponding logic program. The experimental results are summarised in Fig. 2. Our benchmarks are

$$\left.\begin{array}{l} \nu\, x_1 = x_2 \wedge x_n \\ \mu\, x_2 = x_1 \vee x_n \\ \nu\, x_3 = x_2 \wedge x_n \\ \mu\, x_4 = x_3 \vee x_n \\ \quad \cdots \\ \nu\, x_{n-3} = x_{n-4} \wedge x_n \\ \mu\, x_{n-2} = x_{n-3} \vee x_n \\ \nu\, x_{n-1} = x_{n-2} \wedge x_n \\ \mu\, x_n = x_{n-1} \vee x_{n/2} \end{array}\right\} \text{for } n \in 2\mathbb{N}$$

Problem (n)	Time (sec)
1800	33.6
2000	41.8
2200	51.4
2400	60.0
2600	71.7

Fig. 2. The Boolean equation system in [18–p.91] and experimental results

$$\left.\begin{array}{l} \nu\, x_s = y_s \\ \mu\, y_s = \bigwedge_{s' \in \nabla(t,s)} z_{s'} \vee y_s \\ \mu\, z_s = \bigvee_{s' \in \nabla(a,s)} true \wedge x_s \end{array}\right\} \text{for all } s \in S.$$

Problem	$|s|$	$\longrightarrow$	n	Time (sec)
M_{500}	503	505	1006	4.0
M_{1000}	1003	1005	2006	16.4
M_{1500}	1503	1505	3006	39.0

where $\nabla(t,s) := \{s' | s \xrightarrow{i} s' \wedge i \in A\}$
and $\nabla(a,s) := \{s' | s \xrightarrow{a} s'\}$.

Fig. 3. The Boolean equation system and experimental results

essentially the only results in the literature for alternating Boolean equation systems with the alternation depth $n \geq 4$ of which we are aware. Notice that our benchmarks have the alternation depths $1800 \leq n \leq 2600$. Like pointed out in [18], known algorithms based on approximation techniques are exponential in the size of the equation system in Fig. 2, because a maximal number of backtracking steps is always needed to solve the left-most equation.

We tried to use also DLV as the underlying ASP solver on this benchmark, but found that it does not scale as well as Smodels when the size n of the problem grows. For example, for size $n = 1800$ the running time for DLV was over 30 minutes.

In the second series of examples we used a set of μ-calculus model checking problems taken from [16], converted to alternating Boolean equation systems. The problems consist of checking a μ-calculus formula of alternation depth 2, on a sequence of models $M = (S, A, \longrightarrow)$ of increasing size (see Fig. 2 in [16]). Suppose that all transitions of process M in [16] are labelled with a and we want to check, at initial state s, the property that a is enabled infinitely often along all infinite paths. This is expressed with alternating fixed point formula:

$$\phi \equiv \nu X.\mu Y.([-].(\langle a \rangle true \wedge X) \vee Y) \tag{12}$$

which is true at initial state s of the process M. The problem can be directly encoded as the problem of solving the corresponding alternating equation system in Fig. 3. The results are given in Fig. 3. The columns are:

- Problem: Process $M = (S, A, \longrightarrow)$ from [16].
- $|S|$: Number of states in M.
- $| \longrightarrow |$: Number of transitions in M.
- n: Number of equations in the corresponding Boolean equation system.
- Time: The time in seconds to solve variable x_s.

The benchmarks in [16] have a quite simple structure and no general results can be drawn from them. In fact, the equation system in Fig. 3 reduces to a sequence of purely conjunctive equations, whose encoding involves no *choose-1-of-2 rules*, i.e. is a Horn program. A more involved practical evaluation of our approach is highly desirable, and benchmarking on real world systems is left for future work.

7   Conclusion

We present an answer set programming based method for computing the solutions of alternating Boolean equation systems. We developed a novel characterization of solutions for variables in Boolean equation systems and based on this devised a mapping from systems with alternating fixed points to normal logic programs. Our translation is such that the solution of a given variable of an equation system can be determined by the existence of a stable model of the corresponding logic program. This result provides the basis for verifying μ-calculus formulas with alternating fixpoints using answer set programming techniques.

The experimental results indicate that stable model computation is quite a competitive approach to solve Boolean equations systems in which the number of alternation is relatively large. The alternation of fixpoint operators gives more expressive power in μ-calculus, but all known model checking algorithms are exponential in the alternation depth. Consequently, our approach is expected to be quite effective in the verification tasks where there is a need of formulas with great expressive power.

Acknowledgements. We would like to thank Keijo Heljanko for valuable discussions. The financial supports of Academy of Finland (project 53695), Emil Aaltonen foundation and Helsinki Graduate School in Computer Science and Engineering are gratefully acknowledged.

References

1. H.R. Andersen. Model checking and Boolean graphs. *Theoretical Computer Science*, 126:3–30, 1994.
2. A. Arnold and P. Crubille. A linear algorithm to solve fixed-point equations on transition systems *Information Processing Letters*, 29: 57–66, 1988.
3. A. Arnold and D. Niwinski. Rudiments of μ-calculus. *Studies in Logic and the foundations of mathematics*, Volume 146, Elsevier, 2001.
4. G. Bhat and R. Cleaveland. Efficient local model-checking for fragments of the modal μ-calculus. In *Proceedings of the International Conference on Tools and Algorithms for the Construction and Analysis of Systems*, Lecture Notes in Computer Science 1055, pages 107–126, Springer Verlag, 1996.

5. G. Delzanno and A. Podelski. Model checking in CLP. In Proceedings of the Int. In *Proceedings of the International Conference on Tools and Algorithms for the Construction and Analysis of Systems*, Lecture Notes in Computer Science 1579, pages 223–239, 1999.
6. E.A. Emerson, C. Jutla and A.P. Sistla. On model checking for fragments of the μ-calculus. In *Proceedings of the Fifth International Conference on Computer Aided Verification*, Lecture Notes in Computer Science 697, pages 385–396, Springer Verlag, 1993.
7. E.A. Emerson, C. Jutla, and A.P. Sistla. On model checking for the μ-calculus and its fragments. *Theoretical Computer Science*, 258:491–522, 2001.
8. M. Gelfond and V. Lifschitz. The stable model semantics for logic programming. In *Proceedings of the 5th International Conference on Logic Programming*, pages 1070–1080, Seattle, USA, August 1988. The MIT Press.
9. J.F. Groote and M. Keinänen. Solving Disjunctive/Conjunctive Boolean Equation Systems with Alternating Fixed Points. In *Proceedings of the 10th International Conference on Tools and Algorithms for the Construction and Analysis of Systems*, Lecture Notes in Computer Science 2988, pages 436 – 450, Springer Verlag, 2004.
10. K. Heljanko and I. Niemelä. Bounded LTL model checking with stable models. *Theory and Practice of Logic Programming*, 3: 519–550, Cambridge University Press, 2003.
11. M. Jurdzinski. Deciding the winner in parity games is in $UP \cap co-UP$. *Information Processing Letters*, 68:119–124, 1998.
12. D. Kozen. Results on the propositional μ-calculus. *Theoretical Computer Science*, 27:333–354, 1983.
13. K. N. Kumar, C. R. Ramakrishnan, and S. A. Smolka. Alternating fixed points in Boolean equation systems as preferred stable models. In *Proceedings of the 17th International Conference of Logic Programming*, Lecture Notes in Computer Science 2237, pages 227–241, Springer Verlag, 2001.
14. V. Lifschitz. Answer Set Planning. In *Proceedings of the 16th International Conference on Logic Programming*, pages 25–37, The MIT Press, 1999.
15. V. Lifschitz and H. Turner. Splitting a Logic Program. In *Proceedings of the Eleventh International Conference on Logic Programming*, pages 23–37, The MIT Press, 1994.
16. X. Liu, C.R. Ramakrishnan and S.A. Smolka. Fully Local and Efficient Evaluation of Alternating Fixed Points. In *Proceedings of the 4th International Conference on Tools and Algorithms for the Construction and Analysis of Systems*, Lecture Notes in Computer Science 1384, pages 5–19, Springer Verlag, 1998.
17. X. Liu and S.A. Smolka. Simple Linear-Time Algorithms for Minimal Fixed Points. In *Proceedings of the 26th International Conference on Automata, Languages, and Programming*, Lecture Notes in Computer Science 1443, pages 53–66, Springer Verlag, 1998.
18. A. Mader. Verification of Modal Properties using Boolean Equation Systems. PhD thesis, Technical University of Munich, 1997.
19. W. Marek and M. Truszczyński. Stable Models and an Alternative Logic Programming Paradigm, *The Logic Programming Paradigm: a 25-Year Perspective*, pages 375–398, Springer-Verlag, 1999.
20. I. Niemelä. Logic Programs with Stable Model Semantics as a Constraint Programming Paradigm. *Annals of Mathematics and Artificial Intelligence*, 25(3,4):241–273, 1999.
21. C. Papadimitriou. Computational Complexity. Addison-Wesley, 1994.

22. P. Simons, I. Niemelä, and T. Soininen. Extending and implementing the stable model semantics. *Artificial Intelligence*, 138(1–2):181–234, 2002.
23. B. Vergauwen and J. Lewi. Efficient local correctness checking for single and alternating Boolean equation systems. In *Proceedings of the 21st International Colloquium on Automata, Languages and Programming*, Lecture Notes in Computer Science 820, pages 302–315, Springer Verlag, 1994.

Effective Modeling with Constraints

Roman Barták

Charles University, Faculty of Mathematics and Physics,
Institute for Theoretical Computer Science,
Malostranské nám. 2/25, Prague, Czech Republic
roman.bartak@mff.cuni.cz

Abstract. Constraint programming provides a declarative approach to solving combinatorial (optimization) problems. The user just states the problem as a constraint satisfaction problem (CSP) and a generic solver finds a solution without additional programming. However, in practice, the situation is more complicated because there usually exist several ways how to model the problem as a CSP, that is using variables, their domains, and constraints. In fact, different constraint models may lead to significantly different running times of the solver so constraint modeling is a crucial part of problem solving. This paper describes some known approaches to efficient modeling with constraints in a tutorial-like form. The primary audience is practitioners, especially in logic programming, that would like to use constraints in their projects but do not have yet deep knowledge of constraint satisfaction techniques.

1 Introduction

"Constraint programming (CP) represents one of the closest approaches computer science has yet made to the Holy Grail of programming: the user states the problem, the computer solves it." [4] This nice quotation might convince a reader that designing a constraint model for a particular combinatorial problem is an easy and straightforward task and that everything stated as a constraint satisfaction problem can be solved efficiently by the underlying constraint solver. This holds for simple or small problems but as soon as the problems are more complex, the role of constraint modeling is becoming more and more important. The reason is that different constraint models of the same problem may lead to very different solving times. Unfortunately, there does not exist (yet) any guide that can steer the user how to design an efficiently solvable model. This "feature" of constraint technology might be a bit depressing for novices. Nevertheless, there are many rules of thumb about designing efficient constraint models. We also believe that it is important to be aware of the insides of constraint satisfaction to understand better the behavior of the solvers and, as a consequence, to design models that exploit the power of the solvers.

The goal of this paper is to introduce the basic terminology useful for reading further CP texts and to give an overview of modeling techniques used to state problems as constraint satisfaction problems. The emphasis is put to novice users of the constraint technology, in particular to the current users of logic programming

D. Seipel et al. (Eds.): INAP/WLP 2004, LNAI 3392,, pp. 149–165, 2005.

technology that can be naturally extended by constraints. Respecting what has been said above we will first survey the mainstream constraint satisfaction technology. In the main part of the paper we will demonstrate some modeling techniques namely symmetry breaking, dual models, and redundant constraints, using practical examples.

2 Constraint Satisfaction at Glance

Constraint programming is a framework for solving combinatorial (optimization) problems. The basic idea is to model the problem as a set of variables with domains (the values for the variables) and a set of constraints restricting the possible combinations of variables' values (Figure 1). Usually, the domains are finite and we are speaking about *constraint satisfaction problems* (CSP)[1]. The task is to find an assignment of all the variables satisfying all the constraints – a so called complete *feasible assignment*. Sometimes, there is also an objective function defined over the problem variables. Then the task is to find a complete feasible assignment minimizing or maximizing the objective function – an *optimal assignment*. Such problems are called *constraint optimization problems* (COP).

Note that modeling problems as a CSP or a COP is natural because constraints can describe arbitrary relations and various constraints can be easily combined within a single system. Opposite to frameworks like linear and integer programming, constraints in a CSP/COP are not restricted to linear equalities and inequalities. The constraint can express arbitrary mathematical or logical formula, like $(x^2 < y \lor x = y)$. The constraint could even be an arbitrary relation that can be hardly expressed in an intentional form, for example restricted resource state transitions in scheduling applications. Then, a table is used to describe tuples satisfying the constraint.

Fig. 1. A CSP consists of variables (X,Y,Z), their domains (in this case identical [1,2,3,4,5]), and constraints (X<Y, Y<X-2). It can be represented as a constraint (hyper) graph

Solving problems using constraints typically involves three steps. First, the problem is expressed in terms of variables, their domains, and constraints – this is called *constraint modeling*. Second, the constraint model is passed to a generic constraint solver that, hopefully, finds a feasible (or optimal) assignment – *constraint satisfaction*. Finally, this assignment is interpreted as a solution of the original problem. To understand better the important role of constraint modeling let us first look inside the mainstream technique of constraint satisfaction that is a combination of depth-first search (enumeration) with constraint propagation. Despite the fact that

---

[1] There also exist constraint problems over infinite domains, for example over real numbers, but constraint solving over infinite domains is not covered by this paper.

many researchers outside CP put equality between constraint satisfaction and simple enumeration, the reality is that the real power of CP is hidden in constraint propagation. Note however, that some other techniques, for example local search, can also be applied to solve the problems with constraints.

Constraint propagation is based on the idea of using constraints actively to reduce domains of the variables by removing the values that do not satisfy the constraint. Assume that variables X and Y have an identical domain {1,2,3,4,5} and there is a constraint X<Y between the variables. Visibly, the value 1 can be removed from the domain of Y because there is no value *a* in the domain X such that the pair (*a*,1) satisfies the constraint. Similarly, the value 5 can be removed from the domain of X. This domain filtering is realized by a so called *filtering algorithm* that is attached to each constraint. After applying the filtering algorithm, the constraint becomes (arc) consistent, that is for any value in the domain of a constrained variable there is a compatible value(s) in the domain of the other constrained variable(s) such that the pair (tuple) satisfies the constraint. The filtering algorithm is evoked every time a domain of some variable in the constraint is changed and this change is propagated to domains of the other variables in the constraint and so on (Figure 2).

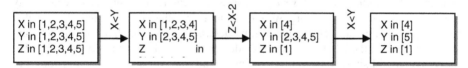

Fig. 2. Constraint propagation does domain reduction by repeated evoking of the filtering algorithms until a fix-point is reached

Notice that a filtering algorithm for a particular constraint may be evoked several times in the propagation loop but because values can only be removed from domains, propagation must finish sometime either by reaching a fix point or by emptying some domain. This basic constraint propagation scheme is called (generalized) *arc consistency* (AC) and it ensures that after finishing the propagation loop each constraint is (arc) consistent. Note however, that arc consistency ensures local consistency only meaning that the values which cannot be part of the complete feasible assignment may still remain in the domains. There exist consistency techniques stronger than AC, like path consistency, but they are rarely used in practice. More frequently, filtering is being strengthened by encapsulating a subset of constraints into a so called *global constraint*. Note finally that the same problem can often be modeled using different sets of constraints leading to different domain pruning and hence the important role of constraint modeling.

Global constraints. Due to its local character arc consistency cannot detect all global inconsistencies. Assume the constraint network on right. All binary constraints are consistent so arc consistency deduces no change of the domains. However, a more global view can discover that values 5 and 6 cannot be assigned to X_3 because they both will be used for X_1 and X_2. If we see the set of primitive constraints as a single n-ary constraint – a global constraint – we can use a special filtering algorithm for this constraint that achieves stronger pruning of domains. Régin proposed an efficient filtering algorithm for such a constraint called all-different based on finding a maximal matching in the bipartite graph with variables on one side and values on the other side [8].

There exist many other global constraints; some of them were designed for a particular problem area. For example, global constraints in scheduling are used to describe resources to which activities can be allocated. Assume a unary resource that can process only one activity at given time. If we model the position of activity in time using its start time S and processing time P then the main feature of the unary resource, namely that no two activities overlap in time, can be modeled using a set of disjunctions $S_i+P_i \leq S_j \lor S_j+P_j \leq S_i$. Again, domain pruning via AC over such a set of disjunctive constraints is weak and stronger pruning can be achieved for example using a global constraint over all S_i and P_i based on a technique called edge-finding [1].

As we mentioned above, arc consistency is a local consistency technique so some infeasible values may still sit in the domains of the variables and thus search (with backtracking) is necessary to find a complete feasible assignment of the variables. This stage is often called *labeling* because the variables are being labeled there – the values from respective domains are assigned to the variables. After each assignment, the value is propagated to other variables using the above described AC scheme – this is called *maintaining arc consistency* during search. If a failure is detected (any domain becomes empty during AC) then another value is tried and if no value remains in the domain then the algorithm backtracks to the last but one variable and so on. In general, the labeling procedure adds new constraints to the system to resolve the remaining disjunctions until domains of all the variables are singleton. For example, finding a value for the variable X with the domain {5,6,7} is equivalent to resolving the disjunction $X=5 \lor X=6 \lor X=7$ which is called *enumeration* (the constraint X=5 is added first, then X=6 is tried, and finally X=7). Resolving $X=5 \lor X \neq 5$ is called a *step labeling* and resolving $X \leq 6 \lor X>6$ is called *bisection*. By adding the above mentioned constraints, the constraint solver actually builds different constraint models in different branches of the search tree so in some sense choosing the right branching scheme is a part of constraint modeling. We will present later how different branching schemes influence efficiency of constraint satisfaction.

Variable and value selection. The labeling procedure needs to be accompanied by heuristics for choosing the variable to be labeled and for selecting the value to be tried first (or, in general, for selecting the branch). If the variables are labeled in a fix ordered then we are speaking about the *left-most* variable selection. Frequently, *fail-first* variable selection is used where the variable with the smallest domain is labeled first (ties are broken randomly). Value selection heuristics are usually problem dependent, for example the smallest value for the time variables is tried first if we are minimizing the makespan (the end time of the latest activity) in scheduling problems.

The standard constraint satisfaction technique looking for feasible assignments can be extended to find out an optimal assignment. Usually a technique of *branch-and-bound* is used there. First, some feasible assignment is found and then, a next assignment that is better than the previous assignment is looked for and so on. This could be realized by posting a new constraint restricting the value of the objective function by the value of the objective function for the so-far best assignment. This is repeated until no feasible assignment is found and then the last found feasible assignment is the optimal assignment.

A deep and general view of constraint programming can be found in [2,6,7,11].

3 Modeling with Constraints

In this section, we will present several example problems and their constraint models. We will use these problems to demonstrate typical constraint modeling techniques like global constraints, symmetry breaking, dual models, and redundant constraints. The main idea behind these techniques is to improve solving efficiency of the models. To allow immediate testing of the presented ideas, the constraint models are programmed using the `clpfd` library of SICStus Prolog [3,9].

3.1 A Seesaw Problem: Symmetry Breaking and Global Constraints

Let us start our journey with a toy combinatorial problem of placing children to a seesaw [7]. Assume that Adam, Boris, and Cecil want to sit in a seesaw in such a way that the seesaw balances. There are five seats placed uniformly on both arms of the seesaw and one seat is placed in the middle (see Figure 3). Moreover, the boys want to have some space around them. In particular, they require that they are at least three seats apart. The weights of Adam, Boris, and Cecil are respectively 36, 32, and 16 kg. To solve the problem, we need to assign the seats to all children (or vice versa). Figure 3 shows one of the acceptable solutions to this problem.

Fig. 3. A seesaw problem and one of its solutions

To model the problem as a constraint satisfaction problem, one needs to decide about the variables, their domains, and the constraints. The natural model for the seesaw problem is using a variable for each boy describing his position on the seesaw: A for Adam, B for Boris, C for Cecil. If we choose carefully the domain for these variables, that is a position on the seesaw: -5,-4,…,+4,+5, then the constraint that the seesaw balances is simply that the moments of inertia sums to 0:

$$36*A + 32*B + 16*C = 0.$$

To restrict the minimal distances between the boys we can use a standard formula for computing the distances that is an absolute value of the difference of the positions. Thus we get the constraints:

$$|A-B| > 2, |A-C| > 2, |B-C| > 2.$$

Note that $|A-B| > 2$ is a compact representation of the disjunctive constraint $(A-B > 2 \lor B-A > 2)$ and that it also ensures that two boys are not sitting on the same seat.

The above constraints describe completely the seesaw problem. To get the solution we need to post all these constraints and to do labeling that is a procedure deciding about the variables' values via depth first search. Figure 4 shows a coding in SICStus Prolog.

```
seesaw(Sol):-
  Sol = [A,B,C],

  domain([A,B,C],-5,5),
  36*A+32*B+16*C #= 0,
  abs(A-B) #> 2,
  abs(A-C) #> 2,
  abs(B-C) #> 2.

  labeling([ff],Sol). % fail-first variable selection
```

Fig. 4. A constraint model for the seesaw problem

Notice that the constraint model for the seesaw problem is fully declarative. So far, we said no single word about how to solve the problem. We merely concentrate on describing the problem in terms of variables, domains, and constraints. The underlying constraint solver that encodes constraint propagation as well as the labeling procedure does the rest of the job.

If we now run the program from Figure 4 we get six different solutions (Figure 5).

```
?- seesaw(X).

X = [-4,2,5] ? ;
X = [-4,4,1] ? ;
X = [-4,5,-1] ? ;
X = [4,-5,1] ? ;
X = [4,-4,-1] ? ;
X = [4,-2,-5] ? ;
no
```

Fig. 5. All solutions of the seesaw problem

An open-minded reader might notice that only three of the above solutions are really different while the remaining three solutions are merely their symmetrical copies. These symmetrical solutions can be removed from the search space by adding a so called *symmetry breaking constraint*. For example it could be a constraint restricting Adam to sit on the seats marked by the non-positive numbers: A≤0.

Rule of thumb – symmetry breaking. Some solutions of the problem can be easily deduced from their symmetrical counterparts. These symmetrical solutions should be removed from the search space to decrease its size and thus to improve time efficiency of the search procedure. The easiest way how to realize it is via adding symmetry breaking constraints that avoid symmetrical solutions and reduce the search space. There exist other techniques of symmetry breaking, for details see [10]. For a more convincing example, how the symmetry breaking constraint improves efficiency of the constraint model, see the section on Golomb rulers.

Let us now try to improve further the constraint model from Figure 4. Usually, the constraint model that propagates more is assumed to be better so our goal is to improve the initial domain pruning. Figure 6 shows the result of the initial domain pruning before the start of labeling (the symmetry breaking constraint is included).

```
A in -4..0
B in -1..5
C in -5..5
```

Fig. 6. Initial domain pruning for the seesaw problem (including symmetry breaking)

As we already mentioned a typical way of improving domain pruning is using global constraints that encapsulate a set of primitive constraints. If we look at the constraint model for the seesaw problem (Figure 4), we can identify a set of similar constraints, namely the distance constraints, that is a good candidate to be encapsulated into a global constraint. Notice that these constraints express the same information as non-overlapping constraints in scheduling. In fact, we can see each boy as a box of width three and if these boxes do not overlap then all boys are at least three seats apart (Figure 7). So the seesaw behaves like a unary resource in scheduling problems.

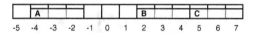

Fig. 7. Allocating boys to seats is similar to scheduling activities to a unary resource

Thus, we can see the seesaw problem via glasses of scheduling and we can use a global constraint modeling the unary resource to substitute the set of distance constraints. For example, the following constraint may by used in SICStus Prolog:

```
serialized([A,B,C],[3,3,3],[bounds_only(false)])
```

The first argument of the `serialized` constraint describes the start times of the "activities", the second argument describes their duration, and the third argument is used for options of the filtering algorithm (above, we asked to propagate the domains completely, not only their bounds). Figure 8 shows the initial domain pruning when the serialized constraint is used. We can see that more infeasible values are removed from the variables' domains and thus the search space to be explored by the labeling procedure is smaller.

```
A in -4..0
B in -1..5
C in (-5..-3)\/(-1..5)
```

Fig. 8. Initial domain pruning for the seesaw problem with the serialized constraint

Rule of thumb – global constraints. More values pruned from variables' domains mean smaller search space so the constraint models that prune more are assumed better. Most constraint solvers use (generalized) arc consistency so the global constraints are the best way how to improve pruning while keeping good time efficiency. Thus the basic rule in the design of constraint models is using global constraint wherever possible.

Typically, the global constraint substitutes a homogeneous set of primate constraints, like differences or distances between the variables. So if such a subset of constraints appears in the constraint model, it is a good candidate for a global constraint. As we showed in the seesaw problem, it is useful to look for global constraints even in the problem areas which do not seem to be directly related to a given problem.

3.2 An Assignment Problem: Dual Models

The second studied problem is more real-life oriented than the seesaw problem. It belongs to the category of assignment problems like allocating ships to berths, planes to stands, crew to planes etc. In particular, we will describe a problem of assigning workers to products.

Consider the following simple assignment problem [7]. A factory has four workers W_1, W_2, W_3, and W_4, and four products P_1, P_2, P_3, and P_4. The problem is to assign workers to products so that each worker is assigned to one product and each product is assigned to one worker (Figure 9).

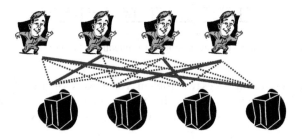

Fig. 9. A simple assignment problem

Table 1. The profit made by workers on particular products

	P_1	P_2	P_3	P_4
W_1	7	1	3	4
W_2	8	2	5	1
W_3	4	3	7	2
W_4	3	1	6	3

The profit made by the worker W_i working on the product P_j is given by Table 1.

The task is to find a solution to the above assignment problem such that the total profit is at least 19.

A straightforward constraint model can use a variable for each worker indicating the product on the worker is working. The domain of such a variable will naturally consists of the products that can be assigned to a given worker. The fact that each worker is working on a different product can be described via a set of binary inequalities or better using the all-different constraint. To describe the profit of the worker, we can use a set of tabular constraints element encoding Table 1. The semantics of element(X,List,Y) is as follows: X-th element of List equals Y. Then the sum of the individual profits must be at least 19. Figure 10 shows the constraint model for the assignment problem in SICStus Prolog.

```
assignment_primal(Sol):-
    Sol = [W1,W2,W3,W4],

    domain(Sol,1,4),
    all_different(Sol),
    element(W1,[7,1,3,4],EW1),
    element(W2,[8,2,5,1],EW2),
    element(W3,[4,3,7,2],EW3),
    element(W4,[3,1,6,3],EW4),
    EW1+EW2+EW3+EW4 #>= 19,

    labeling([ff],Sol).
```

Fig. 10. A constraint model for the assignment problem

By running the above program we get four different assignments that satisfy the minimal profit constraint (Figure 11). The first two assignments have the profit 19, the third assignment has the profit 21 and the last assignment has the profit 20.

```
?- assignment_primal(X).

X = [1,2,3,4] ? ;
X = [2,1,3,4] ? ;
X = [4,1,2,3] ? ;
X = [4,1,3,2] ? ;
no
```

Fig. 11. All solutions of the assignment problem

Frequently, the assignment problem is formulated as an optimization problem. The nice feature of the CP approach is that one does not need to change a lot the constraint model to solve the optimization problem instead of the feasibility problem. Only the standard labeling procedure is substituted by a procedure looking for optimal assignments. In practice, the value of the objective function is encoded into a variable and the system minimizes or maximizes the value of this variable. Figure 12 shows a change in the code necessary to solve the optimization problem where the task is to find an assignment with the maximal profit.

```
     ...
     EW1+EW2+EW3+EW4 #= E,

     maximize(labeling([ff],Sol),E).
```

Fig. 12. A change of the constraint model to solve the optimization problem

The branch and bound technique behind the maximize procedure will now find the optimal solution which is X=[4,1,2,3].

Let us now turn our attention back from optimization to the original constraint model. We decided to use the variables for the workers and the values for the products. However, we could also assign workers to products so the variables will correspond to the products while the values will identify the workers. Figure 13 shows such a dual constraint model.

```
assignment_dual(Sol):-
     Sol = [P1,P2,P3,P4],

     domain(Sol,1,4),
     all_different(Sol),
     element(P1,[7,8,4,3],EP1),
     element(P2,[1,2,3,1],EP2),
     element(P3,[3,5,7,6],EP3),
     element(P4,[4,1,2,3],EP4),
     EP1+EP2+EP3+EP4 #>= 19,

     labeling([ff],Sol).
```

Fig. 13. A dual model for the assignment problem

It may seem that both primal (Figure 10) and dual (Figure 13) models are equivalent. However, somehow surprisingly the dual model requires a smaller number of choices to be explored to find all the solutions of the problem (11 vs. 15). The reason is that the profit depends more on the product than on the worker. Thus, the profitability constraint propagates more for the products than for the workers. Figure 14 compares the initial pruning before the start of labeling procedure for both models. It shows that the dual model propagates more so it is a better model for this particular problem.

The propagation power of both primal and dual models can be combined in a single model. In practice, variables and constraints from both models are used together and

W1 in 1..4	P1 in 1..2
W2 in 1..4	P2 in 1..4
W3 in 1..4	P3 in 2..4
W4 in 1..4	P4 in 1..4

Fig. 14. Initial domain pruning for the assignment problem (left – primal model, right – dual model)

special "channeling" constraints interconnect the models (SICStus Prolog provides the `assignment` constraint to interconnect the models). Figure 15 shows the combined constraint model. Notice that it is enough to label only the variables from one of the original models. Thanks to stronger domain pruning the combined model requires only 9 choices to be explored to find all the solutions of the problem. Figure 16 shows the initial pruning of the combined model.

Rule of thumb – dual models. In many problems, the role of variables and values can be swapped and a so called dual model to the original primal model can be obtained. Comparing the initial pruning of both primal and dual models could be a good guide for selecting one of them. Usually, the best model will be the one in which information is propagated more.

Sometimes, both primal and dual models can be combined together interconnected via channeling constraints. This combined model exploits the propagation power of both models but it also requires overhead to propagate more constraints. Consequently, one must be very careful when combining models with many constraints. Empirical evaluation of the models could be a good guide there.

```
assignment_combined(Workers):-
    Workers= [W1,W2,W3,W4],

    domain(Workers,1,4),
    all_different(Workers),
    element(W1,[7,1,3,4],EW1),
    element(W2,[8,2,5,1],EW2),
    element(W3,[4,3,7,2],EW3),
    element(W4,[3,1,6,3],EW4),
    EW1+EW2+EW3+EW4 #>= 19,

    Products = [P1,P2,P3,P4],

    domain(Products,1,4),
    all_different(Products),
    element(P1,[7,8,4,3],EP1),
    element(P2,[1,2,3,1],EP2),
    element(P3,[3,5,7,6],EP3),
    element(P4,[4,1,2,3],EP4),
    EP1+EP2+EP3+EP4 #>= 19,

    assignment(Workers,Products),

    labeling([ff],Workers).
```

Fig. 15. A combined model for the assignment problem

W1 in (1..2)\/{4}	P1 in 1..2
W2 in 1..4	P2 in 1..4
W3 in 2..4	P3 in 2..4
W4 in 2..4	P4 in 1..4

Fig. 16. Initial domain pruning for the assignment problem with the combined model

3.3   A Golomb Ruler Problem: Redundant Constraints

Lessons learnt in the previous sections will now be applied to solving a really hard problem of finding an optimal Golomb ruler of given size. In particular, we will show how "small" changes in the constraint model, like adding the symmetry breaking and redundant constraints, may influence dramatically the efficiency of the solver.

Golomb ruler of size M is a ruler with M marks placed in such a way that the distances between any two marks are different. The shortest ruler is the optimal ruler. Figure 17 shows an optimal Golomb ruler of size 5.

Fig. 17. An optimal Golomb ruler of size 5

Finding an optimal Golomb ruler is a hard problem. In fact, there is not known an exact algorithm to find an optimal ruler of size $M \geq 24$ even if there exist some best so far rulers of size up to 150 [5]. Still, these results are not proved yet to be (or not to be) optimal. Golomb ruler is not only a hard theoretical problem but it also has a practical usage in radio-astronomy. Let us now design a constraint model to describe the problem of the Golomb ruler.

A natural way how to model the problem is to describe a position of each mark using a variable. Thus for M marks we have M variables $X_1,\ldots, X_M$. The first mark will be in the position 0 and the position of the remaining marks will be described by a positive integer. Moreover, to prevent exploring all permutations of the marks, we can sort the marks (and hence the variables) from left to right by using constraints in the form $X_i < X_{i+1}$. Finally, we need to describe the difference of distances between the marks. Thus for each pair of marks i and j ($i<j$) we introduce a new distance variable $D_{i,j} = X_j - X_i$. The difference of distances is modeled using the all-different constraint applied to all distance variables. Figure 18 shows this base constraint model.

$$X_1 = 0$$
$$X_1 < X_2 < \ldots < X_M$$
$$\forall i < j \; D_{i,j} = X_j - X_i$$
$$\text{all\_different}(\{D_{1,2}, D_{1,3}, \ldots, D_{M,M-1}\})$$

Fig. 18. A base constraint model for the Golomb ruler

The base constraint model already includes several features discussed in the previous sections. In particular, we use a global constraint all-different instead of the set of binary inequalities. We already removed many symmetric solutions by using the ordering constraints (permutation can be seen as a special case of symmetry). There is no doubt about a positive effect of this feature. Still, there is one more symmetric solution to be removed and this is mirroring of the ruler. Assume the optimal ruler [0,1,4,9,11], then the ruler [0,2,7,10,11] is a mirror of this ruler that should be removed from the solution space. The mirror solutions can be removed for example by assuming only the solutions where the distance between the first two marks is smaller than the distance between the last two marks. The symmetry breaking constraint has the following form:

$$D_{1,2} < D_{M-1,M}$$

As we can see from Table 2, adding the above symmetry breaking constraint decreases significantly the running time because the symmetric areas of the search tree are not explored during search.

We can further improve efficiency of the model by adding some *redundant constraints*. The redundant constraint is not necessary to define the solution, it can be deduced from the existing constraints, but it can improve the propagation power. In case of the Golomb ruler, we can derive better bounds for the difference variables. $D_{i,j}$ is a distance between the marks i and j. Notice that this distance consists of the distances $(i,i+1)$, $(i+1,i+2)$ ...$(j-1,j)$. Formally,

$$D_{i,j} = D_{i,i+1} + D_{i+1,i+2} + \ldots + D_{j-1,j}$$

Because all distances must be different, we can estimate the minimal sum of distances $(i,i+1)$, $(i+1,i+2)$ ...$(j-1,j)$ as a sum of $(j-i)$ different positive numbers. In particular:

$$D_{i,j} \geq \Sigma_{j-i} = (j-i)*(j-i+1)/2$$

Let us now try to estimate the upper bound for $D_{i,j}$ using a similar principle:

$$X_M = X_M - X_1 = D_{1,M} = D_{1,2} + D_{2,3} + \ldots + D_{i-1,i} + D_{i,j} + D_{j,j+1} + \ldots + D_{M-1,M}$$

$$D_{i,j} = X_M - (D_{1,2} + \ldots D_{i-1,i} + D_{j,j+1} + \ldots + D_{M-1,M})$$

Again, all distances must be different so we can estimate the minimal sum of distances $(1,2),...,(i-1,i)$, $(j,j+1)$, ..., $(M-1,M)$. There are $(M-1-j+i)$ different numbers so the upper bound for $D_{i,j}$ can be defined as:

$$D_{i,j} \leq X_M - (M-1-j+i)*(M-j+i)/2$$

The above analysis of the problem deduced three additional redundant constraints that can be added to the base model to improve domain pruning. Figure 19 surveys all the additional constraints.

$$D_{1,2} < D_{M-1,M}$$
$$\forall i<j \ D_{i,j} \geq (j-i)*(j-i+1)/2$$
$$\forall i<j \ D_{i,j} \leq X_M - (M-1-j+i)*(M-j+i)/2$$

Fig. 19. An extension of the model for the Golomb ruler

As we can see from Table 2, the model with redundant constraints pays off and the running times are significantly smaller. For the interested reader, the complete code (SICStus Prolog) of the constraint model with symmetry breaking and redundant constraints is given in Appendix.

Table 2. Running times (in milliseconds on Mobile Pentium 4-M 1.70 GHz, 768 MB RAM) to find out optimal Golomb rulers using different constraint models

size	Base model	Base model + symmetry	Base model + symmetry + redundant constraints
7	220	80	30
8	1 462	611	190
9	13 690	5 438	1 001
10	120 363	49 971	7 011
11	2 480 216	985 237	170 495

Rule of thumb – redundant constraints. From the constraints in the base model we can sometimes deduce some derived constraints that bridge the weak domain pruning. These so called redundant constraints are not necessary to define the solution but if they are added to the base constraint model they can improve domain pruning. On the other hand, propagation via the redundant constraints adds overhead to solving time so one must be careful what and how many redundant constraints are added. A good test for adding redundant constraints can be improved initial pruning. A dual model added to the primal model is a special case of redundant constraints.

As we mentioned in the survey of constraint satisfaction technology, efficiency of problem solving is influenced by the constraint model but also by choosing the right labeling strategy. We achieved the above results (Table 2) by using a labeling strategy which selects the variable with the smallest index for assignment (leftmost variable selection) and which uses the step branching scheme (X=Value ∨ X≠Value). We compared two standard variable selection heuristics, namely fail-first and leftmost variable selection, and three branching schemes, namely enumeration, step labeling, and bisection, on the Golomb ruler problem (Table 3). The combination of the leftmost variable selection with the bisection branching scheme seems to be the best option for solving the Golomb ruler problem. Note that different parameters of the labeling strategy may be more appropriate for other problems. Usually, fail-first in the combination with step branching is used as the first choice.

Table 3. Comparison of variable and value selection heuristics for the Golomb ruler problem (runtime is measured in milliseconds on Mobile Pentium 4-M 1.70 GHz, 768 MB RAM)

size	leftmost			fail first		
	enum	step	bisect	enum	step	bisect
7	30	30	30	40	60	40
8	220	190	200	390	370	350
9	1 182	1 001	921	2 664	2 384	2 113
10	8 782	7 011	6 430	20 870	17 545	14 982
11	209 251	170 495	159 559	1 004 515	906 323	779 851

4   Conclusions

Determining the efficiency of different constraint models is a difficult problem and one which relies upon an understanding of the underlying constraint solver. The best model will be the one in which information is propagated earliest [7]. In this paper, we explained the basics of the constraint technology and we presented several techniques that usually improve efficiency of the constraint models by following the above rule on propagating earliest.

Encapsulating a set of constraints into a global constraint is always the recommended way of modeling especially if the appropriate global constraints are implemented in the system. As we showed, sometimes a global constraint intended to a different application area can be applied to the problem so do not be restricted to the subset of the global constraints for your problem area only.

We have also showed that some parts of the solution (search) space can be removed because the solutions from these parts can be easily reconstructed from other solutions. In particular, including so called symmetry breaking constraints always speeds up the solver because they prevent the solver to explore irrelevant (symmetrical) parts of the search space.

Last but not least we presented the idea of redundant constraints. Redundancy means that these constraints are not necessary to define the solution but they can significantly speed up the solver by improving domain pruning (and thus restricting the search space). One example of adding redundancy to the model is combining the primal model with the dual model where the role of variables and values is swapped. However, redundant constraints add overhead necessary to propagate through them so the user must be careful about using them. Empirical evaluation of the models could be a good guide there.

Acknowledgements

The author is supported by the Czech Science Foundation under the contract No. 201/04/1102 and by the project LN00A056 of the Ministry of Education of the Czech Republic. I would like to thank the anonymous reviewers of the preliminary draft for very useful comments and suggestions.

References

1. Baptiste, P. and Le Pape, C.: Edge-finding constraint propagation algorithms for disjunctive and cumulative scheduling. Proceedings of the Fifteenth Workshop of the U.K. Planning Special Interest Group, 1996.
2. Barták, R.: On-line Guide to Constraint Programming, Prague, 1998.
   http://kti.mff.cuni.cz/~bartak/constraints/
3. Carlsson M., Ottosson G., Carlsson B.: An Open-Ended Finite Domain Constraint Solver. Proceedings Programming Languages: Implementations, Logics, and Programs, Springer-Verlag LNCS 1292, 1997.
4. Freuder, E.C.: In Pursuit of the Holy Grail. Constraints: An International Journal, 2, 57-61, Kluwer, 1997.
5. Golomb rulers: some results, 2003.
   http://www.research.ibm.com/people/s/shearer/grtab.html
6. Kumar, V.: Algorithms for Constraint Satisfaction Problems: A Survey, AI Magazine 13(1): 32-44, 1992.
7. Mariot K. and Stuckey P.J.: Programming with Constraints: An Introduction. The MIT Press, 1998.

8. Régin J.-Ch.: A filtering algorithm for constraints of difference in CSPs. Proceedings of 12th National Conference on Artificial Intelligence, 1994.
9. SICStus Prolog 3.11.2 User's Manual.
10. Smith B.: Reducing Symmetry in a Combinatorial Design Problem. Proceedings of CP-AI-OR2001, pp. 351-359, Wye College, UK, 2001.
11. Tsang, E.: Foundations of Constraint Satisfaction. Academic Press, London, 1995.

Appendix

The following code describes a complete constraint model to solve the Golomb ruler problem of size M. More precisely, the largest problem that we have solved was of size 13 and it took almost eleven hours on Mobile Pentium 4-M 1.70 GHz. The code follows the syntax of constraints and built-in predicates of SICStus Prolog 3.11.2 [9]. For example, SICStus Prolog uses the `all_distinct` constraint that implements the Régin's filtering algorithm while the `all_different` constraint implements a simple propagation where the value is removed from domains after its assignment to some variable. The last comment is about the upper bound for the variables describing marks. As the built-in labeling procedure requires the domains of the labeled variables to be finite we decided to use M^2 as the upper bound for these variables.

```
:-use_module(library(clpfd)).
:-use_module(library(lists)).

golomb(M,Sol):-
    UpperBound is M*M,
    ruler(M,-1,UpperBound,Sol),
    Sol = [0|_],           % set the first mark to 0
    last(Sol,XM),          % find the last mark
    distances(Sol,1,M,XM,Dist),
    all_distinct(Dist),    % distances between marks are diff-
    erent
    (Dist=[DF,_|_] -> last(Dist,DL), DF#<DL ; true),
                           % symmetry breaking
    minimize(labeling([leftmost,bisect],Sol),XM).

% generate variables for marks and post ordering constraints
ruler(0,_,_,[]).
ruler(K,PrevX,UpperBound,[X|Rest]):-
    K>0,
    PrevX#<X, X#=<UpperBound,
    K1 is K-1,!,
    ruler(K1,X,UpperBound,Rest).

% generate distance variables and post redundant constraints
distances([],_,_,_,[]).
distances([X|Rest],I,M,XM,Dist):-
    J is I+1,
    distances_from_x(Rest,X,I,J,M,XM,Dist,RestDist),
    I1 is I+1,!,
    distances(Rest,I1,M,XM,RestDist).
```

```
% compute distances between X_I and the rest marks Y_J,  I<J
% and post redundant constraints for distances
distances_from_x([],_,_,_,_,_,RestDist,RestDist).
distances_from_x([Y|Rest],X,I,J,M,XM,[DXY|Dist],RestDist):-
   DXY #= Y-X,
   LowerBound is integer(((J-I)*(J-I+1))/2),
   LowerBound #=< DXY,
   UpperBoundP is integer(((M-1-J+I)*(M-J+I))/2),
   DXY #=< XM - UpperBoundP,
   J1 is J+1,!,
   distances_from_x(Rest,X,I,J1,M,XM,Dist,RestDist).
```

A Local Search System for Solving Constraint Problems of Declarative Graph-Based Global Constraints

Markus Bohlin

Swedish Institute of Computer Science,
Kista, Sweden
markus.bohlin@sics.se

Abstract. In this paper we present a local search constraint solver in which constraints are expressed using cost functions on graph structures of filter constraints of equal type. A similar theoretical approach has previously been used to model a large number of complex global constraints, which motivates the use of such a model in practice. In a local search context, we view global constraints as complex cost functions, encapsulating the structure of the constraints using a graph of variables, values and filter constraints. This representation gives us a declarative model, which can also be used to efficiently compute a cost as well as conflict levels of the variables in the constraints. We have implemented these ideas in a compositional C++ framework called COMPOSER, which can be used to solve systems of graph-based constraints. We demonstrate the usability of this approach on several well-known global constraints, and show by experimental results on two problems that an approach using a graph basis for global constraint modeling is not only possible in practice, but also competitive with existing constraint-based local search systems.

1 Introduction

The constraint satisfaction problem (CSP) is well-known in computer science. Informally, a CSP instance can be defined as follows: Given a set of variables and a set of constraints on these, is there an assignment to the variables such that all constraints are satisfied? A large amount of scientific activity has been spent on solving generic CSP's. One such approach is *constraint programming*, which has evolved from generic systematic search methods since the late 70's. Unfortunately these methods can for certain problems be very time and space consuming.

Another approach for combinatorial problem solving is to use incomplete methods such as local search. Heuristic methods based on such methods for solving constraint problems have evolved during the last fifteen years, becoming one of the most powerful techniques for solving large combinatorial problems, often outperforming complete algorithms. The classical approach for generic constraint solving in local search is to provide a set of *primitive* constraints for modeling [22]. These constraints can then be combined, typically using logic conjunction, to model the declarative semantics of more complex combinatorial substructures. Unfortunately, for several common combinatorial structures there is no simple model, expressed in primitive constraints only, which is acceptable in terms of space and/or time complexity. Global constraints are present in

D. Seipel et al. (Eds.): INAP/WLP 2004, LNAI 3392, pp. 166–184, 2005.

local search systems to give efficient high-level components capturing such combinatorial substructures. This has been demonstrated in several papers on integrating local search and global constraints [7, 9, 12–14, 16]. One such constraint is the well-known alldiff constraint, restricting a set of variables to take disjoint values. A natural decomposition of this constraint reduces to $n(n-1)/2$ binary inequality constraints, where n is the number of variables. In evaluating the effect of a single variable change to such a set of constraints, one must re-examine all $n-1$ inequality constraints on the changed variable. This is unfortunate, since there are more efficient representations of the alldiff constraints.

In this paper we present a local search constraint solver called COMPOSER (referring to the modeling of constraints using graph components in the system), which uses declarative specifications of global constraints in terms of cost functions on filtered graphs of variables, values and arcs. The basic idea goes back to the article [2] by Beldiceanu, where properties on graphs of the mentioned type are used to model global constraints. To be able to implement cost and conflict computation on such a model, we have modified the graph model of Beldiceanu, mainly by replacing the graph properties of Beldiceanu with cost functions.

As we see it, the main benefit of such a parametrized model of global constraints is that practitioners can easily experiment with different cost functions and combinatorial structures, creating modifications and completely new global constraints with minimum effort. Also, the declarative approach we use is not only well-suited for constraint modeling; the resulting constraints can be evaluated efficiently using incremental algorithms.

1.1   Local Search in COMPOSER

The basic technique of constraint solving in COMPOSER is *iterative repair*, which has previously been used with much success for solving constraint problems [7–9, 14, 16, 21]. A problem is described using a set of integer variables with associated finite domains, and a set of constraints. A solution to a problem, where all constraints are satisfied, is found by modifying a total assignment v of the variables in the problem. The assignment v is iteratively refined by evaluation of a *neighborhood* of *transitions* from v. Typically, the transitions are changes in a single variable assignment, denoted as $v[x \mapsto a]$ where x is a variable and a a value, or variable swaps, where the values of two variables are interchanged. A *cost* is used to rate transitions; a transition with lower or minimal cost is selected for application. In COMPOSER, we use a weighted sum of the individual costs of the constraints in the problem as the cost of an assignment. A default weight of 1 is used if this is not specified. Weights are in practice a necessity in order to compensate for the different sizes of the constraint (in terms of variables) as well as the different number of constraints of a certain type. The main benefit of using a common cost basis is that the different cost functions themselves does not have to be balanced.

To speed up neighborhood evaluation, several local search algorithms first select a promising transition subset using a heuristic of moderate accuracy. This subset can then in turn be evaluated more thoroughly to find a transition to apply. A common way to do this in constraint-based local search is to compute a *conflict level* of the variables in the problem, indicating to which degree the variables are responsible for the cost of the current assignment [7, 14, 16]. A set of transitions on the variables with highest conflict level can then be selected for full evaluation. The basic idea is that the variables that are responsible for most of the cost should be investigated first, since they offer more opportunities for large improvements. A common variation on this is to restrict the neighborhood to variables that have a positive conflict level [9, 15].

Conflict level computation of variables are supported in COMPOSER. On a global level, the conflict level of a variable is computed as the sum of the weighted constraint-specific conflict levels of the variable, using the same constraint weights as in the cost computation. In Section 2.3 we describe a generic method for conflict level computation on our model, distributing the cost of the constraints fairly over the variables.

In general, the conflict level computation is more expensive than the cost computation. However, in COMPOSER the conflict levels of the variables are only needed in preprocessing the neighborhood. Therefore, the conflict computation is only done in the actual application of the selected transition; in evaluating the transitions in the neighborhood, it is sufficient to compute a cost only. The automatic conflict computation can also be manually disabled if not needed, for example in local search algorithm which do not preprocess its neighborhood.

1.2   Related Work

COMPOSER and the local search system Comet [14] has a similar basis in incremental evaluation and iterative improvement. The main difference is that in Comet, global constraints are represented by *differentiable objects*, which are implemented using *invariants* (automatically updated incremental expressions) and an imperative language similar to Java. In COMPOSER, we use a declarative model for constraint modeling, where an explicit graph representation is used. On this representation, we then compute costs and conflicts directly. A constraint is then implemented simply by selecting a set of graph components to use.

Galinier and Hao [9] describes a general constraint solver using local search. The solver handles global constraints including alldiff, capa and nbdiff, and is based on hill-climbing and tabu search. Galinier and Hao give costs for the constraints used in their work and demonstrate it on some combinatorial problems. They also propose to use the minimum number of variables that need to be modified for a constraint to be satisfied as the cost of the constraint.

Codognet and Diaz present the local search algorithm Adaptive Search in [7]. This algorithm takes a CSP on a special form as input, and performs local search using variable swaps and Tabu search. Constraints are represented by *error functions*, computing a cost. The conflict level for a variable x is computed by combination (using a combination function) of the costs of the constraints in which x is present. A *cost function* must also be supplied, which the algorithm tries to minimize. In practice, variations of summation are used as both cost and combination functions.

The main difference between COMPOSER and Adaptive Search is that in the former, a full framework of incremental graph components is available to help the user in global constraint modelling, while in the latter the user has no help from the system, and is forced to re-implement efficient incremental error functions, combination functions and ad-hoc cost functions for use in the algorithm. Also, the user has little or no control of which algorithm to use for solving problems.

Global constraints in local search has also been investigated by Nareyek in [16], using an approach where a selected constraint improves the current assignment in a local manner. He also gives costs for some global constraints including `ordered-tasks` and a version of the `serialized` constraint.

Petit, Régin and Bessière use cost-based filtering for systematic constraint programming [18]. The authors also propose two general cost policies for global constraints. The first is to use the minimum number of variables needed to be modified as the cost. The second is to use the number of violated binary constraints that can be used to represent the global constraint as cost. In our work we extend the second approach to constraints that are hard or impossible to represent using binary constraints only.

It has, since the completion of this work, come to our attention that costs based on graph properties in the framework of [2] have also been discussed more recently by Beldiceanu and Petit [4]. These costs are based purely on the graph properties, and the paper does not address computing conflicts for the variables in the constraints, nor does it investigate incremental cost evaluation and necessary extensions of the model, which allows efficient cost computations. Another difference compared to our work is that we have actually implemented the cost evaluation, and also give empirical results on using it in a local search context.

1.3   Organization

The rest of the article is organized as follows. First, Section 2 gives an overview of the constraint model we use. Section 3 continues with an introduction on how to model constraints in COMPOSER, and presents two example applications, showing that parametrized graph constraint modeling for local search is indeed useful in practice. Finally, Section 4 gives some concluding remarks.

2   The Constraint Model

In a local search context, we define a global constraint as a software component with the following characteristics:

- The constraint is dependent only on the current assignment of a set of variables, and constants passed to the constraint at initialization.
- The constraint produces a non-negative *cost*, reflecting to which level the constraint is violated in the current assignment. This cost must be 0 when the constraint is satisfied.
- The constraint can produce a non-negative *conflict level* for a variable in the constraint, indicating how much of the cost of the constraint the variable causes in the current assignment. The conflict level of each variable must be 0 when the constraint is satisfied.

In addition, since constraint evaluation is done for many transitions in each iteration, the constraints should ideally compute their costs and conflict levels as fast as possible. A global constraint is represented in COMPOSER as a directed graph, which we filter and apply a cost function on. The goal is a constraint cost comparable with the cost of a set of semantically equivalent primitive constraints; this cost measurement has been

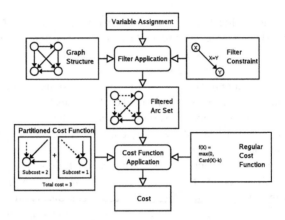

Fig. 1. Illustration of the basic ideas behind the computation of costs for constraints in COMPOSER

used before and is natural for several common global constraints [9, 18], but the main advantage of such a cost is that it is comparable between a large number of constraints. In the COMPOSER system, we describe a global constraint by three components:

1. A *graph structure*, maintaining a set of binary arcs on a set of vertices,
2. A *filter constraint*, filtering the arcs in the graph, and
3. A *cost function*, computing a cost, and optionally conflict levels for the variables.

This division of a global constraint into components gives us an expressive high-level model, which also can be implemented efficiently. The process of computing a cost using modeled constraints is illustrated in Figure 1 and is described in detail in the rest of this section.

2.1   Graph Structures

The graph structure maintains a set of binary arcs on a set of vertices and is used to form a graph of more primitive constraints (called *filter constraints*, see below) for further processing. A graph structure consists of a *vertex generator* and an *arc generator*, where the vertex generator produces vertices for the graph from the arguments to the global constraint — this is the same structure as in the paper of Beldiceanu [2]. Each global constraint has at least one vertex generator. In this paper, we only use identity vertex generators, creating vertices directly from its arguments, and the domain generator, creating as vertices the union of the values in the domains of a set of variables. Which graph structure to use often becomes obvious once we have decided on a filter constraint. For example, if the constraint checks that the number of variables equal to a set of values is within certain boundaries (a cardinality constraint), we would select an equality filter constraint on a graph structure connecting each variable to each value.

Arc generators produce the arcs of the graph. Constraints on binary arcs are quite expressive, and allow modeling of many global constraints [2, 3]. The arc generators we use take either one or two vectors X, W of vertices and produce a set of arcs between these vertices. In this paper, we use only the three arc generators AllUnord, Connect and Bipartite; AllUnord creates arcs between $X[i]$ and $X[j]$ for all integers $i < j$, Connect creates the arcs $(X[i], W[i])$ where $i \in 1..\min(\text{size}(X), \text{size}(W))$,

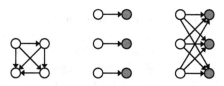

Fig. 2. The three arc generators `AllUnord` (left), `Connect` (middle) and `Bipartite` (right)

and `Bipartite` creates arcs from each vertex $X[i]$, which must be a variable, in the first vector to each vertex in the domain of $X[i]$ in the second vector. These three arc generators are shown in Figure 2. The implementation of the `Bipartite` arc generator is specialized for efficient evaluation of graphs with equality filter constraints. More arc and vertex generators are described in [2, 3] and [5].

2.2   Filter Constraints

A *filter constraint* is a primitive constraint that is applied to the arcs in the graph. The role of a filter constraint is to filter the set of arcs as an intermediate step in computing the cost of the global constraint. This is essentially the same as the elementary constraints of [2]; the difference is that we use filter constraints as a basis for cost computation instead of consistency checking. We use generic binary constraints as filter constraints in this paper. Formally, a filter constraint *fc* is a function taking an arc from the arc set A (produced by the graph structure), and an assignment v for a set of variables X, and returning a Boolean value.

2.3   Costs and Conflict Levels

The cost for a given constraint is formalized by a *cost function cf* of type $AS \rightarrow$ int, where AS is the set of all possible arc sets. In many cases we can construct a cost function directly from a *property p* on the arc set, and a *cost modifier cm*. We refer to such a cost as a *regular cost*. A property $p : AS \rightarrow$ int takes an an arc set and returns an integer — this corresponds roughly to the graph properties of [2], but return a value instead of defining if the constraint is satisfied or not. The properties we use in this paper are the `Card` property, computing the size $|A|$ of an arc set A, and a weighted sum property `WSum`, computing a sum of weights $\sum_{a \in A} w(a)$ for a set of arcs. The cardinality property is useful for constraints whose structure is similar to a decomposition into primitive constraints, and where the consistency is directly dependent on the number of remaining arcs. For constraints where weights are used to determine if the constraint is satisfied, the `WSum` property is often useful. Other properties are used for more complex constraints, but we do not go into detail on this in this paper.

A cost modifier *cm* is a function of type int $\rightarrow$ int, which is applied to the integer result of the property. Cost modifiers are used in those cases where a constraint has a threshold parameter that we need to use in order to check if the constraint is consistent and in computing its cost. The result of the cost modifier application is then returned as the cost of the constraint.

To get a cost that is comparable with other constraint costs, one must select the cost modifier carefully. We use mostly threshold cost modifiers of the type $cm(x) = \max(0, x - k)$ for a constant k, returning the linear distance from the threshold k as cost.

Such costs have been used previously for similar purposes in [9, 14] and fit constraints whose graph structure is closely related to a decomposition into primitive constraints. In other cases for graph structures not directly related to binary decompositions, we use quadratic costs to emulate the cost of a decomposed graph structure.

The conflict level of a variable in a constraint should indicate to which degree the current value of the variable contributes to the cost of the constraint. For a regular cost and a variable x, we use the cost weighted with the ratio between the number of filtered arcs on x and the total number of filtered arcs as conflict level $\text{cl}_c(v,x)$ of the variables; $\text{cl}_c(v,x) = cf(A') \cdot |A'_x|/|A'|$, where A' is the set of filtered arcs, and A'_x is the set of arcs in A' involving x. Note that in the implementation, A' and A'_x are updated incrementally.

Partitioned Costs and Subcosts. Replacing a global constraint with a set of more primitive constraints is an approach which has been used numerous times in the past — for example in local search, see [22]. However, many global constraints have semantics which cannot be efficiently stated by a conjunction of primitive constraints, and often, a regular cost is simply not expressive enough. One example is the gcc constraint[1] of [20]. This constraint takes a set of variables X and two sets of integers L, U of lower and upper bounds, associated to unique values in the union of the domains of the variables in X. gcc is satisfied when, for all values a and an assignment v, the number of variables taking the value a is in the interval (L_a, U_a).

$$\forall a \in \bigcup_{x \in X} \text{dom}(x).L_a \leq |\{x \mid x \in X \land v(x) = a\}| \leq U_a$$

An obvious way to compute a cost for this constraint is to accumulate several costs on the individual values, and then use the sum of these costs as the final cost of the constraint. This technique has been used previously in [9, 14, 15, 19, 21] for similar structures. To be able to express such constructs, we introduce *partitioned costs* cf_Σ and *subcosts*. A partitioned cost consists of a *partition function pf* and a subcost function cf. The partition function *pf* partitions the filtered arc set A' into a vector of disjoint arc subsets $pf(A')$. We then apply the subcost function cf on each arc set in $pf(A')$, and take the sum of the subcosts as the total cost of the constraint; $cf_\Sigma(A') = \sum_{q \in pf(A')} cf(q)$. The subcost can be any normal cost function.

In this paper we only use the Entering partition function, which generate the sets of arcs that all enter the same node x_i. This is usable in situations like the one described for the cardinality family of constraints above. For a partitioned cost, when they are needed, the conflict levels are computed in the subcosts — these are added to form the total conflict level of a variable.

2.4   Incremental Computation

An important characteristic of local search is the efficiency of the cost computation. Typically, a neighbor is constructed by changing the values of a small set of variables. One way of speeding up the cost computation is to take advantage of this small difference between a neighbor and the current solution in the computation of the new cost. This

---

[1] gcc is an abbreviation of *Global Cardinality Constraint*.

is the basis of incremental cost computation; recomputing only the parts of the cost that have actually changed. Incremental computation has been investigated in a general context by Paige and Koenig [17], Alpern et al. [1], and Yellin and Strom [23], as well as for computing local search costs; see for example Michel and Van Hentenryck [14]. The novelty of our work comes from the application of this technique for evaluating declarative models of global constraints.

The incremental evaluation of components in COMPOSER is based on evaluating the change of a single variable assignment. This atomic change can in turn be used to form more complicated changes. For example, value swaps of two variables x, y can be seen as two simultaneous assignments $v[x \mapsto v(y), y \mapsto v(x)]$. For space reasons, we have omitted the details of the incremental updates done in COMPOSER, and focuses on describing the general ideas. We refer the interested reader to [5] for more details.

The basic ideas of the incremental cost and conflict computation of a constraint in COMPOSER is to only evaluate how the cost is affected by addition and removal of arcs due to a changed variable. In addition to this, the total cost and conflict levels are also incrementally updated using finite differencing on the changed costs and conflict levels [17]. Basically, for a transition $v[x \mapsto a]$, where v is the current assignment, x is a variable, a is a value assigned to x, and $a \neq v(a)$, we reapply the filter to those arcs that contain x, and incrementally recompute the affected properties and subcosts, as shown below. Only costs and property values are updated incrementally — the status of filter constraints and cost modifiers are computed more efficiently from scratch.

In doing this for a single constraint, we maintain two sets of added and removed edges respectively. For a regular cost, a new property value can be computed as the old property value p_o and a difference Δp. The common properties used are cardinality and weighted sums, whose differences can easily be recomputed in constant and linear time respectively, as shown in [17]. We can then compute a new cost c_n by application of the cost modifier, so that $c_n = cm(p_o + \Delta p)$.

Next, if they are needed, the conflicts of the vertices are incrementally recomputed. To do this, we also maintain the set of arcs A' satisfying the filter constraint and the partitions A'_x of this set, where for a variable x each arc in A'_x is connected to x. By maintaining and investigating only the arc sets A'_x that have actually changed, we can update the total conflict level efficiently by finite differencing.

A partitioned cost on the other hand is computed as the sum of its subcosts. For a partitioned cost function, we once again can compute a new cost by finite differencing of the changed subcosts. Partitioning the cost of a constraint intelligently can therefore decrease evaluation time considerably. The conflict level of a variable for a partitioned cost is computed as the sum of its subcost conflict levels, and is therefore done in the individual computations of the subcosts.

3   Constraint and Problem Modeling Using COMPOSER

In this section we take a closer look on constraints and combinatorial problem modeling in COMPOSER from a practical point of view. For COMPOSER, all problems were solved using a 1 GHz Pentium III running Linux.

3.1   Constraint Modeling

In this section we will discuss how to model global constraints using the COMPOSER system. More details can be found in [5] and [6]. In COMPOSER, a global constraint is created simply by selecting the graph components used to represent the constraint. As an example of how to model a constraint using COMPOSER, we consider the binarization of the alldiff constraint as presented in Figure 3. Here, a constraint on the variables X is instantiated with a AllUnord graph structure component, which represents arcs between all subsets (x_i, x_j) of variables where $i < j$. An equality filter constraint, VarEqVar, is used, which removes an edge (x_i, x_j) if $v(x_i) \neq v(x_j)$ for an assignment v. Finally, the cardinality of the resulting arc set is used as cost, using the Card property and an implicit identity cost modifier.

```
constraint alldiff (vec[var] X) {
    structure  = AllUnord(X);
    filter     = VarEqVar;
    cost       = Card;
}
```

Fig. 3. The primitive alldiff constraint

Although the model from Figure 3 for alldiff is concise and natural, it has one drawback. It is essentially a decomposition of the constraint into $n(n-1)/2$ binary inequalities, where n is the number of variables. The space complexity of $O(n^2)$ and incremental time complexity of $O(b \cdot n)$, where b is the number of variable changes, is naturally the same as for the decomposition.

However, we can do better than this, given that a efficient implementation of the alldiff constraint should have a space complexity of $O(n+m)$ and an incremental time complexity of $O(b)$, where m is the total number of values for all variables. For structures similar to the alldiff constraint, a bipartite graph can be used, where one partition is the variable nodes, and the other is the set of possible values [9, 14, 15, 19, 21]. The edges of the graph then correspond to assignments. In such a model we can update the cost efficiently by keeping track of the number of variables that are connected to a single value. In COMPOSER we can model the alldiff constraint in this way using the Bipartite graph structure. The model can also be extended to a more generic gcc constraint, shown in Figure 4. In this constraint, two integer arrays L and U are given to the constraint, which are used in the subcost for the value node i to compute $q(\max(0, L[i] - p_i, p_i - U[i]))$, where $q(x) = x(x-1)/2$ and p_i is the number of final arcs connected to i — this is equal to the number of variables taking the value i.

3.2   The n-Queens Problem

In this section we will investigate models and algorithms for solving the n-queens problem, a classical combinatorial puzzle that has been used extensively as an example in the constraint community. In this problem, n queens are to be placed on a chessboard of dimension $n \times n$ so that no queen can attack another queen.

```
constraint gcc (vec[var] X, vec[int] L, vec[int] U) {
   structure   = Bipartite(X);
   filter      = VarEqC;
   cost        = Entering;
   subcost[i]  = QuadBetween(L[i],U[i]);
   property    = Card;
}
```

Fig. 4. A bipartite `gcc` constraint with subcosts

```
Model model;
statevector Q(Queens,"Queen_",0,Queens-1);
vector<int> pos(fromto(0,Queens-1)), neg(fromto(Queens-1,0));
alldiff(model,&Q); alldiff(model,&Q,pos); alldiff(model,&Q,neg);
model.close();
```

Fig. 5. A first model of the n-queens problem

```
constraint alldiff (vec[var] Y, vec[int] M) {
   structure = Bipartite(Y);
   filter    = VarPlusEqC(M) ;
   cost      = Entering ;
   subcost   = QuadAtmostC<1> ;
   property  = Card ;
}
```

Fig. 6. A bipartite `alldiff` constraint with an offset vector M

A Constraint Model. We have solved the n-queens problem in two different ways —
one using a simple assignment neighborhood, and one using a more elaborate swap
neighborhood. Both models are similar in that each queen is represented by a state
variable with domain $0..n-1$. In the first model, shown in Figure 5, we use three
`alldiff` constraints to model that no queen may attack another queen. The `alldiff`
variant with a third argument states that for all variable pairs (x_i, x_j) in Q where $i \neq j$,
the constraint $x_i + m_i \neq x_j + m_j$ should hold where $m_i, m_j \in M$.

In Figure 6, this `alldiff` constraint with offset is modeled in COMPOSER. Note
that similar ideas has been used previously in [7, 14, 15, 21]. The new model is obtained
simply by replacing the filter constraint VarEqC of the original `alldiff` (equal to
$v(x) = i$) with an equality filter constraint using an offset, VarPlusEqC (equal to $v(x) +$
$M[x] = i$). This shows quite clearly the expressiveness of the global constraint modeling
approach of COMPOSER. The cost of this new model of the `alldiff` constraint can
also be represented using $O(n + m)$ space and updated in $O(1)$ time for a single variable
change.

A First Local Search Algorithm. The local search algorithm for the first model of the
n-queens problem is depicted in Figure 7, and is basically the same cost minimization
variation of the min-conflicts procedure [15] found in [14]. The procedure first selects

```
while(model.violation()!=0) {
    int Q = model.getMaxConflicting();
    int V = model.getMinCostValue(Q);
    model.assign(Q,V);
}
```

Fig. 7. Local search algorithm for the n-queens puzzle using steepest descent

Table 1. Experimental results of 11 runs of the n-Queens Problem using Comet (left, from [14]) and using COMPOSER with cost minimization (middle) and cost improvement (right)

	Comet		COMPOSER			
	(minimize)		minimize		improve	
Size n	Sec.	Iter.	Sec.	Iter.	Sec	Iter.
512	0.72	304	0.31	326	0.19	562
1024	2.35	628	1.10	582	0.62	1112
2048	7.50	1100	4.64	1072	2.55	2212
4096	25.51	2092	19.17	2088	10.60	4383
8192	92.07	4040	74.44	4043	43.55	8739
16384	348.58	7968	294.47	7972	178.02	17577
32768	1362.53	15899	1181.63	15924	725.12	35136

a queen with maximum number of conflicts, and then assigns this queen to the position which minimizes the cost. Ties are broken at random. It is worth noting that COMPOSER updates all relevant costs and conflicts automatically in assigning a variable to a value.

We also tried a cost improvement variation, where the first position yielding an improvement in cost was selected. This was implemented simply by using the method getImprovingValue instead of getMinCostValue.

Results. In Table 1 we show the median solution times obtained by running n-queens 11 times for each instance, using our first model. The left column for COMPOSER report times when using the cost minimization strategy shown in Figure 7. This strategy is also used in obtaining the results for Comet [14]. The right COMPOSER column shows the results of using a cost improvement strategy, selecting the first value decreasing the current cost of the assignment. Results for the problem on 256 queens or less were all below 90 ms. for COMPOSER and 290 ms. for Comet.

The results of Table 1 for COMPOSER are clearly competitive with the Comet results on a 1.1 GHz computer, as reported in [14] and shown in the table. As can be seen, for very similar algorithms using cost minimization, COMPOSER has a clear advantage over Comet in all tested instances of the problem. The iteration results are nearly identical on the larger problem instances, which is not surprising considering the similarities between the algorithms used. When considering a cost improvement strategy, the iteration results are roughly doubled for COMPOSER compared with the minimization results, but the execution times have been reduced by almost 40% on the largest problem instance. The results of Table 1 are not directly comparable to those reported by Codognet and Diaz in [7], due to different neighborhoods.

A Swap-Based Local Search Algorithm. The results presented in the previous section are clearly competitive with those reported using other systems. However, previous work on the n-queens problem indicates that a variable swap neighborhood can yield excellent results [7, 9, 21]. If we initialize the queens as a random permutation of 0..Queens -1 and always use swaps between two variables as the transition, it is easy to see that the first alldiff constraint of Figure 5 becomes redundant, since it will be satisfied in all visited assignments. Thus, the second model only differs from the first in that we remove the first constraint, and use a randomized permutation instead of an assignment in the initialization.

```
int Qi,Qj,oldV,iter;
Tabuvector tabu(model.arity(),&iter);
for(iter=0; model.violation()!=0; iter++) {
  Qi = model.getMaxConflicting(tabu);
  Qj = model.getMinCostSwapWith(Qi,tabu);
  oldV = model.violation();
  model.swap(Qi,Qj);
  if(model.violation() >= oldV) tabu.insert(Qi,Tenure);
}
```

Fig. 8. Local search algorithm for the n-queens puzzle using variable swaps

In the new algorithm, we begin each iteration by selecting a queen s with maximum number of conflicts; ties are broken at random. We then find the set of queens t minimizing the resulting cost of swapping queen s and t. Next, we select one of these queens at random, denote this queen as t', and swap the positions of s and t'. We also use a tabu component from COMPOSER to diversify the search on plateaus and to escape local minima [10]. The tabu component for this problem is a vector T of size n, where element T_i stores the iteration when queen i was marked as tabu. This arrangement makes it possible to check if a queen q_i is tabu in constant time, simply by checking the current iteration count against T_i. A similar Tabu structure was introduced in [9] for the progressive party problem. The code for solving the second model is presented in Figure 8. The lines

```
Qi = model.getMaxConflicting(tabu);
Qj = model.getMinCostSwapWith(Qi,tabu);
```

first selects a variable Qi with maximum number of conflicts. We disregard variables that are tabu, and break ties at random. We then select a second random variable Qj, for which swapping Qi and Qj yields the least violation possible. Once again we disregard variables declared as tabu. Finally, the lines

```
oldV = model.violation();
model.swap(Qi,Qj);
if(model.violation() >= oldV) tabu.insert(Qi,Tenure);
```

first save the previous violation of the model, and then commits to the value swap between Qi and Qj. If the new violation is greater or equal to the previous one, we declare Qi tabu. We use a tabu tenure of 10, determined by minor experimentation.

Table 2. Experimental results of 11 runs of the *n*-Queens Problem using the second model and conflict minimization

Size *n*	Adaptive Search (minimize)		COMPOSER			
			minimize		improve	
	Sec.	Iter.	Sec.	Iter.	Sec	Iter.
512	0.06	116	0.03	111	0.01	237
1024	0.22	216	0.12	217	0.02	482
2048	0.82	409	0.67	418	0.09	986
4096	3.23	805	4.03	817	0.31	1984
8192	13.12	1577	19.29	1601	1.20	3959
16384	59.25	3118	83.55	3163	8.78	7981
32768	276.09	6215	349.41	6287	49.29	15942

Previous work on the *n*-queens puzzle has been successful in using a first-descent strategy instead of cost minimization [21]. We therefore modified our search procedure to select an improvement immediately if one existed. The new procedure is equal to the one shown in Figure 8 except that we use the method getImprovingSwapWith to select a second queen. This method works exactly as the one above, except that as soon as a swap which improves the current violation is found, the method returns with this one immediately.

Results. The results of the swap-based steepest-descent algorithm is shown in Table 2, together with results obtained by using the *Adaptive Search* algorithm from [7] on the same computer as the one running COMPOSER. The Adaptive Search framework uses a similar basic model as COMPOSER; the main difference is that in Adaptive Search, each constraint is defined by an *error function*, which has to be implemented by the user. Therefore, the Adaptive Search procedure cannot be adapted without programming skills to new constraints, whereas COMPOSER allows a significantly more user-friendly, declarative specification of constraints.

The reported times for both systems were acquired on the same computer, and are median results of 11 runs. We can see that using COMPOSER with cost minimization, similar to what is used in Adaptive Search [7], is overall marginally slower. This is a result of the declarative model of constraints using an explicit graph structure used in COMPOSER, which imposes a small but not negligible overhead in execution time.

The results on the *n*-queens problem show that using a generic graph-based framework for global constraints is competitive with results previously obtained using local search in [14] and [7]. The results of the modified cost improvement algorithm, shown in the right COMPOSER column of Table 2, also support this. As before, the number of iterations has increased, but the runtime of the new algorithm is overall significantly smaller than the cost minimizing algorithm.

In [15], the conflict minimization strategy is claimed to solve the *n*-queens problem in linear number of iterations. The random queen initialization used in our work makes it difficult to compare the results of Table 2 with the results obtained in [15], where a heuristic preprocessing stage is used. Also, the results presented in [15] is expressed only in number of *repairs* (corresponding to iterations), whereas we express our results in both solution time and iterations. An $O(n)$ time complexity of a repair is also noted

Table 3. Configuration of the Progressive Party Problem. Each boat i has a total capacity k_i (the total number of people allowed on board at the same time), and a crew size c_i. The spare capacity s_i of a boat is formed by subtracting the crew size from the total capacity, $s_i = k_i - c_i$

i	k_i	c_i	s_i	i	k_i	c_i	s_i	i	k_i	c_i	s_i	i	K_i	c_i	s_i	i	k_i	c_i	s_i	i	k_i	c_i	s_i	i	K_i	c_i	s_i
1	6	2	4	7	12	4	8	13	8	4	4	19	8	4	4	25	7	2	5	31	6	2	4	37	6	4	2
2	8	2	6	8	10	1	9	14	8	2	6	20	8	2	6	26	7	2	5	32	6	2	4	38	6	5	1
3	12	2	10	9	10	2	8	15	8	3	5	21	8	4	4	27	7	4	3	33	6	2	4	39	9	7	2
4	12	2	10	10	10	2	8	16	12	6	6	22	8	5	3	28	7	5	2	34	6	2	4	40	0	2	-2
5	12	4	8	11	10	2	8	17	8	2	6	23	7	4	3	29	6	2	4	35	6	2	4	41	0	3	-3
6	12	4	8	12	10	3	7	18	8	2	6	24	7	4	3	30	6	4	2	36	6	2	4	42	0	4	-4

Table 4. Progressive Party Problem analysis for different host configurations

Instance	Host boats	h	g	ratio	Instance	Host boats	h	g	ratio
1	1-12,16	100	92	0.92	7	1-11,21,22	94	92	0.98
2	1-13 (orig.)	98	94	0.96	8	1-9,16-18,22	92	90	0.98
3	1,3-13,19	96	92	0.96	9	1-9,15-17,22	91	89	0.98
4	3-13,25,26	98	94	0.96	10	1-11,22,23	93	92	0.99
5	1-11,19,21	95	93	0.98	11	1,3-11,21-23	91	90	0.99
6	1-9,16-19	93	91	0.98					

in [15]. This is equal to the complexity of evaluating all transition in one iteration of our solution. As can be seen, the time and iteration results in Table 2 are also consistent with these observations.

3.3   The Progressive Party Problem

The progressive party problem is a well-known benchmark problem in the constraint programming community, and have been used in several generic constraint-based local search methods as well [9, 14, 22]. The problem can be described informally as follows. An evening party is to be organized in the setting of a yachting rally. The organizers have decided that the *guest boats* will visit the organizers' boats (the *host boats*) in turn, where the crew of a host boat stays aboard and serves the guests on the visiting guest boats. Every 30 minutes, each guest boat will move to a different host boat. This will go on for a given number of time periods. The organizers have also decided that no guest boat has to visit the same host boat twice, and that two crews must never meet more than once. In Table 3 the different boats and their crews and capacities are shown. We also show the *spare capacities* of each boat, which is simply the number of guests that can safely be taken aboard.

The Model. We have solved the progressive party problem using global constraints in COMPOSER. The problem instances we have considered are listed in Table 4, where the first 6 instances are well-known and previously studied in a local search context [9, 14]. Instance 7 to 11 are new and has not been investigated as far as we know. Also, we have tried to solve the progressive party problem for as many time periods as possible; the constrainedness of the problem increases significantly with each additional time period.

```
statematrix boat(P,G); vector<state*> X(P),Y(P); int p,i,j;
for(p=0;p<P;p++)  capa(model,boat(p),size,spare);
for(i=0;i<G;i++) {
  for(j=0;j<P;j++)  X[j] = boat(j,i);
  alldiff(model,&X);
}
for(i=0;i<G;i++) {
  for(j=i+1;j<G;j++) {
    for(p=0;p<P;p++)  X[p]=boat(p,i), Y[p]=boat(p,j);
    nbdiff(model,&X,&Y);
  }
}
```

Fig. 9. A model of the progressive party problem

```
constraint capa (vec[var] Y, vec[int] C, vec[int] K) {
    structure   = Bipartite(Y);
    filter      = VarEqC;
    cost        = Entering;
    subcost[i]  = AtmostVariant(K[i]);
    property    = WSum1<WVector>(C);
}
```

Fig. 10. A bipartite capa constraint with subcosts

Figure 9 contains the model, similar to the one used in [8] and [14], that we used in solving the problem. A matrix of state variables boat of dimension $p \times g$, where p is the number of periods to run the problem, and g is the number of guests available, represents the guest boats; boat(i,j) holds the host boat that guest j visits in period i. We also use the auxiliary vectors size, which hold the crew size of the guests, and spare which hold the spare capacities of the host boats.

The constraint model consists of three types of modeled global constraints, which were also used in [9, 14]. First, the capa constraint states that for all time periods, the capacity of the host boats most be respected. The capa constraint is actually a restricted version of a general weighted cardinality constraint (which is also easily expressed using COMPOSER), and is shown in Figure 10. This constraint is equivalent with the inequalities $\forall i. \sum_{v(x)=i} w_x \leq c_i$. The nbdiff constraint states that in the two vectors X and Y, at most $k = 1$ pairs (x_i, y_i) may be equal.

A Local-Search Algorithm. The local search procedure used is presented in Figure 11 and was inspired heavily by the two algorithms in [9] and [14]. In short, we use a simple modification of the hill-climbing algorithm, in which the best move is always selected and where ties are broken randomly. As before we use the single-assign neighborhood and a tabu structure, this time over the variables *and* values, to diverge the search. This Tabu structure was proposed by Galinier and Hao in [8]. As parameters we use a tabu tenure of initially 2. This tenure is increased or decreased as the search proceeds, in order to allow exploration of new assignments. We also use a limited backtracking mechanism to improve performance on very hard problem instances. Every time an new best assignment is found, an assignment memory is cleared and initialized by the line

```
model.hist_clear(); model.hist_store();
```

The assignment history component also keeps track of the frequency of the assignments. Whenever `Backtrack` transitions have been done, an assignment in the memory is chosen with probability inversely proportional to the frequency of the assignment. The search then backtracks to this assignment. This will ensure a restart from a good assignment, and also that all currently best assignments are kept in memory for future backtracking reference.

We also use a mechanism restarting from scratch whenever `MaxTries` iterations have passed. We added this feature when we noted that the search got stranded in areas where no improvement was possible. With the restarting mechanism, we were able to get the local search to terminate with a solution in every sample run of every instances of the problem tested.

Results. The resulting median CPU times and iterations of 101 sample runs of PPP are shown in Table 5 and 6, together with results from [14] for the Comet system. Note that in [14], the results of the first two instances has been interchanged [11] — this is reflected in the table. For the first 6 host configurations we see a clear improvement over the results reported in [9, 14, 22] using similar neighborhoods. In CPU seconds COMPOSER is significantly faster than Comet on all problem instances. The results of Galinier and Hao [9] on the original instance using a variable assignment neighborhood is not directly comparable with the COMPOSER results due to different hardware configurations, but COMPOSER is nearly 5 times faster than the results of 67.5 seconds on the largest problem instance from [9], for the original host configuration on a 134 MHz Sun ULTRA

```
int G,H,iter,bestsofar=model.violation()+1,nonimproving,oldV;
Tabumatrix(model.arity(),Hosts,&iter,&bestsofar);
for(iter=0; model.violation()!=0; iter++) {
  oldV = model.violation();
  G = model.getMaxConflicting();
  H = model.getMinCostValue(tabu);
  model.assign(G,H); tabu.insert(G,H,Tenure);
  if(model.violation() < oldV && Tenure > 2) Tenure --;
  if(model.violation() >= oldV && Tenure < TLimit) Tenure ++;
  if(model.violation() < bestsofar) {
    model.hist_clear(); model.hist_store(); nonimproving=0;
  } else {
    nonimproving++;
    if(model.violation()==bestsofar) model.hist_store();
  }
  if(nonimproving>Backtrack) model.hist_restoreProportional();
  if(iter>MaxTries) model.randomAssign();
}
```

Fig. 11. The search procedure for the progressive party problem

Table 5. Median CPU time of 101 runs of the Progressive Party Problem

Hosts/Periods	COMPOSER								Comet				
	3	4	5	6	7	8	9	10	6	7	8	9	10
1-12, 16	0.02	0.04	0.06	0.10	0.18	0.31	0.69	5.23	0.61	0.90	1.17	4.41	21.00
1-13 (orig.)	0.09	0.16	0.27	0.27	0.58	2.51	14.9		0.98	1.64	5.13	90.19	
1, 3-13, 19	0.05	0.10	0.15	0.27	0.57	2.28	22.2		0.90	1.53	5.28	253.92	
3-13, 25, 26	0.06	0.11	0.19	0.31	0.66	2.52	20.8		1.21	1.81	7.02	82.66	
1-11, 19, 21	0.11	0.20	0.40	1.14	6.94				4.50	24.35			
1-9, 16-19	0.13	0.26	0.55	1.81	18.3				6.20	161.16			
1-11, 21, 22	0.11	0.22	0.47	1.41	46.1								
1-9, 16-18, 22	0.13	0.24	0.61	2.26	118								
1-9, 15-17, 22	0.14	0.31	1.11	49.5									
1-11, 22, 23	0.51	4.46											
1, 3-11, 21-23	0.62	3.03											

Table 6. Median iterations of 101 runs of the Progressive Party Problem using COMPOSER

Hosts/Periods	3	4	5	6	7	8	9	10
1-12, 16	62	103	165	256	456	832	1862	13248
1-13 (orig.)	249	430	729	729	1572	6634	37226	
1, 3-13, 19	144	266	405	736	1570	6206	55262	
3-13, 25, 26	164	284	508	841	1812	6609	51681	
1-11, 19, 21	300	559	1143	3256	17853			
1-9, 16-19	372	735	1540	4927	46298			
1-11, 21, 22	298	595	1332	3929	116239			
1-9, 16-18, 22	348	665	1765	6511	291119			
1-9, 15-17, 22	398	885	3162	124017				
1-11, 22, 23	1479	11532						
1, 3-11, 21-23	1780	8090						

1. On the other hand, for 8 time periods, COMPOSER is actually slower than the 1.7 seconds reported in [9]. The reader should note that in the paper by Galinier and Hao, the algorithm for solving PPP for p time periods reuses the solution found for $p-1$ time periods; this can reduce solution time significantly. Comparing iterations, Galinier and Hao also reports 51507 iterations for 9 time periods using reuse solving, which is roughly comparable with the 37226 iterations of COMPOSER. Iterations are not reported for PPP in [14]. The results reported in our work and those reported in [22] are not directly comparable, since Walser uses linear constraints exclusively to model PPP. Also, Galinier and Hao uses an extended neighborhood using variable swaps in [8], which yields excellent results. Due to the different neighborhoods, the results of Table 5 and 6 cannot be directly compared with those reported in [8] for variable swaps.

It is important to note that the local search algorithm does not differ in any substantial way from those used in [9] and [14]. This clearly shows the feasibility of graph-based constraint modeling.

4   Conclusions

In this paper, we presented a particular declarative approach for constraint modeling and implementation using a modified version of the framework of Beldiceanu [2] where global constraints are represented using graph structures, filters, and cost functions. The main point of such a declarative approach for constraint modeling is that it allows great flexibility in experimenting with modification and creation of new constraints — this at a low run-time overhead. In our declarative constraint model, global constraints are parametrized over three main properties of their structure; their *graph structure*, *filter constraint* and *cost components*. Using this parametrization, we have modeled several useful global constraints using COMPOSER. We also showed, by solving two hard combinatorial problems using local search, that evaluating costs and conflict levels for an explicit graph representation of such constraints is not only feasible, but that this model is also highly competitive with existing approaches for constraint modeling and solving.

References

[1] B. Alpern, R. Hoover, B. K. Rosen, P. F. Sweeney, and F. K. Zadeck. Incremental evaluation of computational circuits. In *Proceedings of the First Annual ACM-SIAM Symposium on Discrete Algorithms*, pages 32–42, San Francisco, California, January 1990.

[2] N. Beldiceanu. Global constraints as graph properties on a structured network of elementary constraints of the same type. In *Proc. CP2000*, pages 52–66, 2000.

[3] N. Beldiceanu. Global constraints as graph properties on structured networks of elementary constraints of the same type. Technical Report 2000/01-SE, SICS, 2000.

[4] N. Beldiceanu and T. Petit. Cost evaluation of soft global constraints. In J.-C. Régin and M. Rueher, editors, *Proc. CPAIOR 2004, Nice, France*, pages 80 – 95, April 2004.

[5] M. Bohlin. *Design and Implementation of a Graph-Based Constraint Model for Local Search*. Philosophy Licentiate Thesis No. 27, Mälardalen University, April 2004.

[6] M. Bohlin, W. Kocjan, and P. Kreuger. Designing global scheduling constraints for local search: A generic approach. Technical Report T2002-20, SICS, 2002.

[7] P. Codognet and D. Diaz. Yet another local search method for constraint solving. In *SAGA*, pages 73–90, 2001.

[8] P. Galinier and J.-K. Hao. Solving the progressive party problem by local search. In S. Voss, S. Martello, I. Osman, and C. Roucairol, editors, *Meta-heuristics: Advances and Trends in Local Search Paradigms for Optimization*, chapter 29, pages 418–432. Kluwer, 1998.

[9] P. Galinier and J.-K. Hao. A general approach for constraint solving by local search. In *Proc. CP-AI-OR'00*, Paderborn, Germany, March 2000.

[10] F. Glover and M. Laguna. Tabu search. In C. R. Reeves, editor, *Modern Heuristic Techniques for Combinatorial Optimization*, chapter 3, pages 70–150. McGraw-Hill, 1995.

[11] L. Michel. Personal communication, September 2003.

[12] L. Michel and P. V. Hentenryck. Localizer: A modeling language for local search. In *Principles and Practice of Constraint Programming*, pages 237–251, 1997.

[13] L. Michel and P. V. Hentenryck. Localizer++: An open library for local search. Technical Report CS-01-02, Brown University, January 2001.

[14] L. Michel and P. V. Hentenryck. A constraint-based architecture for local search. In *17th ACM OOPSLA Conference*, November 2002.

[15] S. Minton, M. D. Johnston, A. B. Philips, and P. Laird. Minimizing conflicts: a heuristic repair method for constraint satisfaction and scheduling problems. *Artificial Intelligence*, 58(1–3):161–205, 1992.

[16] A. Nareyek. Using global constraints for local search. In *Proc. DIMACS Workshop on Constraint Programming and Large Scale Discrete Optimization*, pages 1–18, 1998.

[17] R. Paige and S. Koenig. Finite differencing of computable expressions. *ACM Transactions on Programming Languages and Systems*, 4(3):402–454, July 1982.

[18] T. Petit, J.-C. Regin, and C. Bessiere. Specific filtering algorithms for over-constrained problems. In *Proceedings of the 7th International Conference on Principles and Practice of Constraint Programming*, pages 451–463. Springer-Verlag, 2001.

[19] J.-C. Régin. A filtering algorithm for constraints of difference in CSPs. In *Proc. 12th National Conference on AI*, pages 362–367, Seattle, Washington, 1994.

[20] J.-C. Régin. Generalized arc consistency for global cardinality constraint. In *Proc. 13th National Conference on AI*, volume 1, pages 209–215, Portland, August 1996.

[21] R. Sosic and J. Gu. Efficient local search with conflict minimization: A case study of the n-queens problem. *IEEE Trans. Knowledge and Data Eng.*, 6(5):661–668, Oct. 1994.

[22] J. P. Walser. *Integer Optimization by Local Search*, volume 1637 of *Lecture Notes in Artificial Intelligence*. Springer, 1999.

[23] D. Yellin and R. Strom. INC: a language for incremental computations. *SIGPLAN Not.*, 23(7):115–124, 1988.

Realising the Alternative Resources Constraint

Armin Wolf and Hans Schlenker

Fraunhofer FIRST, Kekuléstraße 7, D-12489 Berlin, Germany
{Armin.Wolf, Hans.Schlenker}@first.fraunhofer.de

Abstract. Alternative resource constraint problems have to be solved in practical applications where several resources are available for the activities to be scheduled. In this paper, we present a modular approach to solve such problems which is based on single resource constraints. Furthermore, we present a new sweeping algorithm which performs some "global" overload checking for the alternative resource constraint problem. To our knowledge, this is the first presentation where "sweeping", a well-known technique in computational geometry, was used to perform this checking efficiently.

For a practical evaluation of our approach, we implemented and integrated it into our Java constraint engine `firstcs`. We compared our implementation with the more general `disjoint2` constraint in SICStus Prolog on some benchmark problems: the publicly available *random placement problems (RPP)*.

1 Introduction

Constraint Programming (CP) is the major declarative approach for solving real-world planning and optimisation problems efficiently. With CP, the real-world problem is modelled as a Constraint Satisfaction Problem (CSP) which is solved by general purpose propagation methods. In scheduling situations like course timetabling, medical tool use, or the allocation of railway tracks, we always have to deal with *resources* (e.g. machines) that have to be assigned to activities (e.g. courses or surgeries) exclusively.

Most resource allocation problems can be mapped into a discrete, two-dimensional space where a point (X, Y) represents the usage of a resource Y at time X. Thus, the usage of a resource for some duration can be described as a set of time points. Since each activity is assigned exactly one resource Y for its duration, i.e. some consecutive time points, a task is often geometrically interpreted as a *rectangle*. Thus, the problem of finding an exclusive allocation of tasks to resources can be seen as finding a *rectangle placement* such that any two rectangles do not overlap.

Often, the tasks have to be assigned to any one of a set of *alternative* resources. In CP, there are two main approaches to solve such alternative resource scheduling problems: either by an extension of some single resource constraints [1] or by abstraction and application of a more general non-overlapping

D. Seipel et al. (Eds.): INAP/WLP 2004, LNAI 3392, pp. 185–199, 2005.
© Springer-Verlag Berlin Heidelberg 2005

rectangles constraint. Recent publications [3, 8] have shown that for both kinds of constraints some efficient pruning techniques based on "sweeping" [6] exist.

In this paper, we combine both approaches: the extension and application of pruning algorithms developed for single resource constraints [8] and the development of a new sweeping algorithm for a non-overlapping rectangle constraint. This algorithm performs some overload checks for the early detection of some inconsistency after the application of the pruning algorithms.

2   The Alternative Resource Constraint Problem

Informally, the alternative resource constraint problem is the problem of finding an allocation of non-interruptible tasks to be processed on one of its alternative resources such that they do not overlap on any resource. More formally, the problem is defined as follows:

Definition 1 (Task). *A task t is a non-interruptible activity having a non-empty finite set of potential start times $S_t \subset \mathbb{Z}$, i.e. an integer set which is the domain of its variable start time. Furthermore, a task t has a non-empty finite set of possible durations $D_t \subset \mathbb{N}$, i.e. a positive integer set which is the domain of its variable duration. Finally, a task t has a non-empty finite set of alternative resources $R_t \subset \mathbb{Z}$, i.e. an integer set which is the domain of its variable resource.*

Definition 2 (Alternative Resource Constraint Problem). *Given a finite set of tasks $T = \{t_0, \ldots, t_n\}$ with at least two elements ($n > 0$). An alternative resource constraint problem is determined by such a set of tasks T. The problem is to find a solution, i.e. some start times $s(t_0) \in S_{t_0}, \ldots, s(t_n) \in S_{t_n}$, some durations $d(t_1) \in D_{t_1}, \ldots, d(t_n) \in D_{t_n}$ and some resources $r(t_1) \in R_{t_1}, \ldots, r(t_n) \in R_{t_n}$ such that for $1 \le i < j \le n$ it holds*

$$s(t_i) + d(t_i) \le s(t_j) \lor s(t_j) + d(t_j) \le s(t_i) \lor r(t_i) \ne r(t_j) \ .$$

An alternative resource constraint problem is solvable *if there is such a solution and* unsolvable, *otherwise.*[1]

Assuming that the durations are fixed and the (average) size of all sets of potential start times is m and of all sets of alternative resources is k, the determination of a solution has in general an exponential time complexity of $O(m^n k^n)$. To deal with this exponential complexity in CP, *propagation* is used: An iteration over efficient (polynomial) algorithms pruning the variables' domains such that some – ideally all – values are eliminated not belonging to any solution.

Our aim is the development and implementation of such algorithms for alternative resource constraint problems. Keeping in mind that an alternative resource constraint problem corresponds to a conjunction of single resource constraint problems if the resource domains are singular, i.e. if

$$|R_{t_1}| = \cdots = |R_{t_n}| = 1$$

---

[1] Empty or singleton sets of tasks would define trivial problems.

holds, our work focuses on an generalisation of our previous work performed for *non-preemptive one-machine constraint problems* (cf. [8] following the sugges-tions in [1]). Therefore, in the following, we will use *integer intervals*:

Definition 3 (Integer Intervals). *Given two integers* $n, m \in \mathbb{Z}$ *we define*

$$[n, m] := \begin{cases} \emptyset & \text{if } n > m, \\ \{k \in \mathbb{Z} \mid n \leq k \leq m\} & \text{otherwise.} \end{cases}$$

3   Forbidden Regions

Given a single resource constraint problem determined by a set of tasks T. A *forbidden region* of a task $t \in T$ to be scheduled on a resource r is an integer interval I such that for any start time $s(t) \in I$ it is impossible to schedule another task $u \in T \setminus \{t\}$ on the same resource r either before or after the task t (see Figure 1).

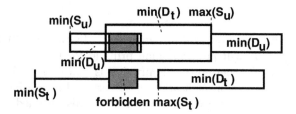

Fig. 1. A forbidden region of a task t with respect to another task u

Assuming that all tasks in T must be scheduled on the same resource r, the application of the pruning rule

$$\forall t \in T \; \forall u \in T \setminus \{t\} \; :$$
$$S'_t := S_t \setminus \bigcup_{u \in T \setminus \{t\}} [\max(S_u) - \min(D_t) + 1, \min(S_u) + \min(D_u) - 1] \quad (1)$$

removes the *forbidden regions* for each task $t \in T$ from its domain of potential start times with respect to all other tasks $u \in T \setminus \{t\}$.

The updated start times S'_t of the task t (primed to emphasise the possible change)[2] will prune the search space correctly (cf. [8] for the correctness poof.)

Considering an alternative resource constraint problem, this means that *after* an allocation of all tasks to their resources this pruning rule and all the other rules presented in [1, 8] are applicable. However, any pruning and consistency checks must be delayed until all tasks' resources are determined. This seems to be rather late and contradicts the principle of *early pruning* in CP. Therefore, we investigated in a generalisation of the pruning rule (1) for alternative resource constraint problems. The result of this investigation is presented in the following:

---

[2] By convention, any update of a set M is emphasised by a prime, i.e. M'.

Definition 4. *Given an alternative resource constraint problem determined by a set of tasks T. Then, for each task $t \in T$ and every resource $r \in R_t$, we define:*

- *a non-empty, finite set of alternative start times $S_t^r := S_t$,*

Now the pruning rule (1) will be generalised. Therefore, let $R := \bigcup_{t \in T} R_t$ be all allocatable resources, $T_r := \{p \in T \mid r \in R_p\}$ be the tasks that may be scheduled on the resource $r \in R$ and $A_r := \{q \in T \mid R_q = \{r\}\}$ be the tasks already allocated on the resource $r \in R$.

If a task t is allocated or may be scheduled on a resource r and the forbidden region of this task t with respect to all other already scheduled tasks u on r will prune the potential start times of t, i.e. the task t cannot be scheduled at start times in these forbidden regions on the resource r:

$$\forall r \in R \, \forall t \in T_r : \tag{2}$$
$$S'^r_t := S^r_t \setminus \bigcup_{u \in A_r \setminus \{t\}} [\max(S^r_u) - \min(D_t) + 1, \min(S^r_u) + \min(D_u) - 1] \ .$$

The replacement of the original pruning rule (1) by the rule (2) for each single resource $r \in \bigcup_{t \in T} R_t$ will perform some pruning for the alternative resource constraint problem. Furthermore, this pruning is still correct, i.e. no solutions are lost: The rule (2) is a specialisation of the original rule; whenever the start times S^r_t are pruned, the start times S_t would be also pruned by the original rule (1) assuming that the task t will be scheduled on the resource r.

However, for further pruning the changes with respect to each single resource must be propagated to the original domains and from one resource to another. Especially, this must be performed if the start times of a task t on a resource r become the empty set (cf. pruning rule (2)) or the potential start times are restricted from "outside", e.g. during a search process. In either case, these changes have to be propagated to the individual resources and back to the common potential start times:

$$\forall t \in T \, \forall r \in R_t : S^r_t \cap S_t = \emptyset \Rightarrow R'_t := R_t \setminus \{r\} \ , \tag{3}$$
$$\forall t \in T \, \forall r \in R_t : S^r_t \cap S_t \neq \emptyset \Rightarrow S'^r_t := S^r_t \cap S_t \ , \tag{4}$$
$$\forall t \in T : S'_t := S_t \cap \left(\bigcup_{r \in R_t} S^r_t \right) . \tag{5}$$

In the first case, there is no potential start time left for a task t and a resource r. Consequently, it will be impossible to allocate the task t to the resource r. Thus, r will be removed from the set of alternative resources. In the second case, the restriction of the start times is propagated to the start times on the alternative resources. Last but not least, the restrictions of the start times which are valid for all alternative resources are propagated to the potential start times.

The application of all these rules in the given order, supersedes an iteration over these rule for the computation of a local fix-point.

4   Global Overload Checking

The application of several single resource constraints for the realisation of the alternative resource constraint benefits from overload checking performed "locally" for each resource (cf. [8]). However, these checks are weak as long as all activities are allocated to the resources: the greater the number of allocated tasks the stronger the pruning based on the rule (2) (see Section 3).

A necessary, global condition for the solvability of an alternative constraint problem determined by a set of tasks $T = \{t_0, \ldots, t_n\}$ is that each non-empty set of tasks $M \subseteq T$ is not overloaded, i.e. the occupied area is not greater than the available area:

$$\sum_{t \in M} \min(D_t) \times 1 \quad \leq$$
$$(\max_{t \in M}(\max(S_t) + \min(D_t)) - \min_{t \in M}(\min(S_t)))$$
$$\times (\max_{t \in M}(\max(R_t)) + 1 - \min_{t \in M}(\min(R_t))) \ .$$

The naive overload checking of all $2^{n+1} - 1$ non-empty subsets of T is not practical. Thus, we suppose to consider the set of at most $\sum_{l=0}^{n} l \times \sum_{m=0}^{n} m = \frac{(n+2)^2(n+1)^2}{4}$ task rectangles, i.e. the set of tasks defined by the Cartesian product of two integer intervals whose bounds are determined by some tasks:

$$[llc(i,j)_X, urc(h,k)_X] \times [llc(i,j)_Y, urc(h,k)_Y]$$
$$:= \{t \in T \mid llc(i,j)_X \leq \min(S_t) \wedge \max(S_t) + \min(D_t) \leq urc(h,k)_X$$
$$\wedge \ llc(i,j)_Y \leq \min(R_t) \wedge \max(R_t) + 1 \leq urc(h,k)_Y\}$$

where the *lower left corners* (the *llc*s) and the *upper right corners* (the *urc*s) are defined as follows:

$$llc(i,j)_X := \min(\min(S_{t_i}), \min(S_{t_j}))$$
$$llc(i,j)_Y := \min(\min(R_{t_i}), \min(R_{t_j}))$$
$$urc(h,k)_X := \max(\max(S_{t_h}) + \min(D_{t_h}), \max(S_{t_k}) + \min(D_{t_k}))$$
$$urc(h,k)_Y := \max(\max(R_{t_h}) + 1, \max(R_{t_k}) + 1)$$

for $0 \leq i \leq j \leq n$ and $0 \leq h \leq k \leq n$ (see Figure 2).

To perform overload checking we use "sweeping" originated and used widely in computational geometry [6]. The recent publication [4] has shown that sweeping is also an efficient pruning technique when adapted and applied to finite domain constraint solving problems, especially for non-overlapping rectangles constraint problems.

While sweeping over task rectangles, it is assumed that the tasks in T are numbered $t_0, \ldots, t_n$ according to an ascending sorting with respect to the order relation

$$t \preceq u :\Leftrightarrow (\min(S_t) + \min(R_t) < \min(S_u) + \min(R_u))$$
$$\vee \ (\min(S_t) + \min(R_t) = \min(S_u) + \min(R_u) \wedge \min(R_t) \leq \min(R_u))$$

such that $t_0 \preceq \cdots \preceq t_n$ holds. Furthermore, we assume that all the corners (llcs and urcs) are also numbered $c_0, \ldots, c_m$ according to an ascending sorting with respect to the order relation

$$c \preceq d :\Leftrightarrow (c_X + c_Y < d_X + d_Y) \vee (c_X + c_Y = d_X + d_Y$$
$$\wedge ((c, d \text{ are both either llcs or urcs } \wedge c_Y \leq d_Y) \vee (c \text{ is an urc } \wedge d \text{ is an llc}))$$

such that $c_0 \preceq \cdots \preceq c_m$ holds. Then, we are sweeping forward, i.e. in ascending order, over the sorted corners:

```
(01) let S := λ be the empty sweep line;
(02) for j = 0, . . . , m do begin (iterate over all corners)
(03)    if the corner c_j is an llc then
(04)       let S := S · c_j; (append c_j to the end of the sweep line)
(05)    else (the corner c_j is an urc) do begin
(06)       let p := 0;
(07)       be S = c_{i_0}, . . . , c_{i_k} the current sweep line
(08)       for l = 0, . . . , k do begin (iterate over the llcs in S)
(09)          if c_{i_l X} < c_{j X} ∧ c_{i_l Y} < c_{j Y} then do begin
(10)             let A := 0 be the (currently) occupied area;
(11)             let A_{i_l, j} := (c_{j X} − c_{i_l X}) × (c_{j Y} − c_{i_l Y})
                    be the available area;
(12)             while ((min(S_{t_p}) + min(R_{t_p}) < c_{i_l X} + c_{i_l Y})
                       ∨ (min(S_{t_p}) + min(R_{t_p}) = c_{i_l X} + c_{i_l Y} ∧ min(R_{t_p}) < c_{i_l Y}))
                    do let p := p + 1;
(13)             for m = p, . . . , n do begin
                    (iterate over the tasks t_p, . . . , t_n)
(14)                if min(S_{t_m}) + min(R_{t_m}) > c_{j X} + c_{j Y} then
(15)                   let m := n; (stop this iteration over the tasks)
(16)                else do begin
(17)                   if min(S_{t_m}) ≥ c_{i_l X} ∧ min(R_{t_m}) ≥ c_{i_l Y} ∧
                          max(S_{t_m}) + min(D_{t_m}) ≤ c_{j X} ∧ max(R_{t_m}) + 1 ≤ c_{j Y}
                       then let A := A + (min(D_{t_m} × 1));
(18)                   if A > A_{i_l, j} then exit ; (there is no schedule)
(19)                end of the else part
(20)             end of the iteration over the tasks
(21)          end of if non-empty rectangle
(22)       end of the iteration over the llcs
(23)    end of the corner is an urc
(24) end of the iteration over all corners
```

The algorithm works as follows: During the forward iteration over the sweep line (cf. lines 08–22) all llcs are considered which might define a possibly non-empty rectangle with respect to the current urc c_j (cf. Figure 2 and lines 09–21). The chosen order relation '$\preceq$' on corners ensures that all rectangles with a positive area $A_{i_l, j}$ are considered. Figure 3 (a) gives some evidence for skipping those llcs that are not "left" or "below" the considered upper-right corner c_j . Then,

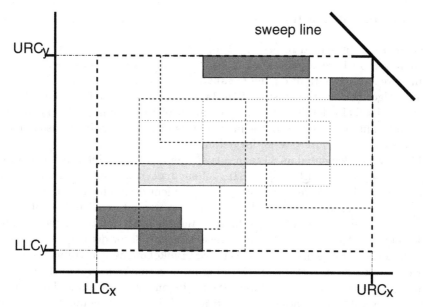

Fig. 2. Determining a possibly non-empty task rectangle

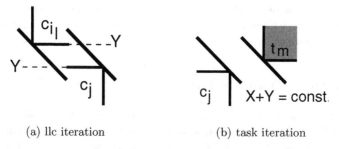

(a) llc iteration   (b) task iteration

Fig. 3. Breaking conditions for the iterations

the available and the occupied areas in the currently considered rectangle are determined (cf. lines 10–11 and further lines 13–20). For the last only the areas of those tasks are aggregated that are contained in this rectangle. Therefore, the tasks which are "left" or "below" (cf. line 12) as well as those which are "right" or "above" (cf. lines 14–15) are skipped. Again, the chosen order relations '$\preceq$' on tasks and corners as well as their compatibility with each other ensure that only irrelevant tasks are skipped. In detail, Figure 3 (b) gives some evidence for stopping the iteration over the tasks. An overload is detected if the occupied area A becomes greater than the available area $A_{i_l,j}$ (cf. line 18): Then, the algorithm stops because there is obviously no feasible solution of the given alternative resource constraint problem.

5   Implementation

The extensions presented in Section 3 as well as the sweeping algorithm introduced in Section 4 are implemented in Java: Both implementations are integrated in our pure Java constraint engine firstcs [5]. Concretely, the forbidden region pruning algorithm in the existing SingleResource constraint implementation was generalised. In detail, the implementation of the pruning rule (1) was replaced by an implementation of the pruning rule (2). This pruning is also realised by a sweeping procedure (see [8] for details).

Then, we implemented an AlternativeResource constraint which generates for each resource $r \in \bigcup_{t \in T} R_t$ a SingleResource constraint which performs pruning for each single resource constraint problem determined by the task set T_r. Thus, pruning for the alternative resource constraint problem benefits from additional pruning rules, like edge finding and not-first/not-last detection also implemented in the SingleResource constraint (cf. [8] for details).

Additionally, we realized in the AlternativeResource constraint the pruning rules presented in Section 3 performing propagation from and to the original domains and between the generated SingleResource constraints. This implementation iterates over these rules until a local fix-point is computed, i.e. any application of the presented rules and algorithms will not further restrict the potential start times or the alternative resources.

Finally, we implemented the sweeping algorithm for overload checking. This algorithm is applied after the computation of the fix-point because it will not change any domains.

6   Empirical Examinations

For empirical examinations, we used the publicly available *random placement problems (RPP)*[3]. All the problem instances consist of 200 activities of randomly generated durations. There are different problem classes which are discriminated with respect to their *filled area ratio*. This is *"the ratio between the size of the placement area and the total area of all objects [activities] ..."*. Their potential start times as well as their alternative resources are randomly restricted to some finite integer intervals. For any of these instances the start times and resources for the 200 activities must be determined such that the resources are exclusively available during the execution of these activities.

From a practical point of view, these RPP instances correspond to simple course timetabling problems [2]: each activity corresponds to a course and its alternative resources to the adequate classrooms, i.e. of sufficient capacity and with the needed equipment. We used the RPP instances to test our AlternativeResource constraint presented in Section 5. Furthermore, we compared our implementation based on the Java Standard Edition, version 1.4.0-03 against the more general disjoint2 constraint in SICStus Prolog, version 3.11.0.

---

[3] online available at http://www.fi.muni.cz/~hanka/rpp/

Table 1. Runtime results for all instances with *filled area ratio* of 80 % without global propagation in SICStus Prolog resp. overload checking in our Java `firstcs` implementation

SICStus Prolog				Java `firstcs`			
80 %	gen./1st prop.	# assigns	1st sol.	80 %	gen./1st prop.	# assigns	1st sol.
gen1	0	393	47	gen1	265	393	1203
gen2	0	389	47	gen2	234	389	1062
gen3	0	388	62	gen3	156	388	1046
gen4	0	393	47	gen4	156	393	1062
gen5	0	397	47	gen5	172	397	1124
gen6	0	393	63	gen6	156	393	1124
gen7	0	390	63	gen7	140	390	1031
gen8	0	394	46	gen8	171	394	1125
gen9	0	390	47	gen9	156	390	1109
gen10	0	386	47	gen10	156	386	999
gen11	0	396	62	gen11	156	396	1109
gen12	0	395	47	gen12	156	395	1108
gen13	0	390	47	gen13	156	390	1031
gen14	0	382	47	gen14	172	382	1046
gen15	0	388	47	gen15	157	388	1046
gen16	0	396	47	gen16	171	396	1140
gen17	0	393	63	gen17	156	393	1046
gen18	16	393	31	gen18	172	393	1077
gen19	0	386	63	gen19	156	386	1000
gen20	0	388	47	gen20	156	388	1046
gen21	0	390	62	gen21	172	390	1124
gen22	0	395	63	gen22	172	395	1093
gen23	0	393	63	gen23	156	393	1093
gen24	0	387	47	gen24	157	387	1108
gen25	0	391	63	gen25	156	391	1078
gen26	0	385	47	gen26	156	385	1093
gen27	16	389	31	gen27	156	389	1078
gen28	0	392	47	gen28	172	392	1124
gen29	0	389	62	gen29	172	389	1124
gen30	0	385	47	gen30	156	385	1031
gen31	0	395	47	gen31	172	395	1140
gen32	0	383	47	gen32	156	383	1031
gen33	16	391	31	gen33	156	391	1061
gen34	0	396	47	gen34	172	396	1109
gen35	0	393	47	gen35	172	393	1077
gen36	0	394	63	gen36	172	394	1124
gen37	0	394	63	gen37	172	394	1093
gen38	0	391	47	gen38	156	391	1062
gen39	16	390	15	gen39	172	390	1124
gen40	0	394	47	gen40	172	394	1171
gen41	0	394	47	gen41	171	394	1078
gen42	0	393	62	gen42	172	393	1046
gen43	16	384	31	gen43	140	384	1031
gen44	0	397	46	gen44	171	397	1109
gen45	16	391	31	gen45	172	391	1155
gen46	0	389	63	gen46	156	389	1062
gen47	0	389	62	gen47	171	389	1093
gen48	0	387	46	gen48	172	387	1109

Table 2. Runtime results for all instances with *filled area ratio* 85 % without global propagation in SICStus Prolog resp. overload checking in our Java `firstcs` implementation

SICStus Prolog				Java `firstcs`			
85 %	gen./1st prop.	# assigns	1st sol.	85 %	gen./1st prop.	# assigns	1st sol.
gen1	15	393	32	gen1	266	393	1140
gen2	0	387	63	gen2	156	387	1031
gen3	0	394	63	gen3	172	394	1156
gen4	0	384	63	gen4	171	384	1078
gen5	0	388	47	gen5	156	388	1125
gen6	0	381	63	gen6	171	381	1062
gen7	0	382	47	gen7	156	382	1093
gen8	0	389	47	gen8	156	389	1062
gen9	15	382	32	gen9	140	382	984
gen10	0	388	47	gen10	157	388	1061
gen11	0	386	47	gen11	172	386	1046
gen12	0	388	47	gen12	156	388	1078
gen13	0	395	47	gen13	187	395	1155
gen14	0	387	62	gen14	157	387	1046
gen15	0	386	62	gen15	156	386	1093
gen16	0	388	63	gen16	156	388	1077
gen17	0	389	62	gen17	157	389	1139
gen18	15	388	32	gen18	156	388	1125
gen19	0	385	47	gen19	141	385	1015
gen20	0	394	47	gen20	172	394	1155
gen21	0	382	47	gen21	157	382	999
gen22	0	389	63	gen22	156	389	1047
gen23	0	395	47	gen23	156	395	1109
gen24	0	385	47	gen24	172	385	1093
gen25	0	389	47	gen25	156	389	1093
gen26	0	389	47	gen26	172	389	1109
gen27	0	383	63	gen27	172	383	1031
gen28	0	388	63	gen28	140	388	1078
gen29	0	392	47	gen29	172	392	1078
gen30	0	391	47	gen30	156	391	1031
gen31	0	393	47	gen31	157	393	1093
gen32	0	387	47	gen32	156	387	1016
gen33	0	392	47	gen33	156	392	1109
gen34	0	386	47	gen34	157	386	1031
gen35	0	391	47	gen35	172	391	1093
gen36	0	385	47	gen36	140	385	1016
gen37	0	388	62	gen37	156	388	1063
gen38	0	393	63	gen38	156	393	1109
gen39	15	391	32	gen39	156	391	1093
gen40	16	385	15	gen40	156	385	1031
gen41	0	386	47	gen41	156	386	1047
gen42	15	394	32	gen42	172	394	1077
gen43	0	378	46	gen43	157	378	984
gen44	0	389	63	gen44	157	389	1046
gen45	0	378	47	gen45	140	378	985
gen46	0	390	46	gen46	156	390	1094
gen47	0	387	47	gen47	156	387	1046
gen48	0	393	47	gen48	156	393	1125

Table 3. Runtime results for some solvable instances with *filled area ratio* of 100 % without global propagation in SICStus Prolog resp. overload checking in our Java `firstcs` implementation

	SICStus Prolog				Java `firstcs`		
100 %	gen./1st prop.	# assigns	1st sol.	100 %	gen./1st prop.	# assigns	1st sol.
gen1	0	379	47	gen1	250	379	969
gen2	0	378	47	gen2	172	378	1000
gen8	0	382	47	gen8	172	382	1109
gen9	0	379	62	gen9	187	379	1016
gen11	0	381	47	gen11	156	381	984
gen14	0	375	47	gen14	157	375	1031
gen16	0	375	47	gen16	156	375	1062
gen17	0	381	63	gen17	203	381	1000
gen18	0	379	31	gen18	187	379	906
gen21	0	376	47	gen21	188	376	1047
gen22	0	382	47	gen22	156	382	1031
gen23	16	385	47	gen23	203	385	984
gen24	0	378	47	gen24	188	378	984
gen25	16	385	31	gen25	141	385	1000
gen28	0	383	47	gen28	141	383	1015
gen30	16	382	15	gen30	157	382	1031
gen33	0	380	47	gen33	156	380	985
gen34	0	381	47	gen34	156	381	1047
gen35	16	379	31	gen35	141	379	1000
gen36	0	376	63	gen36	157	376	1015
gen38	16	377	31	gen38	141	377	922
gen39	0	386	47	gen39	141	386	1016
gen40	0	380	31	gen40	156	380	1015
gen41	0	379	47	gen41	188	379	922
gen42	0	379	47	gen42	203	379	1047
gen43	0	379	47	gen43	188	379	953
gen44	16	382	31	gen44	140	382	969
gen46	0	381	63	gen46	140	381	969
gen48	0	379	47	gen48	156	379	1032

The experiments were performed under Microsoft Windows XP on a PC Pentium 4, 2.8 GHz with 1 GByte RAM.

In both implementations we used standard labelling (simple depth-first search) to determine the start times and the resources: The activities were considered in their given order (activity 1 first, activity 200 last). During the search, for each activity the start time was assigned after selecting the resource. In both cases, the smallest available, not yet tried value was selected. Iin SICStus Prolog, we accordingly used the built-in search `labelling` with the options `[leftmost, up, assumptions(N)]` where N is unified with the number of choices, i.e. assignments made, when a solution is found.

Table 4. Runtime results for some unsolvable instances with *filled area ratio* of 100 % with global propagation in SICStus Prolog resp. overload checking in our Java `firstcs` implementation

SICStus Prolog					Java `firstcs`			
100 %	gen./1st prop.	# assigns	search		100 %	gen./1st prop.	# assigns	search
gen4	16	0	0		gen4	252	0	0
gen6	0	?	> 1h		gen6	204	0	0
gen10	0	0	0		gen10	173	0	0
gen12	0	0	0		gen12	173	0	0
gen13	0	?	> 1h		gen13	188	0	0
gen29	0	0	0		gen29	157	0	0
gen32	0	?	> 1h		gen32	188	0	0
gen37	0	0	0		gen37	173	0	0
gen45	0	0	0		gen45	173	0	0
gen49	0	0	0		gen49	172	0	0
gen50	0	?	> 1h		gen50	173	0	0

Our experiments have shown that all instances with *filled area ratio* of 80 % and 85 % (see Table 1 and Table 2) are solvable. Both implementations found their first solutions backtrack-free and without any global propagation. This means that in SICStus Prolog the `global` option was switched off as well as the global overload checking (cf. Section 4) in our Java `firstcs` implementation. The number of required assignments for finding a first solution are surprisingly identical (see column *# assigns* in Table 1 and Table 2). Further, they are less than 400 (200 resources plus 200 start times) because some variables' values are determined due to propagation. For all these problems, the SICStus Prolog implementation requires on average no measurable time for constraint generation and initial propagation, our implementation requires on average 164 milliseconds (see column *gen./1st prop.* in Table 1 and Table 2 for the required runtime in milliseconds). The labelling process for finding the first solution of one of these problems which triggers some further propagation takes on average 50 milliseconds in SICStus Prolog and about 1079 milliseconds in our Java `firstcs` implementation (see column *1st sol.* in Table 1 and Table 2 for the required runtime in milliseconds).

Additional experiments on the instances with a *filled area ratio* of 100% behave analogously: all instances which are backtrack-free solvable using the SICStus Prolog implementation are also backtrack-free solvable with our Java `firstcs` implementation. Furthermore, all the instances which are detected to be unsolvable using SICStus Prolog are also detected by the use of our Java `firstcs` implementation. In any case, an inconsistency is detected during the initial "global" propagation: SICStus Prolog's `disjoint2` with its `global` option switched on and our implementation with the overload checking presented in Section 4 (see column *gen./1st prop.* in Table 4 for the required propagation time in milliseconds and column *search* for the required search time). In these unsolvable cases, SICStus Prolog used on average 15 milliseconds to detect

Table 5. Runtime results for all instances with *filled area ratio* of 80 and 85 % without global propagation but with the *first-fail* variable selection heuristics in our Java `firstcs` implementation

Java `firstcs` with first-fail				Java `firstcs` with first-fail			
80 %	gen./1st prop.	# assigns	1st sol.	85 %	gen./1st prop.	# assigns	1st sol.
gen1	469	590	2875	gen1	468	593	2954
gen2	187	571	2531	gen2	188	590	2734
gen3	172	582	2625	gen3	203	598	2765
gen4	188	563	2687	gen4	172	631	2781
gen5	188	589	2765	gen5	188	556	2359
gen6	187	578	2547	gen6	188	578	2406
gen7	188	598	2765	gen7	187	561	2391
gen8	187	595	2781	gen8	188	593	2609
gen9	187	563	2438	gen9	188	566	2343
gen10	188	559	2296	gen10	187	599	2766
gen11	203	573	2688	gen11	204	616	3015
gen12	188	561	2594	gen12	188	576	2469
gen13	187	575	2532	gen13	203	625	2891
gen14	172	555	2359	gen14	188	562	2437
gen15	187	617	3094	gen15	203	590	2531
gen16	204	584	2750	gen16	203	613	2844
gen17	188	545	2406	gen17	188	593	2703
gen18	188	565	2500	gen18	188	604	2703
gen19	187	570	2484	gen19	203	575	2500
gen20	188	560	2500	gen20	188	621	2812
gen21	203	582	2485	gen21	171	587	2547
gen22	188	602	2765	gen22	203	569	2578
gen23	187	623	2938	gen23	188	577	2594
gen24	171	561	2500	gen24	203	619	2890
gen25	172	556	2516	gen25	203	600	2781
gen26	188	563	2469	gen26	187	606	2938
gen27	187	592	2703	gen27	188	561	2406
gen28	188	570	2546	gen28	187	588	2672
gen29	187	573	2500	gen29	188	596	2812
gen30	187	555	2360	gen30	187	613	2860
gen31	188	593	2671	gen31	203	588	2594
gen32	188	565	2515	gen32	187	599	2703
gen33	188	558	2531	gen33	187	595	2704
gen34	203	553	2531	gen34	188	570	2468
gen35	188	608	2687	gen35	203	592	2594
gen36	187	573	2734	gen36	172	576	2453
gen37	187	574	2641	gen37	203	604	2812
gen38	188	568	2437	gen38	187	575	2594
gen39	187	567	2469	gen39	203	567	2515
gen40	188	645	3141	gen40	188	563	2437
gen41	187	583	2688	gen41	187	577	2547
gen42	188	593	2625	gen42	188	597	2781
gen43	188	507	2000	gen43	188	568	2328
gen44	203	587	2640	gen44	204	603	2796
gen45	203	581	2500	gen45	203	598	2641
gen46	187	563	2484	gen46	188	585	2547
gen47	187	566	2578	gen47	187	596	2641
gen48	187	578	2547	gen48	203	581	2672

an inconsistency. However, our Java `firstcs` implementation detects further unsolvable instances with *filled area ratio* of 100% during the initial "global" propagation: `100/gen6`, `100/gen13`, `100/gen32`, and `100/gen50`. It takes only 203 milliseconds on average per instance to detect all these inconsistencies. However, the SICStus Prolog implementation is not able to prove the inconsistencies within more than one hour runtime for each of these additional instances.

The described behaviour changes dramatically, if we use the well-known *first-fail* variable selection heuristics instead, i.e. if the variables are selected with respect to their domain sizes in increasing order. Our Java `firstcs` implementation behaves rather stable (cf. Table 5). However, the SICStus Prolog implementation is not possible to find a solution for the instances `gen1` and `gen2` within several hours.

7   Conclusion and Future Work

In this paper, we presented a modular approach for the alternative resource constraint problem based on single resource constraints. Furthermore, we presented a new sweeping algorithm which performs overload checking for the alternative resource constraint problem.

Obviously, the presented "global" overload checking in Section 4 is applicable to more general non-overlapping rectangles problems with rectangles' heights greater than one. Thus, our future work focuses on the combination of our sweeping algorithm with the one presented in [3] yielding better pruning for non-overlapping rectangles problems than other approaches.

Last but not least, our implementation of the pruning rules and algorithms is successfully applied to some online available benchmark placement problems yielding some encouraging results. Compared to SICStus Prolog, the pruning in `firstcs` is even better: Our Java implementation detects more unsolvable problem instances (cf. Table 4) and behaves stable and efficient while using the first-fail variable selection heuristics (cf. Table 5). However, our implementation's runtime is about one order of magnitude slower than the SICStus Prolog implementation. Thus, future practical work will concentrate on runtime optimisation. Therefore, we will replace the currently quadratic pruning algorithms in our `SingleResource` constraint with the recently presented $O(n \log n)$ algorithms [7]. Furthermore, we will try to adopt the underlying ideas to reduce the $O(n^4)$ time complexity of the presented "global" but costly overload checking.

References

1. Philippe Baptiste, Claude le Pape, and Wim Nuijten. *Constraint-Based Scheduling.* Number 39 in International Series in Operations Research & Management Science. Kluwer Academic Publishers, 2001.
2. Roman Barták, Tomáš Müller, and Hana Rudová. Minimal perturbation problem - a formal view. In *Proceedings of the Joint Annual Workshop of the ERCIM Working Group on Constraints and the CoLogNET area on Constraint and Logic Programming*, MTA SZTAKI, Budapest, Hungary, 30 June – 2 July 2003.

3. Nicolas Beldiceanu and Mats Carlsson. Sweep as a generic pruning technique applied to the non-overlapping rectangles constraint. In Toby Walsh, editor, *Proceedings of the 7th International Conference on Principles and Practice of Constraint Programming - CP2001*, number 2239 in Lecture Notes in Computer Science, pages 377–391. Springer Verlag, 2001.

4. Nicolas Beldiceanu and Mats Carlsson. A new multi-resource cumulatives constraint with negative heights. In Pascal van Hentenryck, editor, *Proceedings of the 8th International Conference on Principles and Practice of Constraint Programming - CP2002*, number 2470 in Lecture Notes in Computer Science, pages 63–79. Springer Verlag, 2002.

5. Matthias Hoche, Henry Müller, Hans Schlenker, and Armin Wolf. firstcs - A Pure Java Constraint Programming Engine. In Michael Hanus, Petra Hofstedt, and Armin Wolf, editors, *2nd International Workshop on Multiparadigm Constraint Programming Languages – MultiCPL'03*, 29th September 2003. Online available at uebb.cs.tu-berlin.de/MultiCPL03/Proceedings.MultiCPL03.RCoRP03.pdf.

6. Franco P. Preparata and Michael Ian Shamos. *Computational Geometry, An Introduction*. Texts and Monographs in Computer Science. Springer Verlag, 1985.

7. Petr Vilím. $O(n \log n)$ filtering algorithms for unary resource constraint. In *Proceedings of the International Conference on Integration of AI and OR Techniques in Constraint Programming for Combinatorical Optimisation Problems – CP-AI-OR'04*, number 3011 in Lecture Notes in Computer Science, pages 335–347, Nice, France, April 20–22, 2004. Springer Verlag, Heidelberg.

8. Armin Wolf. Pruning while sweeping over task intervals. In Francesca Rossi, editor, *Proceedings of the 9th International Conference on Principles and Practice of Constraint Programming – CP 2003*, number 2833 in Lecture Notes in Computer Science, pages 739–753, Kinsale, County Cork, Ireland, 30th September – 3rd October 2003. Springer Verlag.

Integrating Time Constraints into Constraint-Based Configuration Models

Ulrich John[1] and Ulrich Geske[2]

[1] DaimlerChrysler AG, Research Information & Communication
Ulrich.John@daimlerchrysler.com
[2] Fraunhofer FIRST
Ulrich.Geske@first.fraunhofer.de

Abstract. Over the last few years, we have been developing the configuration model ConBaCon, which is based on Constraint Programming over finite domains. The model is sound and suitable for building efficient and flexible systems that fulfill all the requirements of advanced configuration systems.

In this paper, we present model extensions that enable time-extended configuration and reconfiguration problems to be solved: Besides "normal" configuration and reconfiguration problems, the extended model can now also solve problems that contain time-dependent resource avaibilities or supply constraints for the ground components included. The general nature of the model extensions introduced seems to be suitable for integration in other (commercial) constraint-based configuration systems/configurator libraries as well.

1   Introduction

Configuration problems can be found in a huge number of business fields. That is why the development of efficient and flexible configuration systems is still a hot topic in computer science. In the last twenty years, with the introduction of the well-known, rule-based configuration system XCON for configuring DEC computers, different approaches have been proposed and investigated for the knowledge-based configuration of products and technical systems. These include various rule-based, case-based and, recently, more and more constraint-based approaches. Overviews of different approaches and systems are given in [19], [18] and [12]. When both research approaches and commercial systems were considered in the past, the following general shortcomings were often found. The problem specification was nondeclarative and hard to maintain. Often, the sequence of interactions during the configuration process was fixed, making a flexible configuration process such as that supported by *ConBaCon* impossible. The simulation of different effects resulting from alternative, interactive decisions is rare and the support of good reconfigurations, which is needed by industry, is inadequate or nonexistent. Furthermore, finding optimal or nearly-optimal configurations is impossible, and there are other problems like the occasional failure of the underlying algorithms to terminate.

D. Seipel et al. (Eds.): INAP/WLP 2004, LNAI 3392, pp. 200–214, 2005.

It is generally accepted that high-quality configuration systems can be realized, especially by using *constraint programming* (cf. [8], [2], [17]).

Our configuration system ConBaCon, based on the CLP language CHIP, overcomes the above shortcomings/problems. The ConBaCon model behind the system is theoretically sound and covers – together with several model extensions – a broad range of technical and non-technical configuration problems (cf. [12]).

A rather interesting problem class is that of *time-constrained configuration problems*. Such problems contain, besides the "normal" problem elements, time-constrained resource availabilities and possible supply times for potential result components.

The practical importance of these problems is highlighted by the following example: Often we have a situation where a customer wants to buy a complex product, for instance a car. Besides some constraints related to the physical configuration of the car like color and equipment, and some optimizing goals like price and consumption, the customer wants the guarantee of delivery by a certain self-appointed date.

Although several software and research companies are working on approaches that tackle these problems, there are neither configuration systems available that are able to handle this problem satisfactorily, nor the authors are familiar with any publication that describe adequate solutions. At best, some approaches offer the opportunity to check the earliest delivery date after completion of the configuration process.

We have developed some extensions of our constraint-based configuration model that allow highly flexible, efficient configuration and reconfiguration processes driven by the fixed delivery date. After giving the delivery date as a hard constraint, the user can explore the possibilities for his/ her car in a flexible, interactive way. All options that cannot be chosen because of the fixed delivery date are marked automatically throughout the configuration process. This enables the user to configure his/ her "dream car" subject to the restriction of the self-appointed delivery date.

The following section outlines the specification language ConBaConL according to our initial configuration model. Section 3 introduces some key aspects of our configuration model and its realization ConBaCon, which allows the configuration of industrial products/technical systems. The model extensions for solving time-constrained configuration and reconfiguration problems are presented in Section 4, where we also give an example for illustrative purposes. The paper closes with a conclusion and some remarks on possible future extensions.

2   ConBaConL

By analyzing the results of design problems for industrial control systems, we developed a formal problem model and, based on this, the largely declarative specification language *ConBaConL*, which allows the specification of relevant configuration problems. Such specifications are composed of three parts: *object hierarchy*, *context-independent constraints* and *context constraints*. Every technical object that can play a part in the configuration problem must be specified in terms of its structure in the object hierarchy. An object can consist of several components in the sense of the *consist_of*-relation, where components may be optional, or the object has some specializations in the sense of the *is_a*-relation. In addition, all attributes of the technical objects are specified. If the attribute values of a technical object are explicitly known, then they are enumerated.

A correct context-independent representation of the configuration problem is created from the object-hierarchy specification by adding the specification of the constraints concerning different attribute value sets on the one hand, and the existence or nonexistence of technical objects in the problem solution on the other. If context constraints exist (e.g. customer-specific demands or resource-oriented constraints), then we have to specify them as problem-specific constraints in ConBaConL. The distinction between problem-specific and context-independent constraints is useful because the technical correctness of the problem solution is ensured if all context-independent constraints are fulfilled.

The constraint elements of ConBaConL can be divided into *Simple Constraints*, *Compositional Constraints* and *Conditional Constraints*. Most of them are introduced below.

2.1   Simple Constraints

Attribute Value Constraints and Existence Constraints

[o, Attr, VS]/not([o, Attr, VS]) ≡
    the attribute *Attr* of object *o* must/must not take a value from *VS*,

exist(Objectlist)/noexist(Objectlist) ≡
    all objects contained in *Objectlist* must/must not be part of the solution.

Relational Constraints Between Attribute Value Sets & Table Constraints

=(T1,T2), *≠(T1,T2)*, *<(T1,T2)*, *≤(T1,T2)*, *>(T1,T2)*, *≥(T1,T2)*. Furthermore, it is possible to specify equations over attributes.

In practice, coherences between solution parts are often specified in the form of tables (decision tables). To avoid a manual, error-prone translation of the table into other kinds of ConBaConL constraints, a table constraint (see [10]) was introduced.

2.2   Compositional Constraints

Compositional Constraints are, besides the above-mentioned Simple Constraints, compositions of compositional constraints: $and([Cons_1,\dots,Cons_n])$, $or([Cons_1, \dots,Cons_n])$, $xor([Cons_1,\dots,Cons_n])$, $at\_least([Cons_1,\dots,Cons_n],N)$/ $at\_most([Cons_1,\dots,Cons_n],N)$/ $exact([Cons_1,\dots,Cons_n],N)$ ≡ at_least/at_most/exactly N of the listed constraints are valid[1].

---
[1] So far, the processing of or-, xor, at_least, at_most, exact-constraints concerning the existence and nonexistence demands of objects has been realized in ConBaCon.

2.3 Conditional Constraints

[if(Comp_Cons₁), then(Comp_Cons₂)] (*[iff(Comp_Cons₁), then(Comp_Cons₂)]*)
If (and only if) the compositional constraint $Comp\_Cons_1$ is fulfilled, the compositional constraint $Comp\_Cons_2$ must be fulfilled.

2.4 Preferences

There are two ways of describing and processing preferences. One is to try encoding the existing preferences as preference rules in the labeling heuristics (see below) within the problem-solution model. Another is to specify weak constraints. So far, specifying *weak simple constraints* has been supported (cf. [10]).

2.5 Modifications

In practice, the specification of product taxonomies/component catalogues has high modification rates. For instance, about 40% of the 30,000 component types of DEC computers used in R1/XCON were updated annually (cf. [4]). There are several reasons for the need to change the product taxonomies/problem specifications. The most common is the fact that new technical modules become available or obsolete ones are withdrawn. A special case of this is so-called versioning. Another reason is the changing of context-independent constraints due, for instance, to changes in laws or government policy. In order to allow subsequent reconfigurations, obsolete information should not be deleted in the specification. Instead, obsolete modules and constraints should be labeled with the keyword *obsolete* in the specification/product taxonomy. New modules and constraints can easily be added to the specifications/product taxonomies. There are two cases in which a new module/object *new_o* is integrated as an alternative to an already specified module o_x. In the first case, o_x is a specialization of an object o. In the second case, o_x is a module of o, whereby a notional object must be introduced at the position of o_x, which acquires the specializations *new_o* and o_x.

Other important elements of ConBaConL are *optimization goals* such as minimization or maximization of indicated attribute values.

A typical specification of ground converters for large electric motors is outlined in [10], together with the problem solution using ConBaCon.

3 Problem Solution Model

When transforming a problem specification, our goal is to obtain a problem-solution model that allows efficient problem solution. The model should also support the option of high-quality user interactions. The model of a constraint-logic system over finite domains is taken as a basis for the solution model outlined below. Thus, the model can also be seen as a global constraint for structural configuration.

3.1   Objects

Each specified object (representing a technical module) that is not marked as obsolete is transformed into a *module object* of the problem-solution model[2]. Moreover, each attribute of a specified object is transformed into an *attribute object*, i.e. a specified object with n attributes is represented by $n+1$ objects in the problem-solution model (Fig. 1).

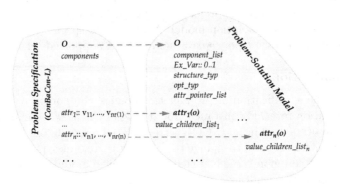

Fig. 1. Transformation of Objects

Objects of the problem-solution space acquire certain model-specific attributes. The attribute *component_list* of object o contains identifiers of the object components (*structure_type* = and-node) and of the specializations (*structure_type* = or-node) of o, respectively. The constraint variable Ex_Var determines whether or not the object is contained in the solution. If the value of Ex_Var is zero, then o is not part of the solution. If the value is one, then o is part of the solution. *opt_type* contains information about whether o is optional or not. Links to the corresponding attribute objects are given by *attr_pointer_list*. Each attribute object stores possible attribute values in *value_children_lists* and in the domain of a corresponding constraint variable. Moreover, identifiers of the value-related children nodes are stored if the object o contains specializations. In this case, the attribute value sets of o are the set unification of the corresponding attribute value sets of the specialization objects.

3.2   CE Constraints

Besides the model objects, constraints are needed in the problem-solution model to ensure the coherences between the objects of the model so that the correctness of the solution and the completeness of the solution process are guaranteed with respect to the problem specification. These constraints we call *consistency-ensuring constraints* (CE constraints). *Consistency-Ensuring Constraints* are

---

[2] Some constellations require the introduction of auxiliary module objects. These are not considered in the present paper. Details can be found in [12].

realized as logical coherences between values of Ex_Var-attributes/attribute value sets of different attribute objects. The most important CE constraints are schematized in Fig. 2. If it becomes obvious that an object cannot occur in

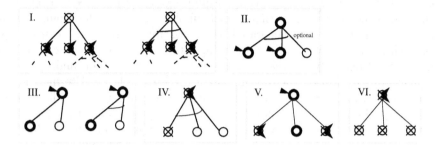

Fig. 2. Consistency-Ensuring Constraints

the solution, then it must be inferred that no component/specialization of it can occur in the solution (I). If it becomes obvious that an object is part of the solution $(Ex\_Var = 1)$, then it must be ensured that all nonoptional components of the object are part of the solution, too (II). The existence of an object in a solution implies in each case the existence of its parent object (III). Furthermore, if a nonoptional component of an object o cannot occur in any solution, then the parent object o cannot occur in any solution either (IV). If the specialization of an object o is part of the solution, then no other specialization of o can be part of the solution (V). If it becomes obvious that no specializations of an object o can occur in any solution, then it must be inferred that o cannot occur in the solution either (VI).

Attribute value sets are kept consistent by a special class of CE constraints. Where a value is deleted in the attribute value set of a specialization of an object o, the value must be deleted in the corresponding attribute value set of o, except if there is another specialization of o that contains the deleted value in the corresponding attribute value set[3]. If an attribute value is deleted in an attribute value set of an object o possessing specializations, then the same value must be deleted in all corresponding attribute value sets of the specializations of o. If an attribute value set of an object o becomes empty, then the nonexistence of o will be inferred by a special CE constraint.

By integrating the introduced CE constraints in the problem-solution model, the structural coherences between objects of the solution model are ensured with respect to their existence, nonexistence and attribute value sets. Moreover, the constraints formulated in the problem specification must be transformed into constraints of the problem-solution model.

---

[3] To avoid intensive checking, the attribute $value\_children\_list$ of the corresponding attribute object is checked and updated after each deletion of an attribute value.

3.3   Specified Constraints

Attribute value constraints and *existence constraints* result in the deletion of attribute values in the problem-solution model or in the setting of Ex_Var-attributes. *Relational constraints* between attribute value sets result in the deletion of attribute values, which become invalid because of the specified relation. If there are other value tuples that do not fulfill the relation, then some appropriate daemons have to be generated which control the relational constraints after each alteration of the attribute value sets in question. *Table constraints* define connections between the attribute value sets in question and existence information (Ex_Var) on the objects listed in the table head. Altering the attribute value sets or existence values results in the marking as invalid of corresponding table lines. If all table lines are marked as invalid, then the table constraint is not satisfied. Conversely, it is ensured that the attribute value sets in question contain only values that are registered in valid table lines[4]. *Compositional Constraints* are normally realized in the solution model by equations and inequations over corresponding Ex_Var-attributes. For each nonexistence statement of an object, the term "$1 - Ex\_Var$" is used instead of Ex_Var in the equation/inequation. *Conditional Constraints* are transformed into conditional transitions of the problem-solution model, which ensure the specified logical coherences within the problem-solution model. In order to substantially reduce the problem space within the problem-solution model, the contrapositions of the specified conditional constraints are also transformed into elements of the problem-solution model.

3.4   Configuration Process

Based on the outlined problem-solution model, a flexible and efficient problem-solution process (Figure 3) was realized within the prototypical configuration system ConBaCon using the CLP language CHIP. In particular, the object-based data management and the existence of *Conditional Propagation Rules*[5] in CHIP facilitated the implementation.

The specified configuration problem is transformed into objects of the problem-solution model. This means that the objects of the solution model are generated, corresponding CE constraints are inferred and set, and the specified constraints are transformed into corresponding constraints of the problem-solution model. The value one is assigned to the Ex_Var-attribute of the target object because the target object must exist in each solution.

Thanks to the generated model with the model-specific CE constraints, a substantial reduction of the search space is guaranteed. In [12] mathematical sentences with their proofs are presented which allow explicit identification of whether a given configuration-problem specification will be transformed by the described procedure into a *strong k-consistency* solution model (backtrack-free

---

[4] For implementation details of table constraints, see [12].

[5] Similar language elements exist in other CLP languages, e.g. Constraint-Handling Rules in ECLIPSE.

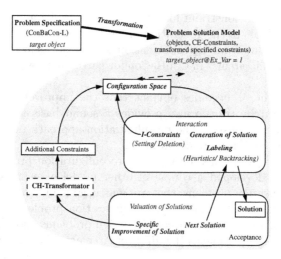

Fig. 3. Problem-Solution Process

solution process is ensured) or not. For specified problems that do not fulfill the required properties, instructions for possible preprocessing steps and – as an alternative – for generating interaction-control procedures for the configuration process are given.

We call the set of the currently active module objects of the problem-solution model *Configuration Space*. Interactive user constraints now can be given (one by one) relating to the existence or nonexistence of objects of the configuration space or to the shape of the corresponding attribute value sets. The user's freedom to decide which object or attribute value set of the configuration space should be restricted by an interactively given user constraint is a distinguishing feature compared with most other configuration models/tools. Governed by the constraints of the problem-solution model, this results in a new configuration space. Thus, a new cycle can start. Users can either give a new interactive constraint or they can delete previously given interactive user constraints. This allows the simulation of several user decisions, which is the prerequisite for a highly flexible configuration process. If no further interactive constraints are required, then the generation of a solution can be started. This is done by labeling the Ex_Var-attributes of the (still) active objects of the problem-solution model. Such labeling can be controlled by heuristics. This allows us to take into account preferences in the form of preference rules for controlling the labeling process. If the solution found is not suitable or fails to pass the solution-quality check, then further solutions can be created by backtracking. If a partial improvement of the solution suffices, then a specific solution improvement can be started by specification and processing of a constraint hierarchy, i.e., the constraints that must be satisfied unconditionally are specified as *hard* constraints, and the solution parts that should, if possible, be in the new solution or desired attribute values are fixed as *weak* constraints. The weak constraints can be marked with several weights. The specified constraint hierarchy is processed in an error-minimization process, which results in the generation of a set of equivalent (hard) constraints of the problem-solution model. Information about the realization and application of constraint hierarchies in ConBaCon for partial improvement can be found in [12].

At second sight, it becomes obvious that the improvement process using a constraint-hierarchy transformer provides a sound basis for reconfiguration, which is needed by industry. The reconfiguration approach using ConBaCon is described in [13], and in more detail in [12].

Besides model extensions for realizing reconfiguration processes with Con-BaCon, we have developed a couple of other model extensions which extend the set of configuration problems that are manageable by our approach. Among them are extensions for tackling large configuration problems (mainly clustering of the model; see [11, 12]), for certain design problems and for optimization-oriented configuration problems (handling of large nets of arithmetic constraints; see [12]).

In the following section, we present the idea of how to integrate time constraints into the solution model in such a way as to enable the solution of time-constrained configuration problems of the sort described in the Introduction.

4   Integrating Time Constraints

Time-constrained configuration problems emerge from classical configuration problems by taking into account availability times of preliminary products, processing times, constraints between these time points/slices and resource constraints regarding the required processing operations. We can distinguish between assembly processes and transformation processes. *Transformation processes* can be connected with all problem objects represented by module objects in the problem-solution model (cf. Section 3). *Assembly processes* are connected with all aggregated objects which are presented in the solution model by module objects with *structure_type = and-node* and their component elements. To be able to specify time-constrained configuration problems, we must of course add, some suitable specification primitives to the specification language ConBa-ConL. In the rest of this section we focus on necessary extensions of the problem solution model.

4.1   Availability Variables

For each module object o of the solution model, an availability FD-variable $avail(o)$ must be introduced, which represents the availability of the module.

The domain of each availability variable must contain the value *zero* as a special element.

If a module is a ground object (supply component), then the domain of the associated variable must contain, in addition to *zero*, all the time values at which the module is available. The domains of availability variables of nonground objects (not supply objects) initially get a proper FD-interval in addition to the special domain element *zero*, e.g. $\langle now, end\_of\_planning\_horizon \rangle^6$.

The inital domains of the availability variables are normally reduced after generating special constraints into the problem-solution model (see below). In order to get better propagation, it is advantageous to delete, in a preprocessing step, values from $\langle now, end\_of\_planning\_horizon \rangle$ that obviously cannot be valid because of the availabilities of the respective components (see next section).

Each processing step (or atomic chain of processing steps) in production can be explicitly associated with a module object. For each object o, we have to introduce an FD-variable *proctime(o)*.

To simplify the description, let us asume that the processing times are always *zero*. This restriction does not affect the quality of the presented model extensions because processing times greater than zero can be easily introduced into the model by proper additional addends (FD variables) in the model.

4.2 Availability Constraints

We must ensure the generation of proper constraints that specify the problem-dependent relations between the availability variables of a solution model. We call them *availability constraints*. In doing so, we must distinguish between *or-objects* (structure_type = or-node) and aggregated objects (structure_type = and-node).

Or-Objects. For each or-node o with specializations $s_1, \ldots, s_n$, we know that o can be available at earliest when one of its specializations s_i is available and the transformation operation possibly associated with s_i is finished. We can realize these dependencies between the availability variables of objects in an or-dependency using the same procedure, which is also used for model extensions relating to large nets of arithmetic constraints in specified configuration problems (for details, see [12]).

For each specialization dependency of a specified configuration problem, this procedure is called with parameters specifying the availability variable of the or-object R and the availability variable list S of the specializations. We have to ensure that values are deleted from the domains of the variables in L (exception: special value *zero*) if the values are deleted in the domain of R. Another procedure ensures that values are deleted from the domain of R if they are removed from the domains of all availability variables listed in L. In our model, this means that R is, in each generated problem solution, equal to one availability variable of L. This gives us the guarantee that the propagation will be done in the desired quality. Thus, the mentioned procedures ensure the consistency between availability value sets of an or-node and its specializations. By doing so, a complete propagation between the availability variables in or-dependencies is guaranteed.

Aggregated Objects. In the case of aggregated objects o with components $c_1, \ldots, c_n$, it is clear that $avail(o) = proctime(o) + max(avail(c_1) + proctime(c_1),$

---

[6] *now* should be greater than *zero*.

..., $avail(c_n) + proctime(c_n))$ if we assume that the assembly process can start at the earliest when all components are available after associated transformation processes are finished. In our solution model, we can realize this relation using the global constraint $maximum(CV,CVList)$ in addition to the predicates which we use for realizing the dependencies between or-objects (see above). The maximum constraint $maximum(CV,CVList)$ ensures that CV is the maximum of the elements of $CVList$.

The propagation realized in the aggregation procedure works in both directions: from the availability variable of the aggregated object o to the availability variables of its components and vice versa. If the availability variable domain of an aggregated object is restricted top-down, then the availability variable domains of all components will be restricted with the same limit. If "no real" availability time point remains, then the variable will be instantiated with the remaining value *zero*.

Initial Reduction of Availability Variables. After generation and activation of the described availability constraints, the initial availability-variable domains that belong to aggregated objects should be reduced before the configuration process is started. This should be done bottom-up with respect to the specified taxonomy. For each aggregated object o, the smallest value *limit* that is able to fulfill the *maximum* relation (see above) is calculated on the basis of the availability-variable domains of the components of o. All values from $\langle 1, limit-1 \rangle$ are deleted in $avail(o)$. Of course, further domain reductions can follow, caused by propagation due to the availability constraints of the model during the initial reduction process.

Constraints Between Availability and Existence. It is intuitively clear that object elements of configuration problems can be part of a problem solution if and only if they are available in time. A remaining task is introducing transformations of these constraints into our problem-solution model.

We can do this by extending the set of CE Constraints (see Section 3.2) by constraints between availability variables and their associated existence variables. To ensure the described dependencies, it is enough to generate, for each module object o, the following conditional constraints:

1. $Ex\_Var(o) = 0 \rightarrow avail(o) = 0$,
2. $avail(o) = 0 \rightarrow Ex\_Var(o) = 0$ and
3. $Ex\_Var(o) = 1 \rightarrow avail(o) > 0$.

4.3   Example of Time-Constrained Configuration

To understand better the way our configuration model works – and the extensions introduced in the previous sections – let us now consider the following example problem shown in Figure 4.

Given is the problem of configuring the complex product a, which consists of the components b, c and d. The specification elements b, c and d are abstract elements. This means that b can be instantiated in the final product either

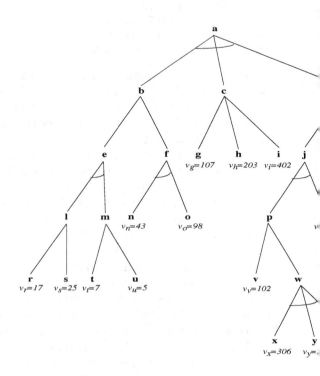

Fig. 4. Taxonomy of Product a with Given Av▮

with e or f, c with g, h or i, and d with j or k, and
components $g, h, i, k, n, o, q, r, s, t, u, v, x, y$ and z are grou▮
may be delivered by a supplier). For each of them, the ea▮
time is listed in the figure; v_s is, for instance, the earliest

For the sake simplicity, we assume that all operation
principle, however they could be greater than *zero*. On th▮
constraints relating to availability could also be integr▮
specification.

Let the specified configuration problem be transform▮
ing (constraint-based) problem-solution model following t▮
Section 3. In addition to this transformation process, av▮
availability constraints are generated as described in Sect▮

After processing the initial reduction of the availab▮
of aggregated objects (see above) and following the dom▮
the constraints realized in the solution model, we obtain
domains:

$\mathrm{dom}(\mathrm{avail}(q)) = \{0, 109\},$
$\mathrm{dom}(\mathrm{avail}(l)) = \{0, 17, 25\},$
$\mathrm{dom}(\mathrm{avail}(m)) = \{0, 5, 7\},$
$\mathrm{dom}(\mathrm{avail}(p)) = \{0, 102, 306\},$
$\mathrm{dom}(\mathrm{avail}(e)) = \{0, 17, 25\},$
$\mathrm{dom}(\mathrm{avail}(f)) = \{0, 98\},$
$\mathrm{dom}(\mathrm{avail}(j)) = \{0, 109, 306\},$
$\mathrm{dom}(\mathrm{avail}(b)) = \{0, 17, 25, 98\},$
$\mathrm{dom}(\mathrm{avail}(c)) = \{0, 107, 203, 402\},$
$\mathrm{dom}(\mathrm{avail}(d)) = \{0, 109, 111, 306\},$
$\mathbf{dom(avail(a))} = \{0, 109, 111, 203, 306, 402\}.$

Now the main configuration process, which is described in Section 3.4 can be started. In addition to the "conventional" questions, which can be answered during the configuration process, we are now able to investigate time-relevant questions as well. For instance, the user can observe that the earliest delivery time for product a is 109.

Also, it is obviously possible to answer questions of the type mentioned in the introduction using the problem solution model. For instance, system users are able to investigate, which configurations of a are available if they set the latest delivery time to 203. This demand is equivalent with the interactively given constraint $avail(a) \leq 203$. Because of the *maximum constraint* between $avail(a), avail(b), aivail(c)$ and $avail(d)$ (see Section 4.2), the value 402 is deleted from $dom(avail(c))$ and the value 306 is removed from the domain of $avail(d)$. This immediately implies the deletion of 306 in $dom(avail(j))$ due to the *domain_aeq_cb constraints* between $avail(c), avail(g), avail(h)$ and $avail(i)$ and between $avail(d), avail(j)$ and $avail(k)$. The deletion of 402 in the domain of $avail(i)$ results in the implication of the nonexistence of i because of the constraint $avail(i) = 0 \rightarrow Ex\_Var(i) = 0$ (cf. Section 4.2). And so on.

As a result of the hard demand that the latest possible delivery time be 203, our solution model deduces that neither the component i nor the component x can be included in the final product.

The configuration process can now be continued in the familiar way (see Section 3.4). Of course, reconfiguration processes can also be started after the generation of a solution.

5   Conclusion

We have presented some fundamental information about our constraint-based problem-solution model ConBaCon for the configuration and reconfiguration of technical systems/industrial products. An idea of the complexity of the configuration problems that can be tackled by the solution model was given by describing the main elements of the corresponding specification language ConBaConL.

The problem-solution model – together with several extensions[7] – was realized using the CLP language CHIP. The resulting ConBaCon system was successfully used with several realistic and abstract configuration problems, including the configuration of power-supply systems for large electric motors and the configuration of computer rack systems.

By substantially reducing the search space, the problem-solution model – together with the underlying CLP system – allows an efficient configuration process that can be flexibly controlled by user interactions. It is ensured that each solution obtained is correct with respect to the problem specification and the underlying constraint solver. In addition, the completeness of the solution process is guaranteed.

The main focus of this paper was on novel model extensions that allow the flexible solving of time-constrained configuration problems. Compared with other configuration systems, this is a distinguishing feature of the resulting problem-solution model. Given the rather general nature of the extensions, we assume that the key ideas presented here can also be integrated quite easily into other constraint-based configuration systems or configuration libraries like ILOG Configurator.

The new features of the problem-solution model were demonstrated by means of an example.

Our extended configuration model offers a broad range of interesting tasks for future work. For instance, the development of extensions for time-constrained multiproduct configurations as well as investigations on the tighter integration of scheduling systems into the problem-solution model are important areas of future research.

References

1. Axling, T.: Collaborative Interactive Design in Virtual Environments. www.sics.se/~axling/3dobelics.html (1996)
2. Axling, T., Haridi, S.: A Tool for Developing Interactive Configuration Applications. Logic Programming 26 (2) (1996) 147-168
3. Fleischanderl, G. et al.: Configuring Large Systems Using Generative Constraint Satisfaction. IEEE- Intelligent Systems 13 (4) (1998)
4. Freuder, E. C.: The Role of Configuration Knowledge in the Business Process. IEEE Intelligent Systems 13 (4) (1998)
5. Geller, S.: Come, and they will build it. Manufacturing Systems (June 1999)
6. Gupta, L., Chionglo, J. F., Fox, M. S.: A Constraint Based Model of Coordination in Concurrent Design Projects. www.ie.utoronto.ca/EIL/DITL/WETICE96/ProjectCoordination/ (1996)
7. Haselböck, A., Stumptner, M.: A Constraint-Based Architecture for Assembling Large-Scale Technical Systems. Proceedings of International Conference on Expert Systems Applications/ AI in Engineering. Edinburgh (1993)
8. Van Hentenryck, P., Saraswat, V.: Constraint Programming: Strategic Directions. J. of Constraints (2) (1997)

---

[7] Links to the corresponding publications are given in the paper.

9. John, U.: Constraint-Based Design of Reliable Industrial Control Systems. In: Bajic, V.(eds.): Advances in Systems, Signals, Control and Computers. IAAMSAD. Durban, South Africa (1998)

10. John, U.: Model and Implementation for Constraint-Based Configuration. Proceedings of the 11th International Conference on Applications of Prolog, INAP'98. Tokyo (1998)

11. John, U.: Solving Large Configuration Problems Efficiently by Clustering the ConBaCon Model. Proceedings of the 13th International Conference on Industrial and Engineering Applications of Artificial Intelligence and Expert Systems, IEA/AIE-2000. Lecture Notes in Artificial Intelligence, Vol. 1821, Springer-Verlag, Berlin Heidelberg New York (2000)

12. John, U.: Configuration and Reconfiguration with Constraint-based Modelling (in German). PhD Thesis Technical University of Berlin. DISKI 255, Aka-Verlag, Berlin (2001)

13. John, U., Geske, U.: Reconfiguration of Technical Products Using ConBaCon. Proceedings of the AAAI'99 Workshop on Configuration. Orlando (1999)

14. John, U., Geske, U.: Constraint-Based Configuration of Large Systems. In: Bartenstein, O. et al: Web Knowledge Management and Decision Support. Revised Papers of 14th International Conference on Applications of Prolog, INAP 2001. Lecture Notes in Artificial Intelligence, Vol. 2543, Springer-Verlag, Berlin Heidelberg New York (2003)

15. Van Parunak et al.: Distributed Component-Centered Design as Agent-Based Distributed Constraint Optimization. Proceedings of the AAAI'97 Workshop on Constraints and Agents. Providence (1997)

16. Pasik, A. J.: The Configuration Invasion. Report, Lazard Frères & Co. LLC, www.selectica.com/html/articles/Lazard1.html. New York (1998)

17. Sabin, D., Freuder, E. C.: Configuration as Composite Constraint Satisfaction. Proceedings of AAAI'96. Portland (1996)

18. Sabin, D., Weigel, R.: Product Configuration Frameworks - A Survey. IEEE- Intelligent Systems 13 (4) (1998)

19. Stumptner, M.: An Overview of Knowledge-Based Configuration. AI Communications 10 (2) (1997)

Distributed Constraint-Based Railway Simulation

Hans Schlenker

Fraunhofer FIRST, Kekuléstr. 7, 12489 Berlin, Germany
hans.schlenker@first.fraunhofer.de

Abstract. In railway simulation, given timetables have to be checked against various criteria, mainly correctness and robustness. Most existing approaches use classical centralized simulation techniques. This work goes beyond that in two main aspects: We use constraint satisfaction to get rid of deadlock problems and the simulation is done distributedly for better performance. This should make it possible to solve very large railway simulation problems.

1 Introduction

This paper is organized as follows: In the first section, I give short introductions to Railway Simulation (Sec. 1.1), Constraint-based Railway Simulation (Sec. 1.2), and Distributed Constraint-based Railway Simulation (Sec. 1.3), each with reference to the current state of the art. Sec. 2 contains the main contribution of this paper: the algorithm DRS. In Sec. 3, I describe our extensive implementation of DRS. Sec. 4 empirically evaluates both algorithm and implementation through a case study. Sec. 5 concludes the contribution, and in Sec. 6, I give some outlook.

1.1 Railway Simulation

A railway system [11, 15] consists of a set of stations, a network of tracks that connects the stations, a set of trains, and a timetable. The timetable assigns to each train and each station this train must pass two points in time: when the train is scheduled to reach the station (*arrival*) and when to leave (*departure*). Each train moves from one station to the next along the network built by the tracks. Signals and additional devices like train-end-detectors ensure safety on the tracks. Blocks are subnets, delimited by signals and train-end-detectors. The railway's today's fundamental safety rule, which applies to all current long-distance railways, is: *There may never be more than one train within one block.*

The issue of *railway simulation* is to virtually let trains run through the network and to check whether the timetable is satisfiable (*correctness*) or stable against perturbations (*robustness*), always under the given safety restrictions. Note that the timetable to be checked is given in advance.

There exist some fundamental approaches for simulating physical systems [4, 7]: continuous vs. discrete event simulation and time driven vs. event driven

D. Seipel et al. (Eds.): INAP/WLP 2004, LNAI 3392, pp. 215–226, 2005.

simulation. Common to all approaches is that the real world system is described in terms of states and events. In continuous event simulation, "state changes occur continuously in time, while in a discrete simulation, the occurrence of an event is instantaneous and fixed to a selected point in time"[7]. Also according to [7], any continuous model can be converted to an equivalent discrete model, such that discrete event simulation can be used to model every physical system. It is obvious that discrete event simulation can be done naturally on modern (discrete) computer architectures.

In time driven simulation, the simulator looks at the virtual system in discrete points in time. You can think of this simulation following a given clock pulse. Event driven simulation, on the other hand, uses an event list, that stores all future events. When an event is processed (the one in the list with the lowest time stamp), this may generate new events which are inserted into the list according to their future time stamp (e.g. [4]). Event driven simulation has already been successfully applied to traffic simulation problems (e.g. [14]).

Distributed event simulation is an extension to event driven simulation. Here, the system to be simulated is divided into parts, which are evaluated on physically distinct (computer) nodes. Events are sent through the simulator's network from where they occur to where they make an impact on. Milestone works on discrete event simulation (e.g. [4, 8]) deal with methods how to asynchronously let some nodes run into the (simulated) future while others still treat the (simulated) past.

1.2   Constraint-Based Railway Simulation

In constraint-based simulation (CBS), we also use discrete time events, but use a completely different modeling: The system to be simulated is described as one complex constraint satisfaction problem (CSP) [10]. This CSP is then solved using well-known and newly adapted propagation and search techniques. A solution to the CSP is finally mapped into a description of a simulation run.

CBS basically works as follows. The railway network is mapped into an abstract discrete model: It is divided into *blocks*, while each *real track section* may belong to more than one block. A block is then the atomic exclusion unit: In no event, one block may be occupied by more than one train at the same time. The way of a train through the network is divided into blocks such that the concatenation of all parts makes up the whole way of the train from its source to its destination. Figure 1 depicts this approach. The blocks are modeled using constraint variables for the starting times and durations, which are connected through arithmetic equations. The timetable is given by minimal departure times for each train and each block (possibly being 0). Note that the arrival times are not directly given as constraints!

The fundamental safety law is ensured using well-known resource constraints (like *cumulative* or *diffn* [1]). Each block is modelled as a set of tasks, that share start and duration times. Each task relates to a track section. And each track section is modelled as an exclusive resource. Assigning start and duration times to each part with respect to its block gives then rather directly a solution to the simulation problem.

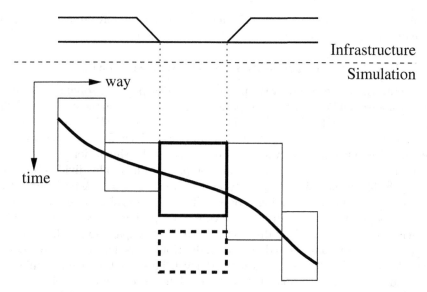

Fig. 1. Constraint-based railway simulation: The upper part of this figure depicts a very simple railway network: one track from left to right, two shunting switches, and two additional tracks, each starting at a shunting, then parallel to the main track.

The lower part describes the way of a train running on the main track, together with (assignment) blocks. The thick line (a so-called *distance-time curve*) depicts the way of the train, going from left to right, through time (vertically, top to bottom) and space (along the track). The train's way is surrounded by blocks (rectangles) that are related to the infrastructure (e.g. the thick bounded one relates to the single track section above). Each block describes the assignment in time of the according train to the block.

The fundamental safety law requires that corresponding rectangles never overlap: The dashed bounded block of another train must not overlap the thick bounded block of this train on one and the same track section

The big advantage of this approach is that deadlock situations are detected very early: constraint propagation does this for us. We can thus prevent most situations where a number of trains jointly lock up parts of the railway network. This is the case for example when one track serves both directions (which is a common situation in Germany) and two opposed trains stand head to head (in theory, a train can't go backwards). This special one-track case has been exhausted in [5].

In contrast to classical approaches, ours does not have a continuous advancing simulation time: Propagation may run from the future to the past. This is untypical compared to classical simulation. Fortunately, this approach has an analogon in our real-world problem: The actual movements of all trains are guided by a real-time train management. This management also looks into the future, when determining the actual train's scheduling, for example to decide which train may leave a certain station immediately, and which one has to wait. Constraint based simulation equivalently uses this information to detect and avoid deadlock cases. We call this approach therefore *look-ahead* simulation.

1.3   Distributed Constraint-Based Railway Simulation

In general, there are several reasons for *distributed* problem solving: reliability, privacy and social boundaries, and performance and load balancing (see e.g. [9]). This work is part of the research and development project SIMONE [13]. There, we want to solve very large simulation problems. Therefore, *performance* (or *scalability*) is our main motivation for distributing the simulation.

In distributed simulation, the simulation problem has to be divided into subparts, which are then simulated in several computing nodes. A meta-algorithm conducts the cooperative solving process. There are several general purpose concepts to cooperatively solve distributed constraint problems: e.g. [3, 16, 19]. Most of them are characterized by distributed search or propagation. I, however, favor a more application-oriented approach: distribution is done on the application level rather than on the constraint network level. This avoids vast communication overhead due to micro-propagation between different computers over some network. Propagation in its very constraint programming sense (e.g. looking-ahead, forward-checking [10]) is done only within one simulator node. Coordination is done by the meta-algorithm.

Regarding railway simulation, there is currently one important work dealing with *distributed* simulation: [12]. Here, a number of local discrete event simulations jointly compute a global simulation. Each local node is responsible for a part of the network and the nodes exchange train information for trains leaving a subnet and entering another subnet. The simulation clocks are synchronized such that all computing nodes know about the global simulation time. This is also the main drawback of this approach: There is usually a lot of synchronization information to be communicated. This bottleneck greatly obstructs scalability of the algorithm.

2   Algorithm

Figure 2 sketches my distributed railway simulation algorithm DRS. Initially (1), the global simulation problem is divided into parts, which are distributed on several computing nodes (see also Sec. 2.1). There, solutions for the local problems are computed (2): the boxes in (2) show very simplified *distance-time curves* like that in Fig. 1. Information regarding the borders of the sub-problems is then communicated (showed by the dashed arrows) between sub-problems' neighbors. While the local problems are globally inconsistent – what can be detected locally – the local simulations are iterated (2), taking into account the neighbors information (see also Sec. 2.2). Finally (3), a globally consistent solution is achieved (see also Sec. 2.3).

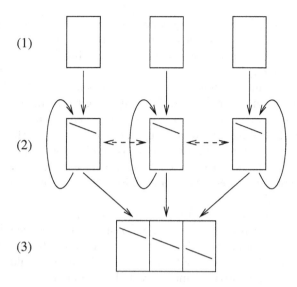

Fig. 2. The DRS algorithm

2.1 Problem Distribution

Each railway simulation problem is kind of naturally distributed: Its track network is spread spatially. Therefore, the natural way to decompose and distribute the simulation problem is along the railway network: We cut the network into subnets.

In our real-world problem, the data is already pre-partitioned. Each track section belongs to exactly one so-called *operating site* (OS, German *Betriebsstelle*). So, each OS o consists of a number s_o of track sections, and to each of o's neighbors o' a number $t_{o,o'}$ of crossing trains. The OSs together with their neighboring relation form a network. The nodes in this network are weighted by s_o, and the edges between two nodes o and o' are weighted by $t_{o,o'}$. We also assume some given k that relates to the number of available computing nodes.

This network is then cut into k parts such that the sum of s_o in all parts is uniformly distributed (there is no part with a sum that is by far greater than the other sums), and the edge cut is minimized. The edge cut is the sum of the weights of cut edges, i.e. edges between nodes that do not belong to the same part. This partitioning is the basis for the problem distribution. The described optimizations imply that the size of the different sub-problems is uniformly distributed and therefore the workload for the computing nodes is balanced, and that the number of crossing trains that have to be communicated between different nodes is minimized, reducing communication and – as we will see – re-computation costs.

2.2 Iterations

The local sub-problems are given by sub-nets of the global track network. In each local iteration, the sub-problem is simulated using the above described constraint-based simulation technique. As soon as such a simulation is finished, the entering and leaving times of all crossing trains are communicated to the node's neighbors. Thus, each node can locally determine which train's simulation is globally inconsistent.

While there are inconsistent trains, the local simulation CSP is extended, such that the local times for incoming and outgoing trains must be *greater than or equal to* the times given by the neighbors. Then, a new solution to the updated CSP is computed, leading to new entering and leaving times. All *new times that are different* from previous solutions, are considered (globally) inconsistent and are therefore communicated to the neighbors. Since each train that crosses parts may trigger re-computations of local simulations, it is obvious that their number should be kept minimal.

Note that the computations of the local simulations can be done interleaved: While one node a is computing, its neighbor b can be finished, sending a the new crossing data. Some moments before, b's other neighbor c finished its work and sent some connection data to b so that b now immediately could recompute its local simulation, taking into account c's work. He would not wait until a finished. This approach makes maximal use of the available computing resources. It is, however, not deterministic: Two (global) simulation-runs on the same problem may not produce the same results, depending on the order in which the local simulation jobs have been executed.

It is a strict requirement (from the railway experts) in the SIMONE project, that simulations *can be* done deterministically. This issue can be solved by synchronizing the simulation processes: All local simulations wait for each other after they have finished their local computations. And when all are finished, all of them communicate and then all of them recompute (in case it is necessary). This algorithm is deterministic and therefore always yields the same results. The drawback here is that the computational resources are used less optimally.

2.3   Formal Properties

Many distributed problem solving algorithms do not terminate on their own in all cases. Mostly, there has to be some algorithm-external termination detection. DRS, however, is guaranteed to terminate, i.e. it always finds a solution (if one exists) in finite time. I proved this termination property together with correctness of the algorithm theoretically. However, due to lack of space, I can't give the proof in detail here.

Its baseline is as follows: The trains are ordered by some pre-defined global priority and treated in each local simulation part accordingly. So, no two trains can displace each other forever: For each two trains there is a major and a minor one and the major one always and everywhere supersedes the minor one. Furthermore, with DRS the simulated departure times of all trains always advance. So, although the timeline is potentially infinite, the global consistency algorithm always converges and terminates finitely.

3   Realization

DRS is designed as a *grid-computing system* [18]: The simulation work should be done by standard workstations that are registered with some central information service and can be used by various clients. Figure 3 shows the global architecture: There is exactly one central server machine, one or more workstations that do the simulation computation, and one or more client machines. All these nodes are connected by some standard Ethernet network.

The server runs the central information service called DIR. This is embedded in a Tomcat server, which is a very stable and operating-system independent platform. Tomcat [2] is an open-source web server written in Java. It is designed as a runtime environment for web services and provides remote management facilities for these. It can thus be used as an application server, as we do it in DRS. The server machine usually hosts additionally a database and CVS service. The latter is used for an integrated development process that allows updating most of DRS' components while the system is running! The DIR must always run since it is the only common service point that all system components must know.

On each workstation there is a WRK service – also running inside a Tomcat – that provides the worker's facilities to the system. The WRK registers itself with the central DIR. The workstations can be shut down, in which case the WRK unregisters with the DIR. Thus, the DIR always knows about all living workers.

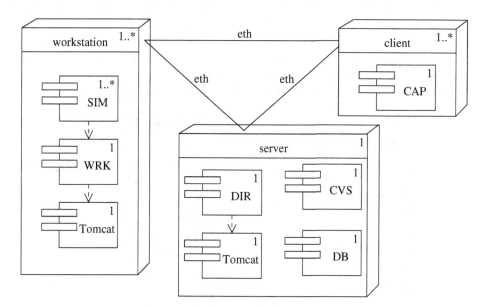

Fig. 3. The DRS architecture

The clients for the user run on some possibly smaller terminals, there may be several clients at a time. The CAP clients contact the DIR to get the list of available workers and – after the user has configured the simulation to be done – reserve there workers for their own use. When the simulation is started, the WRK servers create SIM objects – possibly more than one each – that do the local simulation. The algorithm control is either done centralized inside the CAP or decentralized within the WRKs.

Although it is still a prototype, our implementation is already very stable: The DIR usually runs for weeks without the need for restarting it, and we recently did 900 successive simulations on one and the same running WRK instances.

4   Case Study

The major example, we are working with in the SIMONE project, is based on real world data of a part of the German railway. Table 1 summarizes its characteristics.

Each track section is a part of the railway network, delimited by signals, train-end-detectors, switches, or the like. The example's timetable knows about 1118 trains altogether. It contains, however, data for trains running for example from Monday to Friday, only on weekends, or every day. Thus, only a part of all trains run actually on e.g. Monday. The *Germany* column – taken from [6] – gives you some impression on how the example relates to the whole German railway system.

The main parameters that specify a concrete simulation problem are: the (part of the whole) timetable (e.g. Monday), the trains (e.g. all that start between

Table 1. Characteristics of our example data. The left column describes the whole data set, the middle column the part of the timetable for one day of the week, and the right column roughl the equivalents for the whole German railway network

	Example	Monday	Germany
sum track length [km]	1006.503		65005
operating sites OS	104		
avg track length / OS [km]	9.678		
track sections	7111		
avg track section length [km]	0.142		
avg track sections / OS	68		
avg trains / day	795	781	34950
avg trains / OS	123		
avg OSs / train	11		
avg track sections / train	266		
avg train way / train [km]	43.509	37.844	
avg train way / day [km]	34583.981	29556.384	

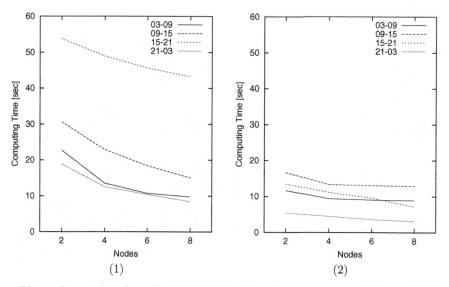

Fig. 4. Experimental results: all 104 OSs (1), and a connected selection of 67 (2)

9 and 10 a.m.), and the spatial parts of the network. For the DRS system, the user additionally can select mainly: the set of workers to be used, the partitioning, synchronized (deterministic) or non-synchronized (non-deterministic) operation, and central or de-central control.

Figure 4 shows some empirical results of DRS: In (1), we simulated the whole example, while in (2) we used only about half of the operating sites or network. In both cases, we separately simulated the trains from 3 a.m. to 9 a.m. ("03-09"), from 9 a.m. to 3 p.m. ("09-15"), from 3 p.m. to 9 p.m. ("15-21"), and from 9 p.m. to 3 a.m. ("21-03"). So, here, we did not do the whole day but different 6-hour timeslices. And, we tried all this on 2, 4, 6, and 8 computing nodes. Each node is equipped with 1GB of memory and 2 AMD K7 processors working at 1.2 GHz and runs Red Hat 8.0 Linux 2.4 and Sun's Java 1.4.0.

We can see from (1) that the computing times for simulating the whole network may differ greatly from timeslice to timeslice: The 15-21 one takes more than 50 seconds on 2 nodes and even on 8 nodes more than 40 seconds, while simulating the trains from 09-15 takes between 15 and 31 seconds. This comes mainly from the different problems' complexity: There are 199 trains in timeslice 03-09, 243 in 09-15, 259 in 15-21, and 199 in 21-03. But although the number of trains in 09-15 and 15-21 are not too different, the latter takes about twice as long as the former. Sometimes there are local problems, that are hard to solve, e.g. when there are many trains very close together. And this is not necessarily exactly the same situation in all timeslices. So, obviously, there is some exceptional problem in the 15-21 slice.

If we take only a spatial part of the network – 67 connected OSs out of the whole 104, see Figure 4 (2) – the simulation times get reduced by an average of 50% and the exceptional problem with one of the timeslices disappears. The overall reason for these differences is that the example contains some very very heavy (or complex) OSs whose local computation takes by far longer than that of the others. And since we do not split OSs when dividing and distributing the global problem, having more computing nodes does not help solving the heavy parts. This may limit the scalability of the overall algorithm, as can be seen in the 15-21 case in (1).

We generated and compared different problem partitionings with 16, 30 and 50 parts. The 30s partitioning turned out to be best for most of the problems. So, the above tests are all based on this partitioning. I already mentioned, that the system can operate in synchronized or non-synchronized mode – here we used the synchronized mode since it always produces the same simulation result for a given problem and therefore should be preferred by most users. In fact, the non-synchronized mode is slightly faster (about 10 to 25%, according other experiments we made). Additionally, we could use central or de-central control. Our implementation allows synchronized operation only in company with central control, so we used this one. We ran each particular test five times and averaged the resulting computing times.

It should be noted that solving the local simulation problem includes solving a job-shop scheduling problem. Each track section can thus be regarded as a machine that is used by *blocks* (see Section 1.2), the jobs. Each job consists of consecutive tasks. Each train uses an average of 266 track sections, thus building 266 tasks. So, in the morning timeslice 03-09, there are about $266 * 199 = 52934$ tasks, $266 * 243 = 64638$ in 09-15, $266 * 259 = 68894$ in 15-21, and about $266 * 199 = 52934$ in 21-03. And all those have to be scheduled onto 7111 machines! So, each simulation problem is quite a large job-shop-scheduling problem. DRS solves them very quickly.

Our example is not very dense, nor did we try to find an optimal schedule for the trains. So, there was very few search needed for finding the *simulation solutions*. The 03-09 time slice took 486 backtracking steps, the 09-15 one took 1635, the 15-21 one took 1485, and the 21-03 one took only 320 steps. Note that these are not average counts because we used the synchronized mode, where each simulation is done deterministically, independant from execution sequences or even the number of computing nodes!

5 Conclusion

I presented here the railway simulation algorithm DRS that uses – in contrast to existing approaches – constraint programming and distributed problem solving. I showed that we have a fast, stable and powerful implementation that proves the algorithms abilities empirically. Some essential features have also been testified theoretically.

6   Outlook

In addition to *simulate* a given timetable, the DRS algorithm could also be used to *generate* a new timetable, rather from scratch. We would only have given the physical characteristics of the trains (together with the exact running time computation), pre-defined train routes through the network, and rough time slots, when the trains should run. The exact timetable could then obviously be computed using DRS and appropriate local simulators.

But, for finding a good timetable, we would need some form of *optimization*: the system should be able to find *good* or *better* timetables wrt. some optimization criterion related to the timetable (e.g. minimal running times of expensive trains, or minimization of transfer delays). This is currently not possible, the trains are always delayed (shifted into the future through the *greater-or-equal* constraints). Optimization could be done through some *controlled cooling*: The trains are computed in the order of their given priority, and in each iteration steps, some high-priority trains keep their exact time slots, while for all lower-priority trains, earlier time slots (than in the previous iterations) could be tried. The frontier between fixed and optimizable trains should then be advanced from iteration to iteration, cooling the system step by step.

With this extension, DRS could be used for railway timetable *construction*. Another possible application is *distributed process scheduling* or *supply chain management*. There, tasks, that are connected wrt. time and content, have to be scheduled and optimized. They could be modelled similarly to our blocks. The schedule would be computed distributedly by DRS.

We could even use DRS as a general labeling procedure for distributed constraint satisfaction problems: There, usually, a number of (distributed) agents each take care of a constraint network. These networks are connected through some shared variables: variables of different agents, that represent the same entity and have to get the same value in a final solution to the CSP. These connecting variables make a large single constraint network out of the distributed local ones.

The intensional equality between shared variables is usually realized by external *equality* constraints, i.e. constraints between different agents. And these external equality constraints could be realized by DRS through the distributed search process: Here we use in each agent (or simulator) a *greater-or-equal* constraint such that when finally a consistent state is reached, all these *greater-or-equal* constraints hold, and thus equality holds between the shared variables.

References

1. A. Aggoun and N. Beldiceanu. Extending CHIP in order to solve complex scheduling and placement problems. *Mathematical and Computer Modelling*, 1993.
2. Apache Software Foundation. *Apache Tomcat*. http://jakarta.apache.org/tomcat/.
3. P. Berlandier and B. Neveu. Problem partition and solvers coordination in distributed constraint satisfaction. In *Proc. Workshop on Parallel Processing in Articial Intelligence (PPAI-95)*, Montreal, Canada, 1995.

4. K. M. Chandy and R Sherman. Space-time and simulation. In *Proc. SCS Multi-conference on Distributed Simulation*, 1989.

5. Elias Silva de Oliveira. *Solving Single-Track Railway Scheduling Problem Using Constraint Programming*. PhD thesis, The University of Leeds, UK, 2001.

6. Deutsche Bahn AG. *Daten und Fakten 2002*.

7. Alois Ferscha. Parallel and distributed simulation of discrete event systems. In *Handbook of Parallel and Distributed Computing*. McGraw-Hill, 1995.

8. Richard M. Fujimoto. Parallel discrete event simulation. *Communications of the ACM*, 33(10):30–52, 1990.

9. Markus Hannebauer. *Autonomous Dynamic Reconfiguration in Collaborative Problem Solving*. PhD thesis, Technische Universität Berlin, 2001.

10. Pascal Van Hentenryck. *Constraint Satisfaction in Logic Programming*. MIT Press, 1989.

11. Daniel Hürlimann. *Objektorientierte Modellierung von Infrastrukturelementen und Betriebsvorgängen im Eisenbahnwesen*. PhD thesis, Eidgenössische Technische Hochschule Zürich, 2001.

12. Volker Klahn. *Die Simulation großer Eisenbahnnetze*. PhD thesis, Universität Hannover, 1994.

13. Dirk Matzke and Maren Bolemant. Modellierung innovativer Systemtechniken der Zugbeeinflussung mit constraint-logischer Programmierung. In *ASIM – Symposium Simulationstechnik*. SCS Europe, 2003.

14. B. C. Merrifield, S. B. Richardson, and J. B. G. Roberts. Quantitative studies of discrete event simulation modelling of road traffic. In *Proc. SCS Multiconference on Distributed Simulation*, 1990.

15. Jörn Pachl. *Systemtechnik des Schienenverkehrs*. B. G. Teubner, 2000.

16. Georg Ringwelski. *Asynchrones Constraintlösen*. PhD thesis, Technische Universität Berlin, 2003.

17. Hans Schlenker. *Distributed Constraint-based Railway Simulation*. PhD thesis, Technische Universität Berlin, to appear.

18. Detlef Schoder, Kai Fischbaum, and Rene Teichmann, editors. *Peer-to-Peer*. Springer, 2002.

19. Makoto Yokoo, Edmund H. Durfee, Toru Ishida, and Kazuhiro Kuwabara. The distributed constraint satisfaction problem: Formalization and algorithms. *IEEE Transactions on Knowledge and Data Engineering*, 10(5), September 1998.

Concurrent Engineering to Wisdom Engineering

Shuichi Fukuda

Tokyo Metropolitan Institute of Technology,
6-6, Asahigaoka, Hino, Tokyo, 191-0065, Japan
fukuda@tmit.ac.jp
http://www.tmit.ac.jp/

Abstract. 21st century will be an age of wisdom, where product development will be replaced by wisdom development. We have been producing products, but from now on, we have to move in such a direction as to satisfy higher level needs in Maslow's Hierarchy. An age of wisdom is a world of combinations and Wisdom Engineering, which developed from Concurrent Engineering through Collaborative Engineering, and which is based upon the world of combinations, will serve extensively for wisdom development.

1   Introduction

Concurrent Engineering at its initial stage was discussed widely in terms of time concurrency. Emphasis was placed upon bringing downstream information more upstream so that adequate decisions can be made at an earlier stage. Time to market was greatly reduced.

With the diversification of society, Concurrent Engineering was interpreted more in terms of space concurrency. Requirements vary from customer to customer. Concurrent Engineering provided a solution to cope with this diversification problem and to satisfy our customers.

But the growing diversification required more and more heads to really solve the problem. Thus, the importance of strategy and team working are emphasized. Concurrent Engineering is now called Collaborative Engineering to emphasize the importance of collaboration.

The 21st century is the age of wisdom. What we sell is not products, but wisdom. Product value is determined by market but wisdom is not. Only wisdom creators know its true value. When people with different grounds meet and discuss, they come up with wisdom that is beyond the sum of their individual knowledge and experience. The wisdom thus created cannot be truly evaluated without them. Thus these people must explore a new market and sell their wisdom.

The age of wisdom will change the whole scene of business. We have been creating products and selling them to market. But from now on, what we have to create is market itself. How we can secure the final functions of a product has long been thought to be the most important issue in product development. In fact, that is why we call this activity 'product development'. But we must be

D. Seipel et al. (Eds.): INAP/WLP 2004, LNAI 3392, pp. 227–244, 2005.

aware that the business situations are quickly changing. Processes themselves are yielding market value as well as the final product functions, as is exemplified by software and games. Thus, the new age will be the age of product, process and market creation. Wisdom will play a central role there.

Concurrent Engineering in this new age should be called Wisdom Engineering, which provides the common ground for people to communicate in order to create wisdom.

2   World Is Changing Now

2.1   Age of Mass Production

Traditional society has been linear. It may be compare to a railroad. We can easily tell our destination. We could predict easily. Problems did not vary too much so that tactics were emphasized (Fig. 1).

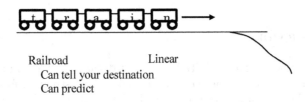

Railroad   Linear
         Can tell your destination
         Can predict

Fig. 1. Linear society compared to a railroad

This age of mass production was a product oriented society.Final product functions alone were emphasized and the process to produce a product has been considered just as a cost increasing factor.

It may also be compared to agriculture. Although the environment changes from season to season, it does not vary too much and we will produce more and better quality products, if we fertilize the farmland properly. The market is fundamentally fixed.

Although we moved from gproduct outh to gmarket inh to cope with the diversification of customersf requirements, chief attention is still paid to the same old market.

2.2   Age of Wisdom

Society from now on will be diversifying more and more so it will become non-linear. It may be compared to a ship going out to sea. We cannot predict easily. We have to examine where we will go and how we can get there. Many factors are involved and they are not easy to cope with. Therefore, strategy becomes increasingly important (Fig.2).

In this age of wisdom, we have to determine first of all where we will head for, or in other words, which market we should explore. We have to create a new

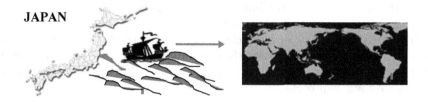

Fig. 2. Nonlinear society compared to ship going out to sea

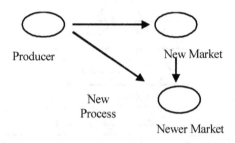

Fig. 3. Process and market oriented age of wisdom

market, and we have to develop a new process to get there. These new processes and markets will create new types of value (Fig.3).

Creating new markets and new processes may be compared to hunting. If we come across the game which is stronger than us, we have to use a new tool, but if this new tool does not work, then we have to look for another game which we can kill.

3   Creating for What?

It is very important for us to look back and ask ourselves once again for what we are creating. Maslow's Hierarchy of Needs [1] provides us with a good perspective. Maslow classified our needs into 5 levels. The first or bottom level is physiological needs. We have to eat for living. The second level is safety and security needs. After we satisfy our appetite, we would like to keep ourselves safe from severe environments. The 3rd level is love and belonging needs. We would like to be a member of some communities. We need a family. The 4th level is esteem needs. We would like to be respected by others. The 5th level is self actualization. Art will satisfy our self actualization needs (Fig.4).

Agriculture and fishing industries may be considered to satisfy our bottom level needs. These needs are primarily important. Housing is the industry to satisfy our second level needs. Note that industries seem to be climbing up the hierarchy. Recently games become very popular. Games may be considered as one of the means to self actualization. Brands may be interpreted as one of the ways to satisfy our 3rd or 4th level needs.

If we are climbing up the hierarchy, then we must be more creative. We have to create wisdom how we can satisfy such needs. We have to ask ourselves for what we are creating. We have to look for a good strategy to produce a new market with a new process.

Fig. 4. Maslow's Hierarchy of Needs

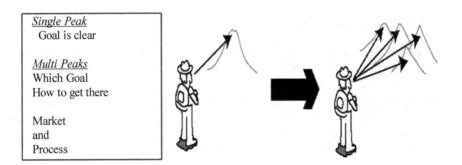

Fig. 5. World of Single Peak to World of Multiple Peaks

In our traditional world, there was only a single peak. But now our world is quickly expanding and there are many peaks around us. So we have to determine which peak we should climb and which path we should take to get there (Fig.5).

4   Combine Type and Overlap Type

When we build up a system, there are two types (Fig.6).

'Combine Type' develops a system by combining independent functional elements, while 'Overlap Type' considers functional overlapping. For example, US robots separate functions into independent elements while Japanese ones assemble many different functions into one.

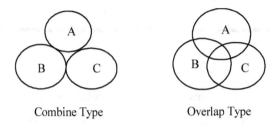

Combine Type   Overlap Type

Fig. 6. Combine Type and Overlap Type

Same difference is found in US and Japanese team working. US teams work together very well at a strategic level but when it comes to tactical level, members work independently. Japanese teams act contrary. They work very closely together at a tactical level, but they do not at a strategic level.

In an age of wisdom, we have to change from Combine Type to Overlap Type and further to Fusion Type. Wisdom is produced when different people with different backgrounds work in a cross functional manner. Better wisdom may be produced if these pieces of knowledge and experience are fused.

To produce such high level wisdom, true collaboration is required both at strategic and at tactical levels.

5   Concurrent Engineering: Looking Back into History

5.1   It Started with DICE

Concurrent Engineering (CE) started with DICE (DARPA's Initiative in Concurrent Engineering). What did DICE CE achieve? They reduced time to market and secured better quality and reduced costs. This was true at this time but does this hold true even now?

Let us consider this problem by looking back into CE history.

5.2   What Does 'Concurrent' Mean ?

Fig.7 shows the definition of 'concurrent' Oxford Dictionary provides. It should be noted that 'concurrent' is not just doing things at the same time. In fact, in a computer world, concurrent processing and parallel processing are very much different. In concurrent processing, data or knowledge is shared and communicated.

1. Running together in space; going on side by side; ----;
associated

2. Geom., Meeting in or tending to the same point

3. ---; Cooperating

4. Agreeing

5. Law, Covering the same ground

Oxford Dictionary

Fig. 7. What does 'concurrent' mean?

5.3   DICE Is Not for New Product Development

It should be noted that DICE project is very much constraint-driven.

Suppose Company A started to produce a product with the final function AF1 within a scheduled time AT1. But Company B later on started to produce another product with a better function BF within shorter time BT. When Company A finds out that Company B is producing a better function product and will be delivering it to market earlier. Company A has to catch up with them. Company A has to change their policy when they find out this and has to produce the same level function AF2 product within the time AT2 (Fig.8).

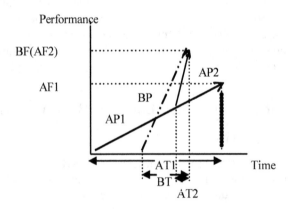

Fig. 8. Why was DICE Concurrent Engineering proposed?

Company A has to use their presently available resources and time is limited. Thus, CE is not a methodology to produce a new product but rather it is the one to find out a solution to how we can deal with the constraints.

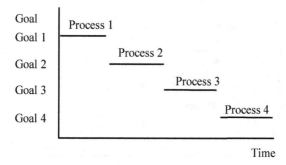

Fig. 9. Product development before DICE

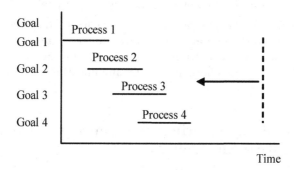

Fig. 10. What DICE Concurrent Engineering attempted

5.4   Product Development Before DICE

Each process had its own goal so that goals changed from process to process. It was a sequential flow and communication among processes were very much limited (Fig.9).

5.5   What DICE Attempted

The primary objective of DICE was to reduce time to market. To realize this goal, they emphasized to bring the downstream processing more upstream. DICE CE at its initial stage was nothing other than parallel processing (Fig.10).

6   Concurrent Engineering: It Grew with Time

Several years were needed for CE to be really 'concurrent'. CE moved from parallel to concurrent processing. Then, goals are coordinated through processes. The importance of strategy and communication among processes were emphasized (Fig.11).

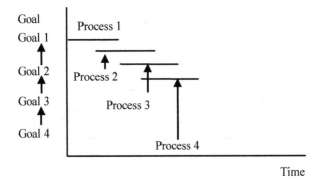

Fig. 11. Improved Concurrent Engineering

DICE CE at its initial stage was in essence a centralized system. Information was integrated only vertically and communication was minimal.

Improved CE was still a centralized system. But information was integrated not only vertically but also horizontally. Communication was encouraged and emphasized.

7   Concurrent Engineering: It Opened the Door to Collaborative Engineering

With the quick spread of Internet in the US, information systems changed from central to distributed systems. In a network, any node can produce an output. Thus, a large degree of flexibility can be introduced and true collaboration becomes necessary as shown in Fig.12.

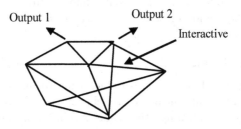

Fig. 12. Network system

8   Concurrent Engineering: Reborn as Life Cycle Engineering

Diversification has been discussed only in terms of variations from customer to customer. But diversification is also found along the time axis. Even a single customerfs requirements change from time to time. So not only spatial variations but also temporal variations must be considered.

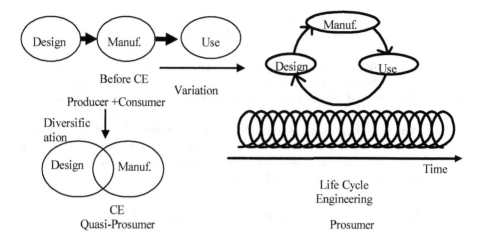

Fig. 13. Concurrent Engineering to Life Cycle Engineering

Before the advent of CE, design-manufacturing-use was processed in a sequential order. But diversification brought design and manufacturing closer together, which was the goal of CE at the later stage. But temporal variation changed CE into Life Cycle Engineering, where a closed design-manufacturing-use loop is repeated throughout the whole product life cycle as shown in Fig.13.

9   Various Types of Concurrencies

We have been emphasizing temporal concurrency because the reduction of time to market has been our primary concern. But it should be stressed that there are other types of concurrencies. Spatial concurrency and technological concurrency.

In a product development, the number of combinations increase as we go downstream, and solution space becomes narrower and the number of constraints

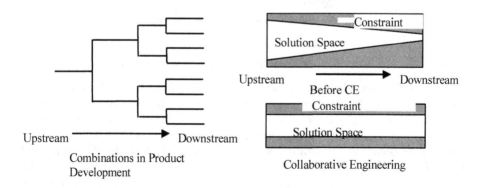

Fig. 14. Temporal concurrency

increases. Collaborative Engineering, or improved CE, was very much successful in distributing the constraints and providing the solution space uniformly all across the different processes from upstream to downstream as shown in Fig. 14.

Spatial concurrency becomes more and more important with increasing globalization. Corporations desire 24 hour operation and it will be possible, if we operate globally. And cultural differences will no longer be the hurdles, but will add another value.

Last, but most important is technological concurrency. To produce wisdom, we have to move from Combine Type to Overlap Type and further to Fusion Type. By this way, we can create new pieces of knowledge beyond just the sum of different pieces of knowledge and experience.

10   Collaboration: How It Changed with Time

Collaboration helps us produce a better quality products. But when it comes to creating wisdom, it is a prerequisite.

Collaboration has evolved from tree to network system. In terms of collaboration level, a tree structure is low and a network one is high (Fig.15).

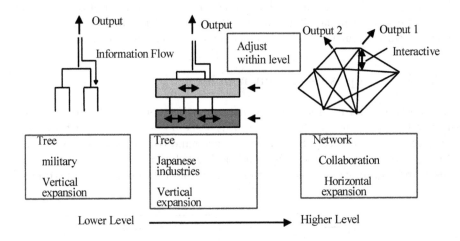

Fig. 15. Collaboration level from tree to network

In a tree structure, information flows one way, from top to bottom and although there may be information flow the other way, it just takes the same way backward. The output node is just one at the top. Typical tree structure is a military system and only vertical expansion is allowed as shown at left.

An advanced tree structure permits communication within the same layer level. This allows adjustments so that the system becomes more flexible. But the expansion is still allowed only in the vertical direction and the output node is, of course, still single as shown in the middle. This type of system is very popular among Japanese industries.

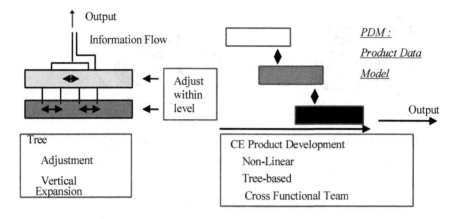

Fig. 16. Product development before Concurrent Engineering

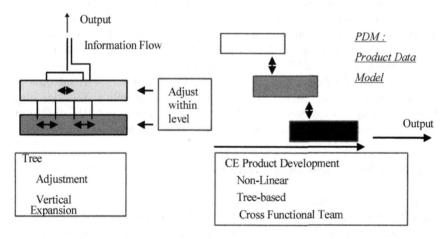

Fig. 17. Concurrent Engineering product development

But when we adopt a network system, it will change the whole scene. We can interact with any one, i.e. any nodes can interact with any nodes. And it allows a horizontal expansion. Any node could be an output node, so that the maximum flexibility will be attained as shown at right.

Let us look at how collaboration evolved by comparing it with the change of product development system.

Fig.16 shows the situation before the advent of CE. The information system was tree-structured, and information was processed sequentially from stage to stage. The concept of Workflow applied to this situation. The whole system was linear.

Fig.17 shows the situation at the time of initial CE. Information was shared and processed concurrently. Product Data Model was developed to share knowledge and experience. But it was still a tree. Although the system allows commu-

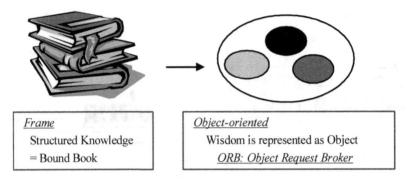

Fig. 18. From Frame to Object

nication, the extent of communication was still limited so that a cross functional team was introduced to solve the problem. But the system was no more linear.

With the transition from a tree to a network, more flexible and adaptive information processing became necessary. Frame was developed for this purpose, but Frame is useful for structured knowledge. It may be compared to a bound book. Adaptability and flexibility was not enough.

So, the concept of 'Object' and object oriented programming were introduced to provide the maximum degree of flexibility and adaptability. Wisdom may most appropriately be expressed in an object-oriented approach. ORB, or Object Request Broker was developed to cope with the situation as shown in Fig.18.

11   Fixed Function and Growing Function

Functions are classified into two types as shown in Fig.19.

Fixed Type is usually observed in hardware. Functions are determined at the start of design and a product is produced and delivered to a customer. Then, it will degrade gradually so that maintenance is required.

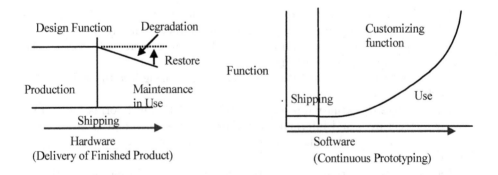

Fig. 19. Fixed function and growing function

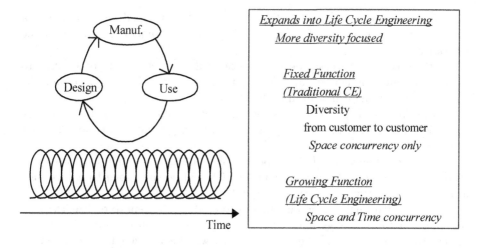

Fig. 20. Life Cycle Engineering

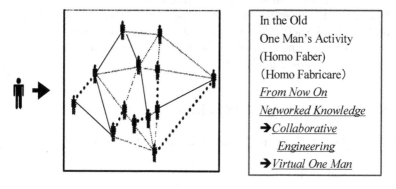

Fig. 21. One physical man to one virtual man

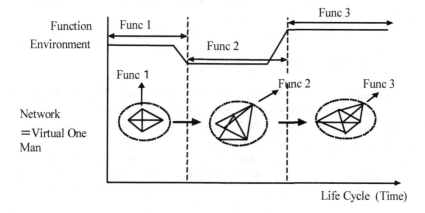

Fig. 22. Collaborative Engineering to Life Cycle Engineering

Software belongs to Growing Type. Software is developed and shipped to a customer with a minimum level of functions and the functions grow with the customer.

In the Fixed Type case, design functions do not change from process to process so that CE can be applied straightforwardly. The producer and the customer are distinguished from each other.

In the Growing Type case, CE is very difficult to apply. Growing function may be achieved by a true prosumer system, where the producer and the consumer work together seamlessly.

Life Cycle Engineering (LCE) repeats a short design-manufacturing-use cycle throughout the product life cycle, so that LCE will be an enabler to realize such a product with growing functions (Fig.20).

Collaborative Engineering may be interpreted as a system to realize a virtual one man. In the old days man produced a tool to produce a product (Homo Faber, Homo Fabricare). The same activity will be realized from now on by networking knowledge and experience. So one physical manfs activity will be realized by one virtual man from now on (Fig.21).

Collaborative Engineering provides a basis for LCE. As the environment varies and we need each different adapting function for each varied portion, Collaborative Engineering provides a different solution for a different portion of the environment as shown in Fig.22.

12   Value in an Age of Wisdom

Traditional Value Engineering defines value in the following way.

Value = Function / Cost

In these days, Function meant the function of a final product and production or manufacturing was considered just as a cost increasing factor, which in other words means it will not add any value.

In the new interpretation, value is given by the following equation.

Value = Performance / Cost

In this definition, performance does not mean just the functions of a final product alone. It also contains satisfaction the production or manufacturing processes provide to the customer and even fashion or brand is also included. In short, performance here includes all kinds of satisfaction a customer enjoys.

Games are sold because the process to get to the goal provides excitement. Housing may be another example. No one would be happy even if a housing firm provides them with the highest quality house. They would like their houses changed to suit their tastes and their voices heard. The process of building a house provides them with joy and with satisfaction. Education may be another example. Art is nothing other than a process. People enjoy art because they interact with their objects. It is self actualization in Maslow's Hierarchy , which is our highest need. Games may also be interpreted as one of the ways to satisfy our self actualization needs. Fashion and brand will satisfy the 3rd and 4th level needs in Maslow's Hierarchy.

13   Creating Wisdom

13.1   Ethnography or Situated Understanding

Schon [2] introduced the concept of a reflective practitioner. A reflective practitioner plans, does, checks and acts as shown in Fig.23, which is nothing more or less than a quality circle.

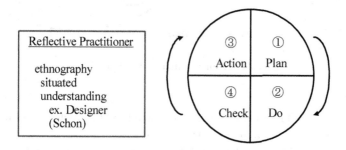

Fig. 23. Reflective practitioner

And in psychology, the idea of ethnography is attracting wide attention these days. They insist that as the situations change very widely and very rapidly, the traditional concept of understanding will no longer be useful. Traditionally, we have been structuring our knowledge and we apply them from case to case. But the amount of our knowledge and experience has become too much enormous and we don't have time and capabilities to use all these pieces of knowledge and experience for an immediate judgment. What is most important to cope with and to adapt to the rapidly and widely changing situations is to determine what to do immediately rather than how to do prudently.

The ethnographic approach will certainly contribute to the realization of LCE.

13.2   From Product to Wisdom Development

Fig.24 shows the transition from product to wisdom development.

Our traditional engineering has been very much analytical. And prediction was easy because we define our problem domain, find out an equation that controls this domain and applied it to solve the problem. It is analog, continuous

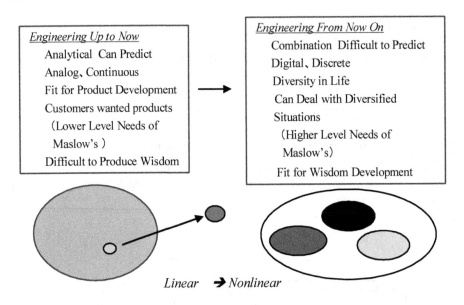

Fig. 24. From product to wisdom

and linear in nature. This world is very well fitted for product development or for satisfying the lower needs in Maslow's Hierarchy.

In an age of wisdom, it is fundamentally a world of combinations so that it is very difficult to predict. And it is digital , discrete and nonlinear in nature. In essence, this is nothing other than our life. Our life is full of diversity and adaptability is very much important there. Wisdom Engineering will satisfy higher level needs in Maslow's Hierarchy.

13.3   Team Working

To produce wisdom, team members should work in a 'Logical AND' manner as shown in Fig. 25.

13.4   Communication

The present framework of communication places emphasis upon how exactly we can convey to others what we think. We have to listen to understand what is happening or what is around us. Thus, we have to develop a new framework for communication to really understand the quickly and widely changing situations. Such a new framework of communication is also needed to establish ethnography.

Another important issue is emotion. Emotion conveys very important messages and intents. If we could communicate emotionally, then we could communicate better [3].

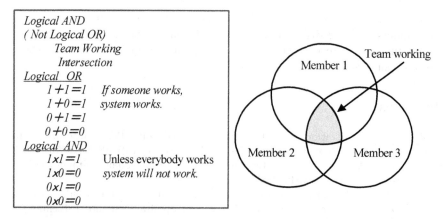

Fig. 25. Team working

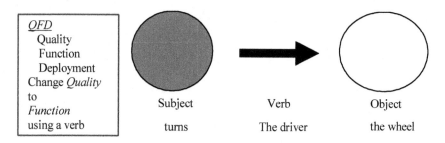

Fig. 26. Role of verb

Another importance issue is the role of verbs in communication. In fact, QFD or Quality Function Deployment uses verbs to define functions(Fig.26). Verbs visualize our images. It should be stressed that Prolog is verb-based. Prolog may help ethnography to grow.

14 Summary

It is pointed out that industries will climb up Maslow's Hierarchy of Needs and Wisdom Engineering help them to achieve this goal.

Wisdom Engineering is based upon the world of combinations, which is digital, discrete and nonlinear. Wisdom Engineering will be an enabler for achieving Life Cycle Engineering, where products vary their functions with the changes of their environments and for producing products with growing functions.

Value will be interpreted in a new definition; value= performance/cost. The manufacturing process will now be considered as a new element to add value and brand or fashion will create a new market.

Wisdom Engineering is more or less ethnographic. Our primary concern is how we understand the situation. To create wisdom, higher level team working and communication are needed, where emotions are communicated and where images are visualized.

References

1. Maslow, A., 'Motivation and Personality',1st edition, 1954,Harper,2nd edition,1970,Harper & Row, 3rd edition,1987,Addison-Wesley,ISBN0060419873
2. Schon, Donald A., 'The Reflective Practitioner: How Professionals Think in Action', 1983, Perseus Books, ISBN0465068782
3. Kostov, Vlaho, 'Computer-mediated Agile Emotional Communication', Doctoral Dissertation, March, 2002, submitted to Tokyo Metropolitan Institute of Technology (in English)

Web Services Based on PROLOG and XML

Bernd D. Heumesser[1], Andreas Ludwig[1], and Dietmar Seipel[2]

[1] University of Tübingen, Wilhelm Schickard Institute for Computer Science,
Sand 13, D – 72076 Tübingen, Germany
{heumesser, ludwig}@informatik.uni-tuebingen.de
[2] University of Würzburg, Department of Computer Science,
Am Hubland, D – 97074 Würzburg, Germany
seipel@informatik.uni-wuerzburg.de

Abstract. This paper describes how the deductive power of PROLOG can be made available across the Internet using standardized Web services technologies. This facilitates the use of PROLOG as a component of distributed information systems and in many new application scenarios. Some of those application scenarios are discussed and one is presented in greater detail. Since a lot of information available on the Internet is nowadays XML based and since Web services technologies use XML based encodings, it is both necessary and useful to be able to process XML documents in PROLOG itself. To make this possible, a new package for SWI–PROLOG called X2P is introduced, making available to PROLOG many of the XML processing facilities of the Libxml2 library, which is a very up–to–date and efficient implementation of most of the current XML related standards.

1 Motivation and Overview

The World Wide Web as we know it today, was initially designed as a platform for information sharing. The core Web technologies, i.e., HTTP, HTML, Web servers and Web browsers, enable the exchange of information in the form of documents.

Web browsers soon became standard tools and it was realized that they can also be used as universal clients to information systems, if these information systems expose their user interface using HTML documents. Most modern information systems use such a Web based architecture. Tools like application servers simplify the development of Web based information systems at the server side.

The development and deployment of distributed information systems, which integrate applications that are distributed on an Intranet or even on the Internet, is still a lot more difficult. The need for such an (enterprise) application integration over the Web was initially generated mainly by business to business (B2B) applications. However, there are a lot of interesting application scenarios aside from B2B, especially in the context of information integration and the Semantic Web [1].

Figure 1 compares the traditional Web with the Web services approach. While the traditional Web is concerned with the interaction between applications and humans, Web services technologies and standards aim at taking the Web one step further by enabling interaction between applications and thereby facilitating application integration.

D. Seipel et al. (Eds.): INAP/WLP 2004, LNAI 3392, pp. 245–257, 2005.

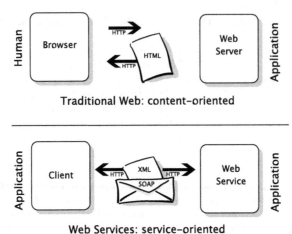

Fig. 1. Traditional Web vs. Web services

Web services are still at an early stage of development, but they certainly have the potential to solve many interoperability problems and are likely to play an important role as a means of implementing distributed information systems in the near future.

We believe that making applications based on the deductive power of PROLOG available across the Internet is very useful and promising, because PROLOG is a very widely used logic programming language, which at the same time enables rule–based programming and rapid prototyping of applications. By adopting the new Web services technologies and standards to facilitate the use of PROLOG based applications across the Internet, we enable the widest range of platforms to integrate such applications.

All Web services standards use XML based document encodings and not all of those documents are transparently handled by the Web services toolkits or middleware, e.g. in the so–called document–style interaction the two interacting applications agree upon the structure of XML documents exchanged between them and must be able to process such documents as requests or responses. Furthermore, a lot of information is made available on the Internet in the form of XML documents. In the context of Web services based on PROLOG, this illustrates that it is both necessary and useful to be able to process XML documents in PROLOG programs.

The rest of the paper is structured as follows: Section 2 describes how XML document processing can be handled in PROLOG. Specifically, it is shown how SWI–PROLOG can be extended with foreign libraries and how this can be used to develop a new package for XML document handling called X2P. In conjunction with this, a term representation for XML documents, the so–called *field notation*, is introduced. The API for the package X2P is described and the package is compared to another standard package for SWI–PROLOG in terms of functionality and performance. Web services, their underlying technologies, standards and tools are the topic of Section 3, while Section 4 shows how in practice all those tools and libraries together can be used to make available Web services based on

PROLOG. Following this, the next section discusses some application scenarios, and the paper concludes with a summary and an outlook on future developments in Section 6.

2   XML **Document Processing in** PROLOG

XML [19] provides a standard way to define the structure of documents that is suitable for automatic processing. This enables the development of generic tools that parse documents and extract their content as well as their structure. Restrictions on the structure of a document can be specified by Document Type Definitions (DTDs) or XML SCHEMAS (however, neither of these provide any semantic information). XML has been widely adopted as the foundation for data representation and formats on the Web. Many parsers and toolkits exist for different programming environments, which implement the XML related standards.

2.1   XML **and** PROLOG

PROLOG is a widely used logic programming language supporting a rule–based, declarative programming approach and enabling rapid prototyping of applications. We use SWI-PROLOG [18], which is available on many platforms.

Since every element in an XML document (except the root element) is nested into another element, we can consider XML documents as term structures, which can be handled nicely by PROLOG and which can then be used to process those terms in a very compact and efficient way.

SWI–PROLOG offers in a package called Sgml2pl an SGML/XML parser, which can also take into account a document's DTD. This parser can parse a document from a file and transform the content into a PROLOG data structure. The data structure used is a nested term of the functor element with three arguments: the name of an XML element, the list of its attributes and the content of this element. The parser uses different kinds of functors to represent other constructs in an XML document (e.g. entities, a DTD declaration or processing instructions). The parsing process can optionally be controlled, e.g. to influence the treatment of spaces.

Libxml2 [8] is the XML parser and toolkit that was developed for the Gnome project [6], but it can also be used standalone and outside of the Gnome platform. This library of C functions implements XML parsers and toolkits for a number of existing standards related to XML, e.g. XPATH [20]. Libxml2 contains functions to parse XML documents supporting validation against an (internal or external) DTD or an XML SCHEMA. It can also handle namespaces and different XML document encodings. The internal document representation follows the DOM interface. The library can also be used to evaluate XPATH expressions.

2.2   **Extending** SWI–PROLOG **with Foreign Libraries**

SWI–PROLOG offers a *foreign language interface*, which can be used to combine code written in a foreign programming language like C with PROLOG programs. This interface can be used in two different ways:

- It provides data types and functions to implement PROLOG predicates in a foreign language, e.g. in C, and hence may use other C functions and libraries. The C code

is compiled to a shared object, and the predicates must be properly registered with SWI–PROLOG as so–called foreign predicates. When a foreign predicate is used, SWI–PROLOG calls the corresponding function from the shared object.
– On the other hand, the foreign language interface can be used to embed the PROLOG engine into a foreign language program. For instance, PROLOG goals can be called and evaluated from a C program.

We use the foreign language interface of SWI–PROLOG in both ways. First, to make some of the functionalities of Libxml2 available to SWI–PROLOG for efficient XML document processing (see the next two paragraphs). Secondly, to provide PROLOG based applications as Web services (see Section 4).

2.3 The X2P Package

We have developed a package called X2P, which makes available through the foreign language interface some of the functionalities of Libxml2 within SWI–PROLOG. X2P is therefore implemented in C and PROLOG and consists of several foreign predicates that encapsulate Libxml2 functions and convert arguments from PROLOG to C and vice versa.

X2P offers predicates for reading, parsing and validating XML documents and for making their content available in PROLOG. There are options available to control some details of this processing, such as the handling of whitespaces, namespaces and entities. Furthermore, X2P allows for the evaluation of an XPATH expression on an XML document. In both cases we recieve the data in the so–called field notation, which serves as a Document Object Model for XML in PROLOG. Sections 2.4 and 2.5 describe the X2P's API and the field notation in greater detail.

Feature	X2P	Sgml2pl
Evaluation of XPATH Expressions	Yes	No
Support for XML Schema	Yes	No
Handling of large documents	Yes	No
SGML Document parsing	No	Yes
Fully implemented in PROLOG	No	No

Fig. 2. Comparison of X2P and Sgml2pl

The differences, as shown in Figure 2, between the X2P package and the SGML parser from SWI's Sgml2pl package stem from the different concepts and history of the two packages. X2P offers the broader range of functionalities for XML documents and the more up–to–date support and implementation of XML related standards. Documents can be validated against an XML SCHEMA document and XPATH expressions can be evaluated only with X2P. X2P can be easily extended to incorporate a current version of Libxml2 offering new functionalities. It offers many more detailed options, influencing the handling of entities, namespaces, comments or processing instructions. However, X2P is limited to XML documents, whereas Sgml2pl can parse all SGML based documents including HTML documents.

Document	SIGMOD	SIGMOD (Old version)	DBLP
Size	478 *KB*	704 *KB*	184 *MB*
Parsing time X2P	0.34 *s*	0.62 *s*	233.17 *s*
Parsing time Sgml2pl	0.32 *s*	0.67 *s*	NA

Fig. 3. Comparison of document sizes and parsing times

In practice it turned out, that in terms of parsing times Sgml2pl and X2P are comparable. However, for large documents X2P seems to be far more efficient: Even with the biggest possible trail stack for SWI (1 GB for SWI–PROLOG on a 64 bit Sun UltraSPARC architecture) Sgml2pl could not parse the XML document containing the data from the Digital Bibliography & Library Project (DBLP, [9]), while X2P could in acceptable time. See Figure 3 for a more detailed comparison of runtimes for parsing the XML editions of DBLP and SIGMOD Record [2].

2.4   The API of X2P

To give an impression of the application programming interface of the X2P package, we describe some of the PROLOG predicates.

The following predicates all make an XML document (or parts of it when evaluating XPATH expressions) available in PROLOG as a term in field notation (or a list of field notation terms).

load_xml_file(+File, -FNTerm)

Reads the XML document from the specified file and returns the field notation representing the document in a term.

load_xml_file(+File, -FNTerm, -Valid)

This predicate is an extension of the above predicate, which additionally attempts to validate the document against the DTD it references. The boolean result of the validation is returned as the third parameter.

load_xml_file(+File, +Schema, -FNTerm, -Valid)

Reads the XML document from the given file, validates it against the specified XML SCHEMA document and returns the corresponding field notation and the validation result.

apply_xpath(+File, +XPathExpr, -FNList, +Options)

The XPATH expression given as the second parameter is evaluated on the specified XML document read from the file and the result of this evaluation is bound to the third parameter (a list of field notation terms). Additional options governing the evaluation process can be supplied in the fourth argument.

For each of these predicates, a corresponding predicate exists, which reads the XML document not from a file but instead from a string. Such predicates are for example necessary when the SOAP server passes an XML document in document–style interaction to the PROLOG engine (see Section 4).

Additionally, many options are available to influence the behaviour of the parser: E.g., if blanks should be conserved or omitted, how namespaces, entities, comments, processing instructions are treated. The predicate xml_file_to_fn allows to pass all of these options to the parser and serves as a basis for the predicates shown above.

Let us take a look at this predicate, which parses an XML document and transforms it into field notation. Its implementation indicates how PROLOG and Libxml2 work together:

```
xml_file_to_fn(File, FNTerm, Options) :-
    process_options(Options, Options1)
    new_parser(Parser),
    set_parser_options(Parser, Options1, Options2),
    parse_xml_doc(Parser,
                   [ source(File), document(FNTerm) | Options2 ]),
    free_parser(Parser).
```

First, some options influencing the parsing are preprocessed. The foreign predicate new_parser uses Libxml2 to initialize a new parser object. The PROLOG predicate set_parser_options calls another foreign predicate to pass the parsing options to the parser object created before. The actual parsing process is initiated by the predicate parse_xml_doc. This predicate calls the foreign parsing routine of Libxml2 and transforms the resulting parse tree into field notation. Finally, free_parser frees the resources allocated by the parsing process.

2.5   Field Notation and FNPATH

Instead of using term structures as the result of parsing an XML document, we map them to the so–called *field notation* (cf. [12]), which we use as the Document Object Model (DOM) for PROLOG. We represent an XML element, which can have attributes and nested elements, by a triple $T : A : C$, where T is the name of the element, A is a list of attribute/value–pairs representing the attributes and their values and C represents the content of the element or the nested elements.

Consider the following fragment of the DBLP XML document describing one of Codd's famous articles:

```
<article mdate="2002-12-04" key="journals/cacm/Codd70">
  <author>E. F. Codd</author>
  <title>A Relational Model of Data for Large Shared Data Banks.</title>
  <pages>377-387</pages>
  <year>1970</year>
  <volume>13</volume>
  <journal>CACM</journal>
  <number>6</number> ...
</article>
```

The resulting representation of the document fragment in field notation is shown below:

```
article:[mdate:'2002-12-04', key:'journals/cacm/Codd70']:[
   author:[]:['E. F. Codd'],
   title:[]:['A Relational Model of Data for Large Shared Data Banks.'],
   pages:[]:['377-387'],
   year:[]:['1970'],
   volume:[]:['13'],
   journal:[]:['CACM'],
   number:[]:['6'], ... ]
```

All the content (and all uppercase tag names) is enclosed in single quotes, since we transform the data contained in elements into atoms.

Based on this field notation we use a powerful and flexible *query language* called FNPATH, which has been introduced in [12]. A detailed description of the field notation and FNPATH can be found there. The FNPATH language allows to address, select and change any part of an XML document. In terms of functionality FNPATH is comparable to XPATH, but it is much more appropriate for using in PROLOG. Additionally it contains features from XQUERY [21] or XSLT [22] like aggregation and efficient transformation mechanisms.

FNPATH defines the :=/2 operator: on the right hand side there is a term in field notation followed by a tree expression addressing some parts of the document. The result of the evaluation of this tree expression is unified with the left hand side.

The tree expressions look like XPATH expression, except that FNPATH uses the operator ^ for separating the location steps.

3   Web Services

The term Web services [3] is not always used with the same meaning. Often, in a very generic meaning, a Web service is simply seen as an application accessible over the Web. We want to use the more specific and restrictive definition given by the W3C's Web Service Architecture Working Group [15] defining a Web service as *"a software system identified by a URI, whose public interfaces and bindings are defined and described using XML. Its definition can be discovered by other software systems. These systems may then interact with the Web service in a manner prescribed by its definition, using XML based messages conveyed by Internet protocols"*.

Web services are still at a very early stage of development and some say that they currently are not more than yet another attempt to master the complexity of enterprise application integration. The Web services movement is a standardization effort that builds on a lot of experience in developing and deploying middleware systems using e.g. Remote Procedure Calls (RPC) or the Common Object Request Broker Architecture (CORBA). Thus, Web services are certainly evolutionary rather than revolutionary.

But if the ongoing standardization effort succeeds and Web services standards become as widely adopted as the Web technologies already have, Web services could become the basis for a seamless and almost completely automated infrastructure for enterprise application integration, because the use of standard technologies reduces heterogeneity drastically.

So the Web services activities try to bridge the gap between what the Web already provides (originally for the interaction between humans and applications, e.g. HTTP as a standard interaction protocol and XML as a standard data format) and what application integration still requires (e.g., interface definition languages, name and directory services, transaction protocols and so on).

Web services assume that some functionality (performed by internal systems) will be exposed as a service and made discoverable and accessible for applications (not humans) through the Web in a controlled manner. Today, three components and proposed standards are the core of Web services, all of them covering different aspects of application integration over the Web: The Simple Object Access Protocol (SOAP) as a way to communicate, the Web Services Description Language (WSDL) as a way to describe services and the Universal Description, Discovery, and Integration (UDDI) project as a name and directory server. Besides these fundamental specifications, which have gone quite some way in terms of standardization and are already implemented and used in practice, some other more high–level concepts are being developed: coordination protocols (concerned for example with transactions) and Web service composition or flow languages (concerned with the composition of Web services clients and services into complex business processes). However, those specifications are at a very early stage of standardization and are still changing rapidly.

We will take a look at the three proposed standards SOAP, WSDL and UDDI, which all use XML based languages to tag the data exchanged, in general and in particular with respect to our goal of making PROLOG based applications available as Web services.

3.1   SOAP, WSDL, and UDDI

The Simple Object Access Protocol (SOAP, [13]) is the communication protocol for Web Services. It provides a standardized way to encode different protocols and interaction mechanisms into XML documents that can be easily exchanged across the Internet. Services can exchange messages by means of standardized conventions to turn a service invocation into an XML message, to exchange the message, and to turn the XML message back into an actual service invocation. The SOAP specification describes in detail a message format, i.e., how information can be packaged into an XML document, a set of conventions for using SOAP messages to implement different interaction patterns (among others the traditional RPC interaction pattern), a set of processing rules that each entity that processes SOAP messages must comply to, and how SOAP messages should be transported on top of HTTP or SMTP. Bindings to other transport protocols can also be defined, but currently HTTP is the most commonly used transport protocol.

SOAP exchanges information using messages. These messages are used as an envelope where the application encloses whatever information needs to be sent. In essence, there are two different interaction styles: document–style and RPC–style. When using document–style interaction, two interacting applications have to agree upon the structure of XML documents exchanged between them, which are then transported from one application to another in SOAP messages. For RPC–style interaction on the other hand, two interacting applications have to agree upon the RPC method signature. The SOAP specification then governs how XML documents representing the request with input parameters and the response with output parameters have to be constructed. This task is typically hidden by the SOAP middleware.

We use gSOAP (see Section 3.2) as a SOAP middleware to provide standalone Web services that make the functionality of PROLOG applications available on the Internet. gSOAP handles the SOAP messaging transparently, so that we are not really concerned with the exchange of messages, the handling of message envelopes or the underlying transport protocol HTTP etc. This leaves us with the task of providing the implementation for the functionality that is to be exposed as a Web service. This implementation differs depending on which interaction style is actually used for the Web service: for RPC–style interaction, we have to provide a function that receives some input parameters (of simple types) from the SOAP middleware and returns the output parameters, while for document–style interaction the implementation must be able to process an XML document as input and produce another XML document as output.

Both interaction styles can be used in conjunction with PROLOG based Web services, but in particular Web services using a document–style interaction make it necessary to be able to process XML documents using PROLOG.

The Web Services Description Language (WSDL, [17] and [16]), is an XML based language that is used both as an advanced form of interface definition language and to describe several aspects of a service that are unique to Web services. This includes the transport protocol (e.g. HTTP) to use when invoking the service and the address where the service can be requested (e.g. an URL when using HTTP as the transport protocol).

We use WSDL documents in conjunction with the Web services middleware toolkit gSOAP for two purposes. First, to let gSOAP generate (for each described Web service interface) stubs and intermediate layers that make requests to the Web service transparent. These stubs are then used as the basis to implement the PROLOG based Web services. Secondly, to publish information about those Web services for use by client applications.

The Universal Description, Discovery, and Integration (UDDI) specification [14] describes how to organize information about Web services and how to build registries where such information can be published (by service providers) and queried (by client service requesters). While WSDL is concerned with the description of service interfaces and information needed to actually access theses services, UDDI offers additional layers of information in a registry that can be used by clients to autonomously discover services and decide whether to use a service or not. Thus, the Web services registry acts as a name and directory server like on other middleware platforms. As a result of a UDDI query, the client recieves a WSDL document describing a Web service. UDDI is currently not used in conjunction with the PROLOG based Web services, although it could of course be used to register the available Web services at the UDDI registry.

3.2 gSOAP

gSOAP [5] is a Web services middleware toolkit for C and C++ developed by Robert van Engelen at the Florida State University. The gSOAP compiler tools offer full SOAP interoperability using a simple API which relieves the user from the burden of SOAP details and thereby ease the development of Web services and client applications in C or C++. The included WSDL parser automates server and client application development and also generates WSDL documents to publish the Web services. gSOAP is available for almost any platform, has shown to be very fast and efficient, and is very well maintained and up–to–date in terms of supporting the latest standards. We currently use gSOAP only for the development of Web services, i.e., not for developing clients requesting those Web services.

4   Putting It All Together

Figure 4 shows how all the technologies and concepts presented so far work together to provide for PROLOG based Web services.

The implementation of a PROLOG based Web service starts with the specification of the function that will be exposed as a service. This is done by supplying a C/C++ header file containing the definitions of data types and a function prototype. The gSOAP compiler generates a C/C++ stub from this header file and a corresponding WSDL document. The stub can then be used to implement the Web service's functionality. In our case, the implementation is merely a C wrapper function, which uses the foreign language interface of SWI–PROLOG to embed the PROLOG engine into the application. For this purpose, a so–called *saved state* of SWI–PROLOG is used, where the predicates of the X2P package already have been consulted and can be used immediately. These predicates again use the foreign language interface to access functions of the Libxml2 library, which leads to the inclusion of this library as a shared object. The top layer of the Web service application consists of a gSOAP runtime library acting as a SOAP server, which transparently handles the SOAP requests and responses.

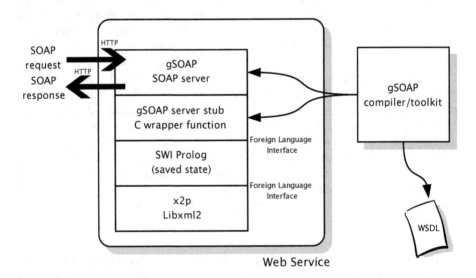

Fig. 4. Architecture of PROLOG based Web services

The WSDL document describing the Web service can be used by a Web service client to locate and request the Web service (HTTP is used as the transport protocol). Upon such a request, depending on the interaction style used, the SOAP server extracts the input parameters (RPC–style) or an XML document (document–style) and passes them to the C function handling the request. In our case, this function uses a PROLOG engine to process the request and produce output parameters or another XML document as a result. This result is returned to the SOAP server, which packages it into a SOAP response that is sent back to the client.

5   Applications

The framework for PROLOG based Web services presented in the last section can be used in many different application scenarios. PROLOG itself can be used as an inference engine for many purposes, and with the advent of the Semantic Web this will gain even more importance. Furthermore, PROLOG enables rapid prototyping of heuristic approaches, especially together with the extensions for XML document processing. The Web services framework for PROLOG then allows us to quickly make such functionality available on the Web as standardized components.

As a simple example, consider a PROLOG based Web service which offers a fuzzy search on the SIGMOD Record XML document. The PROLOG program implementing this Web service receives through the gSOAP middleware and the wrapping C function an XML document (document–style interaction) containing the name of an author. This XML document is then parsed and the author's name is extracted. The SIGMOD Record document is also parsed and transformed into the field notation. The actual search for articles by the given author is fuzzy or fault–tolerant as it can deal (with respect to both the query document and the author names in the SIGMOD Record document) with different name formats, e.g. "firstname(s) lastname", "lastname, firstname(s)", firstnames abbreviated to initials, different spellings and so on. This heuristic approach is well supported by PROLOG, the XML processing facilities and FNPATH resulting in a very compact and elegant program that is easy to maintain. The titles of all articles by the author specified in the query is returned as an (simple) XML document and returned to the calling C program, which passes it to the client calling the Web service.

The main predicate implementing the search is shown below:

```
search_articles(Qname, Titles) :-
    data(sigmod, Doc),
    process_name(Qname, Query),
    findall( T,
        ( Article := Doc^'SigmodRecord'^issues^issue^articles^article,
          [Author] := Article^authors^author,
          process_name(Author, Aname),
          match_names(Query, Aname),
          T := Article^title ),
        Titles ).
```

Notice how the relevant parts of the XML document for SIGMOD Record are addressed using FNPATH expressions. The predicate process_name does some preprocessing for the author name used as a query, while the fuzzy matching is done by the predicate match_names, which is a simple and compact rule–based algorithm. The predicate returns a list of article titles, which are then converted into an XML document and passed back through the layers of the Web services framework.

An approach like this is very promising when used in conjunction with serveral different XML documents from the same domain (e.g. the DBLP and SIGMOD Record documents) or in general for information fusion or information integration tasks, because it enables rapid prototyping of heuristics and services that are easy to maintain.

6   Summary and Outlook

We have presented how the ability to efficiently process XML documents in PROLOG together with the gSOAP Web services toolkit and middleware make it possible to expose the functionalities of PROLOG programs on the Internet as Web services. Due to the thorough standardization of Web services technologies, this enables generic clients to autonomously use such Web services.

Until now, there is very few related work on the topic of combining PROLOG and Web services: In [4], Chen et al. describe the architecture of an intelligent agent that integrates concepts from the Semantic Web with Web Services. This agent system uses SWI–PROLOG as its inference engine for processing semantic information extracted from DAML+OIL documents and SOAP to access other Web services, but it only includes a Web services client and does not provide PROLOG based applications directly as Web services.

Web services technologies are rapidly being adopted by the industry. They are very likely to become the dominant platform for implementing distributed information systems. Just like Web browsers became the universal client for the interaction of humans with information systems, generic Web services clients will be used to discover and autonomously access information systems. For example, major Database Management Systems like IBM's DB2 offer extensions [11] to support Web services both as a provider (i.e. exposing relational data through a Web service) and as a requester (i.e. invoking Web services from within SQL statements using user defined functions). This is also an interesting perspective for our project, because it makes the deductive power of PROLOG available to Database Management Systems.

Another interesting aspect is the implementation of Web services clients for SWI–PROLOG as a complementary technology. This would make the rapidly increasing number of Web services accessible for PROLOG programs. As mentioned in section 3.2, we currently use gSOAP only for the generation of PROLOG based Web services. But given a WSDL document describing a Web service, gSOAP can also generate stub routines for accessing this Web service. These stub routines can then be used to implement PROLOG predicates via the foreign language interface, which access the Web service from a PROLOG program with parameter values determined at runtime and make the responses returned by the Web service available in PROLOG.

We think that PROLOG based Web services can be valuable components of many distributed information systems, for example in an information broker [10] to support complex information gathering and integration strategies or to control a mulit–agent system [7].

References

1. T. Berners–Lee, J. Hendler, O. Lassila. *The Semantic Web*. Scientific American, May 2001.
2. Association For Computing Machinery. *SIGMOD Record in XML*.
   http://www.acm.org/sigmod/record/xml/
3. G. Alonso, F. Casati, H. Kuno, V. Machiraju. *Web Services: Concepts, Architectures and Applications*. Springer, 2004.
4. Y. Chen, W. Hsu, P. Hung. *Towards Web Automation by Integrating Semantic Web and Web Service*. Proc. of the 12th Intl. World Wide Web Conference, 2003.
5. R. van Engelen. *The gSOAP toolkit*. Florida State University,
   http://www.cs.fsu.edu/~engelen/soap.html
6. *GNU Network Object Model Environment*,
   http://www.gnome.org
7. B. Heumesser, R. Schimkat. *Deduction on XML Documents: A Case Study*. Proc. of the 14th Intl. Conf. on Applications of PROLOG (INAP), 2001.
8. D. Veillard. Libxml2. http://www.xmlsoft.org
9. M. Ley. *Digital Bibliography & Library Project (DBLP) XML records*.
   http://dblp.uni-trier.de/xml/
10. A. Ludwig, U. Güntzer. *An Information Brokering Framework*. Proc. of the 7th World Multiconference on Systemics, Cybernetics and Informatics (SCI), 2003.
11. S. Malaika, C. J. Nelin, R. Qu, B. Reinwald, D. C. Wolfson. *DB2 and Web services*. IBM Systems Journal, 41 (4), 2002.
12. D. Seipel. *Processing XML–Documents in* PROLOG. Workshop on Logic Programming (WLP), 2002.
13. *Simple Object Access Protocol (*SOAP*) Version 1.2*, W3C Recommendation,
   http://www.w3.org/TR/soap12-part0/
14. *Universal Description, Discovery and Integration (*UDDI*) protocol*, OASIS Standards Consortium, http://uddi.org/
15. Web Services Architecture Working Group. *Web Services Architecture Requirements*, W3C Working Draft, http://www.w3.org/TR/wsa-reqs
16. *Web Services Description Language (*WSDL*) Version 2.0*, W3C Working Draft,
   http://www.w3.org/TR/wsdl20/
17. *Web Services Description Working Group*, http://www.w3.org/2002/ws/desc/
18. J. Wielenmaker. SWI–PROLOG *Reference Manual*, http://www.swi-prolog.org/
19. *Extensible Markup Language (*XML*) 1.1*, W3C Proposed Recommendation,
   http://www.w3.org/XML/Core/#Publication
20. XML *Path Language (*XPATH*) Version 1.0*, W3C Recommendation,
   http://www.w3.org/TR/xpath
21. XQUERY *1.0: An* XML *Query Language*, W3C Working Draft,
   http://www.w3.org/TR/xquery
22. XSL *Tranformations (*XSLT*)*, World Wide Web Consortium (W3C), August 2002,
   http://www.w3.org/TR/xslt20/

A Contribution to the Semantics of Xcerpt, a Web Query and Transformation Language

François Bry, Sebastian Schaffert, and Andreas Schroeder

Institute for Computer Science, University of Munich
http://www.pms.informatik.uni-muenchen.de/

1 Introduction

Xcerpt [1, 2] is a declarative and pattern-based query and transformation language for the Web with deductive capabilities. In contrast to Web query languages like XQuery and XSLT [3, 4], Xcerpt relies on concepts and techniques from logic programming and automated theorem proving such as declarative "query patterns" and "rule chaining". Xcerpt can also be used for querying Web metadata, like OWL or RDF data [5, 6], and reasoning on such metadata. In contrast to specific languages for OWL and RDF, however, Xcerpt is a general purpose query, transformation, and reasoning language, i.e. it can be used for reasoning not only with Web metadata but also with plain Web data.

Salient aspects of Xcerpt are its nonstandard "query patterns" for retrieving incompletely specified data and its unusual "grouping constructs" *some* and *all* that significantly depart from the standard approaches in logic programming or automated theorem proving. Xcerpt relies on a new, assymmetric unification, called *simulation unification* for evaluating *query patterns* that incompletely specify data. Furthermore, Xcerpt does not rely on meta reasoning for expressing and processing "grouping" constructs corresponding to Prolog's metalevel predicates *setof* and *bagof*.

This article gives a brief overview over challenges of applying logic programming techniques to Web querying. In particular it suggests two different approaches for treating the meta-level grouping constructs *all* and *some* in a proof calculus formalising the operational semantics of Xcerpt.

2 Requirements of a Web Query Language

2.1 Differences to Traditional Logic Programming

The observation that motivated the development of Xcerpt is that Web data formats like XML describe tree or graph structures just like terms in logic programming. However, the usage of these terms differs in several important aspects from the terms used in traditional logic programming, which are discussed below.

Information Representation. In logic programming, a database usually consists of a set of facts, each of which comprises an alternative entry in the database. In

D. Seipel et al. (Eds.): INAP/WLP 2004, LNAI 3392, pp. 258–268, 2005.

the Web, the concept of a database is usually much broader. Besides considering a collection of terms (or documents) as a database, it is very common to represent a complete database within a single term, where the individual entries are *subterms* of the database.

Structure. Whereas logic programming (and relational databases, for that matter) assumes very homogenous sets of data, databases on the Web are in general more flexible and data items of a similar kind often have a slightly different structure. For example, an address book might contain one address entry which has two email addresses and no phone, and another which has no email address but a phone as well as a mobile number.

Schema. Terms in logic programming follow a rather rigid schema, in which both the term label and the arity are fixed (i.e. $f\{a\}$ and $f\{a, b\}$ are instances of different schemas and a query for $f\{X\}$ would match only the first).

Semistructured databases as found on the Web are much more flexible in this respect, mostly due to the heterogeneous and constantly evolving nature of the Web. In particular,

- documents are not required to have a schema at all
- if a schema exists, they do not need to fully comply to it
- schema languages like XML Schema or RelaxNG [7, 8] allow more flexible structures, where subterms might be optional, alternatives, or repeated an arbitrary number of times

For example, $f\{a\}$ and $f\{a, b\}$ might both be instances of the same schema and should thus both match with the query $f\{\{X\}\}$.

Note that this article uses for simplicity reasons a reduced syntax, in which terms are limited to the curly braces { }. Curly braces denote that the order of subterms is irrelevant. The full language Xcerpt [9] also allows a so called ordered term specification with square brackets [ ], which is a more precise representation for XML documents as they are always ordered.

2.2   Partial Patterns and Grouping Constructs

To summarise, a Web query language like Xcerpt needs to fulfill the following requirements:

- it needs to be able to work with partial information about the queried document, as schema information might be missing or incomplete.
- it needs to be able to query several alternatives *within the same document*, which might even differ in their structure.
- it needs to be able to construct new documents in the same manner, i.e. where several alternatives are grouped in the same document.

Xcerpt addresses the first two requirements by extending the notion of terms to *partial patterns* (expressed by double curly braces as in $f\{\{a\}\}$) and by the *descendant* construct (expressed by the keyword *desc* as in $f\{\{desc\ a\}\}$). Partial patterns allow the programmer to specify only the minimum information that is necessary for querying (e.g. in an address book, it is sufficient to specify the name to retrieve an entry). Partial patterns also allow to query several alternatives in a single term, as these can be identified with the different alternative ways of matching a partial pattern with the term (e.g. a partial query for $f\{\{X\}\}$ against a database $f\{a, b\}$ matches either with $X = a$ or with $X = b$). The descendant construct allows to match a pattern at arbitrary depth (e.g. a partial query for $f\{\{desc\ X\}\}$ against the database $f\{g\{a\}, h\{b\}\}$ matches with $X = g\{a\}$, with $X = h\{b\}$, with $X = a$ or with $X = b$).

The last requirement is addressed by the grouping constructs *all* and *some*, which are similar in meaning to the Prolog predicates *setof* or *bagof* in that they collect all possible alternative solutions. Since grouping constructs are very frequently used in Web querying, Xcerpt includes them into the language itself rather than as external predicates. As a consequence, the proof calculi should support such grouping constructs directly, whereas Prolog works around this problem with meta reasoning. An example of an Xcerpt rule containing both grouping constructs and partial query patterns is given in Figure 2.

Xcerpt has many constructs that are not covered here for space reasons. A more detailed introduction into Xcerpt can e.g. be found in [9].

3   Simulation Unification

Simulation unification [10] is a non-standard, asymmetric unification method that respects partial term specifications. Simulation unification is based on a relation called *simulation*, which is a partial ordering on the set of terms. Intuitively, a term t_1 is simulated in a term t_2 if the structure of t_1 can be found in t_2 (see Figure 4).

Simulation unification of a partial term t_1 and a term t_2 computes a *set of alternative substitutions* for the variables in t_1 and t_2 such that the ground instance of t_1 simulates into the ground instance of t_2. For instance, simulation unification of the partial term $f\{\{X\}\}$ and the term $f\{a, b\}$ yields the two alternative substitutions $\sigma_1 = \{X = a\}$ and $\sigma_2 = \{X = b\}$.

The simulation unification algorithm is specified in terms of constraint reduction rules that operate on a constraint store initialised with $t_1 \preceq_S t_2$ (meaning that t_1 should simulation unify into t_2, i.e. after adequate variable bindings t_1 should simulate into t_2). All unification rules decompose a single constraint to a formula containing conjunctions and/or disjunctions of smaller constraints, until no further decomposition is possible (i.e. until either the left or the right side consists of a variable, or a constraint is reduced to one of the boolean values *true* or *false*). If no further rule is applicable, simulation unification creates a set of substitutions by computing the disjunctive normal form of the constraint store, and by replacing all constraints of the form $X \preceq_S t$ by $X = t$. Each disjunct in the disjunctive normal form is an alternative substitution.

It is assumed that the constraint store applies simplification rules as needed (e.g. remove conjunctions that contain a boolean value *false*). Furthermore, the

```
<bib>                                   <reviews>
  <book year="1994">                      <entry>
    <title>TCP/IP Illustrated</title>       <title>Data on the Web</title>
    <authors>                               <price>34.95</price>
      <author>                              <review>
        <last>Stevens</last>                 A very good discussion of semi-
        <first>W.</first>                    structured database systems
      </author>                              and XML.
    </authors>                              </review>
    <publisher>Addison-Wesley</publisher> </entry>
    <price>65.95</price>                    <entry>
  </book>                                     <title>
  <book year="1992">                           Advanced Programming
    <title>                                  </title>
      Advanced Programming ...               <price>65.95</price>
    </title>                                 <review>
    <authors>                                 A clear and detailed discussion
      <author>                                of UNIX programming.
        <last>Stevens</last>                 </review>
        <first>W.</first>                  </entry>
      </author>                            <entry>
    </authors>                               <title>TCP/IP Illustrated</title>
    <publisher>Addison-Wesley</publisher>    <price>65.95</price>
    <price>65.95</price>                     <review>
  </book>                                     One of the best books on TCP/IP.
  <book year="2000">                         </review>
    <title>Data on the Web</title>         </entry>
    <authors>                               ...
      <author>                            </reviews>
        <last>Abiteboul</last>
        <first>Serge</first>
      </author>
      <author>
        <last>Buneman</last>
        <first>Peter</first>
      </author>
      <author>
        <last>Suciu</last>
        <first>Dan</first>
      </author>
    </authors>
    <publisher>Morgan Kaufmann</publisher>
    <price>39.95</price>
  </book>
  ...
</bib>
```

Fig. 1. Two bookstore databases with different structures but similar contents. Note that several alternative entries are contained within the same document and how **book** entries in the left database differ slightly in structure

following rule enforces consistency between different constraints for the same variable and ensures that after the evaluation there exists only a single upper bound for each variable.

$$\frac{X \preceq_S t_1 \wedge X \preceq_S t_2}{X \preceq_S t_1 \wedge t_1 \preceq_S t_2 \wedge t_2 \preceq_S t_1}$$

In case that the two bounds for the variable (t_1 and t_2) are inconsistent, i.e. cannot be unified, one of the constraints $t_1 \preceq_S t_2$ or $t_2 \preceq_S t_1$ is reduced to *false* in further evaluation steps.

```
CONSTRUCT
  books {
     all book {
        var TITLE, price-a { var PRICEA }, price-b { var PRICEB } }
  }
FROM
  and {
     in { resource { "http://bn.com" },
        bib {{
           book {{ var TITLE ⤳ title{{}}, price { var PRICEA } }}
        }} },
     in { resource { "http://amazon.com" },
        reviews {{
           entry {{ var TITLE ⤳ title{{}}, price { var PRICEB } }}
        }} }
  }
WHERE
  or {
     var PRICEA < 40,
     var PRICEB < 40
  }
END
```

Fig. 2. An Xcerpt rule that queries two book databases (given in Figure 1) and returns a list of book titles with price comparisons (given in Figure 3). Partial query patterns are indicated by double braces. A more detailed presentation of Xcerpt can be found in [9]

```
<books>
  <book>
     <title>TCP/IP Illustrated</title>
     <price-a>65.95</price-a>
     <price-b>65.95</price-b>
  </book>
  <book>
     <title>Advanced Programming ...</title>
     <price-a>65.95</price-a>
     <price-b>65.95</price-b>
  </book>
  <book>
     <title>Data on the Web</title>
     <price-a>39.95</price-a>
     <price-b>34.95</price-b>
  </book>
</books>
```

Fig. 3. The XML document resulting from the evaluation of the Xcerpt rule in Figure 2. For each book, the element `price-a` contains the price of the first database of Figure 1, the element `price-b` the price from the second database

3.1   Decomposition Rules

Root Elimination. Root elimination rules compare the roots of the two terms and distribute the unification to the children.

Left Term without Children. This set of rules consider all such cases where the left term does not contain child elements. These cases have to be treated separately from the general decomposition rules below as this would yield the wrong result. For instance, an empty *or* is equivalent to *False* but the result should al-

Fig. 4. A simulation between two graph representations of terms. Note that the sub-term c is contained in the term on the right but not in the term on the left

ways be *True* in case the left term is only a partial specification. In the following, let $m \geq 0$ and $k \geq 1$:

$$\frac{l\{\{ \}\} \preceq_S l\{t_1^2, \ldots, t_m^2\}}{True} \qquad \frac{l\{ \} \preceq_S l\{t_1^2, \ldots, t_k^2\}}{False} \qquad \frac{l\{ \} \preceq_S l\{ \}}{True}$$

As specified by these rules, a term without children, but with a partial specification (double braces) matches with any term which has the same label. If the term specification is not partial, it matches only with such terms that also do not have subterms.

Decomposition. The general decomposition rule eliminates the two root nodes in parallel and distributes the unification to the various combinations of children that result from total/partial specification. If there exists no such combination, then the result is an empty *or*, which is equivalent to *False*.

In the following, let $n, m \geq 1$, and, given two terms $l\{t_1^1, \ldots, t_n^1\}$ and $l\{t_1^2, \ldots, t_m^2\}$, let $\Pi, \Pi_{surj} : \{1, \ldots, n\} \to \{1, \ldots, m\}$ be defined as follows:

- Π is the set of all total, injective functions from $\{1, \ldots, n\}$ to $\{1, \ldots, m\}$.
- Π_{surj} is the set Π restricted to all surjective functions

$$\frac{l\{\{t_1^1, \ldots, t_n^1\}\} \preceq_S l\{t_1^2, \ldots, t_m^2\}}{\bigvee_{\pi \in \Pi} \bigwedge_{1 \leq i \leq n} t_i^1 \preceq_S t_{\pi(i)}^2} \qquad \frac{l\{t_1^1, \ldots, t_n^1\} \preceq_S l\{t_1^2, \ldots, t_m^2\}}{\bigvee_{\pi \in \Pi_{surj}} \bigwedge_{1 \leq i \leq n} t_i^1 \preceq_S t_{\pi(i)}^2}$$

For instance, if the left term has a partial specification for the subterms, the simulation unification has to consider as alternatives all combinations of children from the left term with children from the right term, provided that each child on the left gets a matching partner on the right.

Label Mismatch. In case of a label mismatch, the unification fails. In the following, let $l_1 \neq l_2$.

$$\frac{l_1\{\{t_1^1, \ldots, t_n^1\}\} \preceq_S l_2\{t_1^2, \ldots, t_m^2\}}{False} \qquad \frac{l_1\{t_1^1, \ldots, t_n^1\} \preceq_S l_2\{t_1^2, \ldots, t_m^2\}}{False}$$

Descendant Elimination. The descendant construct is eliminated by adding a disjunction of constraints, which express that the current term t_2 is matched by t_1 or that at least one of the subterms of t_2 is matched by $desc\ t_1$, thus distributing the decomposition to the children of t_2. Let $m \geq 0$.

$$\frac{desc\ t^1\ \preceq_S\ l_2\{t_1^2, \ldots, t_m^2\}}{t^1\ \preceq_S\ l_2\{t_1^2, \ldots, t_m^2\}\ \vee\ \bigvee_{1 \leq i \leq m} desc\ t^1\ \preceq_S\ t_i^2}$$

4   Two Approaches to Proof Calculi for Xcerpt

The suggested calculi are inspired by the SLD resolution used in logic programming. However, traditional approaches like the SLD resolution do not account well for constructs like partial patterns or grouping constructs. Both kinds of constructs have implications on possible proof calculi.

High Branching Rate. In traditional logic programming, there are two elements of nondeterminism that lead to branching in the proof tree: selection of the predicate to unfold in the evaluation of a rule body, and the selection of the program rule used for further chaining. Xcerpt's usage of partial patterns adds a third element: When using partial patterns, there is in general no single way to match two terms. Instead, all possible alternative matchings have to be considered, which leads to a significantly higher branching rate.

Grouping Constructs all *and* some. Unlike Prolog's *setof* and *bagof* predicates, the grouping constructs *all* and *some* are an integral part of the language. It is hence desirable to support such higher order constructs in the proof calculus itself rather than treating them as external predicates.

This article gives a brief overview over possible approaches to proof calculi that are taking into account the above-mentioned issues. The remainder of this section introduces two approaches called "one at once" and "all at once", which differ in that "one at once" follows only a single proof path at a time (like SLD resolution), whereas "all at once" allows to follow a different proof path at each step, regardless of whether the previous path was finished or not.

4.1   Common Properties

The evaluation of the two approaches yields a *set of substitutions* which is constructed in almost the same manner as for simulation unification above. In both approaches, the proof tree is represented as a formula of constraints, the *constraint store*. Such constraints are one of

- *folded queries* represent query parts that have not yet been evaluated (e.g. a query pattern or a conjunction of query patterns) and are expressed as $\langle Q \rangle$.
- *simulation constraints* specify that two terms t_1 and t_2 have to be unified and are expressed as $t_1 \preceq_S t_2$,
- *dependency constraints* specify that the evaluation of one constraint depends on the evaluation of another and are expressed as $(C_1 \mid C_2)$.

Furthermore, the following notations are used:

- $\mathcal{P}_{\text{grouping}}$ denotes the set of all rules in the program $\mathcal{P}$ that contain one of the grouping constructs *all* or *some*
- $\mathcal{P}_{\text{nongrouping}}$ denotes the set of all rules in the program $\mathcal{P}$ that do not contain one of the grouping constructs *all* or *some*
- $\mathcal{T}$ denotes the set of all database terms contained in the program, or referenced by resource specifications

The following constraint reduction rules are also common to both approaches:

Dependency Resolution. The dependency resolution is required for computations that involve the *all* and *some* constructs. A dependency constraint of the form $(t_1 \preceq_S t_2 \mid C_2)$ requires to evaluate the complete proof tree (in case of *all*) or parts of the proof tree (in case of *some*) of C_2 before C_1, and applies the resulting substitution Σ to t_2 (application to t_1 is not necessary, as t_1 and C_2 are variable disjunct).

$$\frac{(\ t_1\ \preceq\ t_2\ \mid\ D\ )}{\bigvee_{t_2' \in \Sigma(t_2)}\ t_1\ \preceq\ t_2'}\quad \Sigma = subst(solveall(D))$$

The actual implementation of the *solveall* function depends on whether the "one at once" or "all at once" algorithm is used. In the "one at once" algorithm, solveall evaluates all paths in the proof tree. In the "all at once" approach, solveall evaluates the complete constraint store.

4.2   One at Once

The "one at once" calculus is similar to the SLD resolution calculus with operational treatment of higher order predicates used in logic programming. Like SLD resolution, the calculus considers only a *single* path at a time. If a grouping construct occurs, the calculus interrupts the evaluation of the current path, visits each of the paths of the queries in scope of this grouping construct in turn and collects the respective solutions, and afterwards continues with the evaluation of the current path.

"One at once" consists of three unfolding rules which are introduced below:

Query Unfolding against Database Term. Unfold a folded query term against a database term t by replacing the folded query term by a simulation constraint between the folded query term and the term t.

$$\frac{\langle t^q \rangle}{t^q \preceq_S t}\ t \in \mathcal{T}$$

Query Unfolding against Rule. Unfold a folded query term t^q against the head t^c of a rule.

1. In case t^c contains none of the grouping constructs *all* and *some*, add a constraint for the simulation of t^q in t^c and add the query part of the rule as a folded query.
2. In case t^c contains at least one of the grouping constructs *all* and *some*, add a dependency constraint such that the unification of t^q in t^c is only evaluated in case the query part is evaluated successfully.

$$\frac{\langle t^q \rangle \quad (t^c \to Q) \in \mathcal{P}_{\text{nongrouping}}}{t^q \preceq_S t^c \wedge \langle Q \rangle} \qquad \frac{\langle t^q \rangle \quad (t^c \to Q) \in \mathcal{P}_{\text{grouping}}}{(t^q \preceq_S t^c \mid \langle Q \rangle)}$$

The dependency part in a dependency constraint (as in the result of the right rule) is solved in an auxiliary calculation. In case t^c contains an *all* construct, or nested *some* constructs, it is necessary to solve the complete query part. If t^c contains only a single *some* construct, it is sufficient to only search for solutions until a sufficient amount is found.

Disjunctive Split. Note that all of these rules need to select both a folded query to continue with and either a rule or a term, and backtrack in case the selected rule or term leads to failure. This selection with backtracking yields a so-called *proof tree*. Both the selection of constraints and of rules/terms is non-deterministic and different search strategies, like the depth-first search used in SLD resolution, are conceivable.

Some of the rules above may yield a disjunction as a result (most notably the dependency resolution and the unification part of the consistency verification). In such cases, the "one at once" approach needs to split the disjunction into different paths of the proof tree (and insert a choice point). The following rule represents this split. Assume that C is in disjunctive normal form:

$$\frac{C_1 \vee \ldots \vee C_n}{C_1 \mid \ldots \mid C_n}$$

"One at once" has the advantage that it only needs to consider a single conjunctive path at a time. On the other hand, only a depth first search is possible and occurrences of grouping constructs externally "interrupt" the evaluation by requiring an auxiliary application of the calculus to certain queries until all solutions are found.

4.3   All at Once

The "all at once" calculus considers all paths in the proof tree at once. Thus, the considered constraint store contains conjunctions as well as disjunctions. Where "one at once" unfolds a query with only one of the alternatives at a time (and then relies on backtracking for finding different alternatives), "all at once" unfolds all possible alternatives simultaneously and adds them to the proof tree. If a grouping construct occurs, it adds a dependency constraint to a certain subtree of the proof tree. The evaluation may then continue at any node in the proof tree. If this subtree is completely solved, the grouping construct can be solved as well.

$$\frac{\langle t^q \rangle}{\bigvee_{t \in \mathcal{T}} t^q \preceq_S t} \qquad\qquad\qquad\qquad \vee$$

$$\bigvee_{(t^c \leftarrow Q) \in \mathcal{P}_{\mathrm{nongrouping}}} (t^q \preceq_S t^c \wedge \langle Q \rangle) \vee$$

$$\bigvee_{(t^c \leftarrow Q) \in \mathcal{P}_{\mathrm{grouping}}} (t^q \preceq_S t^c \mid \langle Q \rangle)$$

This approach has the advantage that higher order constructs are included more naturally into the calculus. Instead of relying on external control for solving higher order constructs, the dependency constraint can be treated by the rules of the calculus.

In addition, the possibility to continue at any node in the proof tree gives rise to interesting considerations about selection strategies. With a depth-first search, the calculus would resemble "one at once" or SLD resolution. Different search strategies might however be auspicious. A cost based A* search that tries to first select such nodes that contribute most to the result could provide performance benefits in practical applications, in particular in the context of the Web where IO costs for remote resources are often considerably higher than for local or even in-memory resources.

As the "all at once" approach works with both conjunctions and disjunctions of contraints, a further interesting aspect is to integrate the evaluation of the rule chaining with the evaluation of the simulation unification. Doing so might allow optimisations of the evaluation, e.g. by interleaving chaining and unification steps when feasible.

5   Related Work and Conclusion

This abstract gives a short overview over issues and problems of applying techniques used in logic programming to the Web query language Xcerpt. Two different approaches for treating Xcerpt's built-in higher level constructs *all* and *some* have been presented.

The language Xcerpt is work in progress. A project website is located at http://www.xcerpt.org. A comprehensive introduction into the language Xcerpt with many examples can be found in [9]. The simulation unification algorithm has first been presented at [10]. A declarative semantics in form of a model theory in the style of classical logic is currently being worked on and first results have been published in [11]. A prototype of Xcerpt exists and has been demonstrated at [12].

Xcerpt is not the only rule-based query language for Web data. Most noteably, the language UnQL [13] first introduced the concept of rule-based querying to the XML world, but it does not provide important features like rule chaining and is not based on logic programming.

The necessity of higher order predicates like *setof* and *bagof* in Prolog have been discussed in numerous articles (see e.g. [14]). Also, a formal semantics has been considered e.g. in [15]. However, such considerations in general do not include support for higher order constructs into the calculus itself but instead treat them as external predicates.

References

1. Schaffert, S.: Xcerpt: A Rule-Based Query and Transformation Language for the Web. PhD thesis, University of Munich (2004)
2. Schaffert, S., Bry, F.: Querying the Web Reconsidered: A Practical Introduction to Xcerpt. In: Extreme Markup Languages 2004, Montréal, Canada (2004)
3. W3C: XQuery: A Query Language for XML. (2001)
4. W3C: Extensible Stylesheet Language (XSL). (2000)
5. W3C: Web Ontology Language (OWL). (2003)
6. W3C: Resource Description Framework (RDF). (1999)
7. W3C: XML Schema Part 0: Primer; Part 1: Structures, Part 2: Datatypes. (2001)
8. Clark, J., Murata, M.:   RELAX NG Specification, http://relaxng.org/spec-20011203.html. (2001) ISO/IEC 19757-2:2003.
9. Bry, F., Schaffert, S.:   A Gentle Introduction into Xcerpt, a Rule-based Query and Transformation Language for XML. In: Proc. Int. Workshop on Rule Markup Languages for Business Rules on the Semantic Web (RuleML' 02). (2002) (invited article).
10. Bry, F., Schaffert, S.: Towards a Declarative Query and Transformation Language for XML and Semistructured Data: Simulation Unification. In: Proc. Int. Conf. on Logic Programming. LNCS 2401, Springer-Verlag (2002)
11. Bry, F., Schaffert, S.:   An entailment relation for reasoning on the web. In: Proc. Int. Workshop on Rules and Rule Markup Languages for the Semantic Web (RuleML'03). LNCS 2876, Sanibel Island, Florida, USA, Springer-Verlag (2003)
12. Berger, S., Bry, F., Schaffert, S., Wieser, C.: Xcerpt and visXcerpt: From Pattern-Based to Visual Querying of XML and Semistructured Data. In: Proc. Intl. Conference on Very Large Databases (VLDB03) – Demonstrations Track, Berlin, Germany (2003)
13. Buneman, P., Fernandez, M., Suciu, D.: UnQL: A Query Language and Algebra for Semistructured Data Based on Structural Recursion. VLDB Journal **9** (2000)
14. Warren, D.H.D.: Higher-order extensions to prolog: Are they needed? In Hayes-Roth, M., Pao, eds.: Machine Intelligence. Volume 10. Ellis Horwood (1982)
15. Börger, E., Rosenzweig, D.: The mathematics of set predicates in prolog. In: Kurt Godel Colloquium. (1993) 1–13

DialogEngines – Dialog Agents for Web-Based Self Service Consulting

Oskar Bartenstein

IF Computer Japan, 5-28-2 Sendagi, Bunkyo-ku,
Tokyo 113-0022 Japan
`oskar@ifcomputer.co.jp`

Abstract. This industrial report discusses design, implementation, and application of DialogEngines, a commercial WWW application service for business-to-consumer web based self service consulting. DialogEngines combines pseudo natural language dialog, recommendation, product presen tation, virtual character rendering with animation and voice to achieve responsive product consulting. The idea is to "help to buy" rather than "sell". Briefly mentioned is a fielded consulting sales application.

1 Overview

Effective consulting is for any non-trivial product a key success factor to help customers to make the right choice. To make websites responsive and effective to answer visitors' questions and satisfy information needs, we developped DialogEngines:

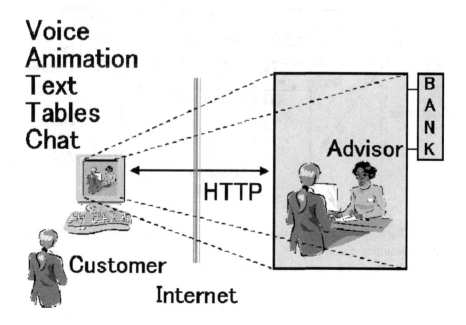

D. Seipel et al. (Eds.): INAP/WLP 2004, LNAI 3392, pp. 269–277, 2005.
© Springer-Verlag Berlin Heidelberg 2005

Intelligent animated conversational agents for Web based self-service consulting. The position in CRM solutions is between human staffed support and keyword search database driven web sites.

The customer accesses the web page as usual, the dialog on the web site is an individual consulting session, much like a staff member of the company personally taking care of the customer.

The agents use detailed product knowledge and dialog knowledge to allow interested customers to explore offers and implicitly build product shortlists based on their requirements.

The system is a commercial internet based URL-embeddable application service. It integrates technologies from research areas including Emotion Engineering, Trust Engineering, Natural Language Processing, Machine Learning, Case Based Reasoning, Web Programming, and Software Engineering.

DialogEngines conduct goal-oriented consulting conversation about given subjects with individual human users in pseudo natural language. Combining emotion engineering and knowledge engineering, DialogEngines present interactive, individual dialogue to web users.

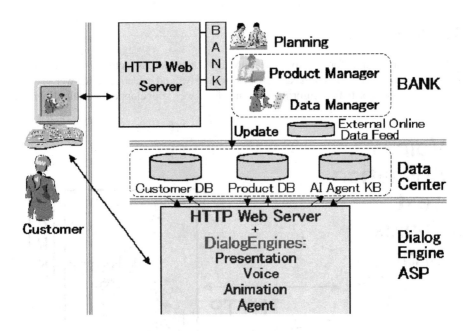

The dialog uses knowledge about products, customers and knowledge about how to conduct consulting dialogs.

The following sections discuss individual components, implementation and applications.

2 Dialog

DialogEngines conduct goal-oriented consulting conversation about given subjects with individual human users in pseudo natural language. The dialog serves three purposes: first, to be friendly, second, to present a solution that satisfies the customers requests, and third, to allow the user to explore the problem space as far as needed to understand not only that a presented solution is good, but also to provide the trust that alternative solutions are not as good.

2.1 Product Model

The product model consists of product specifications and properties.

The target domain of the dialog is an excerpt from an SQL, CSV or XML product data base. The product knowledge defines the scope of the dialog.

Access to the product model beyond the specifications given in the product knowledge base can be extended with words, phrases and conditions, which may be domain specific. This includes access to domain expertise, i.e. mapping from common natural language terms to expert jargon terms defined in the language of the product knowledge base.

2.2 User Model

The user model reflects the result of exploration, understanding, finding, and reassurance.

The dialog is between machine and an individual human user. User input to the agent and user answers to questions by the agent give the data set which drives the user model. Base assumption is that the user wants information about the domain and a specific solution. DialogEngines does not work well with malicious users or in areas outside of the scope of the product knowledge base.

2.3 Agent Model

The agent model details showing, suggestions, confirmations.

Agents can have different characteristics, not only age and sex, but also deeper ones relevant for the progress of the user interaction. Modelled are how polite, explanatory, extrovert, pushy and verbose the agent is. The Agent Model is independent of its rendering in text, voice or animation.

2.4 Dialog Model

The dialog consists of repeated listening, understanding, problem solving, question asking and result presentation actions. Dialog history and strategy, together of course with the product solution space, define the flow of the dialog.

The dialog produces the control information for voice and animation. This is in contrast to traditional animated web sites which present only pre-recorded canned contents.

DialogEngines agents can take initiative and talk actively to the user.

DialogEngines agents can ask intelligent questions to the user, taking into account product knowledge and the context of the conversation.

2.5 Language Model

The language model deals with meaning, ambiguity, conflict resolution, and understanding expressions.

DialogEngines understands user statements using a shallow natural language processing model, the target product knowledge, and additional language knowledge.

Such additional knowledge is domain expertise and semantics for common vocabulary. For example the word "small" will mean different things for different businesses.

Heuristics are used to resolve ambiguities and contradictions. DialogEngines is designed to be practical and useable: like search engines, which sometimes give wrong answers or not all correct answers, DialogEngines language processing is not guaranteed to be sound and complete.

DialogEngines agents make utterances to users according to a knowledge base of example sentences, which can be answers, statements, greetings, questions, requests for confirmation and more.

3 Recommendation

The recommendation component deals with individual preferences, personal taste, and perception of value.

Recommendation is a domain specific optional component that guides the user depending on additional knowledge about individual or general preferences. For example, everything else being identic, one would recommend a bigger hotel room over a small one.

Recommendation is independent of the process of the dialog that understands user needs and presents possible answers. It only uses the result of the dialog. Recommendation works like a traditional expert system. For example in the applications detailed below, recommendation is essential to make a sensible proposal: the dialog benefits from the deeper knowledge processing. In a synergy effect, a good recommendation engine benefits from a user-friendly dialog front end, because it has the potential to gain more goal oriented insight than e.g. a canned questionnaire.

4 Presentation

DialogEngines presents the result of the current dialog as a shortlist, table or similar.

The result of the current dialog is combined with vendor site policies and converted to a lookup in the product knowledge base, then rendered in a user view. Tabular presentations are useful for product shortlists or comparisons. A consulting sales site will typically render photos and prices to the user, in addition to the data that the vendor considers necessary and in addition to the information that was understood to be requested by the customer during the dialog.

This combination is important to the essence of consulting, where both parties inform each other of their needs and also advise the other party on issues that they would have overlooked. A dialog without presentation of the result is technically of course possible, but in practice too difficult to understand for the user. Visualization of product specifications is a research area of its own and not further discussed here.

5 Animation

An animated character (sometimes called avatar) is emotion engineering impact technology. With appearance, stature, facial expressions, and animated gestures, the character conveys emotions and conversational clues that are essential to engaging human interaction.

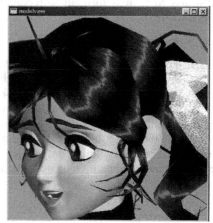

Rendering levels range from simple pictures over animated 2D cartoons to 3D ray trace renderings of body scans of world famous performers.

DialogEngines uses an abstraction layer to generate animation from the ongoing dialogue in real time and render it with the selected rendering technology and character.

DialogEngines is compatible with a wide variety of animation technologies, e.g. with animation renderers by MacroMedia, Microsoft and Nemesys and with with characters developpe dby Microsoft and Nemesys (sample).

6 Voice

6.1 Voice Recognition

Voice recognition can complement or replace character input of user questions. Useful i.e. for intranet applications, CTI systems, customers with special needs, and car navigation. Although we have experience with voice recognition technology by IBM and NEC, it is difficult to recommend voice recognition for the general web public today.

6.2 Voice Output

Voice output is an impact technology especially in combination with animated character agents. DialogEngines can today reliably generate voice in real time and render it in todays internet browsers in FM quality for technical purposes including the consulting sales applications discussed here. Note that voice output can help to understand the flow of a dialog and thus augment communication also with non-verbal utterances, e.g. laughter. DialogEngines can generate abstract "voice" like this just as spoken voice, limited in practice by the rendering capabilities of the text-to-speech component and by the cost to build sufficiently fine grained knowledge bases for the dialog.

7 Implementation

Internet based, modular, multi-client, multi-server, built on widely accepted industry standards, DialogEngines is designed to be configurable for deployment with

DialogEngine

* Standard & Technologies

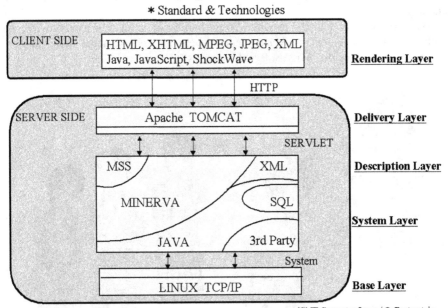

(C) IF Computer Japan / O. Bartenstein

information terminals ranging from standard PCs to mobile phones and car navigation systems. The service is completely Internet based and hosted on a cluster of Linux servers. DialogEngines server side and client side components use *.mss, MINERVA, Java, JavaScript, and other software.

7.1 Technology

Server side DialogEngines is realized as a set of standalone demons and HTTP servlets written in MINERVA and *.mss. MINERVA is a commercial ISO-Prolog compiler hosted in Java. It is used for all natural language processing, understanding, computation of proposals, memory based knowledge base handling, and XML data exchange. DialogEngines makes heavy use of MINERVA libraries including regular expression text processing, XML i/o and blackboards for fast memory based data handling. *.mss is a Web-oriented rendering language companion product of MINERVA, embedded in XML or HTML and used to produce the XML for internal and HTML for external communication. From within MINERVA and *.mss, Java libraries are used for system and network level integration.

Client side DialogEngines for PC/WWW deployment is realized in MINERVA to drive the character animation, Java for system integration, and JavaScript as browser control language. DialogEngines for PC/WWW is compatible with 128bit SSL and does not require cookies, plugins, or any non-default browser settings. We use a very carefully selected subset of browser capabilities to be compatible by design. Extensive tests with browsers by Microsoft, Sun, Netscape, Opera and others confirmed a very high level of interoperability.

7.2 Structure and Scalability

DialogEngines is hosted on a cluster of cooperating but otherwise independent services. Compute-intensive tasks can thus be moved to dedicated or replicated

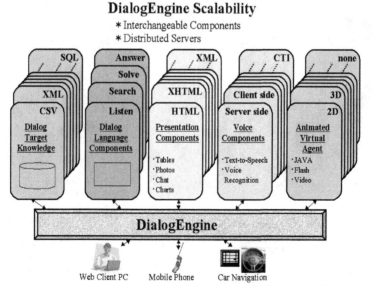

servers if needed for high performance installations, and components like text-to-speech engines can be replaced once better ones become available.

Internal communication makes extensive use of XML for its descriptive power and added level of error detection. Communication between components is exclusively in HTTP. Compared with e.g. direct internet socket communication, this restriction to HTTP places considerable constraints on system design, however HTTP is the best supported and most widely available protocol on the World Wide Web. The demand on network bandwidth is moderate. Measurements show that routing times are more important for comfortable use.

8 Applications

DialogEngines and its configuration variants was designed in response to needs in online consulting by companies operating in financial services, human resources, home entertainment, car driver support, news services, and fashion retail.

A prominent installation is fielded with Paris Miki, the largest optical retail company in Japan, and third largest in the world.

At Paris Miki http://www.paris-miki.com, DialogEngines serves web shop users with in-depth online consulting. The dialog components have access to the full product knowledge base and to an integrated recommendation engine. In 2002, the recommendation component won the Grand Prize of the Nikkei Information Systems Award. The company reported that the recommendation component accounts for about 10% of total sales.

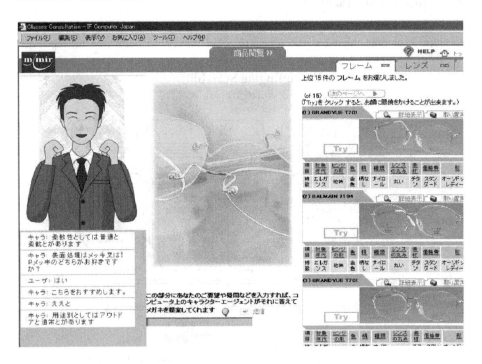

9   Conclusion

We discussed DialogEngines, an interactive front end for recommendation of complex consumer products using pseudo natural language dialog components cooperating with backened problem solvers to conduct individual consulting.

We detailed its implementation as a set of services build with MINERVA, a commercial implementation of ISO Prolog in Java with extensions for scalable web programming.

We explained its commercial deployment on consumer oriented internet web sites based on a cluster of Linux/Java servlet servers combined with rendering of animated and voice-enabled virtual characters on industry standard web browsers.

The application service described in this industrial report is commercially available at http://DialogEngines.com .

Acknowledgements

Many thanks go to my colleages and partners at IF Computer Japan for their exciting contributions and their neverending willingness to build on my ideas; vice versa I am very happy that they allowed me to expand on their ideas and use their amazing software for this work.

I am extremely grateful to our customers who accepted the challenge and the budget to make this work a technical and commercial success.

References

1. DialogEngines http://DialogEngines.com
2. *.mss http://www.ifcomputer.co.jp/inap/inap2001/program/inap_bartenstein.ps
3. MINERVA http://www.ifcomputer.co.jp/MINERVA/

Towards Ubiquitous Maintenance – Defining Invocation of Plant Maintenance Agents in Real Workspace by Spatial Programming

Hiroki Takahashi[1] and Osamu Yoshie[2]

[1] Advanced Research Institute for Science and Engineering,
Waseda University, Kitakyushu-city, Fukuoka, Japan
taka@aoni.waseda.jp
[2] Graduate School of Information, Production and Systems,
Waseda University, Kitakyushu-city, Fukuoka, Japan
yoshie@waseda.jp

Abstract. Recent progress of VR (Virtual Reality) technologies makes it possible to realize the VR space that is synchronized with the real space. We can hereby build virtual workspace through which a worker in real workspace can automatically acquire and invoke appropriate plant maintenance agents. We propose spatial programming which is a manner of VR programming technique, locating various place-dependent agents and web information in VR space, and also describe the interface between agent world and real workspace as an application of spatial programming, towards ubiquitous maintenance.

1 Introduction

In manufacturing systems, to acquire maintenance information and to diagnose quickly and appropriately are important. However, most facilities of manufacturer's factory have some secrecy and its maintenance data is prohibited from sending externally. So, remote maintenance system has large difficulty there, especially it is served and shared with various manufacturers. We have presented *virtual community for plant engineers*[1] or *virtual plant* to prevent this problem, by using plant maintenance agents which are served to each factory from virtual plant. The advantage of this mechanism is that user does not need to send diagnosis data to the external and the agent makes diagnosis process on the computer which is in the factory.

Recently, by the progress of VR technologies, we can now realize the VR space on a computer/network that is synchronized with the real space. Then we can build virtual workspace which contains various programs such as agents and which can work with real world. Basically, diagnosis procedures in the plant depend on each target machine, that is, depend on the place. It is very efficient if it becomes available that a worker can automatically get appropriate plant maintenance agent which is required for one's work of its place from our virtual plant. This also means that the automatic agent service also indicates the

D. Seipel et al. (Eds.): INAP/WLP 2004, LNAI 3392, pp. 278–293, 2005.

workers mission to do there, that is to say, he can automatically get appropriate instruction there. We can regard those place-dependent works as declaratively located processes, so introducing Prolog, which is one of the most popular declarative languages, to our system is useful because of its declarative programming ability.

We have also presented VR space description language[2, 3], which is a manner of VR programming technique, locating various place-dependent programs to VR space. This paper enhances the ability of linking VR space to real space and tries to apply spatial programming to define plant maintenance agents' world which works with virtual plant on the web, towards ubiquitous maintenance.

2   Spatial Programming

Spatial programming, the main idea of this paper, is the place-dependent, declarative programming in VR space.

In the real world, it is often the case that our action is basically place-dependent. For example, if we are at the traffic intersection, which is represented as 'intersection(cross).', we acquire the signal information, which is stated as 'signal(east, red).', and decide 'stop' or 'go' (Fig. 1). But this process is only at traffic intersection, so it is place-dependent. In manufacturing systems, of course, there are many place-dependent information and its processing action such as acquiring diagnosis data and its processing where various agents can flourish, associated with the facility. So, it is natural that which plant maintenance agents are required is place-dependent and user's status-dependent. We noticed this place-dependency and try to use VR space as the environment for building such an agent world linked to real world. Construction of this agent world begins in plain VR space initially, and constructor locates agent's information (strictly speaking, this is the conditions to summon agents) at appropriate position. We call this manner *spatial programming*.

Spatially programmed VR space is presented as 3D virtual space of course, and it can be linked to real space using generic position sensors, such as RF

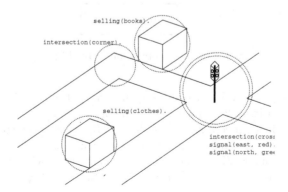

Fig. 1. Place-dependent Information in Real World

tag and its reader which we adopt. This is one of the advantages of spatial programming. Once this link is established, a worker's movement in real space is reflected to VR space. If any place-dependent agent-summoner is located at his position, he can get agents from virtual plant through some devices such as portable PC or PDA (Personal Digital Assistant) and can see information by HMD (Head Mounted Display) such as DataGlass2[1]. Besides it, constructor can also go around in 3D VR space and locate agent-summoner in the space. So it is very intuitive.

Another merit of spatial programming is that it does not need to stop VR space even while agent world's constructor modifies the VR space, because place-dependent description assures independency of descriptions for each object (worker, facility, etc.) in the VR space, so modification of one object does not give influence to other objects' description.

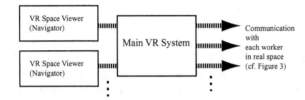

Fig. 2. System Composition of VR space

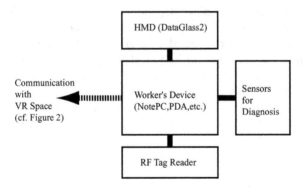

Fig. 3. System Composition in Real Space

The composition of VR space system, that is, spatial programming environment is shown in Figure 2. Main VR system controls time progress of VR space and place-dependent processes. Viewer shows VR space to the constructor with 3D computer graphics, and he can navigate in the space. The viewers are independent of the main VR system and they cooperate each other via network communication, so several constructors can log on the VR space.

---

[1] DataGlass2 is the trademark of Shimadzu Corporation.

The system composition of devices in real space used by worker is shown in Figure 3. Each worker brings this set of devices and receives agent services. Communication between each worker and VR space are established via network.

In the following sections, we describe how to realize the idea described above and the implementation of place-dependent agent world in VR space.

3 Model of Place-Dependent Processing

In the spatial programming, the place-dependent agent-summoner is embedded in the virtual space as virtual object. Agent invocation process is the interaction between embedded summoner object and worker. We named this embedded summoner object *junction*. And we regard worker and facility as kind of objects, which have entities in real space. Our VR system can grasp the position of objects (especially workers) in the real space via position sensors and establish link between object in VR space and entity in real space. When a worker in real space approaches the place where some junction is located in VR space, the mission of agent happens. This corresponds to the interaction between object and junction which contact each other in VR space.Then some mechanism of interaction is required.

Basically, a facility or worker in the manufacturing system has some status. In this paper, we express these things as objects' attributes (e.g. state of 'it is vibrating', state of 'he has a thermometer' and so on). A request for agent also depends on its and his attributes. Agent summoning process has two phases. At first, interaction process must refer to objects' (both worker's and target facility's, but in some case one of them) attributes and must decide which agent he requires, and next, delivers it to the worker.

At the former phase, we adopt blackboard model[4] for this attribute information exchange. Each object has peculiar attributes. Object's attributes are organized to a blackboard, and junction's decision rules that decide which agent should be retrieved will be applied to it. An interaction occurs when an object comes within the effective range of a junction, and is place-dependent and object-attribute-dependent. So, if interactions occur here and there at the same time, different blackboards should be required (Fig. 4). If the organization of blackboard is finished, decision process starts and rules in the junction are applied to the organized blackboard. Each of satisfied rules in decision rules simply enumerates the required agents. The result of decision which is a set of indicators to required agents is written to the object's peculiar attributes temporarily, and then process goes to the next phase.

The latter phase, how to use agent, is object-attribute-dependent, that is, agents' actual invocation process varies due to the worker's situation. For example, if a worker has a sensor processing data is passed from the device, and if a worker should get processing data via file on computer it should be read and passed from file. So, object also has rules how to use agents which are acquired. And in this phase, target object's attributes which contain the result of interaction as temporary attributes are written to the blackboard, and the rules are applied to it. As the result of this, instructions for worker are composed and sent to the worker's

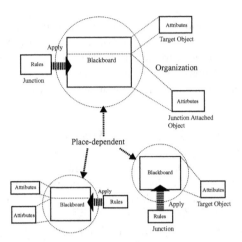

Fig. 4. Local Blackboard Model

device, and agents are appropriately summoned and do expected process on the worker's device. This invocation process is executed for each object.

The advantage of local blackboard mechanism is that description of object and junction has high-level independency because object/junction-dependent description is apart from each object's and junction's description.

We can say place-dependent work is like declaratively located process. In fact, description of attributes on blackboard and decision rules in junction are written declaratively. We adopt Prolog[6] to describe them. Prolog is one of the most famous declarative programming languages, and is also used for artificial intelligence, so it is very useful for our system. Of course, Prolog's whole ability is too great and our demand is not so high, but in the future, its potential is very attractive.

In this system, attributes correspond to facts in Prolog and decision rules correspond to rules. These are written declaratively and separately in the object and junction, and they should be organized when interaction occurs. Prolog's declarative programming paradigm is suitable for this purpose.

We also adopt Java[7][2] language to process actual invocation of agents. Since Java is very strong in network programming, agents are written in Java on the virtual plant. So, it is proper to use Java in our system.

4   Description of Object and Junction

In this system, description of objects, junctions and the space is basically written in XML (eXtensible Markup Language)[8].

XML is the meta-markup language for text documents. It can be used for various fields with user defined tags, and XML documents can contain various

---

[2] Java is the trademark of Sun Microsystems, Inc.

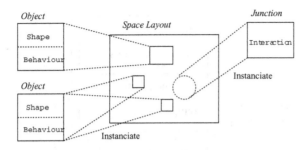

Fig. 5. Configuration of VR Space Description

kinds of descriptions freely, such as Prolog programs. So, we can use XML as description language of VR (which is also real) space and extend it also to be containing description of interaction rules in Prolog and description of actual agent's control in Java.

Description of spatially programmed agent world contains two kinds of definitions. One is of objects in wide sense, such as object and junction located in the space. The other is of VR space itself in which objects and junctions are located. Objects and junctions are instanciated into the VR space when they are located, following object oriented paradigm (Fig. 5). This section describes the definition of object and junction. Definition of VR space and locating process are described in the following section.

4.1 Description of Object

Object has the entity in the real space. So, some basic attributes are naturally possessed by the object such as shape, position, velocity and so on.

Object also has the attributes which are described declaratively and can be referred from junction. Attributes are classified into two types: permanent attribute, and temporary attribute. Permanent attribute is never cleared and always has some kind of value. Temporary attribute can be removed if it is no longer necessary yet, so this is mainly used to pass the pointer of required agents to the object.

Description of object has the following blocks (Fig. 6):

1. Shape Definitions
2. State Variables
3. Permanent Attributes
4. Temporary Attributes
5. Agent Applying Rules
6. Agent Invocation Functions
7. Update Function

'Shape Definitions' block develops object's shape. It is described by combination of primitives.

'State Variables' block consists of state variables such as position, velocity, temperature and so on. These are used in agent invocation functions or by the whole VR system.

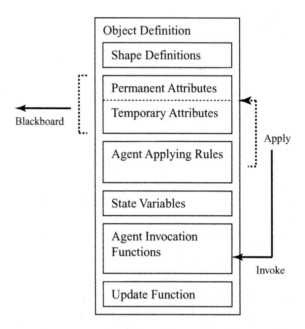

Fig. 6. Description of Object

'Permanent Attributes' and 'Temporary Attributes' block contain declaratively described attributes of the object. Temporary attributes are writable from the outer, and permanent attributes are only changed from agent invocation functions. Description language of those blocks is Prolog.

'Agent Applying Rules' block is to decide how to use the agents, and 'Agent Invocation Functions' block does preprocess of applying agents and compose and send instructions to the worker's device or facility's controller in the real world. The device receives those instructions and actually summons required agents and invokes them obeying the instructions. The functions are written in Java[7]. Retrieved maintenance data should be often processed by in the facility's and worker specific way, so it is proper that this part of composition of instructions is implemented in object, not in junction.

'Update Function' is a function which updates object's state in VR space corresponding to the object in the real world every moment. Detail of this function's role is described in the section 5.

4.2   Description of Junction

Description of junction has following blocks (Fig. 7):

1. Type and Range Definition
2. Agent Summon Rules
3. Interaction Functions

Junction can be classified into two location types and has two types of effective range.

One is 'Fixed' location type junction. This type of junction is fixed in the space, and is interested in only one object which comes into effective range. Another location type is 'Attached' type. This type of junction is attached to specific object, and move with the object. This type of junction is interested in two objects. One is attached object and another is the object which comes into effective range. So, this type can be used as interaction between objects. Usually diagnosis is done by a worker with target facility, so the latter type of junction will be often used.

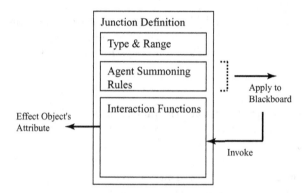

Fig. 7. Description of Junction

Effective range is basically defined by radius. If an object comes into range, junction is activated and indicates the agent summoning instructions to target object. Effective range can be defined as 'contact'. Only attached type junction can have this type of range. If an object contacts another object which has an attached contact type junction, then the junction is activated and indicates the agent summoning instructions to target object. In this case, junction's targets are both objects.

Junction has decision rules that decide which agents should be retrieved and used by the object (strictly speaking, by the worker's device in the real world). The decision rules are described in the 'Agent Summon Rules' block. These rules are applied to organized blackboard which consists of the target objects' attributes (if target is only one, organized blackboard has same contents as the object's attributes) when the interaction is occurred.

After the decision process is completed, appropriate function which composes indicator of the required agents and basic instruction (which should be arranged later by object specific way) of using them according to the result of decision. The functions are defined in 'Interaction Functions' block.

It is allowed that no agent will be summoned. This is used to give massage such as warning to target object.

5   Interaction Process Between Object and Junction

The time of VR space is synchronized with real space and follows real time. To synchronize, objects in the VR space must update their state every moment. Basically in this system, system activates each object's update function in every time interval. So each object can update its own state (e.g. position, equipment etc.) and can communicate with entity in real space (e.g. worker with portable PC) every moment.

System also monitors physical relationship of objects and junctions and can detect that an object is within the range of some junction or contacts another object with junction. Process of system obeys following flow:

```
Do loop
{
  1. While any object exists in junction's
     range (that is, the junction is
     activated).
@{
    1.1. Target object's attributes are
         written to blackboard and junction's
         rules are applied to it.
    1.2. Junction invokes appropriate function
         corresponding to the result of inquiry,
         which gives required agents and its
         instructions to temporary attributes
         of objects.
    1.3. Then, the object applies its rules to
         its attributes. Appropriate function
         in the object is invoked and composes
         final instruction of agents and send it
         to the device in the real world.
    1.4. Object updates its own state and
         removes temporary attributes.
  }
  2. do loop until all objects' actions
     are completed
  {
    2.1. Object updates its own state and
         does other required action.
  }
  3. Clock of VR space is progressed.
}
```

6   Defining and Constructing VR Space

6.1   Description of VR Space

Now, we can define objects and junctions in the space for spatial programming. In this section we describe the structure of the space appearing in manufacturing systems where we and objects can go around, and how to define it.

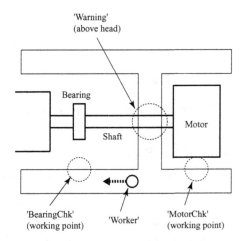

Fig. 8. Sample World

Our VR space fundamentally consists of path and rotary (Initially, no object and junction is located). Path is a straight way that an object corresponding to a worker or other movable object can move along. Rotary is a spot where an object can turn around. Rotaries are connected with path. Rotary is also used as a spot where a worker can access to a facility, because a worker who wants to operate it will turn around there. Each rotary and path has a unique name for system's identification.

For example, consider a plant which has a motor. There are bearing, motor, shaft and so on in this sample factory. Significant facility is motor, bearing and shaft. Motor and bearing require periodic and unexpected maintenance, and shaft is danger when a worker across below it. So, motor and bearing has working point of diagnosis as junction which is named 'MotorChk' and 'BearingChk'. Shaft has 'Warning' junction which warns to worker across below. The facilities' location is indicated in Fig. 8.

At first, user should prepare the structure of the space such as path and rotary. Then, the VR space will be defined as Fig. 8.User can navigate in this space, and can locate object and junction. Next, user should locate objects and junctions in the space to construct VR information world.

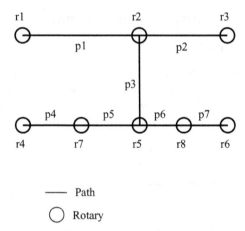

Fig. 9. Sample World's Space Description

6.2   Construction of VR Space

If defining space is completed, we can navigate in it. The next step is locating objects and junctions in it. User should locate objects of facilities in this factory such as motor, bearing, shaft and so on. After locating objects of facilities is completed, the user can define and attach junctions to appropriate objects. In the plant example, the junction 'mc1' is attached to 'm1' and junction 'bc1' is attached to 'b1'. Next, user should define fixed type junction 'wr1' and locate it to appropriate position, crossing the shaft and path (Fig. 10). Lastly, user should locate worker in the space, which is the avatar of worker in the real space.

Located objects are linked to appropriate entities in real space which have the same identifiers as instance names of the objects. These links are automatically established by the system. Then, the objects come to be able to update their attributes, such as position, automatically with time progression.

The interaction process is designed like the following, for example. We consider an interaction between worker and bearing. The interaction is diagnosis of bearing. If the bearing has trouble and the worker has enough equipment to maintain it, the interaction offers plant maintenance agents and the sequence of agent procedures to him. Corresponding to the bearing's vibration trouble, we define the attributes and rules of objects and junction as below.

Attributes of instance 'w1' from object 'Worker':

```
working(ready).
objective(diagnosis).
equip(thermometer).
```

Attributes of object 'b1':

```
sensor(vibration).
status(fault).
```

Rules of junction 'BearingChk':

```
exec(diag(X, Y)) :-
                object(X),
                object(Y, attached),
                attr(X, working(ready)),
                attr(X, objective(diagnosis)),
                attr(X, equip(thermometer)),
                attr(Y, sensor(vibration)),
                attr(Y, status(fault)).
exec(diag(X, Y)) :-
                object(X),
                object(Y, attached),
                attr(X, working(ready)),
                attr(X, objective(diagnosis)),
                attr(X, equip(thermometer)),
                attr(X, equip(vibration)),
                attr(Y, status(fault)).
```

The former rule means that diagnosis should be done if target facility (bearing) has vibration sensor and approaching object (this time, this is a worker) equips thermometer, because vibration data and temperature data are required for diagnosis of bearing. Predicate object/1/2 is a built-in predicate which involves the instance name of object as its argument. Especially, if it takes 'attached' as its second argument, it indicates that the junction is attached to the object. The latter rule means that approaching worker has both vibration sensor and thermometer, so that diagnosis is available and should be done. Then,

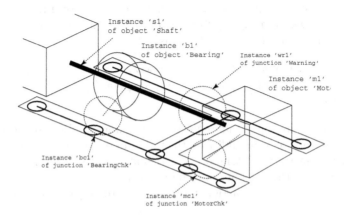

Fig. 10. Composed Sample Information World

if a worker approaches bearing and comes within the range of 'BearingChk', interaction occurs. Blackboard is organized as in the following:

```
attr('w1', working(ready)).
attr('w1', objective(diag)).
attr('w1', equip(thermometer)).
attr('b1', sensor(vibration)).
attr('b1', status(fault)).
exec(diag(X, Y)) :-
                object(X),
                object(Y, attached),
                attr(X, working(ready)),
                attr(X, objective(diagnosis)),
                attr(X, equip(thermometer)),
                attr(Y, sensor(vibration)),
                attr(Y, status(fault)).
exec(diag(X, Y)) :-
                object(X),
                object(Y, attached),
                attr(X, working(ready)),
                attr(X, objective(diagnosis)),
                attr(X, equip(thermometer)),
                attr(X, equip(vibration)),
                attr(Y, status(fault)).
```

Note that each attribute of objects is transformed by setting into predicate attr/2. First argument of attr/2 is the instance name of object, and second argument is attribute itself. This is automatically processed by the system when the blackboard is organized.

Inside the system, inquiry 'exec(F).' gets the answer F=diag('w1', 'b1'). Then function diag(String X, String Y) written in Java is invoked and it composes instructions of bearing diagnosis, e.g.

```
proc([temperature,[vibration, normal,
                fft, peaksearch], do_diag]).
diag('b1').
```

The former predicate represents required agent names and the sequence of procedure. The latter predicate indicates the target of diagnosis. These instructions are added to the worker's temporary attributes by this function. When this process is finished, the blackboard is abandoned.

Next, the phase of interaction process shifts to objects' action. Now, the worker's attributes are:

```
working(ready).
objective(diagnosis).
equip(thermometer).
proc([temperature,[vibration, normal,
                fft, peaksearch], do_diag]).
diag('b1').
```

Suppose the worker's rule is:

```
exec(procdiag(Tgt,Seq)) :- diag(Tgt), proc(Seq).
```

The worker's agent summon rule is applied to its attributes, and inquiry 'exec(F).' gets the answer F=procdiag('b1', [temperature,[vibration, normal, fft, peaksearch], do_diag]). Then worker invokes function procdiag(String Tgt, Vector Seq) written in Java. This function takes two arguments, 'Tgt' and 'Seq'. 'Tgt' is the target of diagnosis and 'Seq' is the sequence of agent invocation. This function composes and sends actual instructions of invocation sequence of agents to the worker's device in the real world, and diagnosis process begins.

Bearing also does its action in the same way, but it does not have anything to do, so it only updates its state.

This is a brief introduction of interaction design. Thus, construction of VR space is completed. In this way, the VR space works as spatial programming environment and now, it can also work as plant maintenance agents' world.

In the next section, we describe how to present the VR space to the user.

6.3   Spatial Programming Environment with VR

Our VR space uses images each of which is associated with specific path or spot to present realistic 3D space. The feature of our VR system is that the real space and the VR space are linked and synchronized. So navigating in this system should be made in realistic environment. Traditional ways to display VR space use 3D modeling, texture mapping and so on. But those methods cost very much. This also causes that rendering process requires very strong machine power.

We adopt the image based rendering[9]. Image based rendering is developed to reduce modeling cost for 3D objects in the space. This method uses a set of real images alternatively and displays image interpolated from those images (Fig. 11). So, image database is very large but this can save human's labor efficiently. This method is especially effective for our VR system with spatial programming, because the number of critical spots or ways is not so big and our movable ways are limited. There is no need to prepare such a large database of images.

User can construct VR space while walking around in it. If he wants to locate an object or junction, what is necessary is to click the button on the browser and input the description of it. Of course, the description can be also loaded from specified text file. After putting it on the VR space, it becomes available to interact immediately without stopping the space.

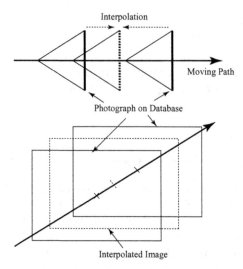

Fig. 11. Image Based Rendering

A user can also interact or receive instructions or message, if user's avatar has appropriate attributes. User can add attribute freely to any object in sight. This function also works for giving instructions to object.

7   Conclusions

This paper describes a way of defining invocation of plant maintenance agents using VR techniques. The basic idea is spatial programming for place-dependent works, one of declarative programming paradigm. This is elegantly achieved by adopting Prolog to implement significant mechanism of spatial programming. The idea is realized by interaction between worker object and junction which is located in VR space as interface of giving place-dependent maintenance procedure with agents to the worker in the real world. In this system, the VR space should be linked to real space, and worker in real space can get various required agents and instructions at real time. Spatial programming also helps a flexible revision of VR space, because user can modify the VR space without stopping or restarting it.

Thus, the VR space which is linked to real space can work as plant maintenance agents' world, and now, we are aiming to realize true ubiquitous maintenance.

Acknowledgment. This work is partially supported by IMS project IRMA.

References

1. Osamu Yoshie, Kyoko Iino, Tatsuya Fukunaga, Nobuyoshi Sato "Supplying High-Quality Knowledge of Machine Diagnosis in Virtual Community," Journal of the Society of Plant Engineers Japan, Vol.12, (2001).

2. Osamu Yoshie, Hiroki Takahashi "VSL-Virtual Space Description Language, and its application to spatial programming," The International Conference on Electrical Engineering, (1999).

3. Tstsuya Inaba, Hiroki Takahashi, Kyoko Iino, Natsuko Hayashi, Osamu Yoshie, "VSL-Trial for Describing Virtual Space in Logic and Its Application to Remote Robot Operation," International Conference on Applications of Prolog, (1999) pp. 50-53.

4. Stuart Russel, Peter Norvig, *Artificial Intelligence*, (Prentice Hall, 1995)

5. Osamu Yoshie, Hiroki Takahashi, Kinjiro Ito, Kageo Akizuki "Building Integrated Homepage by Illustration from Web- and XML- Centric Information Systems," The International Conference on Electrical Engineering, (2002).

6. Leon Sterling, Ehud Shapiro, *The Art of Prolog. SECOND EDITION*, (The MIT Press, 1994)

7. *The Source for JavaTM Technology*. Available at http://java.sun.com/.

8. *Extensible Markup Language (XML) 1.0 (Second Edition)*. Available at http://www.w3.org/TR/REC-xml.

9. E.S.Chen, gQuickTimeVR - An Image-Based Approach to Visual Environment Navigation," Computer Graphics, Proc. of ACM SIGGRAPH95, (1995) pp. 29-38.

A Pragmatic Approach to Pre-testing Prolog Programs*

Christoph Beierle, Marija Kulaš, and Manfred Widera

Praktische Informatik VIII - Wissensbasierte Systeme, Fachbereich Informatik,
FernUniversität in Hagen 58084 Hagen, Germany
{beierle, marija.kulas, manfred.widera}@fernuni-hagen.de

Abstract. We present an overview on the AT(x) approach which is capable of automatically analyzing programs with respect to given tests and a reference solution. In the context of small homework assignments with precisely describable tasks, AT(P), a Prolog instance of the general AT(x) framework, is able to find many of the errors usually made by students and to communicate them in a manner understandable for beginners in Prolog programming. The system is being used in distance education where direct communication between students and tutors is most of the time not possible.

1 Introduction

In distance learning and education, direct interaction between students and tutors is (most of the time) not possible. While communication via phone, e-mail, or newsgroups helps, there is still need for more direct help in problem solving situations like programming. In this context, intelligent tutoring systems have been proposed to support learning situations as they occur in distance education. A related area is tool support for homework assignments. In this paper, we will present a pragmatic approach to the automatic revision of homework assignments in programming language courses. In particular, we show how with the AT(P) system, exercises in Prolog can be automatically analyzed and tested so that automatically generated feedback can be given to the student. We will present an overview on AT(P) which is a Prolog instance of our more general AT(x) framework. Whereas AT(x) is introduced in [BKW03], this paper provides a more detailed description of the AT(P) functionalities.

2 WebAssign and AT(x)

The AT(x) framework is designed to be used in combination with WebAssign, a general system for assignments and assessment of exercises for courses which

---

* The research reported here was partially supported by the *Innovationsfond "Lernraum Virtuelle Universität" (LVU)*.

D. Seipel et al. (Eds.): INAP/WLP 2004, LNAI 3392, pp. 294–308, 2005.

Fig. 1. Structure of AT(x)

was developed by H.-W. Six and his group [BHSV99, Web03]. It provides support with web-based interfaces for all activities occurring in the assignment process, e.g. for the activities of the author of a task, a student solving it, and a corrector correcting and grading the submitted solution. In particular, it enables tasks with automatic test facilities and manual assessment, scoring and annotation. WebAssign is integrated in the Virtual University system of the FernUniversität Hagen [LVU03].

From the students' point of view, WebAssign provides access to the tasks to be solved by the students. A student can work out his solution and submit it to WebAssign. Here, two different submission modes are distinguished. In the so-called *pre-test mode*, the submission is only preliminary. In pre-test mode, automatic analyses or tests are carried out to give feedback to the student. The student can then modify and correct his solution, and he can use the pre-test mode again until he is satisfied with his solution. Eventually, he submits his solution in *final assessment mode* after which the assessment of the submitted solution is done, either manually or automatically, or by a combination of both.

While WebAssign has built-in components for automatic handling of easy-to-correct tasks like multiple-choice questions, this is not the case for more complex tasks like programming exercises. Here, specific correction modules are needed. The AT(x) framework aims to analyze solutions to programming exercises and is such a system that can be used as an automatic correction module for WebAssign. Its main purpose is to serve as an automatic test and analysis facility in pre-test mode.

Instances of the AT(x) framework have a task database that contains an entry for each task. When a student submits a solution, AT(x) gets an assignment number identifying the task to be solved and a submitted program written to solve the task via WebAssign's communication components. Further information identifying the submitting student is also available, but its use is not discussed here. Taking the above data as input, AT(x) analyzes the submitted program. Again via WebAssign, the results of its analysis are sent as feedback to the student (cf. Fig. 1).

Besides its integration into WebAssign, AT(x) has also been coupled to VILAB, a virtual electronic laboratory for applied computer science. VILAB is a system that guides students through a number of (potentially larger) exercises and experiments [LGH02].

3   An Example Session

Before we go into the description of the individual components of the AT(x) system, we want to show an example execution for a Prolog homework task. The task is described as follows:

> Let N and M be integers with $N \leq M$. Define a predicate *between/3* such that a query *between(X, N, M)* is true if N is less or equal to M, and X is an integer between N and M.

Let us assume that the following program is submitted:

```
between(X, N, M) :- var(X), integer(N),
                    integer(M), N =< M,
                    gen_list(N, M, X).
gen_list(N, N, [N|[]]) :- !.
gen_list(N, M, [N|R]) :- L is N + 1, gen_list(L, M, R).
```

Then the system's output is the following:

```
The following query failed, though it should succeed:
    between(10,10,20)
Therefore, your program violates the following property:
    The lower bound N is between N and M
-------------------------------------------------
Wrong solutions were generated for the following query:
    between(A,100,102)
The wrong solutions for this query are listed below:
    between([100,101,102],100,102)
-------------------------------------------------
Solutions were overlooked for the following query:
    between(A,100,102)
The overlooked solutions for this query are listed below:
    between(100,100,102)
    between(101,100,102)
    between(102,100,102)
```

One interesting aspect of the AT(x) framework is the following: the system is designed to perform a large number of tests. In the generated report, however, it filters some of the detected errors for presentation. Several different filters generating reports of different precision and length are available. In the example above, a single representative for each kind of detected error was selected.

4   Structure of the AT(x) Framework

The AT(x) framework consists of combining different tools. Interfaces to different user groups (especially students and supervisors) have to be provided via WebAssign. The design decisions caused by this situation are described in this section.

4.1   Components of the AT(x) System

AT(x) is divided into two main components: the main work is done by the analysis component. Especially in functional and logic programming, the used languages are well suited for handling programs as data. The analysis components of AT(P) (and also of AT(S), an instance of AT(x) for the functional programming language Scheme, cf. [BKW03]) is therefore implemented in the target language (i.e. the language the programs to be tested are written in).

A further component implemented in Java serves as an interface between this analysis component and WebAssign. The reason for using such an interface component is its reusability and its easy implementation in Java. The WebAssign interface is based on Corba communication. A framework for WebAssign clients implementing an analysis component is given by an abstract Java class. Instead of implementing an appropriate Corba client for each of the AT(x) instances in the individual target languages independently, the presented approach contains a reusable interface component implemented in Java (that makes use of the existing abstract class) and a very simple interface to the analysis component.

4.2   The Analysis Components

The individual analysis components are the main parts of the AT(x) instances. They perform a number of tests on the students' programs and generate appropriate error messages. The performed tests and the detectable error types of AT(P) are discussed in Sec. 5 and 6. Here, we concentrate on the (quite simple) interface of this component.

The analysis component of each AT(x) instance expects to read an exercise identifier (used to access the corresponding information on the task to be solved) and a student's program from the standard input stream. It returns its messages, each as a line of text, at the component's standard output stream. These lines of text contain an error number and some data fields containing additional error descriptions separated by a unique identifier. The number and types of the additional data fields is fixed for each error number.

4.3   Function and Implementation of the Interface Component

On the one hand, WebAssign provides a communication interface based on Corba to the analysis components. On the other hand, the analysis components used in AT(x) use a simple interface with textual communication via the stdin and stdout streams of the analysis process. We therefore use an interface program connecting the analysis component of AT(x) and WebAssign which performs the following tasks:

- Starting the analysis system and providing an exercise identifier and the student's program.
- Reading the error messages from the analysis component.
- Selecting some of the messages for presentation.
- Preparing the selected messages for presentation.

The interface component starts the analysis system (via the Java class *Runtime*) and writes the needed information into its standard input stream (which is available by the Java process via standard classes). Afterwards, it reads the message lines from the standard output stream of the analysis system, parses the individual messages and stores them into an internal representation.

For presenting errors to the student, each error number is connected to a text template that gives a description of this kind of error. An error message is generated by instantiating the template of an error with the data fields provided by the analysis component together with the error number. The resulting text parts for the individual errors are concatenated and transferred to WebAssign as one piece of HTML text.

For using this system in education it turns out that presenting all detected errors at once is not the best action in every case. The interface component therefore has the capability of selecting certain messages for output according to one of the following strategies:

- Only one error is presented. This is especially useful in beginners courses, since a beginner in programming should not get confused and demotivated by a large number of error messages. He can rather concentrate on one message and may receive further messages when restarting the analysis with the corrected program.
- For every type of error occurring in the list of errors only one example is selected for output. This strategy provides more information at once to experienced users. A better overview over the pathological program behaviour is given, because all different error types are described, each with one representative. This may result in fewer iterations of the cycle consisting of program correction and analysis. The strategy, however, still hides the full set of all test cases from the student and therefore prevents fine tuning a program according to the performed tests.
- All detected errors are presented at once. This provides the complete overview over the program errors and is especially useful when the program correction is done offline. In order to prevent fine tuning of a program according to the performed tests, students should be aware that in final assessment mode additional tests not present in the pre-test mode will be applied.

4.4   Global Security Issues

Security is an issue that is common to all instances of AT(x). It is therefore addressed by the framework rather than by every individual instance. In [Wid04] it is shown how authentification problems and denial of service attacks are dealt with and by which means malicious code in submitted programs can be detected.

Essentially, WebAssign already provides a filter ruling out denial of service and unauthorized access. Malicious code in students' solutions (e.g. file access, ...) is prevented by the known UNIX security mechanisms. A sandbox approach is possible, but did not prove necessary so far.

5   Requirements for the Analysis Components

The heart of the AT(x) system is given by the individual analysis components for the different programming languages. The intended use in testing homework assignments rather than arbitrary programs implies some important properties of the analysis components discussed here: it can rely on the availability of a detailed specification of the homework tasks, it must be robust against non terminating input programs and runtime errors, and it must generate reliable output understandable for beginners.

The description for each homework task consists of the following parts:

- A textual description of the task. (This is essentially used in preparation of the homework assignment, but not in the testing task itself.)
- A set of test cases for the task.
- Specifications of program properties and of the generated solutions. (This applies especially for declarative languages like Prolog.)
- A reference solution. (This is a program which is assumed to be a correct solution to the homework task and which can be used to judge the correctness of the students' solutions.)

This part of input is called the *static input* to the analysis component, because it usually remains unchanged between the individual test sessions. A call to the analysis system contains an additional *dynamic input* which consists of a unique identifier for the homework task (used to access the appropriate set of static input) and a program to be tested.

Now we want to discuss the requirements on the behaviour of the analysis system in more detail. Concretizing the requirement of reliable output we want our analysis component to return an error only if such an error really exists. Where this is not possible (especially when non termination is assumed), the restricted confidence should clearly be communicated to the student, e.g. by marking the returned message as a *warning* instead of an *error*. For warnings the system should describe an additional task to be performed by the student in order to discriminate errors from false messages.

Runtime errors of every kind must be caught without affecting the whole system. For instance, if executing the student's program causes a runtime error, this should not corrupt the behaviour of the other components. Towards this end, our AT(P) and AT(S) implementations exploit the hooks of user-defined error handlers provided by SICStus Prolog and MzScheme, respectively. An occurring runtime error is reported to the student, and no further testing is done, because the system's state is no longer reliable.

For ensuring termination of the testing process, infinite loops in the tested program must also be detected and interrupted. As the question whether an

arbitrary program terminates is undecidable in general, we chose an approximation that is easy to implement and guarantees every infinite loop to be detected:
a threshold for the maximal number of function calls[1] (either counted independently for each function or accumulated over all functions in the program)
is introduced and the program execution is aborted whenever this threshold
is exceeded. (In the presence of further looping constructs like *while*-loops in
imperative programming, a refined termination control is necessary.) As homework assignments are usually small tasks, it is possible to estimate the maximal
number of needed function calls and to choose the threshold sufficiently. The
report to the student must, however, clearly state the restricted confidence on
the detected non-termination.

6   Analysis of Prolog Programs

Annotation Tests. Due to the declarative character of Prolog, a variety of
tests can be performed on Prolog programs. Certain main properties of a program can be tested by annotations. Our system AT(P) is based on the TSP
approach of H. Neumann [Neu98] where several kinds of Prolog annotations are
proposed, together with an algorithm for their validation with respect to a given
student's program and a reference program. One general kind of annotation is a
positive/negative annotation. Such an annotation consists of a test query, a flag
whether this query should succeed or fail and a description of the property that
is violated if the query does not behave as expected. This description is reported
to the student together with the query and the intended result.

Example 1. Reconsider the predicate *between/3* from Sec. 3. A possible error of
a student's program is to allow for too large values X in a call *between*(X, N, M).
We can detect and explain that by an annotation test where

- the test query is set to "*between(30, 10, 20)*",
- the success flag is set to expected failure,
- the error explanation text is "If X is greater than the upper bound M,
  between(X,N,M) can not succeed".

For instance, if this test fails, the system will generate the following output: *The
following query succeded, though it should fail: between(30,10,20). Therefore,
your program violates the following property: If X is greater than the upper
bound M, between(X,N,M) can not succeed.*

Mode Tests. Mode tests form the class of tests that is probably performed
most often by AT(P). Its aim is to check whether the given program (or more
precisely, the currently checked predicate in this program) behaves correctly for
all intended modes (i.e. combinations of input and output instantiations of the
predicate). Performing a mode test consists of the following steps:

---

[1] In case of Prolog: predicate calls.

1. Generate test queries for all intended modes of the tested predicate.
2. For each generated query perform the following steps independently:
   (a) Evaluate the query with respect to the student's program and collect all generated results.
   (b) Evaluate the query with respect to the reference program and collect all generated results.
   (c) Search for evidence for errors in the generated result lists.

The generation of test queries uses a list of fully instantiated terms that should be provable by the tested predicate and a list of modes the predicate should be applicable with. In the mode list the individual parameter positions are marked as input or output parameter as usual: + denotes an input parameter that must be instantiated, − denotes an output parameter that must not be instantiated, and parameters marked with ? may be either way.

Example 2. Consider the well-known *append/3* predicate as the tested predicate.

```
append([], L, L).
append([H|R1], L2, [H|R]) :- append(R1, L2, R).
```

Some example terms (provable goals) for this predicate are

$$append([], [a, b], [a, b]), \quad append([a], [], [a]), \quad append([a], [b, c], [a, b, c]).$$

Let the list of modes of *append/3* be the following.[2]

$$append(?L1, ?L2, +L3), \quad append(+L1, +L2, ?L3)$$

For the first example term and the first mode declaration we get the following list of test queries:

$$append(L1, L2, [a, b]), \quad append(L1, [a, b], [a, b]),$$
$$append([], L2, [a, b]), \quad append([], [a, b], [a, b]).$$

The other example terms and mode declarations are processed analogously.

Wrong and Missing Solutions. Another part of the test procedure consists of the application of the student program to test queries and checking the resulting substitutions with the reference program. The following steps of comparison are performed:

– Solutions of a student's program are reported as *wrong* solutions if they are falsified by the reference program (i.e. if the query given by the solution fails in the reference program).

---

[2] In contrast to the usual mode declaration *append(?Prefix, ?Suffix, ?Combined)* found e.g. in [SIC01], here we are not interested in the capability of *append/3* to guess list entries when they are not completely given as e.g. in the goal *append(L1, [a, b], L)*.

- A solution of the reference program is reported as *missing* if it is not subsumed by some solution of the student's program. (It is not sufficient for the student's program to *accept* every solution generated by the reference program. The student's program must rather be able to *generate* all these solutions.)
- For some of the test queries the number of expected solutions can be given (*completeness annotation*), and the number of solutions generated by the student's program is compared with this specification.

Example 3. Consider the task of implementing a predicate *perm*/2 that is fulfilled if both arguments are lists which are permutations of each other. Let the analyzed test query be $perm([a, b, c], L)$. Let further the programs generate the following instantiations for L:

	considered values
analyzed program	$[a, b, c]$, $[a, c, b]$, $[b, a, c]$, $[b, c, a]$, $[c, a, b]$, $[c, b, a]$
reference solution	$[c, b, a]$, $[c, a, b]$, $[b, c, a]$, $[b, a, c]$, $[a, c, b]$, $[a, b, c]$

Because of comparing of the solution sequences as *sets*, the system can infer the correctness of the analyzed program with respect to this query.

In case of an infinite number of solutions just a prefix is generated. The system is still applicable to those tasks with infinite solution set if a natural order on the solutions exists and therefore the generated solutions of the student's program and the reference program match. An example of a problem with natural order is the generation of all prime numbers. In contrast, there is no single natural order for generating all words over the alphabet $\Sigma = \{@, \#, \$\}$.

Redundant Solutions. Redundant solutions, i.e. solutions erroneously occurring several times in the sequence of solutions, are detected by an algorithm that interprets *every* repetition of a solution as an unintended one. If repeated solutions are intended by the problem, these messages can be filtered out later.

This procedure turned out to be sufficient since in our context of homework assignments the processed solution sequences are usually quite small.

Supervising Termination and Runtime Errors. The central part of the Prolog analysis component is an original backtracking analyst [Neu98] that evaluates a test query with respect to a program and an expected number of answers, creating a (partial) list of answers and a status report. A query shall be evaluated two times, once with respect to the student's program and once with respect to the reference program. Both programs are held in memory in parallel using different modules.

During the evaluation of a query in a module, its termination behaviour is assessed by a meta-interpreter as follows. Goals for predicates defined in the module are resolved, whereas goals for built-ins or imported predicates are passed to the runtime system using timed-out *call/1*. The interpreter counts the number of resolutions and runtime calls. Upon exceeding the threshold, the current evaluation of the query is aborted and evidence for an infinite loop is reported.

The class of runtime errors contains all errors that are detected by the runtime system and cause the immediate termination of the computation (unless they are caught and processed as in our system). Runtime errors in Prolog programs contain among others

- existence errors (e.g. a non-existing predicate was called)
- instantiation errors (e.g. performing a mathematical computation with unin-stantiated arguments)
- resource errors (e.g. no more memory).

Test evaluations performed by AT(P) are supervised and runtime errors are caught. If a runtime error occurs, the error message is passed to the student via WebAssign and the remaining tests are canceled. This cancellation avoids imprecise results for further tests caused by side-effects of the runtime error.

7   Examples: Partial Specifications of Program Properties

We will present concrete examples of specifications of program properties as they can be expressed in our system. They are provided by the tutor and present a powerful and very flexible means of expressing partial program specifications.

Factorial. Suppose in a Prolog course, the predicate *fac/2* for computing the factorial of a natural number has been introduced, using the calling pattern *fac(+N, ?F)*, i.e., if N and F are such that $F = N!$ then *fac(N,F)* holds provided that the first argument is instantiated. Let us further assume that the following homework assigment is given to the students: *Define a predicate inv_fac/2 that computes both the factorial as well as its inverse, where at least one argument must be instantiated.*

Figure 2 gives a partial specification of *inv_fac/2*. In line 2, *modes/1* has a list of two mode terms expressing the intended usage of *inv_fac/2*. Together with the example term given in line 3, the test queries *inv_fac(5,F)*, *inv_fac(5,120)*, and *inv_fac(N,120)* are automatically generated.

Line 4 contains a so-called completeness annotation (cf. Sec. 6). The general form of a completeness annotation is

   testcase(complete(+TestQuery, +Limit, +Op)).

which causes a check whether *TestQuery* produces a number N of solutions such that N *Op Limit* holds, with $Op \in \{<, <=, =, >=, >\}$. Thus, line 4 specifies that *inv_fac(_N,1)* has exactly 2 solutions (the factorial of both 0 and 1 yields 1).

Lines 5–17 contain four positive (5–12) and four negative (13–17) annotations. In general, for a positive annotation

   testcase(pos_ann(+TestQuery, +Annotation)).

TestQuery should succeed. If it fails, *Annotation* is violated. For instance, if the query *inv_fac(N, 720), fac(N, X), X = 720* fails, then the annotation *'inv_fac(N,F) and fac(N,X) => F = X'* has been violated (lines 9-10). Note

```
% Import: fac/2                                                    % 0
:- load_files([library('fac.pl')], [compilation_mode(assert_all)]). % 1
modes([inv_fac(+_N, ?_F), inv_fac(?_N, +_F)]).                     % 2
examples([inv_fac(5,120)]).                                        % 3
testcase(complete(inv_fac(_N,1), 2, =)).                           % 4
testcase(pos_ann((inv_fac(0, F), F = 1),                           % 5
                 'inv_fac(0,F) => F = 1')).                        % 6
testcase(pos_ann((fac(6, F), inv_fac(X, F), X = 6),                % 7
                 'F > 1 and fac(N,F) and inv_fac(X,F) => N = X')). % 8
testcase(pos_ann((inv_fac(N, 720), fac(N, X), X = 720),            % 9
                 'inv_fac(N,F) and fac(N,X) => F = X')).           %10
testcase(pos_ann((inv_fac(5,F), fac(5,F)),                         %11
                 'inv_fac(N,F) => fac(N,F)')).                     %12
testcase(neg_ann(inv_fac(_N,100),                                  %13
                 'not fac(N,F) => not inv_fac(N,F)')).             %14
testcase(neg_ann(inv_fac(_N,0), 'not inv_fac(_N,0)')).            %15
testcase(neg_ann(inv_fac(_N,-1), 'F < 0 => not inv_fac(_N,F)')).  %16
testcase(neg_ann(inv_fac(-1,_F), 'N < 0 => not inv_fac(N,_F)')).  %17
```

Fig. 2. Specification of program properties for *inv_fac/2*

```
modes([between(?_X, +_N, +_M)]).                                   % 1
examples([between(1,0,3)]).                                        % 2
testcase(complete(between(_X,100,102), 3, =)).                     % 3
testcase(complete(between(_X,5,5), 1, =)).                         % 4
testcase(neg_ann(between(_X,6,5), 'If the lower bound N is greater % 5
 than the upper bound M, between(X,N,M) can not succeed')).        % 6
testcase(pos_ann(between(10,10,20), 'The lower bound N is          % 7
 between N and M')).                                               % 8
testcase(pos_ann(between(20,10,20), 'The upper bound M is          % 9
 between N and M')).                                               %10
testcase(pos_ann(between(20,20,20), 'N is between N and N')).      %11
testcase(neg_ann(between(20,30,40), 'If X is less than the lower   %12
 bound N, between(X,N,M) can not succeed')).                       %13
testcase(neg_ann(between(30,10,20), 'If X is greater than the upper %14
 bound M, between(X,N,M) can not succeed')).                       %15
```

Fig. 3. Specification of program properties for *between/3*

```
modes([subterm(+_SubTerm, +_Term)]).                              % 1

examples([subterm(p(X), q(a,p(X),y,p(p(X))))]).                   % 2

testcase(pos_ann(subterm(p(X), p(X)),                             % 3
  'forall T: [atomic(T) or var(T) or compound(T)] => subterm(T,T)')).  % 4

testcase(neg_ann(subterm(p(X), p(Y)),                             % 5
  'var(X) and var(Y) and not X == Y => not subterm(p(X),p(Y))')).  % 6

testcase(neg_ann(subterm(p(x), p(X)),                             % 7
  'atomic(A) and var(X) => not subterm(p(A),p(X))')).             % 8

testcase(neg_ann(subterm(p(x), p(q(x))),                          % 9
  'T1 does not occur as substring in T2 => not subterm(T1,T2)')).  %10
```

Fig. 4. Specification of program properties for *subterm/2*

that the annotations are given as text strings, intended as error explanations for the students.

Analogously, the test query in a negative annotation should fail. For instance, if the query *inv_fac(_N,100)* succeeds, the annotation *'not fac(N,F) => not inv_fac(N,F)'* has been violated (lines 13-14).

Let us now suppose that the tutor wants the students to develop a more general version of *inv_fac/2* where both of its arguments may be uninstantiated. The specification of program properties given in Figure 2 can be adapted to this modified task easily by just replacing line 2 by

```
modes([inv_fac(?_N, ?_F)]).
```

specifying the generalized mode situation.

Between. A partial specification of program properties of the predicate *between/3* (Sec. 3 and 6) is given in Figure 3. Note that here, the tutor has choosen rather verbal annotations as error explanations, instead of more formal ones as for *inv_fac/2*.

Subterm. Let the following homework assignment be given: *Define a predicate subterm/2 with calling pattern subterm(+SubTerm,+Term) that holds if SubTerm is a subterm of Term, where every term is a subterm of itself, and a subterm of an argument of some term T is a subterm of T as well. For instance, p(X) is a subterm of p(X) and of q(a,p(X),Y), but not a subterm of p(Y).* Figure 4 specifies various properties of *subterm/2*. If we want to extend the task by requiring that in the case of multiple occurrences of *SubTerm* in *Term* the predicate should succeed only once, we could adapt the partial program specification of Figure 4 by adding the completeness annotation

```
testcase(complete(subterm(a, p(a,g(a,a),a)), 1, =)).
```

8   Implementation and Experiences

Both AT(P) and AT(S) are fully implemented and operational. The analysis components run under the Solaris 7 operating system and, via their respective Java interface components, serve as clients for WebAssign.

During the summer semester 2003, AT(P) was used in the framework of a course on deduction and inference systems at the FernUniversität Hagen, and both AT(P) and AT(S) are currently being used for a course on logic and functional programming. Part of all programming exercises in the course are supported by the system, but not yet all of them. Thus, since currently the system is available just for selected homework tasks, using the system means sending in homeworks on two different ways (WebAssign for the selected available tasks, "plain paper" sent in by mail or e-mail for the remaining tasks). Nevertheless, two thirds of the students chose to use the system. Feedback from the students was positive in general, mentioning both, a better motivation to solve the tasks, and better insight in the new programming paradigm.

9   Related Work

In the area of testing and analysis of Prolog programs there have been many proposals, ranging from theorem proving (eg. [Stä98]) to various forms of debugging (eg. [Duc99]) and systematic testing. Here we shall only refer to proposals with a strong declarative bias, i. e. using logical assertions (or annotations) for representing and/or validating program properties. The proposals differ along several axes: static or run-time analysis, restricting the target language or not, expressiveness of the annotation language.

Some authors restrict the target language by throwing out "impure" predicates. LPTP [Stä98] is an interactive theorem prover for a pure (no `cut`, `var` or `assert`) subset of Prolog. LPTP's language is a first-order logic, enriched with connectives for success, failure and universal termination. GUPU ([Neu97], [NK02]) is a teaching environment for a pure subset of Prolog. Before a student is allowed to feed in some clauses for a predicate, a partial specification (as a set of annotations) must be supplied. In GUPU the tutor supplies a reference solution as well [NK02]. GUPU's annotation language can express examples, counter-examples and termination statements.

Yet other authors take the challenge of the "full" or standard Prolog language. The first approach to validation of full Prolog seems to be the ADVICE package [O'K84]. It was followed by a theoretical work [DM88] on static validation. Some current practical approaches, performing run-time validation, include the language of annotations of the CIAO-Prolog [HPB99] and the NOPE system of annotations [Kul00]. The TSP system [Neu98], at the heart of our AT(P), performs run-time validation of full Prolog, and its annotation language can express examples, counter-examples, modi and numerical constraints on the number of computed answers.

Whereas e.g. LPTP is a powerful theorem prover and GUPU is a fully integrated teaching environment, we would like to stress the fact that the aim of AT(P) is a different one. It is an approach to support Prolog programming in distance education for beginners in logic programming. In such a context, the AT(P) assumption to have a correct reference solution available and to check the student's program with respect to this reference solution (rather than, say, with respect to a program-independent specification), seems to be justified. Furthermore, our particular system requirements of a completely WWW based system without intensive interaction characteristics on the one hand and the requirements for robustness with regard to program errors, runtime-errors, non-termination, etc. on the other hand, led to the pragmatic approach of coupling the analysis component AT(P) to WebAssign, thereby reusing WebAssign's communication and administration facilities.

10   Conclusions and Further Work

We have presented a brief overview on the AT(x) approach which is capable of automatically analyzing programs with respect to given tests and a reference solution. In the framework of small homework assignments with precisely describable tasks, AT(P) is able to find many of the errors usually made by students and to communicate them in a manner understandable for beginners in Prolog programming (in contrast to the error messages of most compilers).

There are other programming aspects that are not covered by AT(P). Examples are the layout of Prolog code, use of "imperative" programming style, etc. While there are systems dealing with such aspects (e.g. enforcing a particular layout discipline), in our AT(P) approach they are currently handled by a human corrector in the final assessement mode. Whereas it should not be too difficult to extend AT(P) in this direction, our priority in the design of AT(P) was the focus on program correctness by fully automated pre-testing of Prolog programming assignments.

Acknowledgements. The basis for the analysis component of AT(P) is taken from the TSP system, which was designed and implemented by Holger Neumann [Neu98]. TSP offers a variety of different tests and turned out to be extremely stable; the partial specifications presented in Sec. 7 were adapted from [Neu98]. We also thank the anonymous referees for helpful comments.

References

[BHSV99]   J. Brunsmann, A. Homrighausen, H.-W. Six, and J. Voss. Assignments in a Virtual University – The WebAssign-System. In *Proc. 19th World Conference on Open Learning and Distance Education*, Vienna, Austria, June 1999.

[BKW03]   C. Beierle, M. Kulaš, and M. Widera. Automatic analysis of programming assignments. In A. Bode, J. Desel, S.Ratmayer, and M. Wessner, editors, *DeLFI 2003. Proceedings der 1. e-Learning Fachtagung Informatik*, volume P-37 of *Lecture Notes in Informatics (LNI)*, Bonn, 2003. Köllen Verlag.

[DM88]   W. Drabent and J. Małuszyński. Inductive assertion method for logic programs. *Theoretical Computer Science*, 59:133–155, 1988.

[Duc99]   M. Ducasse. Opium: An extendable trace analyser for prolog. *J. of Logic Programming*, 39:177–223, 1999.

[HPB99]   M. Hermenegildo, G. Puebla, and F. Bueno. Using global analysis, partial specifications, and an extensible assertion language for program validation and debugging. In K. Apt, V. Marek, M. Truszczynski, and D. S. Warren, editors, *The Logic Programming Paradigm: A 25-Year Perspective*. Springer-Verlag, 1999.

[Kul00]   M. Kulaš. Annotations for Prolog – A concept and runtime handling. In A. Bossi, editor, *Logic-Based Program Synthesis and Transformation. Selected Papers of the 9th Int. Workshop (LOPSTR'99), Venezia*, volume 1817 of *LNCS*, pages 234–254. Springer-Verlag, 2000.

[LGH02]   R. Lütticke, C. Gnörlich, and H. Helbig. VILAB - a virtual electronic laboratory for applied computer science. In *Proceedings of the Conference Networked Learning in a Global Environment*. ICSC Academic Press, Canada/The Netherlands, 2002.

[LVU03]   Homepage   LVU,   Fernuniversität   Hagen, http://www.fernuni-hagen.de/LVU/. 2003.

[Neu97]   U. Neumerkel. A programming course for declarative programming with Prolog. http://www.complang.tuwien.ac.at/ulrich/gupu/material/1997-gupu.ps.gz, 1997.

[Neu98]   H. Neumann. Automatisierung des Testens von Zusicherungen für Prolog-Programme. Diplomarbeit, FernUniversität Hagen, 1998.

[NK02]   U. Neumerkel and S. Kral. Declarative program development in Prolog with GUPU. In *Proc. of the 12th Internat. Workshop on Logic Programming Environments (WLPE'02), Copenhagen*, pages 77–86, 2002.

[O'K84]   Richard A. O'Keefe. *advice.pl*. 1984. Interlisp-like advice package.

[SIC01]   *Swedish Institute of Computer Science. SICStus Prolog User's Manual*, April 2001. Release 3.8.6.

[Stä98]   Robert F. Stärk. The theoretical foundations of LPTP (a logic program theorem prover). *J. of Logic Programming*, 36(3):241–269, 1998. Source distribution http://www.inf.ethz.ch/~staerk/lptp.html.

[Web03]   Homepage WebAssign. http://www-pi3.fernuni-hagen.de/WebAssign/. 2003.

[Wid04]   M. Widera. Testing Scheme programming assignments automatically. In *Trends in Functional Programming*. Intellect, 2004. (to appear).

Author Index

Lecture Notes in Artificial Intelligence (LNAI)